TOWARDS THE
EFFECTIVE SCHOOL

TOWARDS THE EFFECTIVE SCHOOL:
The problems and some solutions

Ken Reid, David Hopkins and Peter Holly

Basil Blackwell

© Ken Reid, David Hopkins, Peter Holly
First published 1987

Published by
Basil Blackwell Ltd
108 Cowley Road
Oxford OX4 1JF
England

ISBN   0 631 14722 5

Typeset in 10 on 12pt Sabon by Oxford Publishing Services, Oxford
Printed in Great Britain

To teachers everywhere – members of a greatly misunderstood profession

Foreword

I would like to thank my co-authors David Hopkins and Peter Holly for the effort and thought which they have put into their writing and into the collaborative stages involved in producing a book of this kind. I should also like to thank James Nash for all his help and patience. Finally, I am deeply indebted to Denise Johns for typing the manuscript.

Ken Reid
Swansea, April 15th, 1986.

Contents

Preface   viii

Section A: Setting the scene   1
  Foreword   2
  1 Introduction – towards the effective school: context and
  strategies for improvement   3
  2 Some characteristics of effective schools   22

Section B: The problems: perceived outcomes of secondary schooling   33
  3 Disadvantaged and disaffected pupils: social, parental and
  school processes   35
  4 Discipline and disruption   47

Section C: Traditional remedies   65
  5 Pastoral care   67
  6 Non-comformist pupils: school processes   81

**Section D: Promoting school improvement: external and internal
influences**   97
  7 Combating disaffection   99
  8 Teacher research and school self-evaluation   115

Section E: Creating effective schools   137
  9 Beyond the saber tooth curriculum   139
  10 Moving beyond the cult of the individual   162

Section F: Facing the future   207
  11 The developing school   209
  12 Conclusions   261

Further reading   271
Bibliography   273
Index   301

Preface

There is now considerable agreement on what constitutes an effective school. Recent empirical studies on school effectiveness concur on two things. First, in contradiction to the major studies of the 1960s, such as the Coleman (1966) and Plowden (1967) Reports, and the important embryonic work of Jencks *et al* (1972), schools can and do make a difference to a pupil's achievement in school. Second, these differences in outcome are systematically related to variations in the schools' climate, culture or ethos, and their quality as social systems.

The literature is also in agreement on two further issues. First, positive features of 'effective schools' are to do with process-type manifestations of schooling such as strong leadership, high expectations, a clear set of goals, school-wide staff training, and efficient systems for monitoring pupils, rather than with extraneous aspects like the age of the school buildings and teachers' salaries. A more extensive list of the process measures would include: teachers being well prepared for lessons; having an effective disciplinary style that is positive rather than negative; structuring the curriculum; and, as a staff, providing consistent policies for the pupils in the school. In particular, research (Rutter *et al* 1979) suggests that policies which promote pupil responsibility and achievement, both in and out of the classroom, are the most successful. Research also indicates, perhaps surprisingly, that class size is less important than a teacher's ability to manage, control and structure his or her lessons sensibly, and generally teach well.

The second aspect on which the literature is in agreement is that all these features are amenable to alteration by concerted action on the part of the school staff. This is not an easy task; many more qualitative school-based studies will be needed before the fundamentals of really good practice are ascertained. Nevertheless, the implications of our existing knowledge are already apparent and must be transmitted to teachers if schools are to change their present direction and practices and become really efficient and effective agents of pupils' learning and development.

Towards Effective Schools has been written in an attempt to summarise and synthesise what is presently known in the search for truly effective schools. We hope our book will provide secondary teachers, headteachers, advisers, students, parents and all those interested in education, with a survey or overview of the literature, together with a discussion of the strategies that can be used to assist in making schools more effective. The book may be read as a whole or individual chapters may be used in their own right. In part, this reflects the imbalance of our existing knowledge and the great deal of work that remains to be done before schools can be judged to be truly effective institutions (Gray, 1981; Reynolds and Reid, 1985).

The text is unusual in that it focusses on different, but related, themes in the effective/ineffective school debate. The six sections reflect the state of our existing knowledge. The content of these sections deliberately moves from the negative to the more positive features of secondary schools. At the same time, whenever possible, we atempt to *concentrate* on the implications of recent research for practitioners and to provide some workable schemes for staff to implement in their schools and classrooms. In this way, the text marries theory with practice.

Section A sets the scene for the present deliberations on school effectiveness as far as that is possible, given the disparate nature of the research which has been undertaken. Throughout this section, and later in the book, relevant findings from work undertaken in Britain, the United States, Canada, Europe and elsewhere are included at appropriate points.

Section B concentrates on some of the problem areas of secondary schooling – disadvantages, disaffection, indiscipline and disruption. These topics reinforce the negative effects of much secondary schooling which are so often highlighted by the popular media and in books like *Truancy and School Absenteeism* (Reid, 1985) and *Disaffection From School* (Reid, 1986).

Section C analyses the present state of knowledge drawn on by schools in attempting to overcome deviant behaviour, illustrating some of the more traditional remedies such as the preventative work employed by pastoral care staff. Taken together, Sections B and C reflect the realities of life for many pupils and teachers in our secondary schools today. Sadly, this is especially true for a large proportion of schools located in deprived regions, with a majority of disadvantaged, lower-ability pupils who themselves come from unfavourable social backgrounds. It is equally true for many schools situated in inner-city areas in which there is a pervading anti-education neighbourhood culture.

Section D begins the second half of the book and the positive phase of our writing. It examines some of the ways of promoting school improvement. In particular, it investigates some of the external and internal remedies which can be tried to redress the balance in schools. The first chapter focuses on combating disaffection and looks at ideas which can be used to good effect. This chapter concludes the first major theme of the book – on schools' problems. It is followed by a key chapter on teacher research and school self-evaluation, both of central importance to notions of accountability, effectiveness and professionalism.

Section E takes these points a stage further. First, in *Beyond the Saber*

Tooth Curriculum, we analyse the state of curriculum development, which is crucial to deliberations on school improvement. Then in *Moving Beyond the Cult of the Individual*, we highlight the necessity for a collaborative partnership between schools and providing agencies, which is so vital in school-focused in-service. Without additional training, how will many school managers and teachers attempt to improve either their own institutions or their own contributions?

In *Section F*, we look to the future by proposing a model which can be used to develop the effectiveness of secondary schools. Finally, we conclude by reinforcing some of our earlier points, while at the same time stressing the importance of managerial practices and learning within schools. The whole book is predicated on the assumption that if schools are to be judged effective, a first priority is to have teachers and managers who are properly trained and know what they are doing.

The purpose of our book, therefore, is to provide a guide to educationalists and social scientists on how schools can gradually become more effective. The book is not a panacea; no such easy remedies are available. As in most things, change requires hard work. All we have attempted, given the lead from recent research on effective schools, is to outline some strategies and methods for working that can help schools to make a difference. We have reviewed much of the research, and tested it against our experience in developmental work in schools. Consequently, we feel that the strategies and methods advocated in the rest of the volume hold the promise of genuine improvement.

At various points in the text, we use case data gathered from our own research, either specifically for this book or for other reports or research projects. We hope this data will provide meaningful insights for practitioners. Details of these studies can be found in the further reading lists at the back of the book.

Inevitably, in a collaborative book of this kind, the co-authors have taken the lead on different chapters. In this case, David Hopkins is responsible for chapters 8, 9 and part of chapter 1. Peter Holly put together chapters 10, 11 and 12. Ken Reid is responsible for chapters 1 – 7, and the editorial and production stages associated with the book.

We sincerely hope the book will make a contribution to the literature and be of assistance to teachers, managers, students and lecturers alike. If so, the effort and endeavour which has gone into it will prove to have been worthwhile.

Ken Reid
David Hopkins
Peter Holly

Swansea and Cambridge,
April, 1986.

Section A: Setting the Scene

In these first two chapters we set the scene for what is to follow, and summarise many of the findings on school effectiveness which have so far been published. In particular, in Chapter 1, we highlight the difficulties associated with defining the term 'effective' and distinguish between the effective schools/school improvement debate. In Chapter 2, we concentrate upon *some* of the characteristics of effective schools, looking at the evidence drawn from research. These characteristics are sub-divided into eleven categories: school leadership; school management; school ethos; discipline; teachers and teaching; the curriculum; student learning; reading; pupil care; school buildings; and school size. We then summarise these findings before discussing, what is as yet, not known. For the sake of brevity, we have excluded a lengthy, and necessarily complicated, discussion on the methodological difficulties associated with such work. Fortunately, this is already available elsewhere (Gray, 1981; Reynolds and Reid, 1985) and does not need duplicating.

Chapter 1

Introduction – Towards the effective school: Context and strategies for improvement

Schools are different. Some are lively, some are happy. By contrast, others are dour and somewhat forbidding. When we walk into schools, and more so when we live and have our history in them as pupils and teachers, we can feel the differences. Schools have their own tone, their own vibrations and soul that set them apart and make them unique. This tone or culture or ethos or climate, as it has been variously called, is a result of the way in which the individuals in the school interact, how they behave towards each other and their expectations of one another. A school's culture has a very powerful influence on the life of those within it and on the success, in academic, social and personal terms, that the individuals within the school achieve. To say this is not to say anything new. We all know it from our own experience. If we do not feel it on a day-to-day basis, our memory soon conjures up images and feelings from our past. We can all put our own achievement into its proper context – the social milieu, the good and bad teachers, the successful and unsuccessful moments and so on.

Despite the authenticity of our feelings, it is only since the late 1970s that educationalists have begun to come to terms with what the culture of the school is all about. A number of major research reports in the 1960s and early '70s denied that school differences had any importance for pupil learning. The British *15000 Hours* study (Rutter *et al*, 1979), which was instrumental in arguing for the impact of individual school differences on pupils, put it like this:

There was a widespread pessimism about the extent that schools could have any impact on children's development and Basil Bernstein's (1970) view that 'Education cannot compensate for society' was generally accepted. However, it is important to recognise that there was immense disagreement on just what did have an influence on children's behaviour and attainments. Jensen (1969) saw hereditary factors as predominant; Jencks (1972), on the other hand, mainly put it down to 'luck'; many people saw family influences, especially during the preschool years, as the most important factor (eg Coleman *et al*, 1966; Plowden, 1967; West and Farrington, 1973) whereas sociologists were more inclined to see the roots of inequality in the economic and political structure of society itself.

Thus, Bowles (1971) (see also Bowles and Gintis, 1976) argued that 'educational inequalities are rooted in the basic institutions of our economy, class sub-cultures and social class biases in the operation of the school system itself.

Clearly, there is considerable disagreement about the influence of schooling on children's development. At first sight, too, there appears to be a hopelessly confusing chaos of contradictory research findings. In fact, that is not so. (Rutter *et al*, 1979 p 2)

Rutter and his colleagues went on to demonstrate that individual schools do make a difference to pupils' behaviour and attainment. Although their results have been criticised on methodological grounds (Goldstein, 1980), the substance of their argument stands. Moreover, other British researchers (Reynolds *et al*, 1976; Gray *et al*, 1983; Reynolds, 1985) and many Americans (eg Purkey and Smith, 1983) have published books and research reports with similar findings, all of which support the notion that schools are different and can have an important impact on the lives of their pupils, teachers and communities. We summarise many of these in Chapter 2 and in later chapters of this book. What is particularly interesting about this developing field of work is not only that schools can and do make a difference to pupils' achievement, but that these differences in outcome are systematically related to variations in the schools' climate, culture or ethos, and their 'quality' as social systems.

By implication, therefore, two pupils from similar social backgrounds and of similar intellectual abilities can perform differently at two outwardly similar schools because of the unique blend of academic and social circumstances to be found within the two establishments. If this thesis is correct, and the evidence in support of the contention is mounting, then teachers and schools have more control over their outcomes than has hitherto been realised. Equally, they have the ability to change their present direction and become really efficient and effective agents of pupils' learning and development – or do just the opposite. Thus, good schools may increase pupils' achievements. Bad schools decrease them. The importance of this correlation cannot be overemphasised. It is a crucial matter, especially in a competitive society and in an era of accountability – which leads us to another point.

It is all very well to keep talking about 'effectiveness' but what does it mean? There is always more than one view of what 'effectiveness' really is. For instance, is 'effectiveness' simply about producing people most likely to contribute to the nation's wealth? Alternatively, is it about producing educated, autonomous individuals?

There again, how does one really define 'school effectiveness'? While most laymen probably think they know what effectiveness means ('capable of producing desired results,' 'efficient' or something close to it), the term is particularly hard to define in an educational sense. In fact, it is noticeable that the literature is devoid of definitions despite the amount recently written on the topic.

The practical difficulties associated with defining 'school effectiveness' can be gauged from the extracts now presented. These extracts were written down by experienced teachers, senior teachers and headteachers while on full-time secondment, studying for a master's degree in education at the West Glamorgan Institute of Higher Education. They highlight the problems very well. The teachers were asked to define what school effectiveness means. Here are some of their better responses.

To be effective means the best possible use must be made of what is available to achieve the desired end. Therefore, effective schools must capitalise on their staff, resources and the pupils' abilities to achieve the required outcomes (Scale 2 female teacher).

The efficient organisation of curricular and staff resources to give a meaningful education which is balanced, has breadth and fits the children for life (Female deputy head).

The school utilising all its resources to the full to develop the pupils' potential (Unpromoted female teacher).

The ability of the school to be successful in achieving its aims and objectives and in preparing pupils to reach their potential for the next stage of life (Scale 3 female teacher).

Providing a system of schooling that meets the value of judgements of those directly engaged within the service as well as those whose value judgements are held to be of importance in the wider community. This includes meeting national needs, moral and economic requirements as well as the needs of a rapidly changing technological age . . . (Male headteacher).

The diversity of these answers speak for itself. So does the lack of precision. Yet, in a sense, they are all right. Each answer has something to offer, to commend it. Yet none of them is watertight or accurate enough. This is hardly surprising when we consider the scope of the topic. For example, what is covered by the term effective:

- the atmosphere of the school which should be one conducive to learning?
- the teachers' motivational skills, enabling pupils to develop socially and academically?
- self-evalution and school evaluation on a professional level?
- a suitable, well-taught and balanced curriculum?
- consistent discipline?
- good managerial practice?

We could go on, but the point has been made. School effectiveness is implicit in all these tasks, and many more besides.

The same students experienced similar problems when they attempted to respond to three related questions.

1 How would you prove to an external agent that you participated in an effective school?

2 As a form or subject tutor, how would you prove to your headteacher that you are effective?

3 How could you help make your school more effective?

These are all difficult and complicated questions which demand a great deal of time and thought. They reflect the different everyday uses of the word 'effective'. The students' answers indicate that an individual can be effective at one level, on one topic, with one class, but not at another level, with different topics or groups. Hence, the whole concept of effectiveness is fraught with definitional difficulties. Yet an understanding of the concept is important because it is currently central to the debates in education about accountability, the curriculum, management, cost-effectiveness, teacher education and much more. If we cannot confidently define 'school effectiveness' and its many derivatives, we should at the very least reflect on its meaning and question what we are doing in schools. After all, it is a crucial part of being a competent, thinking and informed professional.

Without debating the points further, it is worth noting the teachers' criteria for effectiveness as expressed in answer to the three questions above. First, they considered how to prove to an external agent that they were participating in effective schools.

Their answers suggest such proof would lie in:

a the creation of policy documents and/or guidelines on the whole curriculum;

b the processes involved in teaching and learning being constantly available for inspection, even at a moment's notice;

c the school devising its own evaluation practices and monitoring pupils' progress regularly;

d thorough, periodic teacher assessment;

e pupil profiles and records of achievement being readily available for inspection;

f in-service training (school-based and otherwise) being continuously conducted and monitored, staff maintaining their skills and keeping up-to-date with new developments;

g worthwhile liaison being conducted between parents and the school's board of governors;

h progress in school/community links in as many ways as possible;

i the maintenance and improvement of a school's record of academic achievement as measured by external examination passes;

j good sporting performances and a second record of cultural achievements;

k the monitoring of pupils' outcomes after they have left school;

l an outstanding record on pupils' behaviour and attendance;

m good managerial and organisational practice;

n evidence that they were making the best use of their resources and possessed the latest technology and other equipment;

o ensuring that the school's programmes are suited to a pupil's age, ability and aptitude, so that the less able can achieve relatively as much as the high fliers;

p parents taking an active part in school life;
q a school ethos conducive to learning and favourable to pupil-pupil and pupil-teacher interaction;
r staff and departmental meetings being regularly held to discuss schemes of work, pupils' progress, staff and curriculum development issues;
s efficient pastoral care;
t regular marking of pupils' work;
u good classroom displays of work;
v the maintenance of standards on all these issues throughout the year and in succeeding years.

Clearly, this list is far from exhaustive. But it is sufficiently long to show how demanding a task it is to create really effective schools. Ask yourself how many schools could claim to succeed on these levels now? Do you know any?

The teachers thought that form or subject tutors could prove their effectiveness by:
a thorough preparation;
b yearly and termly pupil forecasts;
c planning rigorous learning programmes for children;
d providing a calm working atmosphere;
e being pupil- and subject-centred;
f attending in-service courses whenever possible;
g varying teaching strategies;
h encouraging external agents to question pupils on their classroom experiences and progress;
i making favourable peer reviews of teaching performance;
j producing regular reports on their performance with groups/forms of pupils;
k proving they had dealt with or could remedy perceived teaching deficiencies;
l meeting the school's aims and objectives;
m collaborating with parents and other external agencies as required;
n participating in extra-curricular activities;
o showing examples of pupils' progress using samples of their work;
p being aware of children with special needs or learning difficulties;
q participating in school working parties, duties and other activities as required;
r consistently working hard and working equally hard with all classes, irrespective of ability.

Again, this list is not exhaustive. But it shows how many and varied the skills required by form tutors and subject teachers really are. It also highlights how stupid some people are when they demean the attributes needed for teaching. This varied list reinforces the enormous dedication and vitality required to teach today. Furthermore, it is a cogent retort to those who disbelieve that teaching is a professional activity, achievable by anyone. Finally, the skills outlined indicate that being judged effective means being accountable to third parties as well as oneself. The era of teacher autonomy is fast coming to an end. Whether this will make any difference to professional standards must remain an open question.

The last question the teachers were asked was: how could you make yourself and your school more effective? On this issue there were shorter answers and increased consensus. The teachers considered this would require:

a a knowledge of self and school assessment programmes such as GRIDS;
b setting high personal standards at all times, being a good team player, maintaining a school's and a department's aims and objectives;
c school-based in-service and staff development programmes;
d appropriate educational expertise and knowledge, particularly in psychology, guidance, curriculum development, management and child development;
e a school being able to identify its own needs, weaknesses and strengths and implement programmes accordingly.

These are among the very issues which the rest of the book concentrates upon; but a great deal more needs to be known about them. We hope you might feel a little wiser after reading the rest of our book.

School effectiveness research in the United States: Does it have any meaning for us in the UK context?

To what extent is American investment and rhetoric relevant or irrelevant to our needs? Do we 'value' what they are saying? Rowan, Bossert and Dwyer (1983) contend that the trend in the US has been for research which –

'. . . has defined school effectiveness narrowly as instructional effectiveness and has measured this construct using standardised achievement tests. The approach ignores the variety of school goals and yields messages of school effectiveness that are invalid and unreliable.'

Not all commentators in the United States are convinced of this line of enquiry. Cuban (1984) makes much the same point. His claim is that school leaders in the United States are being poorly served by the research into school effectiveness which offers an incomplete theory of school improvement and which is decontextualised. He warns of some of the unintended consequences of effective school practices that employ top-down strategies to achieve the narrow goal of raising test scores. Cuban also advises his readers to beware of the trendy jargon which promotes such indicators (of a good school) as high expectations, instructional leadership, an orderly environment, a positive climate, and consensus over academic goals. Above all, he identifies the dangers of unreflective acceptance of the instrumental rationality of 'tight-coupling' in organisations, which involves the 'locking in' of objectives, instructional goals, evaluation of student outcomes through test scores, etc. Advocates of this ends-means model also believe in the appropriateness of transplantation; that what is good for one school is good for the rest. The problem, says Cuban, is that while research findings are never clear cut, 'practitioners, who must take decisions every day, are anxious to locate those decisions in a technical rationality'. The authority dependency within hierarchical systems has this important 'spin off' – a naive belief in the efficacy of expert advice and the wave of the magic wand. 'Unlike the way things happen in Fairy Tales', says Cuban (1984),

school reform requires more than a kiss to convert a frog into a stunning prince. Furthermore, productive schooling entails more than raising (standardised) test scores.

Consequently, he continues:

the familiar pattern of a burst of romance followed by frustration and disappointment appears to describe the trajectory of the effective schools enthusiasm (I was about to write the word movement).

Cuban then makes these six telling points:
1 no one knows 'how to grow effective schools'.
2 there is no agreement on the central definitions, like 'effectiveness', 'leadership', etc.
3 the concept of effectiveness (commonly applied) is much too narrow. Cuban, for instance, argues that –

educators and parents prize other outcomes of schooling that transcend current definitions of effectiveness. . . . Some of those outcomes are sharing, learning to make decisions, developing self-esteem, higher order thinking skills, and a sense of the aesthetic.

4 research methodologies leave much to be desired. Unlike Britain, one important consideration to take into account is that the vast majority of the research activities have been conducted in elementary schools. Does such research have any meaning for secondary schools?
5 little attention has been paid to the potentiality of school districts (and LEA's) in terms of local mobilisation of school improvement.
6 The deep seated effects of mandation are too little understood.
 Cuban reviews the literature of effective schools (which emphasises goal-setting, targetting, academic aims, establishing and maintaining high expectations, frequent monitoring, etc) and concludes that not only is it 'conceptually simple' but it leads to policies which 'promote tighter

coupling between organisational goals and the formal structure, while relying on a traditional top down pattern of implementation'.

This 'organic tautness' rests on centralised (and, therefore, consistent) normative control, the mandate of a planning process for each school and the production of evaluation instruments (aligned with the predetermined goals). ·

Cuban concludes:

District officials pursuing policies that fasten individual schools to the central office believe they have found just the right hammer to pound in a nail . . . (but) encouraging a decision with a bang of the gavel is not the end of a process but merely the beginning of a sequence of events, many of them unanticipated, in the complicated process of implementation (see Fullan, 1982).

Mandation, of course, 'can produce compliance with the letter of the order without also leading to improvement'.

This line management model, resting on a 'chain of command', is based on two key assumptions; that

- a body of knowledge can be applied to increase productivity
- 'managerial savvy' (Cuban's words) can 'weld a consensus in a mission to drive an organisation forward'.

According to this model, says Cuban, the teachers become the 'problem', the 'solution', the 'scapegoats'. They stand in the way of and, therefore, reduce developers' 'hit-rates'.

It has been argued that a research style is a 'cultural artefact' (MacDonald, 1976) and that the objectives model, so influential within the literature of effective schools, is 'as American as popcorn . . . an ideological model harnessed to a political vision'. MacDonald continues:

The inclination of so many American curriculum developers and evaluators to perceive educational change as a technological problem of product specification and manufacture, is by itself unremarkable. Mechanistic analogies have a peculiar appeal for a people who see themselves as the raw materials of a vision which can be socially engineered. Their culture is characteristically forward-looking, constructionist, optimistic and rational. Both the vision and the optimism are reflected in the assumption that goal consensus, a prerequisite of engineering, is a matter of clarification rather than reconciliation. In contrast British culture is nostalgic, conservationist, complacent and distrustful of rationality. Our schools are the agents of continuity, providing discriminating transmission of a culture that has stood the test of time and will continue to do so, given due attention to points of adaptive growth. Goal consensus is neither ardently desired, nor determinedly pursued. Such pursuit would entail a confrontation of value-systems which have so far been contained within an all-embracing rhetoric of generalized educational aims. . . .

The theory and practice of the objectives model of evaluation is thus wedded to an American view of society, and an American faith in technology. Pluralist societies will find it difficult to use. Unified societies will use it, and discover they are pluralist.

Yet for several years, the DES, with its various publications, has been advocating the introduction of aims and objectives as part of deliberate planning. In *Ten Good Schools* (1977) a rather curious amalgam of US and UK 'wisdom' emerged. While the objectives approach is linked to strong leadership vision and shared values, schools are encouraged to become 'institutions for learning', linking with the local community and having a 'climate . . . conducive to growth'. Demonstrating the influence of Hoyle's (1975) concept of the creative school, this same publication also stresses the importance of consultation, team work, participation, power-sharing and delegation. It is interesting to note that Fullan (1985), who is able to survey the research literature in both the United States and the United Kingdom from his Canadian vantage point, acknowledges not only the received wisdom from the US when he stresses the importance of instructionally focused leadership (clear goals, monitoring, etc), but also the importance of 'process variables'. The latter are described as the 'four fundamental factors underlying successful improvement processes', ie

- a feel for the improvement process on the part of leadership
- a guiding value system
- intense interaction and communication
- collaborative planning and implementation.

In the UK context, Reynolds (1985) summarises research this far; he lists the kind of indicators used in the Rutter study (1979) (academic development, delinquency roles, levels of attendance and employment prospects, and school 'ethos'); and he nods in the direction of the American research and mentions the significance of a school's history (its biography and reputation). Reynolds points out that there has been little research in Britain on the desirable qualities of leadership, unlike in the USA where the effective school principal is seen as 'goal setter, enabler and mixture of Attila the Hun and Jesus Christ'.

Reynolds goes on to pose the central question – how do we make schools good? He concludes:

Some schools clearly have the potential, the willingness and the ability to change. . . . How one reaches the poor school with any personnel change is clearly the vital issue of the 1980s. Top-down solutions of the 1960s clearly do not work – for insecure teaching staffs, outside pressure is likely to only generate personal barriers to change.

Clearly poor schools must be partners in attempted change; they must in part 'own' the attempt. Yet exactly how outsiders and teachers work in partnership or alliance without the existence of any ground rules is unclear. To find means of ensuring that schools actually change is clearly a major undertaking which has yet to be embarked upon.

Gray (1981a and b) makes some interesting points concerning the dimensions of effectiveness. Are schools judged to be effective over time? Are they reviewed across the board; for example, academically and socially? What criteria are used to make such judgements and who does the judging? What, for instance, is HMI's vision of a good, effective school? What do parents actually believe? And the pupils? And the teachers themselves?

Is the effective school one that:
- maximises student achievement?
- maintains both student discipline and individual welfare?
- successfully prepares the students in both vocational and life skills?
- establishes harmonious relationships with the community? . . .

Four problems arise here. First, any attempt at a definition of school effectiveness automatically limits the range of indices to those mentioned in the definition; second, whenever a definition is offered, some people will approach it as 'tips for schools' – as a rather crude, over-simpified recipe for success; third, any definition is based on value judgements, not divorced from ideological considerations; and finally, arising from this question of ideological commitment, it is inevitable that any definition will depend on one's 'perspective' – as parent, stock-broker, educationalist, Marxist, etc. This book has a perspective, and that perspective is composed of value positions; the factors deemed of 'value' are:
- the improvement of both teaching and learning
- the development of the school as a 'learning institution'
- the humanisation of schooling
- the total involvement of staff in both collaboration and democratic collegiality; on awareness of the benefits of both process and product
- the research-based, INSET-based nature of school development

It could be argued that effective schools develop effectively – and they develop effectively by examining both the normative and procedural dimensions. This leads to the drawing of a vital distinction between a 'good' and an 'effective' school. The latter develops successfully in *any* direction; the former develops successfully according to an agreed, 'superior' and intrinsically worthwhile agenda. But in a pluralist society . . . ?

School effectiveness and change processes

Several commentators (the Schmucks, 1974; Cuban, 1984; Fullan, 1985; Purkey and Smith, 1985, Hopkins 1986a etc.) have argued that because 'change is a process not an event', schools need to improve – and make more effective – not only their 'change process capacity', but also their understanding of the dynamics of change. The goal is effective implementation of innovations; it is the *effecting* of change. 'Policy', argue Pressman and Wildavsky (1979), 'is effectively "made" by the people who implement it.' Within what Holly (1986) refers to as a 'development culture', schools are encouraged both to recognise this fact and to support their teachers in adopting and implementing desired changes effectively. Fullan (1985) makes much the same point when he maintains that teachers, administrators and support agents should 'share the considerable burden of development required by long-term improvement'. In this same paper, Fullan raises two further points of some relevance here: that

– the incremental, innovation-focused strategy (as above) needs to be established on a school-wide basis (as in the GRIDS approach). 'When successful improvements are accomplished', says Fullan, 'they involve individuals working in small groups and other collective ways, obtaining technical mastery, a sense of success, and new meanings';

– successful implementation involves what could be described as the exploration of opposites. The Berlaks (1982) and Holly (1986) have highlighted some of the dilemmas involved in the generation of change in schools. Fullan's view is that:

effective approaches to managing change call for combining and balancing factors that do not apparently go together – simultaneous simplicity – complexity, looseness – tightness, strong leadership-participation (or simultaneous bottom-up-top-downness).

Fullan (1981), in arguing for the importance of evaluation *for* development, utilises the stance taken by Berman and McLaughlin (1976) who maintain that:

although student outcomes might be the ultimate indicator of the effectiveness of an innovation . . . projects must go through the complex and uncertain process of implementation before they can affect students, it makes sense to put first things first and to measure the effectiveness of implementation before examining potential student aspects.

Purkey and Smith (1985) and Holly (ed. 1986) also stress the importance of evaluation within, and on behalf of, the developmental process. 'At the risk of stating the obvious', says Purkey and Smith:

We note that some means of measuring change is necessary as evidence that schools have indeed advanced or to show where further improvement must take place. A base-line must be established to which schools can be periodically compared.

What is recommended here is an ipsative approach; each school's progress being reviewed against its own baseline (as previously 'evaluated'). Yet, as Cuban (1984) has argued so cogently, the 'effective schools movement' in the US is taking a different route to school assessment (which entails a mixture of criterion- and norm-referencing). The central question within this approach is: how do schools measure up? How do they perform against both certain (agreed) criteria and the 'norm'? Are they above or below average? What are the standardised test scores in this and other schools? Unfortunately, however, this approach is no longer just a North American phenomenon following the recent publication by ILEA's Research and Statistics Branch of the 'Junior School Report'. In 'Summary of the Main Report' (1986), a spokesperson for the commissioning authority has announced that the research would be used to identify those primary schools not achieving appropriate standards and which 'fell below average'. Armed with this research:

the authority will be able . . . to bring the task force into such schools and help them improve to the level of other schools. This particular study provides a kind of educational slide-rule which allows us to measure one school against another.

(quoted in the TES, 18/4/86)

This particular piece of research identified twelve 'measures of effectiveness' pertinent to ILEA's junior schools. The list contains such indicators as purposeful leadership, staff involvement, intellectually challenging teaching, a work-centred environment, maximum communication between teachers and pupils and a positive climate. Yet the report heavily emphasises pupil progress as the chief criterion for school effectiveness. Thus, the report included such statements as 'three out of ten schools in the sample were found to be very effective in terms of the progress pupils made'; and 'effective schools jack up the progress of everyone in them'. Progress, in fact, is judged in terms which are both cognitive (reading, mathematics, writing and oracy) and non-cognitive (attitudes, behaviour, attendance and self-concept). While not wanting to question the validity of this research, we would make the following points:

- Often it is not the research itself which is debatable, but the way it is then used. Research findings often suit political purposes.
- While, according to Purkey and Smith (1985), a more qualitative approach to researching effectiveness is not inappropriate, quantitative analysis is 'relatively objective, it gains validity and acceptability, particularly when viewed by parents, the media, politicians and so on'. It is the expected mode of research.
- Deal (1985) has argued that, in the US context, the symbolic importance of the effective schools movement has led to the recasting of the value of research studies:

The findings of the effective schools research may be more important as symbols than as facts. Our society presently places more faith in science than in ordinary knowledge or common sense. Conclusions of researchers have more value than the judgement of practitioners. Although educators have claimed all along that schools make a difference, the Coleman Report (1966) demonstrated empirically that they did not. The facts overwhelmed the opinions of professionals, even though other social scientists hotly contested the facts. Coleman's method of proof was challenged by others who themselves believed in quantitative research. Despite the challenges, the facts fractured the faith. It took new quantitative evidence that schools can make a difference to shore up belief and confidence dampened by previous findings. One of the main contributions.of the effective schools research is to restore the myth of education lost in the 1960s and 1970s.

This, of course, explains the enormous popularity of the Rutter Report (1979) in the US. What looked like 'research' was saying just what the Americans wanted to hear – that schools can make a difference. Cuban (1984), in noting the initial impulse behind the study of effective schools (which was to react against the Coleman Report and attempt to improve student academic performance in low-income, largely minority schools), warns against the 'trendy jargon' of effective schools research which results not only in mandation but also in a reductionist drive which squeezes out 'the ineffable elements of teaching as an art – tempo, improvisation, drama and excitement of performance'. Cuban also queries the appropriateness of the 'implicit theory of change embedded in in-service programs, which are instituted to remediate situations after ineffectiveness has been diagnosed. The understanding is that:

faculties and administrators, as individuals and small groups, need additional knowledge and skills in order to implement research findings: change individuals and the school will become effective.

Elliott (1983) attacked this managerialist 'deficiency model' of (individual) staff training. Purkey and Smith (1985) have recommended the introduction of an in-service approach in which:

instead of a few teachers receiving in-service credit for attending a class at a local college, the entire school's staff would be offered credit for in-school workshops or for participating in collaborative improvement efforts.

Cuban (1984) rounds off his critique of the 'effective schools movement' by asking a central question – does the lack of focus on schools with high test scores mean that they are OK? Purkey and Smith (1985) argue that 'using test scores alone to evaluate and compare individual teachers and administrators is likely to have a chilling effect'. They go on to say that collaboration is 'most likely to occur in an atmosphere that supports innovation and risk-taking' but grading teachers is hardly conducive to such an environment. Fullan (1981) agrees, insisting that the political use of evaluation data can 'inhibit effective implementation'. Purkey and Smith (1985) continue:

Staff development that explicitly recognises the experience and expertise of staff members and encourages them to work together to change their school . . . (and which involves) the collaborative identification and solution of the school's problems . . . should be based on the expressed needs of teachers as revealed in the process of analysing school weaknesses (and strengths) and planning schoolwide correctional strategies. The focus should be on issues relevant to the organisation as a whole, not on 'fixing' individuals.

In the effectively developing school, then, its staff are *the* resource; they provide the creative power. The task, however, is to remain creative over time. As Pressman and Wildavsky (1979) have pointed out:

The advantages of being new are exactly that: being new. They dissipate quickly over time. The organisation ages rapidly. Little by little the regulations that apply to everyone else apply also to it. Accommodations are made with the other organisations in its environment. Territory is divided, divisions of labour are established, favours are traded, agreements are reached. All this means that the new organisation now has settled into patterns of its own which it defends against interruption. Youth has gone and middle age has come, hopefully more powerful, certainly more experienced, inevitably less innovative.

The staff of an effective school will find ways of achieving periodic rejuvenation. An effective school, within the UK context, will consider successful, 'good' schooling as both a product (an achieved set of outcomes) and a process. The 'product' perspective is the one normally emphasised: does a school achieve certain goals? Does it produce the 'goods'? Does it 'make a difference'? And this does not have to be a one-dimensional approach; cognitive and non-cognitive aspects can be considered, including (crucially) the maximisation of challenging and enjoyable learning experiences for all pupils. Such an approach aims to be able to list the school's accomplishments. But it is the manner in which those accomplishments are achieved (ie the quality of the process) that is also vital. The Schmucks (1974) were right to point to the importance of a 'humanised' process of schooling. The process is educative for all learners, students and teachers alike. Relationships can engender learning. Such a school will have an 'effect' (ie have an impact, make a lasting impression) *in the doing* of teaching and learning. This entails *having* an effect over time. The medium is the message; the effective school is an affective one. And the medium is also the process of change and development. The effective school effects change (ie develops) effectively. It establishes a development culture; it is ready for both change (and the learning through dissonance that goes with it) and the release of creative synergy.

The effective schools/school improvement debate

There are two strands in the current effective schools/school improvement debate. The effective schools literature is concerned to develop criteria that characterise the effective school; to provide a model for effective schooling. The schools improvement studies, on the other hand, are more action and developmentally oriented. They embody the long-term goal of moving towards the vision of the 'problem-solving' or 'thinking' or 'relatively autonomous' school and are more concerned to promote and evaluate school improvement strategies. These two approaches are, of course, complementary, so we will briefly review them both before looking at their similarities and outlining a strategy for implementation. We begin by considering some of the lessons learnt from school improvement studies.

We have recently been involved in an international school improvement project that provides a good example of work in this area (Van Velzen *et al* 1985; Hopkins 1987). The current OECD/CERI International School Improvement Project (ISIP) defines school improvement as:

... the change of the teaching-learning process and/or the internal conditions in one or more schools with the ultimate aim to accomplish the educational goals by the school(s) more effectively.

The International School Improvement Project has identified six areas of focus which reflect the contemporary emphasis on school improvement. These are:
1 school-based review for school improvement;
2 principals and internal change agents in the school improvement process;
3 the role of external support in school improvement;
4 research and evaluation in school improvement;
5 school improvement policy;
6 conceptual mapping of school improvement.

Most writers on the topic argue that the prime goal of school improvement is the induction of a capacity for problem solving within the school. School-based strategies mark a radical departure from the centralised change strategies of the 1960s and '70s. Ironically, their utilisation and increasing popularity are based on extensive research and development that has emerged out of the failure of the educational reforms of the past two decades (Lehming and Kane, 1981; Fullan, 1982). School-based strategies have as a major goal school improvement; implicit in these strategies is a set of assumptions about how change occurs. David (1982:1–2) has defined these assumptions as follows:

One assumption is that change does not occur unless the particulars of a school and its context are taken into account. A second is that school staff will not be committed to a change effort unless they have had the opportunity to be involved in decisions concerning the shape of the project. A third is that effective schools are characterised by a school-wide focus – a set of shared goals and a unified approach to instruction as opposed to several separate, uncoordinated projects and approaches. Finally, proponents of school based strategies believe that any planning effort that encourages self-awareness and reflection on the part of school staff will greatly increase the chances that behaviours will change.

If school improvement is used as a generic team, then it can be regarded as constituted by a set of differing activities (school-based in-service, school self-evaluation, organisation development, school-based curriculum development, participatory decision-making, etc.), each of which is underpinned by a set of assumptions about change similar to those suggested by David. This idea can be represented diagrammatically as in Figure 1.1

Figure 1.1   The ecology of school improvement

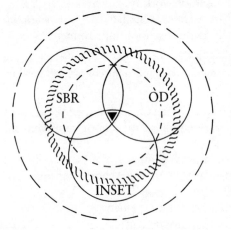

▼   School improvement
----   Assumptions about change
\\\\   School ethos/climate
___   Ecology of school
NB Inner circles representing SBR, OD and INSET are only examples of the nexus of activities that comprise school improvement – there are other activities and the combination will vary from school to school.

The following eight factors are representative of the so-called organisation factors that are characteristic of effective schools:
1 curriculum focused school leadership
2 supportive climate within the school
3 emphasis on curriculum and instruction (eg maximising academic learning)
4 clear goals and high expectations for students
5 a system for monitoring performance and achievement
6 ongoing staff development and inservice
7 parental involvement and support
8 LEA support.
Commenting on a similar list, Fullan (1985:400) says that these factors:

say nothing about the dynamics of the organisation. To comprehend what successful schools are really like in practice, we have to turn to additional factors which infuse some meaning and life into the process of improvement within the school. In reviewing material that more closely addresses process issues, there are four fundamental factors which in my view underlie successful processes.
1 A feel for the process on the part of leadership
2 A guiding value system
3 Intense interaction and communication
4 Collaborative planning and implementation
It is these process factors that fuel the dynamics of interaction and development of the previous organisation variables.

The relevant literature will have to be consulted for a detailed explanation of these factors; in particular Fullan's (1985) paper. A few illustrational comments on the process factor list (drawn from Fullan, 1985) are in order. A feel for the process of leadership is difficult to characterise because the complexity of factors involved tends to deny rational planning. A useful analogy would be that organisations are to be sailed rather than driven. A guiding value system refers to a consensus on high expectations, clear and explicit goals, clear rules, a genuine caring about individuals, etc. Intense interaction and communication refers to simultaneous support and pressure at both horizontal and vertical levels within the school. Collaborative planning and implementation needs to occur both within the school and externally, particularly in the LEA.

Another set of process type variables is given by David Clark and his colleagues (1984) who undertook a useful analysis of the two sides of the debate. They conclude their paper with a list of variables that characterise both the school improvement and effective schools approach.

Lessons from America's best-run schools
Thomas Peters and Robert Waterman (1982) unleashed a blockbuster best seller about America's best-run companies, *In Search of Excellence*. The book is an articulate and relaxed summary of what the authors learned by visiting 35–40 successful companies, serving as consultants for many years to both successful and unsuccessful firms, and reviewing rather carefully contemporary theory and thought about organisations. They began their presentation by noting and commenting very briefly on attributes they asserted characterised excellent companies. It is our desire to attempt the same brief summary for schools.

1 *Commitment* Good schools project a *raison d'être*. The school's mission that is asserted by individual staff members may seem imprecise, but collectively the staff has arrived at an agreed upon set of behaviours and outcomes that are sufficiently specific to acculturate new organisational members and control the behaviour of veteran members. They are organisations with a sense of themselves.

2 *Expectations* Good schools and school systems are populated by confident people who expect others to perform to their personal level of quality. The attitude of success crosses categories and feeds on itself. Teachers expect students to achieve. Students know they are expected to achieve and they expect in turn, to have involved, competent teachers. Principals are surprised by teachers who fail. Teachers are surprised by administrators who ask little of themselves and others.

3 *Action* People in good schools do things. They have a bias for action, proclivity for success, and a sense of opportunism. They plan for now, seize decision options when they arise, try new ideas, drop bad trials, and play within their strengths.

4 *Leadership*   Peters and Waterman pressed the point that 'innovative companies foster many leaders and many innovators throughout the organisation'. People with high levels of efficacy and expectancy who are trying and experimenting cannot be restricted to designated leadership positions. Effective educational organisations spawn primary work groups and individual 'champions' in unusual numbers. The designated leaders create an environment for trial and a tolerance for failure so that leaders can emerge and be sustained at all levels of the school system.

5 *Focus*   Good schools pay attention to the task in hand. Student achievement in the classroom commands the attention of teachers and administrators. More classroom time is allotted to academic learning; more of the allotted time is engaged academic learning time for students. Staff development programmes concentrate on classroom-orientated skills and understandings. Good schools know what their core tasks are and focus on those jobs.

6 *Climate*   At a minimum, good schools maintain an orderly and safe environment for students and teachers. But they are much more than orderly. Successful schools work for all people in the building. They are not schools for students; nor are they schools for teachers and administrators. They work for adults and children and adolescents. Good schools are good places to live in and work, for everybody.

7 *Slack*   Good schools have a reasonable level of human resources and slack time. Time is necessary for teachers to participate in staff development activity and to incorporate new practices into their already crowded professional lives. Good practice is facilitated by a reasonable level of organisational redundancy and slack at the classroom level. Tolerance for failure, encouragement of experimentation, and the capacity to invent and adapt innovations are not achievable in organisational settings where effectiveness is regularly traded off for efficiency.

All this may sound a little abstract, but the importance of these somewhat nebulous characteristics cannot be underestimated if the staff of your school are going to make a difference. How does a school or school staff become more effective? Figure 1.2 (taken from Fullan, 1985) illustrates the interaction between the organisation and process factors which we have just discussed.

It must also be remembered that schools generate an individual culture (Sarason, 1982). This internal culture has been variously described as the school ethos or school climate, and in many cases reflects the internal capacity of the school to change. The external ecology is composed of environmental pressures which are a function of government policy, social climate, local culture, etc. These two influences are also represented on the diagram. Conceptualising school improvement in this way assists in understanding why activities vary from country to country and within national and local boundaries.

Figure 1.2 The interaction between the organisation and process factors

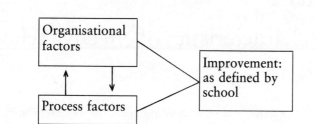

We can contrast these aspirations and their rather global perspective with the more specific concerns of the effective schools research. Not only does the effective schools research conclude that schools do make a difference, but there is also broad agreement on the factors that are responsible for that difference. The review conducted by Purkey and Smith (1983) is well known, and their distinction between organisations and process factors widely accepted. Although more attention has been paid to the former, the latter are arguably the most important.

The process factors provide the means for achieving organisational change; they lubricate the system and 'fuel the dynamics of interaction'. The process factors remain similar from setting to setting; be it a large American urban school, a Welsh rural school or a multi-national company. It is the organisational factors that may vary from context to context and so it is important that we are clear about our criteria for effectiveness.

In summarising this section we maintain that there is a commonality between the school improvement and effective schools movements. We characterise the type of school envisioned by these two sets of literature as the 'problem solving' (for want of a better phrase) school. It is our argument, based upon our experience and research in schools, that a problem solving school might well have some or all of the following processes built into its metabolism.

- school-based review
- coherent staff development
- the capacity to monitor change
- continuous curriculum development

Some of the following chapters, especially Chapters 9 to 12, will look more closely at each of these processes.

Chapter 2

Some characteristics of effective schools

This chapter focuses on the dissemination of research into school effectiveness undertaken on both sides of the Atlantic. First, however, it is necessary to put the ensuing discussion into context. There is no simple combination of variables that will produce an effective school (Brookover *et al*, 1979). Consequently, there is no universal recipe for success. While all reviews assume that effective schools can be differentiated from ineffective ones, there is no consensus yet on just what constitutes an effective school. Every school is unique, a miniature society (Shipman, 1967). Therefore, each school has its own characteristics which are shaped by such factors as its location, pupil intake, size, resources and, most importantly, the quality of its staff.

The literature is also deficient on how schools can be altered in order to make them more effective, something we shall be tackling later in this book. Obviously a school with a weak staff simply cannot redeploy or replace ineffective teachers at will. Senior managers are forced to improve their institutional strengths through time-consuming activities such as staff development schemes and in-service training. There is a world of difference between theoretical and practical solutions which will work on the 'shop floor'.

These practical difficulties impose considerable constraints upon researchers and often leave them open to the charge of providing unworkable or unrealistic solutions. However, researchers themselves are frequently placed in invidious positions. What will work at one level in one school will not prove effective in another. There is no certainty that the same combination of ingredients, used in different schools at various times, will produce similar results. There are simply too many intangibles for teachers and researchers to control. Research is undertaken in the real world; it is impossible to eliminate all the negative features of schools, however hard we try. We cannot, for example, control pupil intakes or pupils' socio-economic backgrounds. Sometimes, therefore, researchers have either been unsure quite what to recommend to improve certain schools, or thought that specific proposals were not necessary (Purkey and Smith, 1983).

We are constrained, too, by the limited information which is presently available, by the kind of studies which have been undertaken, and by the methodological difficulties inherent in research into school differences and school effectiveness (Gray, 1981; Reynolds and Reid, 1985). Before we can generalise findings across school boundaries, there is a need for a much fuller appreciation of what each school and each school system is trying to achieve. For instance, many of the differences between schools are subtle and qualitative. Without access to additional data and multivariate procedures, any judgement of school effectiveness, particularly as it is often made on the basis of crude examination results, is likely to be erroneous. Bryan and Digsby (1983) caution that a balanced appraisal of the effectiveness of school and schools systems is essential, particularly at times when certain patterns of schooling and curricula are being dismantled or attacked for political or economic, rather than educational, reasons. In such circumstances, studies of school effectiveness are in danger of being turned into projects of expediency and accountability.

The search for results, too, has other problems. For example, in focusing on school management and school improvement we cannot ignore other levels of a school's system. A school is a combination of 'nested layers' (Barr and Dreeben, 1981) in which each organisational level sets the context and defines the boundaries for the layer below, although there is a reciprocal influence. If the locus of the educational process is at the lowest structural level, the classroom, it is nevertheless the adjacent level, the school, that forms the immediate environment in which the classroom functions. The quality of the process at classroom level will be enhanced or diminished by the quality of activity at the level above it (Purkey and Smith, 1983). In practical terms, this might mean running the school in such a way that the sanctity of the class period is seldom violated by external interference (Stallings, 1981). Alternatively it might lie in supposing that classroom discipline or good management is a necessary, though not sufficient, prerequisite for learning for most students (Duffy, 1980). Just as order in the corridors is enhanced by order in the classroom (Stallings and Hentzell, 1978; Glenn, 1981), control is difficult to maintain behind a classroom door if the hall, dining room and other classrooms are in chaos.

Hence, if we are concerned with making entire schools more successful, it is logical to treat the school as a whole entity. Only when schools maximise the chance of efficient learning taking place in every classroom for every pupil will they be judged effective. It is only then that teacher-specific or management-led interventions will succeed. As we shall see in later chapters, this is very far from the case in many disaffected schools in Britain and the United States at the present time (Reid, 1986).

It is within these limitations that the remainder of this chapter, and many of the others, are written. It is almost impossible to *prove* that a school is well managed or effective, even when it is. Intuition is no substitute for scientific certainty. In the meantime, too many writers are applauding the concept of managing schools effectively (Edmonds, 1978; 1979a, b; 1981a, b; Austin, 1979; 1981; Hersh *et al*, 1981) without critically analysing that concept or showing how to prove outcomes. This is a mistake. It is, however, quite understandable. It may even be a necessary stage as we continue in our search for effective schools, effective teaching and effective pupil learning.

The evidence from research

Studies into school differences and school effectiveness have been conducted at three levels: case studies, small-scale investigations and large-scale enquiries. Each of these kinds of projects has its own strengths and weaknesses (Smith and Purkey, 1983; Reynolds and Reid, 1985). For the rest of this chapter we have deliberately concentrated less on methodology and methodological considerations in favour of reporting outcomes under a number of distinct headings. We hope in this way to inform practitioners rather than to complicate issues or contribute to a technical debate. In any case, such literature is available elsewhere (Reynolds, 1985; Reynolds and Reid, 1985).

A breakdown of research to date shows that findings from studies into school effectiveness can be divided into 11 categories. These are: school leadership; school management; school ethos; discipline; teachers and teaching; the curriculum; student learning; reading; pupil care; school buildings; and school size. Much more is known about some of these issues than about others.

School leadership
Successful school leadership is associated with:
1. Setting a strong administrative example (Weber, 1971; Brookover *et al*, 1979; Edmonds, 1979a, b; 1981a; California State Department of Education, 1980; Glenn, 1981);
2 Principals who recruit their own staff (Austin, 1979; 1981);
3 Leaders being fully supportive of teachers (Levine and Stark, 1981);
4 Skilled leadership in providing a structural institutional pattern in which teachers can function effectively (Levine and Stark, 1981);
5 High levels of parent-teacher and parent-principal contact (Armor *et al*, 1976);
6 Principals who achieve a balance between a strong leadership role for themselves and maximum autonomy for teachers (Armor *et al*, 1976);
7 Strong instructional leadership (Trisman *et al*, 1976);
8 Principals who are firm disciplinarians and provide strong behavioural role models for teachers and pupils alike (NIE, 1978).

School management

Effective school management is related to:

1 Goal-specific staff development programmes (Venezky and Winfield, 1979; Phi Delta Kappa, 1980);

2 Worthwhile and efficient inter-departmental meetings and planning exercises, assisted by staff development programmes (Levine and Stark, 1981);

3 High teacher morale (NIE, 1978; Hunter, 1979; Doss and Holley, 1982);

4 Staff having a sense of control over the school programme (Hunter, 1979; Doss and Holley, 1982);

5 Clear autonomy of the school from the district/local education authority (Hunter, 1979);

6 Teachers who have high job satisfaction levels and who are in general agreement with the heads' educational and procedural style of management (NIE, 1978);

7 Material and moral support from the central administration for staff (NIE, 1978);

8 An emphasis on academic success, with individual achievement and improvement rewarded (NIE, 1978).

School ethos

A favourable school climate or school ethos is linked with:

1 An atmosphere of order, purposefulness and pleasure in learning (Weber, 1971);

2 A co-operative atmosphere in the school (Venezky and Winfield, 1979);

3 Discipline and order in a supportive atmosphere (Glenn, 1981);

4 Joint planning by teachers in staff development programmes (Glenn, 1981);

5 An efficient, co-ordinated scheduling and planning of activities, resources and people (Glenn, 1981);

6 A general sense of educational purpose (California State Department of Education, 1980);

7 Unique features of schools which operate differently within every institution (California State Department of Education, 1980);

8 A strong school spirit (NIE, 1978);

9 Students' sensing that the school as a social system is not a meaningless environment in which they can exert little control over what happens to them (NIE, 1978);

10 Staff consensus on the values and aims of the school as a whole (Rutter *et al*, 1979);

11 The establishment of clearly recognized principles and guidelines for student behaviour (Rutter *et al*, 1979);

12 A formal attitude and expectation for academic success coupled with

specific actions which emphasise those attitudes and expectations (Rutter *et al*, 1979).

Discipline

Good and well-disciplined schools are related to:

1 Better control or discipline (Lezotte *et al*, 1974; New York State Department of Education, 1974a, b; 1976; Brookover and Schneider, 1975; Spartz *et al*, 1977; Austin, 1978).

2 Principals interpreting rules in a manner that enhances rather than reduces effectiveness (Levine and Stark, 1981);

3 Clearly stated rules that are consistently, fairly and firmly enforced (NIE, 1978);

4 The maintenance of orderly classrooms (Armor *et al*, 1976);

5 The link between a school's structure of order and academic success (NIE, 1978);

6 Classroom management that keeps students actively engaged in learning activities (Rutter *et al*, 1979);

7 Classrooms in which praise is freely given and discipline applied infrequently but firmly (Rutter *et al*, 1979);

8 Giving a high proportion of students responsibility for personal and school duties and resources (Rutter *et al*, 1979);

9 Having organisationally 'tight' regimes that attempt high expressive control of pupils (Rutter *et al*, 1979; Millham, 1982);

10 Having a form of balanced control neither harsh nor weak (Reynolds, 1982).

Teachers and teaching

Efficient teaching is associated with:

1 Positive leadership from a group of teachers, that includes the sharing of responsibility for decision-making and implementation (California State Department of Education, 1980);

2 Teacher accountability for student performance and the provision of accurate information on that performance (California State Department of Education, 1980);

3 On-going in-service training related to the instructional programme (California State Department of Education, 1980);

4 In-service training programmes concentrating on topics determined by teachers, together with frequent informal consultations among teachers in implementing reading programmes (Armor *et al*, 1976);

5 Teachers' strong sense of efficacy and high expectations for students (Armor *et al*, 1976);

6 Teacher flexibility in modifying and adapting instructional approaches (Armor *et al*, 1976);

7 Reduced teacher-pupil ratios (Doss and Holley, 1982);

8 Cohesiveness amongst teachers (NIE, 1978);

9 Demonstrated staff concern for individual and group student welfare (Rutter *et al*, 1979);
10 Positive teacher expectations from all pupils (Douglas, 1964; Rist, 1970; Williams, 1976; Cuttance, 1980).

The curriculum

A good school curriculum is associated with:
1 The co-ordination of curriculum, instruction and testing to focus on specified objectives achieved through careful planning and staff development (Levine and Stark, 1981);
2 A programme which focuses on the needs of low-achieving students (Levine and Stark, 1981);
3 A programme which emphasises high-order cognitive skills such as reading, comprehension and problem solving (Levine and Start, 1981);
4 The assured availability of materials and resources necessary for teaching (Levine and Stark, 1981);
5 Minimising burdensome record-keeping tasks by designing simple procedures for tracking students and monitoring class progress and achievement (Levine and Stark, 1981);
6 Co-ordinating required homework with the maths and reading curriculum, together with improving the quality of homework assignments and improving parental involvement in students' learning (Levine and Stark, 1981);
7 Providing immediate feedback to students on what is acceptable performance at school (Rutter *et al*, 1979);
8 The academic demands of courses, students' concern for and commitment to academic values, the amount of time spent on study and homework and, in general, a climate of high expectations on the part of students and their teachers alike (McDill, 1969; Brimer and Madaus, 1978; Madaus *et al*, 1979; Marjoribanks, 1979; Rutter *et al*, 1979; Madaus, 1980);
9 Ensuring a favourable psychological atmosphere within classrooms (Walberg, 1969; Rosenshine, 1970; Rosenshine and Furst, 1971; Walberg and Anderson, 1972; Moos, 1979; Frazer, 1981; Frazer and Walberg, 1981);
10 Positive learning outcomes in the classroom achieved through obtaining the right 'mix' of cohesiveness, satisfaction, task difficulty, formality, goal direction and democracy. Negative learning outcomes are related to friction, cliquishness, apathy, disorganisation and favouritism (Haertel and Walberg, 1981).

Student learning

Effective student learning is related to:
1 High expectations for children's achievement (Trisman *et al*, 1976;

Hunter, 1979; Brookover *et al*, 1979; Edmonds, 1979a, b; 1981a; California State Department of Education, 1980; Glenn, 1981);

2 An orderly atmosphere conductive to learning (Edmonds, 1979a, b; 1981a);

3 An emphasis on basic-skill acquisition (Edmonds, 1979a, b; 1981a);

4 Frequent monitoring of pupil progress (Edmonds, 1979a, b; 1981a);

5 Efficient use of classroom time (Tomlinson, 1980);

6 Using parents to help keep children on task (Tomlinson, 1980);

7 Fostering high levels of parental contact and involement (Phi Delta Kappa, 1980);

8 Schools that encourage 'direct' instruction (Austin, 1979; 1981);

9 Low pupil/teacher ratios (Phi Delta Kappa, 1980);

10 An emphasis on instructional leadership by the principal or another staff member (Smith and Purkey, 1983);

11 Comparative monitoring of student progress on a class-by-class basis (Levine and Stark, 1981);

12 A good school's 'social' system (quality of peer group relationships, order and sub-cultures) (Brookover *et al*, 1979);

13 Amount of time spent on instruction (Brookover *et al*, 1979);

14 Staff commitment to student achievement (Brookover *et al*, 1979);

15 The use of competitive team games in instruction (Brookover *et al*, 1979);

16 Ability grouping procedures (Brookover *et al*, 1979);

17 The use of appropriate reinforcement practices (Brookover *et al*, 1979);

18 A clear focus on basic skills, small-group instruction and evidence of interchange of ideas among staff (Trisman *et al*, 1976);

19 Class size or school organisation calculated to increase the sense of personal relationships between student and teacher (NIE, 1978);

20 Students' belief that school subject matter is relevant and valuable (NIE, 1978).

Reading

An effective school with a good learning environment includes:

1 A strong emphasis on reading (Weber, 1971);

2 High reading expectations from students (Weber, 1971);

3 The availability of additional reading personnel to help students (Weber, 1971);

4 The use of reading in the phonics programme (Weber, 1971);

5 Individualised reading programmes (Weber, 1971);

6 Careful evaluation of students' reading progress (Weber, 1971);

7 An environment with a high achievement orientation orginating from the principal down, as opposed to a human relations emphasis (Venezky and Winfield, 1979);

8 A reading curriculum that requires mastery of complex reading skills (California State Department of Education, 1980);
9 A reading programme which is well integrated with other subject areas (California State Department of Education, 1980).

Pupil care

Effective pupil care is probably associated with:
1 The treatment of students in ways that emphasise and assure their success and potential for success (Rutter *et al*, 1979);
2 More favourable teacher-pupil relationships in classrooms (Reynolds *et al*, 1976);
3 Encouraging pupils to participate in the running of their schools (Reynolds *et al*, 1976; Rutter *et al*, 1979);
4 Schools which offer rewards rather than punishments (Rutter *et al*, 1979);
5 Schools which avoid the heavy use of physical punishment (Clegg and Megson, 1968) and caning (Reynolds *et al*, 1976).

School buildings

There are suggestions that effective schools are linked with:
1 The provision of a clean, comfortable and well-maintained physical environment for students (Rutter *et al*, 1979);
2 Schools which take trouble over building upkeep and maintenance of their grounds (Pablant and Baxter, 1975).

School size

Effective schools are likely to be:
1 Smaller (Barker and Gump, 1964; Coleman, 1966; Cohn, 1968; Garbarino, 1973; 1980; Wicker, 1979; Garbarino and Asp, 1982).

Summary of what is known

What emerges from this mass of evidence in different areas suggests that:
1 The leadership role of the principal and the senior management team is vital – although there is little scientific evidence to support this frequently reported assertion.
2 It is crucial for schools to be well-managed organisations. In this context, a 'happy', efficient staff is of key importance. So is the part played by in-service training. Staff operating on agreed, united policies appear to be the most effective.
3 A favourable school ethos or school climate is necessary for positive outcomes to accrue – how to achieve such an atmosphere is less well documented.
4 Effective schools are orderly at all times, both inside and outside classrooms.

5 The quality of teaching staff is perhaps the single most important factor. Schools with weak staff will never be as effective as those with a strong staff.

6 Schools need to concentrate much of their endeavour upon teaching *per se* while at the same time promoting empathetic pupil care and learning-centred approaches in the classroom.

7 The curriculum should be as important for low-achieving as for high-achieving pupils.

8 Regular feedback on performance needs to be given to all pupils.

9 The academic demands of courses, allied to a commitment to traditional academic and behaviour values, is extremely important.

10 Pupils should expect and receive high professional standards from teachers at all times. When this happens, it seems that pupils will reciprocate.

11 Proper use must be made of classroom teaching time as part of standard practice within schools.

12 Traditional 'core' subjects should be emphasised by schools, particularly reading, writing and maths. It seems that reading standards are vitally important. Once pupils fall behind in the basics, student disaffection may replace a desire to learn.

13 Pupils should be encouraged to participate in the running and organisation of their school. When pupils identify with their school and its staff, they will be more respectful and show more positive behavioural and learning features.

14 Pupils are more likely to feel part of a school unit in buildings which are clean and well cared for, and in schools whose organisational structure does not make them feel 'lost'.

What is not known

Far too little is known about school differences and effectiveness in primary education in Britain (Mortimore *et al*, 1985). The search for effectiveness in primary education is hampered by the lack of a clear consensus as to the outcomes of this stage of education. There are no public examination results, for example, which can be used as a basis for the formulation of an operational definition of efficiency. Research undertaken in primary schools is ambivalent in its support of one teaching style over another, hence the sterility of the debate over the relative merits of progressive as compared with traditional approaches to learning. The literature is, however, clear on one point. So long as teachers know what they are doing and why, and their teaching styles correspond with their aims and objectives, then the likely effectiveness of their teaching is enhanced. When staff do not have clear aims and objectives, but instead muddle through their curriculum, the likelihood of ineffective outcomes is considerably increased. A challenge to teacher education, both pre- and in-service, is to enable teachers to acquire a vocabulary which allows them to articulate their intentions and describe the match between these and the learning performance of children in classrooms (Robinson, 1983).

Amongst areas in secondary education where the volume of literature is at present too small or too contradictory (Reynolds, 1982) to permit a reliable assessment are:

a Curriculum range, content and style of presentation. Our knowledge in this field would soon be enhanced if a national curriculum was introduced.

b Principal characteristics, methods, relationships with colleagues, etc. There are, however, numerous studies previously reported which make general statements on this theme and stress the crucial link between positive school leadership and effectiveness.

c School/community relationships and school/parent relationships. Nevertheless, research consistently shows the vital importance of good parent-pupil, parent-school relationships (Newsom and Newsom, 1984).

d Teacher characteristics – cognitive, effective, organisational and relational.

e School organisation – academic, pastoral, cultural, sporting, etc.

Issues on which further research is necessary before too many firm conclusions are drawn include the effects of: resource levels/expenditure per pupil; quality/quantity of plant/buildings per pupil; class size/pupil-teacher ratio; and school size. For example, there are hints that expenditure on teachers' salaries may have some effect on outcomes (Thomas, 1962; Bowles and Levin, 1968). Strangely, evidence on class size suggests this factor is of doubtful importance (Davie, 1972; Wiseman, 1974; Rutter *et al*, 1979; APU, 1981a, b, c) contrary to many teachers' and parents' intuition. It seems possible that school size may be important up to a certain 'threshold'. Above this level, further increases in size may not be associated with a corresponding decline in effectiveness (Garbarino and Asp, 1982). It is equally possible that large schools may be able to generate a level of smooth functioning characteristic of smaller institutions when they react appropriately (Reynolds, 1982).

Many other factors remain to be explored. To what extent are school effects consistent over time? Jencks *et al* (1972) report that schools judged effective one year are not necessarily effective the following year. By contrast, Rutter *et al* (1979) suggest there is a consistency of 'effectiveness' or 'ineffectiveness' over time.

Most studies (Rutter *et al*, 1979; Purkey and Smith, 1983) agree that socio-economic variables continue to play a stronger part in school outcomes than educational ones (Coleman, 1966; Jencks, 1972; Rutter *et al*, 1979; Purkey and Smith, 1983). A minority disagree (Madaus, 1980). But, which children are most influenced by their schools?

Children of low ability, as suggested by Coleman (1966)? Or high socio-economic status children as argued by Barnes and Lucas (1974)? Which range of outcomes do schools have greatest influence upon – cognitive or social (Reynolds, 1982)? Which countries exhibit the greatest school effects – developed or underdeveloped (Coleman, 1965)?

It follows that an effective school is one 'characterized by high evaluations of students, high expectations, high norms of achievement, with the appropriate pattern of reinforcement and instruction' in which students 'acquire a sense of control over their environment and overcome the feelings of futility which . . . characterize the students in many schools' (Brookover *et al*, 1979, p. 243).

However, the quest to discover how to increase the academic achievement of students from all walks of life has not been overwhelmingly successful. Many factors have been shown to have a dramatic influence on student learning. But many of these, like family background and related variables (Coleman *et al*, 1966; Jencks *et al*, 1972) are not easy to manipulate, at least in the short run.

Other variables that can be measured and, in theory, changed relatively easily, usually by spending money, have been found to bear little relationship to achievement. These include decreasing class size, raising teacher salaries, buying more library books, changing the reading series, constructing new school buildings, or adding compensatory education programmes (Coleman, Jencks and Stephens, 1967; Averch *et al*, 1972; Murnane, 1980; Hanusher, 1981; Mullin and Summer, 1981).

It is clear, however, that effective schools require strong leadership by the principal and other staff. Teachers should aim as high as possible for their students at all times. They should formulate a clear set of academic goals for students and place an emphasis upon learning within the school. This may well necessitate the introduction of school-wide staff development training programmes in every educational institution, as well as a system for the monitoring of student progress.

A great deal of important information and many leads have been ascertained since the 1960s, particularly during the late 1970s and early '80s, but much more research is necessary before too many firm conclusions are drawn. Without this knowledge, our search for effective schools will never be complete. The search for reliable information on effective schooling is one of the greatest challenges facing educationalists today. It is a process in which everyone connected with education can play a part. We hope it is a challenge educationalists will accept with relish.

Section B: The Problems: The unacceptable outcomes of secondary schooling

The 1980s will be remembered as the era of disaffection in education for many different reasons (Reid, 1986). In chapters 3 and 4 we concentrate on some of the background information required to understand why some schools are less effective than others. In Chapter 3 we consider the social, parental and school processes associated with disadvantaged and disaffected pupils. This is important background material for anyone who has to combat or manage disaffection. Chapter 4 focuses on discipline and disruption. In order to make the chapter a more enjoyable read, we introduce the chapter by highlighting the differences between Hillbourne and Bampton Comprehensive Schools. This is followed by a consideration of research undertaken in the United States and Britain and by relating this data to school aspects and to practical school management; a theme developed in later chapters.

Chapter 3

Disadvantaged and disaffected pupils: Social, parental and school processes

Writing a chapter on disadvantage and disaffection and relating it to school effectiveness is not an easy exercise. The reason for making this assertion is fairly simple to understand. While there is now quite a lot of work on what makes a good school in academic terms, much less is known about what generates good social results. In fact, the authors of some studies have found it virtually impossible to find out what it is about some schools that produces a good level of attendance, a low delinquency rate or a group of pupils with positive self-esteem (Reynolds, 1985a).

There are some hints in the literature – little else – that some schools do particularly well for low-ability pupils but not for high-ability pupils. Just what these schools are like remains unclear. They are also a minority. Since they may represent authentic positive discrimination in action or be true working-class comprehensives, we really do need to find out how they manage to excel. Ironically, some of these schools may be regarded less highly by the general public than others because of their poorer external examination results.

Perhaps the major problem, though, is that while we have only a limited idea of what makes a good school, we have as yet no idea at all of how to prevent disadvantage and disaffection taking hold of some schools. The vicious circle whereby failure generates reactions which ensure the continued failure of siblings, lives on. These processes themselves may, in turn, lead to confrontation between teachers and pupils in a variety of ways (McLouglin, 1983).

The literature on disadvantage and disaffection is full of the social, psychological and institutional 'causes' and 'effects' of these phenomena (Wedge and Prosser, 1973; Rutter and Madge, 1976; Delamont, 1980; Mortimore and Blackstone, 1982; Reid, 1985; 1986). It is less complete on the ways of improving disadvantaged and disaffected pupils' circumstances and opportunities, particularly in schools. There are several reasons for this state of affairs.

First, the importance of the school as a contributory factor in pupils' disadvantage and disaffection has only recently begun to receive increased attention. In the 1950s and '60s, for example, few schools, apart from a limited number of secondary moderns, were thought to experience major problems of violence, vandalism, disruption, absentee-ism and pupil disaffection. After all, as we discuss in more detail in Chapter 4, by the end of the 1970s HMI (DES, 1979) were commenting that the great majority of schools were orderly, hard working and free from any serious problems. Estimates by McNamara (1975) of the prevalence of 1.5 per cent of disruptive pupils at grammar schools and only 4.2 per cent in schools located in socially deprived areas led to similar conclusions being drawn.

By the mid-1980s, this view was being challenged (Reynolds, 1984). There was mounting evidence that:

a Absenteeism is a major problem in parts of Britain (Reid, 1985).

b 2000 out of 30 000 schools were the victims of suspected arson in 1979 (Geddes, 1982).

c Underachievement is seen as the disease of the age, especially among lower and middle ability pupils. These pupils appeared to receive too little of everything – resources, the best teachers, adequate curricula, praise and parental support (Davie *et al*, 1980; Hargreaves, 1982).

d Malaise in the teaching profession has reached epidemic proportions (Reid, 1986).

e Pupils' conduct in schools is becoming far more brazen and defiant (Pack, 1977).

f Vandalism of school buildings in some parts of Britain and the United States is rife. Vandalism and thefts, for example, are costing Welsh education authorities more than half a million pounds every year (Stephenson, 1986).

Second, the educational significance of research into disadvantage and disaffection is beginning to be acknowledged. New legislation, together with DES and Welsh Office proposals, is aimed at making teachers and their schools increasingly more accountable for their actions and outcomes. Influential in this trend have been the publication of findings from HMI inspections of schools, the publication of schools' annual examination pass rates, the moves to increasingly involve parents in schools' decision-making processes, and the publicity given to findings obtained from the schools' differences group, notably the impact made by *15,000 Hours* (Rutter *et al*, 1979).

Third, the search for the school factors involved in pupils' disaffected behaviour has now begun in earnest, after a very slow, cautious and uncertain beginning. Explicitly, much educational and social research conducted before the mid-1970s emphasised the strong association between a range of social variables (pupils' home backgrounds, social class origins, housing and location...) and absenteeism, truancy, disruption and underachievement. The view was often expressed that teachers and schools were the victims of their pupils' home and social backgrounds and innate intellectual capabilities rather than anything related to their schooling (Tyerman, 1968). After all, it seemed that these views had a factual base. For example, important work carried out in the United States suggested that individual schools only had weak and few independent effects upon their pupils when compared with the greater consequences of social class (Jencks *et al*, 1972; Bowles and Gintis, 1976).

Similar results appeared to emanate from research in Britain. Galloway's work, for instance (1976a, b), reported that the strongest link between absenteeism and schooling lay in the number of pupils who had free school meals.

Of course, it is now known that these pioneer studies were heavily loaded towards familial and social rather than educational variables. Hence, a correlation between identifiable school attributes and pupil outcomes could not have been achieved (Reynolds *et al*, 1980; Reynolds and Reid, 1985). Retrospectively, we can now also see that researchers who attempted to undertake school-based studies into institutional factors involved in absenteeism, disruption, underachievement and other manifestations of disaffection were hindered by the lack of clear leads from earlier studies, as well as methodological difficulties (Acton, 1980; Goldstein, 1980; Hargreaves, 1980; Reynolds and Sullivan, 1981; Reynolds and Reid, 1985); problems of confidentiality (Smithells, 1977); and territorial imperatives (Power *et al*, 1967; 1972). Nevertheless, educational researchers were slow to respond to certain clues. For instance, the link between school policies and social outcomes became apparent following the work of Hargreaves (1967) and Lacey's (1970) school studies. The William Tyndale Enquiry (Auld, 1976) is but one practical example which showed that a clear relationship existed between perceived bad practice in schools and educational outcomes.

Set against this background and the slow and uncertain beginning, it is now possible to argue that a great deal has been achieved in the search for key school factors in a comparatively short amount of time since the mid-1970s. But much more work remains to be done, both of a quantitative and qualitative kind (Reynolds and Reid, 1985; Hopkins, 1985). Research to date on the effects of schooling leave far too many questions unanswered, especially in the area of disadvantage and disaffection (see Chapter 2).

We write this chapter, therefore, bearing in mind all these limitations. Rather than remaining stagnant or negative in our prognosis, we will deliberately endeavour to move the debate forward by leaning heavily on thinking and research which is aimed at promoting more effective schooling for both disadvantaged and disaffected pupils. But first it is necessary to reiterate briefly some of the known 'causes' of disadvantage and disaffection.

Disadvantaged and disaffected pupils are, in the main, those who fall into some of the following categories – absentees, truants, delinquents, vandals, maladjusted pupils, disrupters, the less able, children with special educational needs, underachievers, girls (in certain subjects) and black and other minority groups of children. They include:

1 Children from families at the lower end of the social scale, often those in which the father is employed in either unskilled or semi-skilled work.

2 Children from families where paternal unemployment or irregular employment is the norm.

3 Children from families where the father is away from the home for long periods, either for reasons of work (merchant seaman) or other reasons.

4 Children from families on low incomes.

5 Children from families where maternal unemployment, inability to find work, or full or part-time employment in low income occupations is rife.

6 Pupils from families with an above average number of children.

7 Pupils from families living in overcrowded conditions.

8 Pupils from families living in poor and/or old housing, frequently council or rented rather than privately owned.

9 Pupils from families overcoming or experiencing marital disharmony such as parental divorce or separation.

10 Children from one-parent families.

11 Children from families in which there are poor material conditions within the home.

12 Children from families in which the parents are unable to cope with a single or variety of social pathologies that threaten their lifestyles and lead to abnormal conditions within the home. These conditions include alcoholism, mental and physical illness, violence, family disorganisation, child abuse, incest, debt, a parent in prison *et seq.*

13 Children from families closely involved with the social services for social, economic or health reasons.

14 Children from families in which the parents are unco-operative and/or hostile to authority in general, especially to school personnel.

15 Pupils from families in which the parents are not interested in their children's progress.

16 Pupils from families in which the parents do not insist that their offspring attend school, or take no notice of their absence, and/or do not insist on prompt attendance at school (as manifested by their children oversleeping or being late).

17 Children from families whose circumstances entitle them to free school meals.

18 Children from families in which the parents are passive victims of a dreadful environment (tower blocks, urban decay) and are unsure of their constitutional rights.

19 Children from families which have a handicapped sibling or relative.

20 Pupils taught in lower ability or less able groups, often with the least experienced or least qualified staff.

21 Pupils who change school frequently, or attend poor academic or confrontation-orientated institutions.
22 Pupils who suffer from unfortunate physical circumstances, behavioural or social traits.
23 Girls who dislike or are treated as second-class citizens in, for example, science and maths classes.
24 Asian, West Indian or other children who have linguistic or other social or educational problems.
25 Children who have suffered one long or several short illnesses which have seriously interrupted their schooling.

You can imagine, even from a quick reading of this list, how difficult it would be for schools to devise their own 'at risk' registers of pupils who fall into one or more of these categories. It would be even more difficult and time-consuming to maintain regular interviews and assessment sessions with them in some institutions. This situation is yet another example of teachers having insufficient time to do all the things they would wish to in schools. It is any wonder, therefore, that so many schools do so badly by their disadvantaged and disaffected pupils? Is it any wonder that such pupils commonly make allowances for their parents but not for their teachers (Reid, 1983c, d, e)?

School processes

We will now briefly consider some of the school processes related to disadvantage and disaffection. These include home-school links, parental perspectives, the curriculum, underachievement, deviance, school differences, rules and regulations, teachers' expectations, teacher-pupil and peer group relationships, and bullying. Information related to other school processes, such as pastoral care, is discussed later in the book. We have deliberately chosen to focus on home-school links and parental perspectives because of the increasing interest shown in these aspects by a variety of sources, not least the Department of Education and Science itself.

Although unhappy childhood experiences are no longer considered to be irreversibly damaging, Rutter (1975) believes there is little doubt that 'parents help shape the child's behaviour by means of their selective encouragement and discouragement of particular behaviours, by their discipline and by the amount of freedom which they allow'. Inconsistent and lax discipline as well as parents adopting different criteria and operating on different planes within the home, appears to have negative effects on children. So does the timing and quality of parental responses.

Maintaining effective and consistent standards of discipline in the home is never easy, as any parent will testify. Parents have to cope with a number of pressures and distractions on a daily basis. Nevertheless, Rutter claims that the parents of troubled children differ quite early on from other parents in being less good at intervention, in giving less encouragement and praise for good behaviour, in responding erratically to bad behaviour and in giving naughty children too much attention for their misdemeanours.

In a particularly revealing study, Rutter *et al* (1975) compared families in two contrasting geographical locations – the Isle of Wight and an Inner London Borough. They found that parents in the inner-city region suffered from more social disadvantages. These included worse housing conditions, greater family discord, more mental disorder and an increased incidence of criminality. In addition, their offspring were twice as likely to have emotional, behavioural and reading problems. Broken homes were associated with delinquency and psychiatric disorders in children. Varlaam's (1974) ILEA literacy survey accords well with Rutter's work and shows similar associations between home and social background, behaviour and reading attainments. Such findings led the Court Committee (1976) to conclude that there is now extensive evidence to show that adverse family and social environments retard physical, emotional and intellectual growth, educational achievement and personal behaviour. Interestingly, however, outcomes for single-parent homes are no different from those of two-parent homes, once allowance has been made for economic factors (Davie *et al*, 1972; Mortimore *et al*, 1983).

Other home factors, too, can affect the natural development of children and have consequences for school behaviour. These include:
1 Circumstances which force children to acquire adult status too early – either because of their domestic situation or for other reasons. Thereafter, school life can seem boring, irrelevant, petty and restrictive. Such attitudes often lead to withdrawal and conflict (Jones, 1976; Bird *et al*, 1980; Grunsell, 1980).
2 Well-integrated families who are notably anti-school, anti-authoritarian and anti-establishment. Sometimes these negative familial attitudes are supported by a prevailing neighbourhood culture which devalues schooling and overvalues alternative ideals like work, or fosters anti-social tendencies – sometimes through group identities (teddy-boys, skinheads, punks) (Mays, 1972; Phillips, 1978; Grunsell, 1978).
3 Families which suffer from too much intra-familial friction such as unstable parental relationships (constant arguing), violence in the home, difficult sibling relationships and very poor parent-child relationships which can be hurtful, derisive, neglectful, punitive, harsh, overdemanding or characterised by minimal contact or affection (Seabrook, 1974; Bird *et al*, 1980; Grunsell, 1980).

One of the least publicised facts about some teachers and social workers is that they themselves may never have had to endure social or familial deprivation like so many of their pupils. Such teachers and social workers can sometimes find it harder to relate to children and clients from less fortunate social or home backgrounds because of the culture gap which exists between them. Although many studies have found that a high proportion of non-graduates or college-trained teachers come from working-class backgrounds (Lacey, 1977), there is now good evidence to show that a clear majority of university postgraduate-trained teachers have favourable social class origins (Reid *et al*, 1980; Patrick, Bernbaum and Reid, 1982).

The work of Feldhusen *et al* (1973), undertaken in the United States, remains one of the most impressive of those studies conducted into the relationship between a student's home and social background and school indiscipline. Feldhusen investigated 1550 children in grades 3, 6 and 9 who exhibited persistent prosocial or aggressive-disruptive behaviour. They found that aggressive-disruptive youths were disadvantaged in terms of their home, family and parental backgrounds when compared with prosocial peers. Their list of psycho-social correlates of classroom misbehaviours and home circumstances includes:

1 lax or inconsistent paternal discipline;
2 maternal inadequacy in the supervision of the offspring;
3 poor parent-child relationships including indifference and hostility;
4 a disunified family in terms of corporate spirit and social and household activities;
5 disagreements between parents about child rearing;
6 poor husband-wife relationships;
7 parents who disapproved of many traits in their children;
8 mothers who felt unhappy in the community in which they lived;
9 parents who were unable to control their tempers and who had a tendency to resort to angry, physical punishment when their children misbehaved;
10 parents who belittled their own influence upon their children and who thought that other children exerted bad influences upon them as well;
11 parents whose leisure time was devoid of purposeful activity or included few cultural or intellectual engagements;
12 parents who were not members of a church or only attended spasmodically;
13 parents who are less well educated than the average population and, if employed, were in lower-level occupations of a semi-skilled or unskilled type.

Analysis of the school factors showed that the disruptive children had an average nine points deficit in their intelligence quotient (IQ) levels, significantly lower reading and mathematics test scores, and were more inclined to drop out of school. In a follow-up study, Feldhusen *et al* (1977) found that some of the best long-range predictors of disruptive behaviour were: the original behaviour status as identified by teachers, IQ, reading scores and father's educational level.

British studies confirm many of Feldhusen's findings. Rutter (1975) reports that conduct-disordered children tend to be impulsive, unpredictable and unmalleable; aggressive and assertive in their relationships; less responsive than their peers to praise and encouragement; and to show little concern or feelings for others. Rutter also found that conduct-disordered children tend to be educationally backward. The Cambridge longitudinal study of delinquency (West and Farrington, 1973) ascertained that the best predictors of delinquency were teachers and peers' ratings of troublesomeness in earlier years.

In Reid's (1984b, c) study into persistent school absenteeism, the form teachers completed Scale B of the Rutter Children's Behaviour Questionnaire (1967). The results showed that the persistent absentees (note: not disrupters) tended to behave worse in class than good attenders from the same forms and from academic bands. They also manifested higher levels of antisocial and neurotic tendencies in a minority of cases. When the criterion variables (such as 'truants from school') were excluded from the analysis, the differences between the groups were much reduced. Therefore, they displayed some behavioural traits which were not solely related to their non-attendance. Like most earlier work on truancy and absenteeism, the non-attenders in Reid's sample came from significantly more deprived home backgrounds than the good attenders with much lower social class origins.

Tattum (1982) has suggested that many disruptive children are socially inept and lack the skills necessary to handle difficult situations. Such pupils can, for example, be verbally abusive when disciplined, as part of their 'normal' reactions. Whereas other children tend to be quiet when problems arise in class, some disrupters appear to feel the need to defend themselves irrespective of cause, attempting to save face even when there is no need – part of the 'it's not my fault' syndrome.

Taken collectively, most studies tend to suggest that much more thought and attention needs to be given to combatting early signs of behavioural problems. Unless action is taken at their inception, disaffection and disruption are likely to develop as pupils grow in confidence with age. Among other aspects requiring particular attention are: early signs of behavioural problems in primary schools; problems which manifest themselves during the crucial period of transfer between primary and secondary schools (often badly handled) and between grades especially for 'at risk' pupils; overtly unfavourable parental attitudes towards school; *and* repeated parental non-attendance at parents' evenings or meetings arranged in schools.

Generally speaking, liaison and communication between schools and parents and vice versa is not always as efficient or effective as it might be. Whether increasing parental involvement in schools will improve this matter must remain an open question. Given the present nature of governing bodies, it seems unlikely that too many of them will concern themselves with such matters as disaffection, disruption and absenteeism. If they did, things might start to improve. Who knows, some radical attitudinal changes and innovations might even take place.

Despite the aforementioned evidence, it is quite wrong to assume that all disaffected or disruptive pupils come from lower streams and unfavourable home circumstances – although most probably do. When, however, an able child from a favourable home background manifests disaffected or disruptive conduct, the outcry is often out of all proportion to the event. Care should be taken by teachers not to generalise in specific cases as the circumstances in each incident usually differ; at least in the finer detail.

Parental perspectives

As with pupils' perceptions, there have been comparatively few studies into parents' perspectives of their children's learning and behaviour at school, especially the latter. This is surprising considering the credence given to their role on governing bodies. Without this information, teachers are denied crucial insights into parents' values and requirements from the education service. It seems probable that rates of absenteeism, disruption and disaffection would probably be substantially reduced if teachers could be more certain of parental support when dealing with non-conformers.

Perhaps the best-known study into parental perspectives of children's behaviour at school in Britain is the work of Newsom and Newsom (1983; 1984). Their longitudinal data derives from a long-term study of child rearing in the East Midlands, based on a social-class-stratified random sample of 700 children. The findings were obtained from semi-structured interviews of about three hours each conducted with mothers when their children were aged 11 and 16. At 16, the children were also interviewed separately. As the implications of this work are so important for an understanding of the relationship between disaffection and schooling, the findings are now presented and discussed in considerable detail. We will deal with them in three stages: results at 11 and 16 followed by overall conclusions.

At eleven

a Children's disruptive behaviour in school is seen by parents as something which the teacher ought to be able to control. It is also seen as part of a pattern which threatens the child's work and which exemplifies the teacher's inability to interest and persuade the child effectively. Parents have both admiration and sympathy for teachers but they are often critical on specific issues, usually relating to so-called 'new' education.

b 26 per cent of the mothers in the study were aware that their children were bullied at school: 4 per cent seriously and another 22 per cent in streets on the way to and from school. A few parents admitted that their own offspring were inclined to bully other children.

c One-third of the parents were unhappy about at least one of their child's friendships at school. Working-class mothers were more likely than middle-class mothers to worry about their children being led astray by their friends into delinquency. Aggressive behaviour *per se* was not seen as a serious problem at 11. Stealing was then the focus of much parental anxiety.

d 65 per cent of mothers thought regular homework should be given in the final year at junior school. Only 3 per cent of the 11-year-old children received homework from their teachers at this time.

e The parents were more concerned about teachers' aggression than that of their children at 11. This specifically included shouting by teachers at children in school. The findings show that there is a striking link between pupils liking a teacher and being 'very happy' at school. 14 per cent of social class I and II children had specific difficulties with a teacher compared with 7 per cent for all other classes. Overall, 15 per cent of the parents did not like or had strong reservations about their children's J4 class teacher. The findings suggest that middle-class parents are less easy to please than others and may put more pressure on to their children than working-class parents.

f Some 60 per cent of the parents claimed that they normally react to their children's criticisms of teachers by supporting the member of staff. On the whole, it takes extreme distress on the part of 11-year-olds to make mothers complain to schools or teachers. What parents seem to want from junior schools is 'effective organisation applied in a benevolent manner'.

At sixteen

a Parental emphasis changes from organisation to discipline – reflecting their offsprings' adolescent, exploratory stage. Parents regard the two worst features of secondary schools as being poor at maintaining discipline and containing pupils, often deviants, who are likely to adversely influence their child. The best things are 'the staff', followed by equal mentions of 'facilities' and 'good discipline or ethos'. The findings show that parents have a natural fear of their children getting into trouble. Working-class mothers fear that their children's friends will involve them in trouble with the law. Parents with high vocational aspirations for their children see the distraction of undisciplined friends and acquaintances as a direct threat to their children's future qualificational needs and employment prospects. 35 per cent of all mothers were unhappy about the 'bad influence' of particular friends on their children; 22 per cent were specifically concerned about the friend's delinquency. More than twice as many mothers from unskilled and semi-skilled backgrounds worried about this aspect compared with mothers from skilled manual and middle-class backgrounds.

b 47 per cent of middle-class children (rising to 57 per cent in class I and II) undertook homework in the evenings compared with only 18 per cent in the working class. 53 per cent of working-class children never did any homework, compared with only 7 per cent of those in the top two groups (classes I and II). Clearly, these findings are related to pupils' intellectual levels and vocational aspirations. They also confirm how schools reward able pupils at the expense of others (Hargreaves, 1967; Hargreaves *et al*, 1975). Inevitably, such discrepancies will prejudice pupils' and parents' views of their schools and influence behaviour patterns, levels of alienation and disaffection and home-school links.

c Social class, sex and family size differences were discerned amongst troublesome children at 16. Non-amenability and delinquency showed a strong predictive association. Thus, children who were troublesome in their parents' estimations at 11 tended to remain so; this confirms a trend previously reported in the NCD studies (Davie, 1972). Tense and anxious 11-year-olds are likely to become troublesome in a more positive way at 16. There is a strong association between troublesomeness at 16 and negative feelings about school at the same age.

Overall conclusions

a Parents are likely to know a great deal about their child's experience at school, if only because they so often have to deal with its consequences. For example, many children take it out on their families when they arrive home from school angry or depressed. Quite often children will display their real feelings only in front of their parents. Many pupils regularly suppress or modify their conduct and opinions when they are in the presence of more formal authority.

b The suggestion by teachers that troublesome children misbehave in school because of the way their parents are handling them currently or have handled them in the past is at best an oversimplification, possibly a myth. Children's behaviour at school is much more complicated than that. Most parents are certainly sensitive to potential situational problems. Generally, they endeavour to deal with them before they reach extremes. They are also aware of many of their children's emotional and constitutional difficulties and endeavour to circumvent them as best they can.

c Early antecedents to troublesomeness at school include children's vulnerability to stress and anxiety and negative attitudes. These findings suggest, when compared with environmental experiences such as family-cohesion and father-participation, that there is an important constitutional component in children which affects their behaviour. This is supported by the fact that many mothers can easily identify particular children as being especially difficult to rear, in terms of temperament, from a very early age.

d The child's intellectual competence does have some effect on how far he or she is able to enjoy school. Failure to enjoy school is linked with troublesomeness.

e Constitutional idiosyncracies, environmental forces and their interaction with the school provide a complex tapestry which in some ways is too difficult to describe. Generalising behavioural patterns from individual and collective data is an extremely risky business. Schools have experience of children which is not available to parents and vice versa. However, where parents make judgements of their children which go against the grain, these beliefs are likely to be credible because they are often so painful to make. This is one reason why teachers need more regular contact with as many parents as possible. At present, teachers see too few parents, too irregularly and often at the wrong times of the year. Parents' evenings, for instance, are more useful and effective when they are held near the beginning of the academic year rather than at the end. Parents and teachers need to forge close partnerships because they are both working towards the same goal – the intellectual and social development of the child.

In another important study, Fogelman (1976) presents the findings obtained from the National Children's Bureau longitudinal data on pupils' rates of absenteeism at the age of 16 based on pupils', parents' and teachers' perceptions. The results show that on average the parents thought their children attended school more regularly than either the pupils themselves or their teachers maintained. In fact, the pupils admitted far more non-attendance than either of the other two groups, and this shows the variance which is possible in such work. According to the 16-year-olds, many of them miss the odd day for one reason or another when they feel like it. On balance, Fogelman concluded that the teacher assessments were probably the most accurate of the three; some parents might have wished to protect their offspring or been unaware of their children's occasional or persistent absences, while some pupils were keen to exaggerate their truancy. What is clear from Fogelman's work is that occasional non-attendance at 16 is not solely confined to the less able adolescent or to pupils from working-class backgrounds. As we shall see in later chapters, school variables play a considerable part in the process.

Chapter 4
Discipline and disruption

Hillbourne comprehensive contains roughly 1000 pupils. The organisation and structure of the school is typical, apart from the fact that it has been granted educational priority status, houses a very small sixth form and places a strong emphasis on the provision of pastoral care. The senior management team includes the head, three deputies (academic and curriculum, pastoral care and head of upper school) and five year heads. Irrespective of remuneration, these staff feel that they have more status within the school than their subject centred colleagues.

Senior staff consider that the emphasis on pastoral care is necessary given the low socio-economic backgrounds of most of the pupils and the substantial levels of disaffection towards schooling endemic amongst the pupils. Despite the provision of pastoral support, this disaffection is manifest in the large numbers of pupils who wander up and down the school drive, leaving and entering at will; in the fourth and fifth years fewer than half the pupils are present in school on some days. Inside the classrooms learning is secondary to the maintenance of order; the latter being rigidly enforced by senior staff who, to an outsider's eye, often appear to instigate measures which border on the harsh. The so-called pastoral support sometimes appears to be little more than an extension of the administrative and organisational structure of the school's disciplinary policies. For instance, irrespective of need, pupils continue to be sent home for failure to comply with school uniform regulations; the cane was much in evidence prior to being banned by the local council and detentions continue to be a daily event.

Hillbourne's modern purpose-built campus stands out amidst the surrounding gloom. Many of the parents live on traditional council estates in an area prone to high unemployment, where good second jobs for married women are rare, prospects for young school leavers limited and evidence of vandalism and graffiti rife. It is hardly surprising that a school with the sort of ethos described above, existing in such a deprived catchment area, finds itself out of favour with a large proportion of disenchanted parents who show their lack of interest in traditional educational values by encouraging their children to stay at home or by turning a blind eye to their non-attendance.

In earlier times the school used to find difficulty in recruiting suitable permanent staff because of its unfavourable location and non-academic reputation. These days, Hillbourne maintains control, but at a high cost. The price is paid in poor teacher-pupil relationships, very low external examination pass rates, reluctance to enter the sixth form and unacceptably high levels of daily absenteeism – three and four times above the national average.

Bampton School is located some three miles away. It is twice the size of Hillbourne with a flourishing sixth form containing some 200 pupils, and boasts a proud academic record. The school contains special units for difficult and disruptive pupils and for the teaching of English to immigrant pupils. Despite being located in a similarly deprived catchment area to Hillbourne, and having a long history of coping and dealing with pupils with behavioural problems, the school does not have educational priority status – probably because two others already have.

The organisation and structure of Bampton School could not be more different from that of Hillbourne. The school is subdivided into three large independent units with a deputy head in charge of each – the upper, middle and lower schools. Apart from these personnel, there are no pastoral staff *per se* although the school does contain a counsellor, an education social worker, a youth leader and two full-time education welfare officers. The three deputies, therefore, assume the major pastoral function supported by senior and junior heads of department, form and subject teachers.

Like Hillbourne, absenteeism rates are very high especially in the third, fourth and fifth years with pupils entering and leaving the school grounds at will. Unlike Hillbourne, however, a large number of pupils remain on the premises but absent from lessons daily. These pupils appear to wander around or hide away in disaffected cliques; they will attend some lessons but not others. Again, unlike Hillbourne, disruptive behaviour and indiscipline are commonplace in some classrooms and a number of teachers are unable to cope. The constant stress of many lost battles is apparent on the faces of some staff. Outbreaks of bullying, racial rivalries and extortion are by no means unusual according to an education social worker who works permanently from an office in the school's buildings. Instances of pupils staying away from school because they are afraid to return have been reported.

All the available evidence suggests that control in Hillbourne is bought at a high price – while academic success in Bampton continues in spite of attendant behavioural problems. Perhaps a clue to the different orientations of the two schools lies in the fact that Hillbourne was originally designated a secondary modern whereas Bampton was the local grammar school. Maybe old traditions die hard. Whatever the case, the only real similarities between these two neighbourhood comprehensives are their location and intake. Even the atmosphere within the two staff common rooms is very different. In Bampton, the teachers could not be more obliging. Conversely, in Hillbourne the staff appeared suspicious of researchers – perhaps with reason.

Despite their close proximity, Hillbourne and Bampton comprehensives have little in common apart from the social origins of their pupils and high rates of absenteeism, pupil disaffection and substantial disciplinary problems. While Hillbourne endeavours to cope with these latter difficulties through overt punitive measures, staff at Bampton take a more empathetic approach towards their deviant pupils. Paradoxically, both schools are equally unsuccessful at overcoming their related problems of disaffection, alienation and disruption.

Helen, 14, is registered at Hillbourne. Her father, a manual labourer, is currently unemployed. Her mother is a part-time cleaner. Although only in the early part of the fourth year at school, she has already decided to leave at the first opportunity. She hopes to become a hairdresser. Meanwhile, Helen attends school as rarely as possible. On most days, she remains at home to help her mother – mainly by looking after her two younger sisters. The Hughes family dislike the values upheld by Hillbourne staff intensely. On one occasion, for example, Mrs Hughes had a major argument with one of the deputies, Mrs Price, over Helen's non-attendance and failure to wear school uniform. This led to Mrs Hughes swearing at Mrs Price and threatening to keep her daughter away from school indefinitely. Now, whenever Helen attends school, she quickly finds herself in further trouble – usually for cheeking staff during lessons. To date, she has been excluded from school on two occasions for repeated abuse to staff and suspended on another for allegedly setting fire to the home economics room.

Jane, 15, attends Bampton. Like Helen, she is in one of the lower ability bands. But unlike Helen, she has an excellent attendance record. Jane's problem is that she dislikes her teachers intensely and considers the content of most of her lessons to be irrelevant for her future needs. She claims that she would like more maths and English lessons and is upset by her inability to come to terms with reading, writing, spelling and mathematics. Jane blames her lack of achievement on large classes, minimal individual attention, the constant hassle between some teachers and her classmates and poor teaching. She believes that pupils like herself (in the 'C' stream) are treated differently from her more able peers. Explicitly, Jane is resentful of the fact that she is never given any homework and always seems to get the 'worst teachers' every year.

Helen and Jane are typical of large numbers of disaffected pupils in the two schools. While Helen expresses her alienation through her non-attendance and disruptive conduct, Jane manifests hers through a lack of effort. The behaviour of both pupils is symptomatic of schools which have poor teacher-pupil relationships and staff who have too little time to help pupils in need.

John teaches at Hillbourne. He originally started in the school as a supply teacher but became permanent a year later after failing to find another post. Although trained at a former college of education as a secondary subject specialist, he now teaches a variety of subjects including maths, humanities and English. John believes his opportunities of promotion within the school are strictly limited. He contends he is opposed to the 'harsh regime' which runs the school but admits he has never publicly spoken out in staff meetings. He thinks that to do so would only be to his own disadvantage in the long run. John considers the headmaster to be an administrator, remote and unapproachable. He thinks that the real power behind the throne is one of the deputies, whom he dislikes intensely because of her attitude towards the pupils and male staff. He believes the school is failing its pupils and will get nowhere without a significant change of personnel and a massive change of policy. Interestingly, when asked, John thought that Bampton had a worse reputation than his own school and appeared to take comfort from the fact.

Bob teaches at Bampton. Like John, he originally started in the school on supply. Unlike John, Bob believes that Bampton is going places and cites the fact that his friend is deputy head and often uses him as his right-hand man in times of need. (Bob also trained at a former college of education as a one subject specialist and now concentrates on general subjects with lower ability band pupils.) He contends that the school's main problems are a lack of resources, poor parental support, a few weak teachers and unacceptably high rates of non-attendance. He is proud of the fact that he is personally attempting to do something about the latter and charts the progress of certain pupils daily. Bob is scathing of practices at Hillbourne, an attitude based on information gleaned from pupils who have been transferred. He says he is happy at the school and has no desire to teach anywhere else. To him every day is a challenge with battles to be fought, won or lost.

Despite the different ethos and reputations of the two schools, both John and Bob think that their school is better than the other, although their evidence for making this statement is limited mainly to hearsay. It seems, therefore, that staff support what they have become used to and are influenced very much by colleagues and senior management. When asked, John described Helen as a 'vicious trouble-maker who comes from a very difficult family which has a history of violence'. Bob thought Jane was 'a born loser who did very little to help herself'. It is interesting that the long-term prognosis for both Helen and Jane is similar, given existing economic factors, despite the fact that one is a disruptive absentee while the other is a classic underachiever. Eventually, both may have difficulty in finding secure permanent employment because of their lack of educational qualifications. Whether and how the two teachers and schools could have done more to help Helen and Jane might be considered as you read on.

Evidence from the United States

Owing to the media's penchant for highlighting cases of violent conduct and indiscipline in schools, it is frequently forgotten that poor conduct has been manifested by a minority of pupils since the Middle Ages (Pallister, 1969; Gawthorne-Hardy, 1977). Different countries have different policies for dealing with naughty and difficult pupils. For instance, as far as is known, disruptive behaviour in schoolchildren is not a problem behind the Iron Curtain. French, West German and Spanish schools attempt to pre-empt indiscipline through central and rigid policies. In Sweden, the liberal' regimes of the 1960s and '70s led to a growth of indiscipline and related offences causing some classrooms to be locked between every lesson in large towns and cities. In the United States the picture is even bleaker; successive studies have shown that levels of disruption are not only high but increasing and indiscipline within schools and classrooms is rife (Children's Defense Fund, 1975; Bayh, 1977; NIE, 1977; Gallup, 1977; Rubel, 1977). A substantial proportion of pupils and teachers alike fear for their safety. Parents are concerned not only about the safety of their children when travelling to school but also when attending classes.

In one survey, three-quarters of teachers claimed that disciplinary problems in schools impaired their effectiveness to teach and considered their schools had done too little to help them with their difficulties. In 1978/79 alone, 5 per cent of the respondent teachers had been physically assaulted at least once (roughly 100 000 assaults). Of these, 10 per cent required medical treatment for their physical injuries. 8 per cent needed treatment for subsequent emotional trauma (NEA, 1979). This evidence is supported by the fact that Congress accepted a report which estimated that 70 000 teachers in the United States are physically assaulted every year (Bayh, 1977).

A review of the available literature shows that assaults on teachers and students in the United States are increasing – so is teacher stress, vandalism, extortion, rape, robbery and weapon violence in schools (Reid, 1986). These findings make depressing reading. In one year, for example, no fewer than 100 000 teachers had their private property vandalised. In any given month estimates reveal that an average 2.4 high school students have something stolen, 282 000 are attacked and 112 000 forcefully robbed on school premises. Violence, indiscipline and anti-social behaviour is especially concentrated at the junior high school level (12–15 years). Over two-thirds of robberies and half the assaults on youths occur on pupils in this age group particularly in deprived urban areas like Chicago and New York. Black pupils are more at risk than their white peers in some quarters (NIE, 1977).

Evidence from Britain

In Britain, evidence on the state and amount of disruptive conduct in schools from a host of reports and research projects provides a fairly patchy and uneven picture of schools today. The Essex County Teachers' Working Party (1976) on disruptive behaviour in schools, for example, reported no wholesale breakdown of discipline within the county. Significantly, however, they added that in recent years the disruptive influence of a minority of pupils had caused increasing difficulties within the authority. By contrast, giving evidence to the same Working Party (NUT, 1976), the Berkshire Association of Secondary Heads reported a rise in physical attacks upon teachers and in serious acts of disobedience.

The Pack Committee Report (1977) on truancy and indiscipline in Scotland provides some guarded support for the latter view. The Report concluded that indiscipline in Scotland could be on the increase in some areas but probably not in others. Acts of disruptive behaviour were not out of control nor of alarming proportions. Nevertheless, and here is a crucial statement, the Committee believed that the character of disruptive behaviour in schools had changed in recent years, making it harder to control. In particular, some pupils had become more brazen. It seems, therefore, that as schools have changed and become increasingly more humane, so have some pupils become bolder. Thus, individual staff are left to determine their own standards of acceptable and unacceptable behaviour.

Fortunately, evidence from surveys suggests that there is no overall breakdown in discipline in education in Britain – just in certain areas, schools and classrooms. British teachers can take some heart from the fact that things are nothing like as bad as in the United States. It is, however, a moot point as to whether disaffection and disruption in British schools is encouraged by prevailing economic circumstances and attendant parental plight and social distress. Only time will tell.

Despite numerous methodological problems (Tattum, 1982; Galloway *et al*, 1982; Reid, 1985), surveys undertaken in Britain show that the incidence of disruptive behaviour in schools is low. For instance, only 24 of 1065 schools in Lowenstein's first survey (1972) reported that violence was a common occurrence, although 622 stated that it had occurred. In his follow-up survey in 1975, Lowenstein reported an average of 0.53 violent incidents per 100 primary school pupils, 0.41 per 100 middle school pupils and 0.64 per 100 secondary school pupils. Instances of disruptive behaviour averaged out at 1.62, 1.45 and 4.48 per primary, middle and secondary school pupil respectively. Lowenstein also reported that boys were more likely to be involved in these forms of behaviour than girls, and that the final year of compulsory education was the peak period. Size of school was not a factor. Nevertheless, he considered that the larger the school the more difficult it is to ensure that each member of staff cooperates in being observant and vigilant and willing to report appropriate incidents to colleagues.

Lowenstein listed 13 categories of violent conduct in schools (in order of frequency, not intensity): physical attacks on other children; disruptive or unruly behaviour; truancy; verbal abuse of other children; vandalism; extortion; breaking and entering of school property; gang violence; attacks on teachers by pupils; attacks on other children; miscellaneous manifestations; racial violence; and attacks on teachers by parents. From the data on violent conduct, Lowenstein ascertained that the most serious problems in primary schools were physical attacks on other children and disruptive and unruly conduct. In middle schools, truancy was ranked third behind the other two. In secondary schools, disruptive and unruly behaviour easily came top, followed by physical attacks on other children, vandalism and verbal abuse of teachers.

Contrary to previous findings, on the evidence of data obtained from a 40 per cent response rate from a sample of 1600 NAS/UWT members, Comber and Whitfield (1979) concluded that indiscipline is a serious problem which imposes considerable stress upon teachers. Tattum (1982) challenged these findings. He argued that Comber and Whitfield were wrong to have based such a conclusion on evidence obtained from a minority of respondents. Tattum suggests that researchers such as Comber and Whitfield should not overemphasise the negative side of school life.

In any event, Comber and Whitfield's conclusions are out of step with the majority of findings reported from other surveys. The DES (1975) study found that the number of pupils involved in violent incidents in all types of schools was very low, although these were three times more common in secondary than primary schools. Violence towards teachers was less usual than towards other pupils. Boys were far more likely to be involved than girls. The Report largely blamed pupils' home and social circumstances for the disruptive behaviour; in particular, marital break-up and domestic tension. The DES Report considered that the most appropriate remedies for schools to apply, at that time, were better cooperation and communication between and within schools, improved pastoral care and community relationships, and decisive school leadership, supported by effective help on the part of the social services.

In 1979 the HMI secondary survey looked at a large sample of all maintained schools in England with fourth and fifth year intakes. It found that only 6 per cent of schools indicated that they had a considerable disciplinary problem. Less than 1 per cent thought it was serious. Approximately 2 per cent of the schools expressed a lot of concern over violence between pupils. Only one school in the entire survey thought violence between pupils was a serious problem. Similarly, hostility toward staff was a minority concern. 60 per cent of schools indicated that they had no disruptive pupils. Perhaps more surprisingly, only 13 per cent of schools thought they had more than ten disruptive pupils on their rolls. The overwhelming mass of headteachers claimed, therefore, that their schools only suffered from minor problems of indiscipline. Interestingly, absenteeism was regarded as a much more serious problem than indiscipline, especially parentally-condoned non-attendance. Over 20 per cent of all secondary school headteachers indicated that they had a serious or considerable problem over their pupils' rates of attendance. Disruptive conduct emerged as a much greater issue in inner-city schools than others – particularly those with a large number of pupils with learning difficulties and located in deprived areas with older housing; just the sort of schools depicted in the case data at the start of the chapter.

HMI concluded that indiscipline and disruptive behaviour are small-scale in secondary schools in England. When, however, such behaviour takes place, it is out of all proportion to the event. The Report considered that effective discipline in schools depends to a large extent upon good internal management of the curriculum, teachers' abilities and teaching styles and an empathetic pastoral care system.

Evidence from other surveys accords well with HMI's findings. The Cumbria Working Party on disruptive pupils (Sidaway, 1976) ascertained that 4 per cent of their total secondary school population was described by teachers as aggressive, bullies and disrupters. The overall figure was distorted by the age of the pupils. For instance, 10 per cent of pupils in the fifth year in Cumbria were included in the overall statistic. This may provide a pointer to where resources need to be concentrated, especially as less able and difficult pupils traditionally tend to receive fewer resources than their more able peers. This is, perhaps, hardly surprising when external examination results can mean everything to outside assessors.

Mills (1976) made a study of 16 secondary schools containing pupils aged 13 to 16. He found that schools generally contain a hard core (some 3 per cent) of disrupters. These vocal deviants were supplemented by another 10 per cent who sometimes became involved. The most common deviant or non-conformist activities were rejection of school uniforms, persistent truancy, missing individual lessons and misbehaviour calculated to destroy lessons. Like other studies, Mills reported that assaults on teachers were rare. Bullying rates were assessed at eight per thousand pupils.

In another study, McNamara (1975) found that rates of disruptive behaviour varied between schools from 1.5 per cent in selective grammar schools to 4.2 per cent in those secondary schools located in difficult and deprived areas. Finally, Rutter *et al* (1979) reported little evidence of serious misbehaviour in their twelve Inner London secondary schools. They acknowledged that some teachers had more problems in controlling classes than others but felt the blackboard jungle image of city schools was unjust.

Despite the dearth of supporting statistical evidence for an increase in indiscipline and disruptive conduct in schools in Britain, many, including sections of the media, would have us believe that disciplinary standards in schools are constantly declining. The truth of this statement is hard to verify for a number of reasons. First, the precise extent to which individual schools and classrooms are prone to indiscipline is very hard to detect.

Second, there has been a lack of research into discipline in schools, partly because of the emotive nature of the topic, but also because of the difficulties associated with measuring the subject (Wright, 1973) as well as opposition which can come from inside and outside schools (Power *et al*, 1967). Hence, obtaining reliable and objective data on indiscipline is a difficult enterprise in itself – particularly as schools which are prone to high levels of disaffection and disruption prefer to avoid unfavourable publicity. Such schools tend to regard their problems as in-house matters, for the sake of staff and parental morale if for no other reason. Often, therefore, potential researchers are unwelcome guests.

Third, a substantial amount (possible in these days, a majority in some parts of the country) of abusive behaviour, disruptive conduct and indiscipline lies undetected, or, more accurately, goes unreported. If some staff reported every bit of bad behaviour they came across they would never sit down! In any event, different teachers have different tolerance and threshold levels. Whereas one teacher will always report pupils who swear or smoke, others prefer to ignore the behaviour. Therefore, what may be regarded as indiscipline by one teacher (eating sweets, walking across a room without permission) may not be so considered by another (Hargreaves *et al*, 1975). A pupil who is well-behaved in one teacher's class, may regularly misbehave in another.

Fourth, every outbreak of indiscipline tends to be spontaneous and unique. Consequently, many young teachers are unprepared for some everyday classroom situations and learn to cope with experience. Postgraduate student-teachers, for example, believe that maintaining order in the classroom is the one aspect of their teaching practice which can make or break them (Patrick, Bernbaum and Reid, 1982). This is not a criticism of existing initial training schemes; simulation exercises, for example, can provide at best only a partial answer.

Fifth, different situations appertain in different schools and classrooms. For instance, some subject teachers only teach certain years or classes whereas their colleagues may teach predominantly lower and less able bands. Controlling well-motivated sixth and fifth form examination pupils is very different from handling disaffected pupils in third, fourth and fifth year groups.

This brings us to another fundamental, often forgotten, point. Most teachers and parents regard punishing children as a regrettable but necessary part of the process of bringing them up as social beings. The intention behind punishing children in schools is to stop them behaving in undesirable ways and, in theory, to train them in self-control so that they can be relied upon to behave appropriately when they are not being directly supervised. Paradoxically, children are punished so that further punishment will become unnecessary. Where this syndrome ends and negative reinforcement begins is a complex and little understood matter. Therefore, definitions of indiscipline and disruptive behaviour in schools (Lowenstein, 1972; Parry, 1976; SED, 1977; Lawrence *et al*, 1981; Galloway *et al*, 1982; Tattum, 1982; Topping, 1983) generally take account of the fact that most children are not always good or bad. Behaviour consists of a continuum which ranges from extremely cooperative to totally unacceptable. The behaviour of children in school changes as their teachers, age and family circumstances alter and is influenced by such factors a teachers' tolerance levels and managerial skills, as well as circumstances which pertain in lessons (peer group relationships, the curriculum, mores of the classroom). This is why disturbances occur more frequently in some lessons than others. Definitionists usually recognise that acts of indiscipline effectively disturb the education of individual disrupters as well as the remaining children in the class at the same time.

School aspects

The precise relationship between school systems and indiscipline or disruption is a complex subject because schools vary so much. There is some evidence to show that indiscipline is more likely to happen in long lessons and at the end of a school day, when teachers and pupils are tired and comparatively minor incidents can erupt. Findings also show that such occurrences are more likely in mid-week, mid-term and mid-year, particularly November, February and March (York *et al*, 1972; Lawrence *et al*, 1981; Galloway *et al*, 1982).

The Pack Committee (SED, 1977) took the view that difficulties in schools could be related to the raising of the school leaving age: the fact that maturation occurred earlier than in previous generations; pupil confusion arising from a period of rapid educational change in schools; disenchantment and apathy with the curriculum and the kind of secondary education provided especially for non-academic groups; teacher shortages, high rates of staff turnover, high teacher-pupil ratios and poor teacher-pupil relationships; and poor and weak teaching in some cases. Undoubtedly, today, unfavourable or uncertain employment prospects can be added to this list.

With one exception (Madaus, 1980), research into school differences in Britain continues to suggest that institutions have less effect on pupil behaviour than home background. Whether this is really true remains to be seen as some researchers are beginning to suggest that the influence of schools is much greater than has hitherto been thought (Reynolds and Reid, 1985). Very little is known about the relationship between discipline and school differences although early pioneer studies into pupils' perceptions of their schools and teachers (Phillips and Callely, 1981; 1982) provide some clues. There are several reasons for this lack of information, including confidentiality and territorial imperatives which can provide researchers with difficult obstacles to overcome. As previously mentioned, whereas research into reading difficulties or relating to handicapped children is frequently welcomed by teachers and local authority advisers and administrators, the reverse is often true on a delicate subject like school discipline.

Evidence obtained from research into differences between schools shows that substantial variations occur in rates of delinquency (Power *et al*, 1967; 1972); child guidance referrals (Gath, 1972); behavioural problems (Rutter, 1972); use of off-site units for disruptive pupils (Bird *et al*, 1980); action taken to cope with disruptive behaviour (Tattum, 1982); rates of suspension (Grunsell, 1980; Galloway *et al*, 1982) and absenteeism (Reynolds *et al*, 1976; Rutter *et al*, 1979) which are not solely attributable to differences between catchment areas.

Reynolds *et al*'s (1976; 1980) study of eight secondary schools in a homogeneous South Wales valley found that high attendance schools are characterised by small size, lower institutional control, less rigid enforcement of certain rules on pupil behaviour, higher co-option of pupils as prefects and good parent/school relationships.

Rutter *et al* (1979) reported that in the most successful schools there was a prompt start to lessons, a strong emphasis on academic progress and attainment, relative infrequency of punishment and a high rate of recognition for positive achievements. Well-cared-for buildings and a feeling by pupils that they could approach teachers for help when needed were other significant pointers. Likewise, the HMI Report (1977) on ten good schools suggested that favourable regimes are characterised by careful preparation, variety of approach in lessons, regular and constructive correction of pupils' work and consistent praise and encouragement being given to pupils for their endeavours.

Indiscipline in schools can be reduced and academic achievement maintained, if not actually improved, when proper guidelines are followed by staff in schools (Mortimore, 1980; Hastings, 1981; Gillham, 1984; Lawrence *et al*, 1984). Like most other things about education, it seems that everything probably depends upon the calibre of staff in schools – particularly levels of motivation, competence and professional interest. Generally speaking, research to date suggests that academic criteria in schools have to take precedence over social consideration if attainment is the prime goal. This is often acknowledged by schools in their hierarchical patterns where, for example, academic deputy heads normally take precedence over the pastoral deputy heads in terms of seniority. The evidence on the precise relationship between effective schooling and discipline is strictly limited given the lack of reliable information and, to some extent, the contradictory nature of existing findings. Rutter *et al* (1979) and Millham (1982), for example, suggest that organisationally 'tight' regimes are most effective. By contrast, Reynolds *et al* (1976; 1979) argue that schools with high institutional control which are rigid and harsh are more ineffective than their counterparts. Likewise, the evidence from Finlayson and Loughran (1976) and Rafilides and Hoy (1979) implies that harsh, authoritarian and 'custodial' school regimes can have adverse effects upon pupils as typified by Helen in Hillbourne at the beginning of the chapter. Conversely, Hargreaves (1967; 1979; 1980; 1981; 1982) contends that disorganised and weakly-controlled schools can have the same negative effects upon certain pupils.

Existing research appears to suggest, therefore, that effective schools are characterised by a form of balanced control (Reynolds, 1982), which should be organisationally 'tight' while at the same time managing to remain pupil-centred. This contention is supported by present findings which imply that schools which attempt to control pupils by offering rewards rather than punishment are more effective (Rutter *et al*, 1979), as are those which avoid liberal use of physical punishment and the cane (Clegg and Megson, 1968; Reynolds *et al*, 1982).

Practical school management

Interest in the ways in which schools can combat indiscipline and disruption is increasing. There appears to be a measure of agreement among educationists on the need for schools to introduce coherent staff policies on organisational matters if they are to combat indiscipline and disruption. Successful schools aim to prevent too many difficulties from arising rather than being exceptionally skilled in coping with them once they have occurred (Ouston, 1981).

McDaniel (1984) has developed a three tier model on the stages of discipline development for professional teachers. Many new teachers often start at level 1 and graduate at differing rates to level 3 dependent upon their personal strengths and weaknesses. At level 1 he suggests that:

Effective discipline begins with a teachers' knowledge of subject matter, curriculum, and methods of instruction and evaluation. The implication of this instructional stage, is that teachers can practice their pedagogy and will demonstrate to their students how learning can take place in the classroom. Teachers can demonstrate skills and strategies which will be a framework for their pupils' learning. This stage of development should maintain a positive learning atmosphere for most of the students, most of the time.

At level 2 he suggests:

Effective discipline requires a teacher to provide both control and support for student actions. Teachers should, therefore, accept their role in establishing values and rules. Teachers must learn how to manage and reinforce cultural norms for these rules and values. Teachers must also learn techniques which will diffuse difficult or unruly classroom situations which can present themselves for a number of reasons even with the best possible instruction.

At level 3, McDaniel suggests that:

Effective discipline depends ultimately on students developing self-discipline, internal controls for behaviour and mature decision-making processes. Teachers have to create conditions which enable their pupils to improve their self-concepts, desire to learn and respect for others.

It is extremely important that teachers get to know their pupils as well as possible. If you know your pupils you will be able to respond to their needs. For example, if you know that a pupil in your classroom is an avid hockey player it may be possible to draw an analogy when trying to teach him or her a difficult concept, for instance that of the angle of incidence equalling the angle of refraction as a physical property of light. In this way, you could avoid frustration which could develop from an unlearned concept.

Similarly, the knowledge that a pupil is having a difficult time at home should lead to appropriate empathy and accommodation in the classroom. The teacher, with the advice of others, will have to be sensitive to the importance of developing a degree of independence from the situation outside of school as it might affect the classroom.

Research (Tattum, 1982; Galloway *et al*, 1982; Mortimore *et al*, 1983; Woods, 1984; Frude and Gault, 1984; Gillham, 1984; Reid, 1986) shows that the following measures can be successfully used to overcome indiscipline in schools.

1 Changing existing timetabling structures so as to reduce the 'slack' time when vandalism and conflicts between children, or between children and teachers, tend to occur. Effective measures include the use of staggered lunch-breaks and reducing the number of pupils out of class at any one time; making for easier control and less pressure on open space.

2 Agreement between staff on united and coherent policies to reduce opportunities for deviant behaviour and teacher-pupil confrontations to take place: enforce a minimum (rather than maximum) number of indispensable school rules; provide an adequate system of remedial education; ensure good lesson plans and viable classroom management policies. Staff should be consistent in their interpretation of rules in the classroom and endeavour to overcome erratic, unfair or idiosyncratic sanctions.

3 Paying particular attention to organisation at the beginning and end of lessons and avoiding confusing commands. It helps to specify seating arrangements to keep mutually-provocative pupils apart and prevent unseemly scrambles for seats. Teachers should ensure the work they set is suitable to all levels of ability in the group, and make certain that less able children experience success as well as the able. Shouting or 'gunning' for pupils should be avoided; sometimes misdemeanours can be more successfully dealt with privately after the lesson rather than immediately – giving time for the situation to calm down and for rational processes to reassert themselves.

4 When confrontation occurs, defusing the process by taking firm immediate action. It is important not to over-react. Sometimes cracking a joke can help. On other occasions, removing a pupil from the classroom may be a last resort.

5 Starting lessons promptly and finishing on time.

6 Making use of effective rewards. Regular praise for the recognition of good behaviour, work and achievement is strongly associated with high achievement in schools.

7 Promoting pleasant working conditions in schools and encouraging pupils to take an active part in the daily life of the institution. Schools should ensure physical conditions are as pleasant as possible. It is important to give pupils opportunities to assume responsibility through monitor and prefect schemes, and for looking after resources and equipment, as well as encouraging their participation in meetings and assemblies.

8 Openness and honesty from teachers about their problems with individual pupils, groups of pupils and difficult forms. Colleagues should not regard such frankness as a sign of professional incompetence or weakness. Even the most experienced teachers make mistakes in their handling of classroom crises.

9 Considering pupils' perceptions. Pupils seem to prefer teachers who are strict but fair, have a sense of humour, are approachable and are empathetic in manner. They dislike teachers who are soft, ineffective, rigid, harsh, uncaring and whose demeanour provokes classroom confrontations. Pupils particularly dislike staff who fail to learn their names.

10 Taking account of group dynamics in class. Teachers should look for leaders or troublemakers and if necessary, find ways of changing the group layout. A useful strategy is for the teacher to stand in different places.

11 Avoiding a tendency to accuse groups of troublemaking when only one or two pupils are involved. Similarly, teachers should not punish whole classes for offences committed by individuals.

12 Giving pupils the benefit of the doubt if they make excuses which cannot be checked – such as a stomach ache.

13 Trying not to become too personally involved in confrontation. Irrespective of 'cause', keep your true feelings to yourself. A teacher who is in a bad mood can over-react and this is often the worst possible response. If you do decide to have a confrontation, have it on your own ground and on your own terms. Never be led into events. Know exactly what you are going to say in advance and choose your words carefully.
14 Using punishments wisely and sparingly. Do not over punish for a minor misdemeanour.

Implications for teachers

The evidence to date seems to suggest that schools have to find ways of striking a balance between overt disciplinary measures and laxness. In practice, this means that teachers need to be able to maintain control at all times while creating a relaxed atmosphere conducive to successful learning and harmonious interaction.

In reality, the acquisition of these skills depends as much upon outlook, personality and temperament as anything else. It needs to be remembered that while effective pastoral care teams support and prop up weak teachers, they cannot replace or change incompetence or ineffective work overnight. Change takes time. Helping weak teachers overcome their difficulties should be one of the main thrusts of good school-based in-service and staff development, practised through and under the auspices of the headteacher. Regrettably, too few schools practise this art at present.

These days, teachers have to rely increasingly on their own skills to maintain order in the classroom. The times when pupils feared the whole school regime, as portrayed in *Kes* or *John Brown's Schooldays*, are over – except, perhaps, in a few state and public schools. Similarly, the era when the cane provided a strong deterrent is (almost) over as well. Although many teachers believe that they have fewer and fewer options open to them in handling disobedient and disruptive pupils, the fact remains that more and more staff are learning to use their own skills to combat and counter potential and actual outbreaks of indiscipline.

Encouragingly, teachers' attitudes towards discipline are changing too. Many more teachers now realise that merely sending a pupil out of a classroom is no answer. Such solutions are the outcome of lost battles. In a way, the same is often true when teachers have to raise their voices, shout, or threaten pupils. We are, of course, painting a hopelessly idealistic picture; there will inevitably be situations from time to time when teachers need to distance themselves from aggressive and disruptive pupils. Nevertheless, this is no reason for teachers abandoning their objectives. If some teachers can achieve near perfect disciplinary records with pupils, then others should be able to improve with practice. Charisma is not everything – but it can be a great help!

Having to cope continually with disaffected and potentially difficult pupils is obviously more difficult than handling strongly motivated and well-adjusted high fliers. Indeed, the stress on certain teachers from continually working with difficult pupils is often greater than working amongst other groups (Kyriacou and Sutcliffe, 1978).

To summarise, therefore, much remains in the hands of individual teachers and schools. All the available evidence suggests that schools, headteachers and their staff set the disciplinary standards within their institutions. Clearly, tasks are made easier or more difficult by a host of related factors such as location size, and staff and pupil attitudes. So, for example, just as order in the corridors is enhanced by order in the classroom (Stallings and Hentzell, 1978; Glenn, 1981), so good discipline within the classroom is more difficult to maintain if the halls, dining room, playground and nearby classrooms are in chaos. To end the chapter, let us take a practical example which is commonplace in most schools.

A group of third year boys return from their physical education lesson after playing soccer. They arrive at their maths lessons five minutes late, exuberant, hot and in a high state of outrage after a last minute dubious penalty award which cost their class victory. Meanwhile, the girls in the form arrive at the same classroom on time after a movement lesson. The subject teacher has to cope with both sets of pupils: keep the girls happy until the boys arrive, quieten the latecomers down and re-integrate both groups into an atmosphere conducive to good academic learning. Hence, the teacher has to start the lesson late and adjust his or her work scheme accordingly; hardly a recipe for a successful lesson.

Next door, a colleague is taking a fifth-year examination class with exam time looming. The pupils, conscious of their impending examination, and its importance, enter the room quickly and quietly and start their revision exercises at once, pausing only occasionally to ask relevant questions.

In these examples, the managerial skills required of the first teacher are much greater than those demanded from the second. Given the variability in teaching, however, the subsequent lesson might well see the situations reversed with the first teacher in a more favourable situation than the second. Clearly, therefore, teachers have to be adaptable, in order to cater for all kinds of eventualities. This is why personality, temperament, intuition, educational knowledge and levels of classroom skills are key aspects of teachers' professional armouries. All these aspects play major parts in determining whether teachers are successful or unsuccessful at maintaining order in the classroom and dealing with ebullient and disruptive pupils.

Maintaining order and control in schools is a complex phenomenon. Aspects which appear to be related to disciplinary outcomes include: school location; history, status and ethos of the school; the age of the pupils; the day and time of year; socio-economic factors; parental values and support; teacher-pupil relationships; interaction within the classroom; the personality, qualifications, experience and ability of the teaching staff; school organisation (such as academic-pastoral divisions); the behaviour of the pupils themselves; external support from the local education authority, governors and advisers; features of the curriculum; staff attitudes (pupil centred, subject centred, self-centred); teacher stress; the amount and degree of pupil alienation and disaffection; the views and policies of the head and senior management staff; school and teachers' policies for combatting indiscipline; the skills of pastoral staff and/or school counsellors; resources, facilities and extracurricular activities – among many others.

There is no ready-made panacea which will enable schools to overcome their problems – only hard work. Just as one teacher can keep control with 5X and another cannot, so some schools appear to maintain disciplinary standards better than others. It may well be that the time is fast approaching when unsuccessful schools and teachers will feel the consequences of their actions – as moves to measure the effectiveness of schools and teachers begin to bite.

Section C: Traditional remedies

Chapters 5 and 6 analyse some of the traditional remedies used by schools to combat deviant conduct. Chapter 5 concentrates upon pastoral care. The text considers a wide range of matters including the organisation of pastoral care, the constraints upon pastoral care, pupils' perceptions of pastoral care and the evidence from research into school differences and school effectiveness which is relevant to the practice of pastoral care. Chapter 6 looks at other school factors which are associated with disaffected or non-conformist behaviour in schools. These include the curriculum, underachievement, school rules, teacher expectations, teacher-pupil and peer group relationships, and bullying.

Chapter 5
Pastoral Care

Nowadays, pastoral care is regarded as an integral part of secondary school organisation in most institutions. It is considered essential for the social and educational well-being of all pupils, particularly those from disadvantaged backgrounds. Despite this general consensus, there is surprisingly little evidence which highlights the differences between effective and ineffective pastoral care (Galloway, 1985). As much as anything else, this is probably due to the lack of research on pastoral care in action (Best *et al*, 1983). Perhaps, therefore, the key questions we should be asking are: Is there any such thing as really effective pastoral care? If so, how do we recognise it? Before we can attempt to answer these questions, it is first necessary to review all the evidence. However, this too will have to wait until we have set the scene.

The organisation of pastoral care

Pastoral posts suddenly mushroomed in secondary schools in the mid- and late 1960s. Prior to this, there was usually no division between caring and learning in most institutions. Teaching was still regarded as a vocation. In theory, every teacher cared equally for the academic and social dimensions of school life. However, with the introduction of comprehensive schooling, which came about partially in response to the demands for equality of educational opportunity for everybody, there developed a feeling that large, integrated, all-through schools required specialists in – and for – pupil's welfare.

Between the late 1960s and mid-1970s, the overwhelming majority of comprehensive schools established posts at senior or middle management level for pastoral care. Responsibility for academic and pastoral care became separated. Suddenly, a new breed of teacher was born, the expert on pupils' social and human needs. In many parts of Britain, and also overseas, these moves coincided with the upsurge of interest in counselling and the appointment of counsellors; something which sadly proved to be a short-lived growth area. These new professional and positional opportunities provided a two-tier organisational structure in most schools which (counsellors apart), continues not only to exist but to thrive. Nevertheless, it remains a fine and debatable point as to whether the subdivision of academic and pastoral responsibility within schools is a good thing or the most effective or wisest way of organising staff (Galloway, 1985; Reid, 1985a; 1986a,b; Reid and Milner, 1987).

Whatever the merits or demerits of pastoral care, over the last 20 years or so a science of guidance and counselling work in schools has developed. Debates remain, however, about the extent of its parameters. Hamblin (1977), for example, suggests that pastoral care should focus exclusively on pupils' progress and adjustment at school. He contends that teachers should not attempt to do much about problems related to pupils' home backgrounds because they cannot hope to achieve anything. Therefore, they should not waste their time. He also argues that the paramount priority of senior staff is to lead effective pastoral teams, since he believes all teachers should be involved in pupil care. Middle managers should not usurp the role of form tutors. When they do, their actions are liable to rebound on them as the tutors could well vote with their feet.

More recently, however, Hamblin – the doyen of guidance – has come out openly with the view that pastoral care has failed and *is* failing for a variety of reasons. These include confused aims and objectives, misguided and too discipline orientated administrative practices inside schools, and the non-introduction of worthwhile pastoral curricula (Hamblin, 1986a,b).

The evidence from research supports some of Hamblin's assertions. Difficulties with the implementation of pastoral care lie in role conflict (Dunham, 1977) and, as previously mentioned, the tendency for pastoral specialists to obviate or override the interest of subject staff and form tutors (Button, 1981; Galloway and Barrett, 1982). In addition, some middle managers are perceived by staff and pupils alike as spending too much time on non-essential or out-of-school issues such as pupils' home lives (Spooner, 1979; Galloway, 1981); truancy (Reynolds and Murgatroyd, 1977); and the maintenance of school rules and regulations (Frude, 1984). It was for these reasons that the Teachers' Action Collective (1976) criticised the whole concept and process of pastoral care in schools. They suggested that the reality of pastoral care lay in its function as a necessary and controlling agent of school life. It was control which lay beneath much of the caring rhetoric. They argued that the provision of pastoral staff and special units has diverted much-needed financial resources away from basic education. It has also removed too much responsibility from the form and subject tutor. The Collective argues, therefore, that pastoral care in schools is ultimately untenable because of the range and number of difficulties involved, some of which are 'caused' by the creation of pastoral posts. They suggest that some so-called pastoral care experts cause as many problems as they solve, while at the same time making others worse.

There is another argument against pastoral care. To date there is no evidence to indicate that schools which do not distinguish between academic and pastoral responsibilities fare any worse than those which do. In fact, some schools which can be described as 'guidance orientated' may be guilty of providing profoundly unsatisfactory environments for teachers and pupils alike (Galloway, 1985). Some research suggests that it is the *ethos* of pastoral care teams as much as anything else which is important in producing favourable outcomes (Rutter *et al*, 1979; Reynolds *et al*, 1980; Reynolds and Reid, 1985). Establishing this favourable climate is, however, never easy – as the rest of the chapter will demonstrate.

Constraints upon effective pastoral care

The literature on the relationship between school effectiveness and pastoral care is not only sparse but probably too thin to make accurate judgements possible at present (Reynolds, 1983). The same, incidentally, is true for the existing evidence on the organisational features of institutional life when related to school effectiveness. In order, therefore, to glean clues, we will now consider some of the constraints upon effective pastoral care. Later, we will begin sifting the evidence in search of further leads.

Reid and Milner (1987) carefully divided the numerous factors which impose their own kinds of constraints upon effective pastoral care in schools into three sorts – role, pupil and institutional aspects. They then further subdivided these three major strands into 30 contributory areas some of which are outlined below.

Role factors

The inherent role factors which impinge upon the practice of effective pastoral care in many schools include:
a external constraints (societal change, the effects of the media, malaise and LEA policies as well as matters relating to educational research);
b the way pastoral staff are selected and appointed;
c the lack of initial and in-service training on guidance-related issues for postholders;
d the pastoral-academic dichotomy in many schools;
e the pressure of workloads;
f the absence of certain professional support, especially from outside agencies;
g the demise of counsellors and counselling *per se* in schools;
h personality and territorial imperatives;
i managerial aspects such as imprecise job descriptions and inadequate role definitions.

Pupil-related factors

Pupil-related factors which impose constraints upon effective pastoral care include:
a the extent and diversity of 'problems' in schools;
b the degree and amount of underachievement, alienation, disaffection, absenteeism and disruptive conduct;
c the number of remedial pupils and those with special educational needs;
d the tenor of the school 'ethos' and its effects upon pupils' perspectives and their participation in school life.

Institutional factors

These can be sub-divided into 11 areas:
a school administration;
b teacher expectations;
c teacher stress;
d teacher-pupil relationships;
e classroom management and organisation;
f the curriculum;
g school rules;
h pupil profiles and record-keeping systems;
i resources and buildings;
j the ability of form tutors;
k home-school links.

The quality of pastoral postholders' performance in schools is generally affected by the interplay between many of these aspects. For example, some middle managers receive more training than others. Some schools have fewer difficult pupils than others. Some heads of year have better and more effective form tutors than others.

In order to reinforce these points, and to show how they effect the quality of pastoral care inside schools, we now present a few informative and illustrative case extracts. These were obtained from interviews with selected staff in a largish comprehensive in South Wales. Fuller details on the organisational structure of this school are available elsewhere (Reid, 1986). Suffice for now to say that the school contains approximately 1200 pupils and is located in a fairly deprived region of South Wales. In many ways, apart from its denominational status, it is not atypical of many similar-sized comprehensives throughout Britain.

Comments included in the text are drawn from semi-structured interviews with the Head, the Deputy Head in charge of pastoral care, a head of year, a head of department and two form tutors. The extracts are fairly revealing and largely self-explanatory. They show how opinions between teachers on the effectiveness of pastoral care in one school can differ. Presumably if they differ here, they will also differ elsewhere.

Quite frankly, I pride myself on the pastoral work done in this school. I think I can fairly say it is one of my finest achievements. Look at the books on my shelf, they're nearly all on pastoral care and counselling. (The Headteacher).

Pastoral care here is a joke. I have more truants in my form than attenders on some days. I have three loud-mouthed yobs. You can only call them that. One is a constant thorn in my side. For three years I've tried to have something done about him. You should try to teach him. I've given up. Mr Fielding (the Head of Year) doesn't seem to care or want to know. He's always only been interested in the high fliers. I don't know how he got the job in the first place. He used to be much better in his old job. I respected him then. (A third-year tutor).

Since the latest round of reorganisation, things have really improved here. The Head spoke to us – his three Deputies – and made certain role and organisational changes. Now we're really beginning to respond and get to grips with the main issues. Our truancy problem, apart from a minor hiccup last term, is much better. So too is our disciplinary record since we started suspending more pupils. Most of all, however, staff morale is improving. (Deputy Head in charge of Pastoral Care)

This is strictly off the record . . . I'd say I do as much pastoral care as anyone else on the staff. The pupils and many staff seem to come to me naturally. They don't like . . . (A Head of Department)

If I could get rid of say, half a dozen of my staff, I'd have fewer overall problems tomorrow. (Headteacher)

It's about time some of the staff got off their backsides. They leave everything to us. Pastoral care is supposed to be about team work, not just extra work for a few. (A Head of Year)

I used to report everything. Now I don't bother unless its really serious. It's a waste of time. Nothing ever gets done. You're just wasting breath. (A fourth year tutor)

If I had a really difficult school, I don't know how I'd manage. In many ways, we're really lucky here. (Headteacher)

In one or two forms here, its battle warfare. Fortunately, we don't have too many serious problems below the third year. It's mostly the fourth and fifth years, and then only certain forms. This year we started on a new policy, we gave up bothering chasing any of the fifth formers' problems. You never achieve anything so why bother? (Deputy Head in charge of Pastoral Care)

You ask about our truancy problem. Well, frankly, I'll tell you. I'd rather teach 20 than 30. Wouldn't you? It's common sense. We've got ten per cent of troublemakers here. They spoil everything for everybody. Its not fair on the rest. (Fourth year tutor)

Some of us had a chat in the staff room last term and agreed on one thing. We're no better off with heads of year than before they were introduced. We can't see the point of the changes. (Third year tutor)

I've got two or three really good form tutors – one in particular. Then I've got a couple of indifferent ones and two who are both awful. Funnily enough, its some of my older staff who are the worst. (A Head of Year)

I never take my problems to my co-called head of year. I despise him after what happened in our last confrontation. Last year was different because Mr James knew how to handle things. This . . . person now seems to think that because I've got a problem it's always my fault. He keeps looking at me as if I was an idiot. I've been here fifteen years and have never been treated like this before. I know he

talks behind my back because Mrs Smales told me so. I loathe him. You may as
well know the truth. (Fourth year subject tutor)

I think I can safely say that I've got one of the happiest and most efficient staff
in this part of Wales. There's only one problem. They're an ageing staff. I could
really do with a few youngsters for all kinds of reasons. I'd support job rotation if
it meant I could have some new blood. (Headteacher)

Even a cursory glance at these statements is sufficient to note the
contradictory views of the staff. They show the need for the staff in the
school to pull together. The underlying problem appears to be a failure of
management. As the extracts reveal, the head believes he has an effective
guidance set-up; a view not entirely shared by all his staff.

There is mounting evidence that successful pastoral work will only be
achieved when all the staff operate together, assisted by workable
policies and agreed aims and objectives (Hamblin, 1978; Galloway,
1985). To achieve this, special staff meetings may have to be called to
formulate policies and agree upon strategies (Gillham, 1984). Such
endeavours do work, whether they involve disruptive, disaffected or
absentee pupils (Jones, 1980; Reid, 1982; 1985; 1986; Tattum, 1982).
Each school needs to work out its own individual blend and approach to
pastoral care, dependent upon the educational philosophy held by the
head and other key staff. Its effectiveness can only be judged by
determining whether it provides a framework within which the individual teacher is able to act when faced with pupils who have special
needs or problems, experience learning difficulties or cause trouble (Bird
et al, 1980; Johnson *et al*, 1980).

The aims of pastoral care

The literature suggests that the aim of most pastoral staff in schools is to
enable children with difficulties to overcome them as smoothly and as
quickly as possible, in order to ensure that the educationally damaging
consequences for children at risk are minimised. When, however, such
intervention fails, especially with deviant children, staff usually resort to
more formal sanctions. These sanctions can range from the use of short,
sharp, shock treatments – like lines and detention – to the wielding of the
cane, which was fashionable in former times. For continued misbehaviour, a series of measures dependent upon individual circumstances is
generally considered: these range from the provision of remedial
education, to more severe options like suspension or court proceedings
(Reid, 1986).

Evidence to date suggests that schools vary considerably in the type of
response they make to their pupils; in the level of resources and options
open to them; in the order in which these options are deployed; and in
the speed with which punitive sanctions replace welfare-orientated ones.

Schools tend to be idiosyncratic in their responses to their pupils' needs, dependent both upon their policies and their assessment of individual situations. It is often forgotten, however, that one of the inherent dangers of enforcing overly primitive measures is that schools can sometimes reinforce the very behaviour which they are seeking to overcome (Reynolds and Murgatroyd, 1977). Alternatively, schools can occasionally find themselves isolated when they make stands against totally unacceptable behaviour. In October, 1985, for example, five staff in Manchester were suspended after refusing to teach pupils who had daubed disgusting slogans about their families on school walls. It is in such situations that teachers not only feel isolated and misunderstood but lose morale.

The literature suggests that good schools (DES, 1977) endeavour to achieve a very high proportion of success with pupils – and do so. Theoretically, this means arriving at effective solutions for every needy pupil within their care. Such lofty but laudable ideals are very hard to achieve without a great deal of dedicated hard work on the part of staff, especially in schools located in deprived or difficult areas or those with an abundance of disaffected or alienated pupils. Persistent absentees, for example, are unlikely to be successfully re-integrated if they are immediately sent home on their return to school for failing to wear the proper school uniform or if they are 'punished' for falling behind with their school work. What they need is help, not victimisation (Reid, 1982a; 1985).

It is widely recognised that good schools aim to identify actual and potential problems at a very early stage in their development. Thereafter, pastoral staff need to liaise between teachers and parents as and when necessary, link with outside agencies, and provide the right conditions for empathetic and practical help to be given, irrespective of individual circumstances (Schools Council, 1973; Clegg and Megson, 1973). Unfortunately, inadequate educational training often prevents many pastoral staff from implementing the right procedures in every case, often because they have too little understanding of the function and network of outside agencies (Fitzherbert, 1977). Also, in far too many schools, a few weak links are undoing the good work of the majority of staff.

The practice of pastoral care

As mentioned at the beginning of the chapter, the literature is deficient in systematic evaluations of the effectiveness of pastoral care systems and school counselling in meeting the needs of pupils or changing their behaviour. In fact, much of the literature concentrates on guidance and support systems, making suggestions as to how these should be carried out or giving examples of practice from case studies (Moore, 1971;

Lytton and Craft, 1974; Marland, 1974; Blackham, 1978; Hamblin, 1978, 1981; Jones, 1984). Similarly, writers on counselling tend to examine the role of the counsellor within schools and the nature of counselling as it is practised within the school setting (Holden, 1969, 1971; Hamblin, 1973, 1974; Lewis and Murgatroyd, 1976; Galloway, 1981; McGuiness, 1982).

The authors of these texts and articles have noted that there is a considerable imprecision about the way in which terms such as 'pastoral care', 'counselling', and 'guidance' are used and in the meanings assigned to them. Given the enormous structural differences which exist between schools in the implementation of their pastoral care set-up, it is hardly surprising that preliminary studies on pastoral care in action reveal considerable variations in the effectiveness of certain systems in monitoring pupil well-being and providing a satisfactory support structure for teachers (Best *et al*, 1980).

Explicitly, Johnson *et al* (1980) describe the pastoral care practice in schools in two Outer London Boroughs which they studied. They ascertained that most teachers felt pastoral care systems were able to cope with the conflicting demands made upon them. A minority of staff, however, considered that some of the disciplinary or administrative procedures were incompatible with the caring functions. Interestingly, some pupils commented that there were too many people in schools interested in finding out about their problems. Generally, the evidence suggests that most pupils are able to build up close relationships with individual teachers who may or may not have some form of pastoral responsibility for them. The authors found that a good relationship between pastoral staff and pupils within schools normally bore little or no correlation to pupils' problems outside schools.

In another study, Bird *et al* (1980) found differences between schools in the latitude which they allowed to pupils in expressing dissent, as well as in the firmness with which disaffected behaviour was identified and followed up with disciplinary or remedial action by pastoral care staff. The continuum ranged between action being taken at the first sign of disturbance to staff only taking notice of the most overt symptoms of distress or dissent. Clearly, these differences in emphasis are related to the extent of a school's problems just as much as organisational and personality factors.

Some of these points are reinforced in Galloway *et al*'s (1982) Sheffield study. They also found significant differences between schools in the practice of pastoral care. Some schools, for example, seemed to succeed in allowing class teachers to consult with colleagues informally and receive advice on how to handle difficult pupils, thereby helping to defuse potentially explosive situations. Conversely, other systems, frequently those which required teachers to refer pupils to specialist heads of year, often diverted attention from the source of the problem and increased the danger of turning minor incidents into major confrontations. In schools which operated the latter structure, Galloway *et al* found an increased likelihood of suspension being used. This may well be due to the earlier intervention of heads of year in the decision-making process.

Pupils' perceptions

Regrettably, also, too few studies have examined pupils' perceptions of aspects of their schooling (Furlong, 1976; Phillips and Callely, 1981; Reid, 1983a,b,c,d,e). This may be due to suspicion on the part of some authorities as to the potential use and outcomes of such studies (Power *et al*, 1967; 1972). Alternatively, it may be related to methodological or credibility factors. Either way, it is ironic that those studies which do exist are in some ways encouraging. Phillips and Callely (1981), for example, found that even fourth year pupils do not find everything about their schooling too distasteful. In fact, a high proportion of pupils seem to look forward to their time in school because they like the work involved, they enjoy learning and being with their friends. This study is particularly encouraging because it was conducted in South Wales, where there are known to be a higher and disproportionate number of social and educational problems from many other parts of England and Wales (Fogelman and Richardson, 1974; Carroll, 1977; Reynolds, 1982; Brace, 1982; Reid, 1985).

If studies on pupils' perceptions of their schooling are not common, pupil comments on their experiences of pastoral care systems are even rarer. Murgatroyd (1977) undertook a survey of pupils' perceptions of counselling in a school with a highly developed and praised (DES, 1977) counselling service. He found that counsellors were regarded by pupils as senior teachers with considerable administrative duties, including major responsibility for checking attendance registers for truancy and reporting truants to the education welfare officer. Therefore, they were not seen as major sources of help with personal problems.

By contrast, Hooper (1978) found the reverse to be true. He analysed pupils' perceptions of counselling in a school in South West England. He reports that children in this establishment were quite willing to approach the counsellor with personal problems and others arising out of the school setting. He suggests that school differences may be related to whether counsellors are client-centred or institution-orientated. Presumably, the same may well be true for pastoral care.

Siann *et al* (1982) investigated pupils' perceptions of the effectiveness of counselling services in a secondary school in Scotland which had a well developed guidance system and a high degree of commitment to it. Pupils were asked to read eight problems: four were school-based, and four were personal/familial problems. Half the sample were given a list of possible sources of assistance, including guidance staff. The other half were unprompted. On personal and familial problems, the unprompted group were as likely to cite pastoral staff as being sources of assistance as were the prompted group. The researchers took this to mean that guidance staff were spontaneously seen as sources of help on these matters. The respondents also completed a semantic differential test. Analyses of these data confirmed that counselling staff were seen in more pastoral terms than other teaching staff.

In this study, pupils regarded the majority of school staff as caring and as potentially helpful in crises, particularly those related to school. Nevertheless, guidance staff were seen as more caring and more pastoral in character than the subject teachers the pupils were asked to rate. In addition, in both experimental groups, the pupils saw guidance staff as being more likely to be helpful than other teachers in the event of personal/familial problems. Siann *et al* concluded that these findings were inter-related. Guidance and counselling staff are probably more effective within schools which are supportive of their work and their values than in those which are not.

In another similar experiment, Reid (1982b; 1983c; 1985) found that persistent absentees were unlikely to take their problems to any of their teachers, including form tutors. The teachers were perceived as agents of an educational system they had already rejected. Using Kelly's (1955) repertory grid technique, Reid found that pupils preferred their parents, family and friends to their teachers, even in cases where it was known that the absentees had difficult home circumstances. It seems, therefore, that natural loyalty ties may be important in work with deviant groups. The absentees were prepared to give the benefit of the doubt to their parents but not to teachers. This experiment shows the invidious position in which guidance staff find themselves when endeavouring to work with pupils who have been repeatedly admonished by schools.

Pastoral staff suffer from other difficulties, too. Miller and Russell (1978) found that the amount of time available to teachers of guidance to see pupils individually was so limited as to preclude pastoral staff getting to know all their charges well. In fact, two out of three fourth-year pupils reported that they had only met their guidance teachers once in an an interview setting.

Smith (1976) asked 217 teachers, 'What aims, if any, should a guidance system have?' He grouped responses into seven categories. Three of these were regarded as being concerned with the counselling aspects of guidance. Slightly over half of the staff endorsed 'letting pupils discuss problems' (54%) and 'showing interest in pupils' (54%); only fifteen per cent endorsed 'inculcating values/moral guidance.'

While the work of Siann *et al* (1982) is encouraging and shows that guidance *can* work in schools, the national Scottish data of Gray (1980) are extremely discouraging. In a major study of client evaluation of guidance in Scottish secondary schools, he found that only a minority of pupils considered teachers to be a help with their personal problems. Of his cohort of 1975/76 school-leavers in Scotland, one in five reported that 'a lot' or 'quite a lot' of help had been given to them in the personal area. Half of the respondents stated explicitly that they had not been helped at all. As Gray's question referred to 'teachers' in general rather than 'guidance teachers' in particular, pastoral staff may or may not have accounted for all the limited help that was noted. Gray concluded from his survey that 'guidance teachers have had either a very small or an uncertain influence on "personal matters"' in pupils' schooling.

The research to date suggests that pastoral work inside each school generates its own ambience. It may well be that such an ambience powerfully affects the behaviour and perceptions of pupils as well as teachers. As we noted in Chapter 2 and we will see again shortly, this may be one reason why researchers in the United States have placed such emphasis and credence upon the concept of school climate.

Research evidence from the school differences studies

The evidence from research into school differences and school effectiveness seems to suggest that effective pastoral care is related to some or all of the characteristics below. These conclusions must be treated cautiously, however. Further research is needed before firm conclusions are reached. In any event, a number of unanswered questions remain.

1 Effective pastoral care is probably related to the disciplinary orientation of schools. Institutions which attempt to control pupils by offering rewards rather than punishments seem to be most effective (Rutter *et al*, 1979), as do those which avoid the heavy use of physical punishment (Clegg and Megson, 1968).

2 Effective pastoral care is almost certainly related to the degree of pupil participation in school life. Encouraging children to participate in the running of schools appears to be conducive to good attainment, attendance and behaviour (Reynolds *et al*, 1976; Rutter *et al*, 1979) as well as to their enjoyment and favourable perception of school life (Purkey and Smith, 1983).

3 The views of teachers and teachers' expectations of pupils seems vital. Studies consistently show that teachers' views and positive expectations of pupils affects outcomes (Rit, 1970; Williams, 1976; Cuttance, 1980; 1985). For instance, when teachers hold negative views of their pupils' home backgrounds, they are likely to get negative conduct in return (Reynolds, 1979; Wadsworth, 1979).

4 The size of schools, classes and the teacher-pupil ratio *may* be important but possibly only under certain conditions. To date, however, there is too little evidence to be certain. Reynolds *et al* (1976) suggest

pupils achieve better in schools with more favourable pupil/teacher ratios. Data from successive Assessment of Performance Studies (APU 1981a,b,c), Wiseman (1974) and Rutter *et al* (1979) have all indicated that school and class size are not crucial factors. In one sense this is surprising. Most teachers will freely admit that it is easier to give pupils individual attention in classes of 20 than of 30.

5 Effective pastoral care may be related to the form of institutional control which is practised within schools. Once again, the evidence so far on this measure is somewhat contradictory. Rutter *et al* (1979) and Millham (1982) suggest that organisationally 'tight' regimes which attempt high expressive control of pupils within their school lives are most effective. Conversely, Reynolds *et al* (1976) and Reynolds (1979) argue the opposite – schools with high institutional control are most ineffective. Finlayson and Loughran (1976) and Rafalides and Hoy (1979) have both reported that harsh, authoritarian, 'custodial' regimes have an adverse effect upon pupils' perceptions. So too, it seems, do disorganised or 'anomic' institutions, by generating a weakly-controlled environment which causes pupils to lose respect for staff (Hargreaves, 1979; 1980; 1981). Research to date seems to suggest that effective schools may be characterised by a form of *balanced* control (Reynolds, 1982b). The implications for middle managers are obvious.

6 The psychological environment of the classroom is very important in effective schools. The evidence from small, large and multi-national studies all show that positive learning outcomes are highly associated with cohesiveness, satisfaction, degree of task difficulty, formality, goal direction and democracy. Negative associations are found in atmospheres conducive to friction, cliqueness, apathy, disorganisation, inequality and favouritism (Walberg, 1969; Rosenshine, 1970; Rosenshine and Furst, 1971; Walberg and Anderson, 1972; Moos, 1979; Frazer, 1981; Frazer and Walberg, 1981; Haertel and Walberg, 1981). There are clear indications here, too, for form tutors to be positive. Effective form tutors will use their time wisely on, for example, materials relating to the implementation of pastoral curricula (Hamblin, 1986b).

7 The academic environment of the school is crucial in effective schools. Research shows that pupils like to be kept busy on worthwhile activities, including homework (McDill, 1969; Brimer and Madaus, 1978; Madaus *et al*, 1979; Marjoribanks, 1979; Rutter *et al*, 1979; Madaus, 1980; Garbarino and Asp, 1982). Important factors in affecting positive achievement are: the academic demands of courses; the students' concern for and commitment to academic values; the amount of time spent on study and on homework; and, in general, a climate of high expectations on the part of students and their teachers (Reynolds, 1982b). It may be that one of the most crucial jobs of pastoral staff, therefore, is to support academic staff and learning in the school whenever possible, and not pull in the opposite direction.

8 The professional outlook of staff in a school is another aspect related to effective guidance. There are hints that expenditure on teachers' salaries may have some effect on outcome (Bowles and Levin, 1968; Averch *et al*, 1971), particularly in eras of disaffection, strife and malaise (Reid, 1986). Despite this, successive studies on resource levels, expenditure per pupil, and the quality and quantity of buildings suggest that these are relatively unimportant features (Coleman, 1966; McDill, 1969; Jencks *et al*, 1972; Reynolds *et al*, 1980), even in split-site schools (Rutter *et al*, 1979) or in schools with a lot of old buildings (Reynolds *et at*, 1976; Rutter *et al*, 1979).

Some of these findings may appear surprising to many teachers, particularly as Her Majesty's Inspectorate (DES, 1985) have linked quality to the state of buildings. There is evidence to suggest, however, that it is the day-to-day upkeep of buildings, rather than their age or appearance, which may be associated with positive school outcomes (Pablant and Baxter, 1975; Reynolds, 1982b).

9 Studies on pupils' perceptions and pastoral care in action suggest that a school's atmosphere is very important to effective pastoral care. The concept of school ethos (Rutter *et al*, 1979) or school climate (Reynolds, 1985) is gaining in momentum. Many of the reported differences between schools, in terms of both their overall effectiveness and the effectiveness of their pastoral care systems, are critically related to their atmosphere, policies and many of the non-cognitive aspects of schooling (Reid and Jones, 1983; Reynolds and Reid, 1985). For the moment, these non-cognitive aspects remain very difficult to measure, precisely. Certainly, studies undertaken in the United States repeatedly stress the importance of a school's social climate to educational outcomes (Brookover *et al*, 1979; Purkey and Smith, 1983).

Despite much of this direct and tangential evidence, there remain a number of important questions which need to be answered before we can be certain just what leads to effective pastoral care in schools. These include:

a What relationship does the training, personality and educational background of pastoral staff have with effective pastoral care, including work undertaken by form tutors and counsellors?

b What differences can the attitude and policies of the headteacher make to effective pastoral care?

c How can headteachers, deputies and middle managers foster and promote corporate spirits and policies amongst all their staff, particularly those with pastoral care responsibility, and make sure a favourable school climate is discerned by pupils in the school?

d Are better pastoral staff located in the most effective schools? If so, why?

e Is pastoral care equally effective in year groups of 250 compared with those of 75, 125 or 150?

f Is effective pastoral care related to the ratio of pupils' problems in school rather than size *per se*?

g What consequences for effective pastoral care do good parent-school relationships have? To what extent do the views of parents (Newsom and Newsom, 1984) influence the perceptions, behaviour and performance of pupils, particularly in relation to guidance in schools?

h What is the evidence for effective pupil care in primary schools?

We now return to the questions we posed at the beginning of the chapter: Is there any such thing as really effective pastoral care and, if so, how do we know it? The answer to the first question must be 'Yes'. The answer to the second, however, is much more complex and cannot be stated unequivocally. Presumably, teachers and pupils know intuitively when their guidance systems are effective as the Siann *et al* (1982) study suggests. Guidance staff are probably most effective when they receive total support from every member of staff and when all teachers operate in unison to carry out agreed policies. In such circumstances, all teachers will take a real interest in the social as well as the educational interests of their pupils. The children will be known by name and feel wanted and cared for in school. That is, *every* child. Not solely the bright or most socially gifted. School will be a rewarding place and will promote and foster emphathetic approaches in teacher-pupil relationships. The staff will conduct themselves in such a way as to merge their academic and pastoral concerns.

Under these circumstances, it is more likely that the pupils will manifest their affection for their school by working hard, behaving well and participating in extra-curricula activities. This is not 'pie in the sky'. It is what effective pastoral care is all about.

Chapter 6
Non-conformist pupils: school processes

This chapter concentrates on some of the institutional processes related to deviant behaviour within schools. Topics include the curriculum; underachievement; the real relationship between deviance, underachievement and disaffection; school differences, disadvantage and disaffection; school rules; teacher expectations; teacher-pupil and peer group relationships; and, bullying.

The curriculum

Relatively little work has been done on the relationship between the curriculum and disaffection. However, most writers are in accord that disadvantaged and disaffected pupils often have unsuitable and unfavourable curricula to follow at school. In fact, the literature abounds with adverse comments about the way the curriculum is organised for less able children, especially as so many disaffected pupils tend to experience serious learning difficulties, are backward and/or inclined to underachieve. Falling behind with school work can be one of the initial reasons why some pupils first start to miss school or show disruptive symptoms (Anderson, 1980; Buist, 1980; Welsh Office, 1984).

Research suggests that there are four ways in which pupils' experiences of the curriculum adversely affect them: when they find it irrelevant, too academic or too demanding and, importantly, when it leaves them with a sense of failure (Bird et al, 1980). Undoubtedly, repeated failure in assignments set by teachers in school reduces many pupils' academic self-concept and tends to lower their general levels of self-esteem as well as raising their degrees of alienation from school (Reid, 1981, 1982a).

Despite the introduction of new curricula into some schools through TVEI and micro-electronic programmes, there is little doubt that what is taught at secondary level is inappropriate to the needs of industry, commerce or the pupils themselves. For example, in one school, the head of department asked a maths student to teach fractions and decimals to middle band fourth year pupils. These 14 and 15-year-old pupils should have learnt these mathematical concepts years earlier. When one of us investigated the matter further, some of the pupils stated they were learning fractions and decimals for the second or third time – others had never done so. This incident exemplifies the lack of structure in the curriculum. In some schools the content of a subject curriculum changes with every new teacher, which must confuse many parents and pupils alike. In this respect, the absence of agreed national guidelines for the secondary school curriculum is a handicap and can trigger off both disruption and disaffection – particularly when pupils become bored or uninterested in the content of their lessons. Sometimes, who can blame them?

We will avoid further detailed discussion of the institutional effects of the curriculum at this point because this subject is considered in depth in chapters 9, 10, 11 and 12.

Underachievement

Underachievement is a massive educational problem which is undoubtedly related to the curriculum as well as to a whole host of other factors, such as teachers' abilities and class size. As such, it should be a major concern for everyone involved in education.

One of the biggest drawbacks to establishing the precise link between disadvantaged and disaffected behaviour and underachievement lies in the fact that underachievement is a difficult and imprecise concept to measure. Underachievement is not a stable or single commodity. For this reason, researchers tend to measure aspects of underachievement by using such instruments as standardised achievement tests in, for example, reading or mathematics, which provide only partial answers. These endeavours rarely take account of behavioural underachievement or mass underachievement either in schools or throughout a region. Moreover, most projects on underachievement are unable to glean accurate information on the quality of teaching or unsuitable curricular *et seq.*

Despite this lack of precision it is essential that the concern felt by many secondary teachers about their pupils' lack of achievement is not ignored. Many teachers who use the term underachievement assume, because of their general knowledge of the pupil, that the necessary potential is there. This is a reasonable assumption to make. Most young children have the potential to learn to read although, for some, progress is slow. Similarly, most adults who wish to, eventually learn to manipulate the complex controls of a car. There are, of course, some tasks that are beyond the capabilities of most of us: rapidly understanding complex scientific theories; gaining complete fluency in a new language in a short period; becoming a first-rate musician if we are born tone deaf ... Thankfully, however, for most tasks undertaken in secondary schools, careful tuition, hard work and a high level of motivation can lead to the growth of skills and understanding.

Achievement is not, however, uniform. There are clear differences in all three of the above components (tuition, application and motivation), and thus pupils vary markedly in their performance. At the level of individual pupils this is understandable. After all, talents and motivation occur to quite different degrees. Similarly, the quality of teaching in schools also varies.

There have been no completely satisfactory arguments put forward to explain the causes of underachievement. There are, however, a number of important correlates of group underachievement (Mortimore, 1982). These include social disadvantage, peer influence, school influence, the secondary system, sexism and racism.

Although it is wrong to blame home background for underachievement at school, it is clear that pupils who experience social disadvantage such as low income, poor housing, marital disharmony, inconsistent discipline, unemployment or come from one parent families, are less likely to do well at school than their more advantaged peers (Mortimore and Blackstone, 1982). The evidence overwhelmingly suggests that the combination of bad housing, low income, poor health care and familial stress, has a powerful effect on the school performance of some pupils. Nevertheless, it needs to be borne in mind that some pupils from deprived working-class backgrounds achieve well at school and in later life.

From a variety of data sources it is clear that from the age of seven onwards there is a considerable difference in achievement between pupils from homes where the parent has a non-manual occupation, and those where the parents are considered 'working class'. In reading, mathematics and in referral rates for special education, these class differences persist over time (Davie *et al*, 1972; Fogelman *et al*, 1978).

Halsey *et al* (1980) reported that, despite the increase in the provision of higher education, the chances of a pupil from a working class home going to university are no better now than before the First World War. Even after accepting the fact that many of these pupils may not have chosen to go on to higher education, the occupational limitations remain considerable. Upward social mobility is still the exception rather than the norm for most children from working-class origins. In this era of high unemployment, the consequences of underachievement may be particularly serious.

Rutter (1979) suggests that the influence of peers is especially important for pupils as they make educational choices (subject choices etc) during secondary school. Even in schools where teachers highlight the advantages to pupils of taking a wide curriculum, some pupils will insist on following rigidly stereotyped choices. Thus, although research on the influence of peer groups is not as fully developed as studies of family background, it seems probable that friendship influences have a strong effect on certain children – especially teenage pupils. In some cases this peer pressure is only part of a much wider influence encompassing family and society.

Recent studies of school effectiveness have shown that individual schools can have a powerful effect on pupil achievement (Edmunds *et al*, 1978; Rutter *et al*, 1979). The impact of the school *may* not, however, be sufficient to overcome the combined effects of social disadvantage. The available evidence seems to suggest that good schools raise the performance of *all* pupils. The reverse is also probably true. Poor schools have negative effects on the achievement of their pupils. As shown in Chapter 2, critical factors which impinge on pupil performance appear to be effective teaching strategies; positive teacher expectations; well-structured courses; a favourable school ethos; adequate resources; well managed departments and schools; the provision of regular homework; and the quality of feedback given to pupils and parents alike (Brophy and Good, 1974; Rosenshine, 1978; Mortimore and Mortimore, 1981). Of course, it is easier to be a good teacher in some schools than in others. Researchers have frequently drawn attention to the negative effects of bad behaviour, high absence rates, low morale and the generally unfavourable school climates within some institutions.

While the organisation and curriculum of secondary schools remain dominated by public examinations it is difficult to see how, even with 'good' schools, the underachievement of some groups of pupils can be avoided (Mortimore, 1982). Conventional examinations are highly competitive. Pupils from disadvantaged home and social backgrounds compete with those who, throughout their lives, have experienced every possible support. For most pupils in secondary schools the chances of achieving sufficiently high grades to pass external examinations like 'O' level or GCSE are low. Small wonder then that so many pupils give up towards the end of their secondary schooling or once they perceive their limitations. Truancy and disruption present alternatives which, for some pupils, are probably very had to resist.

Sexism is commonly associated with certain kinds of underachievement particularly for girls in science subjects and for girls raised within, for example, some Asian homes where women are treated as second class citizens. A knowledge of issues related to sexism can influence the expectations and career aspirations for girls held by teachers, parents, male peers, employers and, indeed, the girls themselves. But the evidence about sex differences in achievement is not straightforward. Overall, girls appear to perform as well or slightly better than boys at all stages up to 'A' level examinations. In some subjects, however, there appear to be major differences between the sexes. For example, Assessment of Performance Unit (APU) surveys show that girls underachieve in most mathematical tests (HMSO, 1980; 1981b). Boys appear to underachieve in French and some modern languages. In the physical sciences, girls are under-represented. But they do not underachieve. In fact, although the proportions of girls entering for physics and chemistry examinations are relatively small, those who do enter perform rather better, on average, than the boys. Needless to say the proportions of girls entering technical subjects and of boys entering home economics are minimal.

Even though more girls than boys go on to higher education, a much smaller number go on to high status courses. In 1981, for the first time, a slightly higher proportion of female than male applicants for university places were successful. Overall, however, there were still far more male applicants – and thus entrants – to university (UCCA, 1982). For girls, therefore, the term 'underachievement' is somewhat misleading. In reality, it is a combination of underachievement and under-representation that creates barriers to equal opportunity.

On teacher training courses within universities in England and Wales women graduates predominate in modern languages and arts subjects. Males continue to be in a majority in maths and physics and, to a lesser extent, in chemistry. Biology and primary education are female domin-ated. Teaching is increasingly becoming a female dominated profession (Reid *et al*, 1981; 1981b).

Racism is another important contributory factor in underachievement. Racism, however, is an extremely complex subject, as the variation in school performance between pupils of different Asian family back-grounds demonstrates. Racism, in the form of direct aggressive actions, such as bullying in school, clearly causes concern to many pupils from minority groups and this worry undoubtedly affects pupils' learning. However, in describing ethnic groups, there is always a danger of overgeneralisation, particularly when pupils from so many different cultures are involved. Moreover most black pupils now in school are of British nationality, and have been born and educated in this country.

Generally speaking, evidence on the achievement of black pupils is difficult to find, as ethnic background has seldom been systematically researched – partly because of the delicate nature of the topic. To date, research suggests that:
a The proportions of black school leavers going on to some form of further education are high.
b The parents of some black pupils are especially keen for their children to do well at school.
c Underachievement is common among black pupils with family backgrounds from the Caribbean (HMSO, 1981; Taylor, 1981).

Options open to teachers in attempting to boost underachievers include: personal tuition/tutor schemes; extra work being given in school and at home; additional help in lunch times and out of school hours; the provision of extra tuition by peripatetic staff; and the systematic use of positive reinforcement measures (Harrop, 1984). Too often large classes, onerous teacher responsibilities and shortages of resources forestall much endeavour with underachievers. In practice, this means that specialist 'booster' schemes tend to be reserved or given to a few of the most deserving cases; only a proportion of those that need them. Often these 'booster' schemes are reserved for pupils in the remedial or special units attached to the school. This may mean that some of the pupils who leave school without any qualifications might, with more concerted attention, have achieved a reasonable number of passes.

Deviance, underachievement and disaffection

The extent to which underachievement precipitates absenteeism, disaffection and/or disruption is even less easy to gauge. Reynolds (1982b) and Reynolds and Murgatroyd (1981) argue that secondary education in Wales tends to generate underachievement among pupils partly because there is too much concentration upon the higher-ability child. In 1979/80, for example, 25.1 per cent of pupils left schools in Wales with no formal qualifications compared with 12.2 per cent in England.

Evidence from research suggests that disruptive behaviour causes more concern to teachers than any other form of deviant behaviour (Blackham, 1967; Dunham, 1977). This is because it destroys the learning process, produces threats to the teachers' established order and cannot be ignored (see Chapter 4).

When making their own internal assessments, schools should attempt to discover the underlying 'causes' of each pupil's problems, whether they are related to behaviour or learning or both. Schools have to decide whether individual non-conformers misbehave because of institutional, teacher-related, social or behavioural difficulties. Such assessments are never easy especially as most teachers and middle managers are exceedingly busy people.

Studies into the relationship between disadvantage, disaffection and behaviour can be sub-divided into three kinds: local; national and epidemiological; and longitudinal. Perhaps the best-known local study in Britain remains Shepherd *et al*'s (1971) study of 6000 Buckinghamshire schoolchildren. Teachers were asked by the researchers to assess children's behaviour, using a list of 21 statements such as 'not interested in school work.' The findings obtained from these data revealed that:

a A slight majority of the children showed no manifestations of behaviour problems.

b Boys were more likely than girls to manifest adverse behavioural traits.

c Girls were more often rated as being quiet or withdrawn. By contrast, boys were more frequently reported as aggressive, lacking interest, uncooperative, lying and stealing.

d Across the entire age-range of pupils, only four per cent of boys and nearly two per cent girls were considered to be uncooperative in class. As with surveys on disruptive behaviour, there was a marked increase in prevalence among pupils in their final two years of compulsory schooling.

e There was striking evidence that poor behaviour and poor attainment are inextricably linked.

The National Child Development (NCD) Study is probably the most widely regarded and acclaimed national investigation into the health, educational attainments and behaviour of children in England and Wales. Successive teams of researchers studied cohorts of all children born in one week in March 1958 in England and Wales. These children have been followed up at different periods from early childhood to adulthood and looked at from a variety of standpoints.

When these children were aged seven, their form teachers were asked to complete an original version of the Bristol Social Adjustment Guides (BSAG) devised by Stott (1963). From the findings, Davie *et al* (1972) reported that teachers regarded 64 per cent of the children as stable, 22 per cent unsettled and 14 per cent maladjusted.

At the age of 16, Rutter's (1967) 26 item behaviour questionnaire was preferred and used instead of the BSAG. From these data, Fogelman (1976) found that 18 per cent of children were regarded by teachers as being disobedient. Irritation and overhasty reactions applied, to some extent, to 20 per cent of the pupils.

Both the Buckinghamshire and National Child Development Studies have strengths and weaknesses. Their strength lies in the originality, size and location of their cohorts which provide county-wide and national pictures. Their weaknesses lie in the fact that the Buckinghamshire children may not be representative of pupils in places such as Liverpool, Glasgow, Belfast, Cardiff, London or Birmingham, while the NCD teams had to rely on screening techniques completed by a wide variety of professional personnel throughout the country.

The most detailed and widely accepted epidemiological studies of behaviour problems in English children were conducted by Rutter and his team in the Isle of Wight and in an inner London Borough (Rutter *et al*, 1970; 1974; 1975a,b,c). These studies analysed pupils' health, educational attainment and family backgrounds as well as their behaviour. As would be predicted from the chosen locations, almost twice as many children in London (19%) as in the Isle of Wight (11%) were found to be deviant on the basis of their scores on the Teachers' Behaviour Questionnaire (Scale B) devised by Rutter in 1967. Two important findings stand out from these data. First, considered overall, parents expressed concern about roughly the same number of children as the teachers when interviewed by a social scientist or psychiatrist, using an interview schedule of known reliability (Graham and Rutter, 1968). Second, children who were regarded as disruptive at school were not always so considered at home, nor vice versa. Therefore, in this study, although the parents and teachers agreed on the percentage of children with behavioural problems, they did not always agree on their assessment of individual children.

The evidence suggests that teachers are prone to associate disruption more with extroverts than with occasional or introverted offenders. Parents, who probably know their children rather better than most teachers, appear to be more able to identify withdrawn children as disruptive. This suggests that teachers often fail to recognise signs of disturbance which do not involve noisy or aggressive outbursts in class or in schools. Finally, information obtained from the schools and families in Rutter *et al*'s comparative study conclusively show that the greater prevalence of deviant behaviour in London children than in those in the Isle of Wight is associated with higher rates of disadvantage within the pupils' home backgrounds and inside the schools rather than with other factors.

It is all the more regrettable, therefore, for a number of different reasons, that progress in meeting the requirements of the 1980 Act, which followed publication of the Warnock Report (1978), remains fairly slow, despite a great deal of endeavour and lip-service being given to the concept of children with special educational needs. There can be little doubt that large numbers of new (Reid *et al*, 1980; Patrick, Bernbaum and Reid, 1982) and established teachers are inadequately prepared for dealing with children with special educational needs. This is not altogether surprising given resource, capitation and manpower shortages. Time constraints, too, on initial training courses pose difficulties for course planners in determining just what to include and exclude (Thomas, 1985). A great deal more work needs to be undertaken before all children with special education needs in schools are properly catered for educationally and socially.

School differences: disadvantage and disaffection

Research into differences between schools highlights some of the organisational features associated with differing rates of pupil absentee-ism and disaffection. Reynolds *et al* (1976; 1980) investigated eight secondary schools in a homogeneous South Wales valley. They found that these schools varied considerably in the amount of non-attendance they experienced. They reported that high attendance schools were characterised by small size, lower institutional control, less vigorous enforcement of certain key rules on pupil behaviour, higher co-option of pupils as prefects and closer parent-school relationships. The high truancy schools appeared to be narrowly custodial in orientation, with high levels of control, harsh and strict rule enforcement and an isolation of the formal staff organisation of the school from potential sources of support amongst both pupils and parents.

Rutter *et al*'s (1979) research undertaken on twelve Inner London comprehensives found that in the most successful schools there was a prompt start to lessons, a strong emphasis on academic progress and attainment, generally low frequency of punishment and a high rate of recognition for positive achievements, well-cared for buildings and a feeling by pupils that they could approach teachers for help when they had a need.

Rutter *et al* (1979) reported that the more emphasis there is on pastoral care, the worse the academic attainment. MacMillan and Morrison (1979) agree with this conclusion. They point out that when a reduction in disruptive behaviour is a school's prime objective, it is likely to be achieved at the expense of attainment. The HMI Report (DES, 1977) on ten good schools reinforces many of Rutter's findings. Their work suggests that favourable regimes are characterised by good preparation, variety of approach, regular and constructive correction of pupils' work and consistent praise and encouragement being given to pupils for their endeavour.

The work of Ayllon and Roberts (1974) provides some evidence to the contrary. Their study shows that disruptive behaviour can be reduced and academic achievement maintained, if not actually improved, when proper guidelines are followed by staff in schools. Like most other things about education, it seems that everything probably depends upon the calibre of staff in schools – particularly levels of motivation, competence and professional interest. Generally speaking, research to date suggests that academic criteria in schools have to take precedence over social considerations when choices have to be made, if attainment is the prime goal. This is acknowledged by schools in their hierarchical patterns; academic deputy heads for example, generally take precedence over pastoral deputy heads in terms of seniority.

The effect that school policies and staff attitudes can have upon pupil outcomes had been commented upon repeatedly in the literature even before the school differences studies were conducted. For instance, Clegg and Megson (1973) were particularly concerned with the way in which school practices sub-divided the slow children from the bright, reinforcing the disadvantages of the weaker children. Hargreaves (1967) was among the first to draw attention to the alienation felt by low achievers in many schools. A lot of schools inadvertently operate double standards, rewarding the able and leading the less able to draw their own conclusions by manifesting disaffected behaviour. Despite the introduction of comprehensive schooling, one of the greatest challenges facing educationalists today is to provide equal opportunities and equal facilities for all pupils (Hargreaves, 1982). Too many schools are comprehensive in name only. In some parts of South Wales, for example, they are really neighbourhood rather than comprehensive schools in the true meaning of the word.

Inside schools

School rules, teacher expectations, the quality of teacher-pupil and peer group relationships and bullying are all aspects that are undoubtedly related to the quality and practice of education within schools.

School rules

All schools have rules of one sort or another for reasons of safety, common sense and need. School rules can be sub-divided into two kinds. General prescriptive rules concern dress, personal decoration and interpersonal relationships – the 'no running down the corridor' or 'do not wear eye make-up in school' ilk. These rules are often perceived by pupils as being petty and can lead to confrontation in school, some of it totally unnecessary.

A second sort of rules operate in classrooms. These relate to behaviour, movement, talk and academic practice. In an important study, Hargreaves *et al* (1975) analysed the rules which operate within classrooms and the manner in which routine deviance is expressed by pupils and imputed by teachers. They described the methods of social typing used by teachers to define certain pupils as potential troublemakers. They also noted the main strategies adopted by teachers to maintain order in the classroom. Hargreaves *et al* conclude that like rules, teachers can be sub-divided into two sorts – moralists (stringent enforcers) or pragmatists (who take action geared to the need of the prevailing situation).

Breaking school or class rules may be the first stage in deviant conduct in the eyes of teachers. Some pupils break school rules for fun, or as a challenge; others because of their social circumstances, while others do so maliciously. Most pupils unquestioningly accept the need for rules in primary schools. Challenges to authority in secondary schools appear to increase with age, often as pupils mature and begin to feel that some rules are an unfair imposition upon their maturity. In some schools most pupils will wear uniform, in others a majority do not or will not. Once some pupils manage to 'get away' with breaking a rule, the evidence suggests that others soon follow. In some schools, especially those located in working-class neighbourhoods, anti-school counter-cultures exist which operate their own group mores. Usually, these working class groups reject the norms and regulations sought by traditional, academic schooling (Hargreaves, 1967; Willis, 1977; March *et al*, 1978; Corrigan, 1979) and engage in 'bovver' and aggravation, testing teachers' patience to the limits.

Staff should never underestimate the degree of sophistication which pupils indulge in as they intuitively react to the moods and petty rules of particular teachers. Individual staff foibles, rules, needs and requirements are so complicated that they defy accurate description. In fact, with every class change throughout the day in secondary schools, pupils have to alter their conduct according to different criteria set by different staff. Moreover, some teachers vary their own standards considerably on a daily or hourly basis dependent upon who they are teaching, the needs of the pupils, subject or syllabus and/or inclination. For instance, staff not feeling '100 per cent' due to a cold or hangover rarely teach as well as when they are fully fit.

It is often reported that disaffection and indiscipline in schools increase with age. This is partly because schools do not always adjust sufficiently to the fact that many pupils are young adults once they reach adolescence. The onset of puberty has occurred much earlier over the last hundred years while youth has become increasingly more self-confident and assertive, with a culture of its own. Yet, at the same time, the school-leaving age has been progressively raised. There is no doubt that many pupils greatly resent being treated like 'kids' by teachers (Marsh *et al*, 1978; Tattum, 1982). The fundamental nature of the school, with the demand for compliance and the lack of pupil-power, may cause some older pupils to rebel (Pollard, 1980). This problem can be exacerbated by the fact that some pupils exercise considerable power and freedom in their daily lives outside school. Leading a double life can be just as difficult for pupils as for teachers. Many youngsters have to suspend their adult status, power and privileges while at school which is one reason why sixth form and tertiary colleges are so popular with the 16–19 age group.

Frude (1984) makes the point that most school 'offences' which constitute disruption in the classroom (making a noise, smoking, making sarcastic comments, daydreaming) are purely situational offences. In adult contexts they would be ignored. Hence certain kinds of disruption may be construed by pupils as merely asserting a freedom which is normally given to adults. By failing to comply with what they perceive as 'petty' rules, some pupils see themselves as resisting the child-status assigned them by their institutions. Research highlights the need for teachers to defend a limited number of agreed major rather than minor school rules (Woods, 1984; Gillham, 1984).

Teacher expectations

Another vexed area is that of teachers' expectations. Since the beginning of state intervention in education, it has been apparent that working–class children generally achieve lower levels of academic attainment than their peers from more favoured social backgrounds. By common consent, state schools now strive for equality of educational opportunity. Since the 1944 Act educational legislation has been devised in the hope of achieving this goal. Despite the legislation and subsequent introduction of comprehensive schooling beginning in 1965, many people rightly believe that while the main constitutional barriers have been breached, society has found more subtle ways of preserving educational inequalities. Consequently, many working class children and children of ethnic minority groups still function badly in state educational establishments and remain disadvantaged throughout their lives; a tendency which appears to be passed on through successive generations (Bernstein and Brandis, 1974; Kamin, 1974).

Rosenthal and Jacobson (1968), Rosenthal (1975), Nash (1976) and Banks (1979) are among those who have suggested that one of the main reasons for this state of affairs is teacher (and parent) expectations. They suggest that teachers expect less academic success from deprived, working class children and so try less hard with classes mainly comprised of less able or middle band pupils. In any event, comebacks from working-class as opposed to middle-class parents are less likely in schools as these parents generally expect lower attainment levels from their offspring.

Research suggests that differential teacher expectations can exert a strong influence on the academic performance of children in classrooms, although there is little evidence about how these differential expectations are formed or how they are manifested in the classroom. A survey of the literature engenders the belief that contributory factors encompass sex stereotyping and views of the role of women in society, black intelligence quotients and the effect of pupils' physical attractiveness upon teachers (Insell, 1975).

Rist (1974) contends that teachers possess mental images of ideal types of pupils which are based upon social class criteria and subjective evaluations. These ideal typologies are related to the individual pupil's intellectual abilities. From these mirror pictures teachers sub-divide their classes into fast and slow learners. The fast learners are then accorded more of the teacher's attention and are subjected to reward-directed behaviour while the slow learners are given less time and subjected to more control-orientated behaviour. These patterns of interaction become established; in the child's later school years, teachers no longer have to rely on subjectively interpreted information but utilise data related to past performance. Pupils so treated then perform as they are expected to and these expectations become self-fulfilling prophecies. In this way academic failure can be guaranteed by teachers unwittingly having low expectations and being biased against certain pupils (Labow, 1975).

There is, of course, a corollary to this phenomenon. If adverse teacher expectations can lower achievement in some pupils, equally positive expectations may raise it in others. Hence, the vital role of teacher-pupil relationships discussed in the next section.

Although many secondary pupils do not experience formal methods of assessment within schools before the fifth year (particularly since the abolition of the 11-plus in most areas), it is abundantly clear that children receive clear, informal messages about their abilities and attractiveness to teachers in a number of ways. These include: observing the success of their peers in class (undoubtedly mixed ability situations highlight these differences); teachers' personal interest, talk and reactions towards them in class; and the degree of subject help they need and receive as well as marks written on books. Most children are bright enough to know when they are not doing very well with their classwork, failing their parents or falling behind their peers.

Many teachers probably underestimate the genuine difficulties which some children have in understanding what is required of them in class and in keeping up with new material (Anderson, 1980; Sharp, 1981). Many pupils, too, despise staff who favour 'A' band pupils at the expense of the less able. Sometimes even bright pupils are conscious of this difference. There is a greater emphasis on academic learning in the lessons of able pupils and in their out-of-class teacher conversations compared with the more disciplinary-orientated nature of teaching and discussion in lower ability bands.

Schools, like teachers, can generate self-fulfilling prophecies. School practices, as well as individual teacher practices, can differentiate between deviants and conformers, the less able and the able. This is especially true in some difficult, disadvantaged schools where the 'truce syndrome' operates. Poorly-managed schools in which truce syndromes are manifest tend to be those in which pupil absence is ignored, pupils are sympathetically excluded from certain lessons and bartering takes place in classes for good behaviour by allowing individualised rather than mainstream programmes to be followed (Reynolds, 1975; 1976; Bird *et al*, 1980). This is all part of 'the anything for peace and quiet' ethos which is apparent in some difficult schools and classrooms. Once teachers break or give in, it is hard for them to pick up the pieces again. It is interesting to note that truce situations are far more widespread in lower ability bands than in academic bands. It seems that many teachers simply do not want to teach low ability groups. Whether this is because they find it demeaning or harder work is difficult to ascertain. Perhaps their attitudes reflect their own educational experiences. Or perhaps it might have something to do with their lack of training in discipline or remedial education. Whatever the reasons, some teachers who manage very well with 4A seem to struggle with 4X.

Teacher-pupil relationships

Ensuring that pupils accept the authority of teachers and maintaining order and discipline in schools is of vital importance to the teaching profession. Without such order there would be chaos. Teaching would become twice as difficult, if not impossible. Teaching is now recognised as such a stressful occupation for heads, deputies and classroom teachers (Dunham, 1977; Kyriacou and Sutcliffe, 1978; Knutton and Mycroft, 1986) that it is near the top of the stress league. Such stress can be exacerbated by teaching large numbers of disillusioned and disaffected pupils, particularly those in their final years at school (Jones, 1980). Despite this, teachers need to remember that there is a subtle difference between authority conferred by institutions and authority earned through good leadership and meaningful teacher-pupil relationships. The latter is related to respect; the former to status. Ducking out of confrontation is an easy way of losing pupils' admiration.

Once pupils or classes gain a reputation for troublemaking, it is hard to lose. Experienced and new teachers alike tend to stereotype the individuals involved. Undoubtedly, deserved or undeserved bad reputations adversely prejudice teacher-pupil relationships both in formal lessons and within school generally. In fact, it is sometimes difficult for confirmed deviant pupils like absentees and disrupters to convince staff that they have turned over a new leaf, even when it is true (Hargreaves *et al*, 1975).

Staff-room 'gossip' can establish longstanding and unfavourable reputations for pupils (Delamont, 1976). Many teachers are prone to make hasty and irrational judgements about individuals and groups of pupils based on very little evidence. They can, for example, make assumptions and judgements about likely disrupters on the basis of teacher talk, pupils' appearances, pupils' academic abilities, memories of unpleasant experiences with the pupil's siblings or of one particular incident in class. Such hasty opinions, if they are transmitted to pupils, are likely to be interpreted as 'offences of unfairness' (Marsh *et al*, 1978).

All pupils test out teachers, especially new teachers, from time to time. However, some teachers are better than others at maintaining order in the classroom and in the way they handle and relate to pupils. A few teachers are over strict in class and tend to overreact to challenges to their authority (Hargreaves *et al*, 1975). Excessive strictness can provoke adverse reactions from pupils. Pupils particularly appear to dislike being called names, being physically manhandled and being constrained too much in class (Shostak, 1982). The literature suggests that most pupils like variety in lessons, they enjoy being taught and being given plenty of encouragement and praise when they do well. They also like acting on their own initiative in class. Fortunately, the evidence suggests that most staff, including new teachers (DES, 1982), appear to maintain order in their classrooms and have good relationships with their pupils. Nevertheless, individual teacher-pupil relationships vary widely, as does the quality of these interactions (Delamont, 1976).

Despite disagreement about what constitutes a 'good' teacher and longstanding criticisms of this paradigm, most research suggests that pupils prefer teachers who are strict but fair, who are approachable and have emphathetic attitudes towards them. They dislike teachers who are soft, ineffective, rigid, harsh, or uncaring and those whose demeanour provokes classroom confrontations (Rutter *et al*, 1979; Sharp, 1981).

Teachers need to take great care when handling pupils. Many pupils are highly sensitive people. Pupils are notoriously sensitive of their teachers' views of them and will interpret any sign or gesture as indicators of their perceived worth. Frude (1984) states that pupils see the fact that their name is known or not known by the teacher, or that they are chosen or left out of various classroom selections, as signs or indicators of their standing with the teacher. This in turn is likely to affect their behaviour. Hence, a child who feels disliked by a particular teacher may live up to such expectations by becoming troublesome.

Inevitably in any classroom teachers will value and prefer some pupils to others. A teacher who is a keen footballer, for instance, may well enjoy and prefer the company of the captain of the school team rather than someone who detests the game. This is only natural. Of course, it is always harder to discipline and punish a favoured pupil than another. But ideally, teachers should not have favoured pupils: only some who they know better than others. For this reason, Hargreaves *et al* (1975) suggest that teachers should focus on acts in class rather than on persons. This guarantees equality of approach. Pupils who are rebuked will then tend to define the teachers' actions as impersonal and find it easier to respond normally in the future.

Peer group relationships

The influence of peers and friendship groups on behaviour in schools, inside classrooms and within the local environment should never be underestimated, especially among teenagers who are at a vulnerable age. Sociologists have found that deviance is often associated with the prevailing neighbourhood culture. The 'Tiger Bay' and 'Toxteth' way of life often transcends generations (Mays, 1972). Miller (1958), for instance, argues that lower working-class culture is characterised by trouble, toughness, smartness, excitement, fate and autonomy – the kind of behaviour depicted by James Dean and Marlon Brando in films of the 1950s and '60s and manifest by Clint Eastwood *et al* today. These so-called 'focal concerns' are in theory supposed to motivate working-class youngsters in their search for status in their surrounding neighbour-hood.

Likewise, strong feelings can bind peer groups and can and do lead to 'counter cultures' within schools. These friendship or common culture groups can generate strong anti-school feelings within classrooms and schools and have profound consequences upon teacher-pupil relationships (Hargreaves, 1967; Lacey, 1970; Hargreaves *et al*, 1975; Willis, 1977).

Teachers today need to recognise that pupils belong to a variety of peer groups within schools, notably in their registration and teaching forms. Many pupils will have been together for a number of years, perhaps ever since they started in nursery or primary schools. The influence of such sub-cultures is all-important in learning situations. Each form, for example, tends to have its own 'heroes', 'wags', 'isolates', and potential disrupters. Competition between groups, pupil harassment, polarisation of attitudes and in-cliques can all effect and/or influence classroom outcomes. How teachers react to and handle each sub-group is often vital to learning and conduct within the classroom.

Some pupils, though they lose all formal interest in school, continue to use its facilities for their own compensatory social reasons. Reid (1985), for example, found that good attenders sometimes have lower opinions of their teachers and schools than bad attenders, even though they are in the same form groups.

Bullying

The thorny question of bullying in schools has received comparatively little attention in Britain possibly because of the delicate and complex nature of the subject (Olweus, 1978, 1984; Beynon and Delamont, 1984). Evidence is beginning to increase however, which suggests that some pupils miss school either because they are bullied or because they are involved in other clandestine activities such as extortion. Acts of bullying in schools interfere with the mental as well as the physical presence of children. In some cases, acts of bullying cause untold misery which is out of all proportion to the event.

Although there has been little research the literature indicates that bullying poses a greater threat to pupils in some schools and classrooms than in others. According to research undertaken in the United States, schools at risk are often situated in deprived, low socio-economic regions with a high proportion of black children on their roll (Tattum, 1982).

In the next chapter we will develop some of these points further as we consider the effects of ill-discipline and disruption in school and suggest some ways of combating disaffected behaviour (Reid, 1985; 1986). As we shall see, these are far from simple matters. Moreover, there are no easy answers – apart, perhaps, from a great deal more hard work.

Section D: Promoting school improvement, external and internal influences

Chapter 7 and 8 begin the second half of the book. The first few chapters have concentrated on some of the reasons why so many of our secondary schools today could be classified as being disaffected or ineffective. The remaining chapters suggest some of the ways staff in schools can begin to make their schools more effective; hence the title of the book. Chapter 7 ties up the loose ends by bringing a positive dimension to the theme of combating disaffection. This long chapter, in a field on which too little has previously been written (Reid, 1986), examines the need for attitudinal change within the profession and ways of improving: pastoral care, the work undertaken by form tutors, and classroom managers. It goes on to consider the important ILEA Report on *Improving London's Secondary Schools* (Hargreaves, 1984).

Chapter 8 sees a change of style as we consider teacher research and school self-evaluation. This chapter is fundamental to the book as it critiques the notion of teacher research and provides different practical ways for educationalists to begin to come to terms with analysing their own institutions. Armed with this information, teachers can become more knowledgeable and their schools more effective.

Chapter 7
Combating disaffection

Between Chapters 2 and 6 we described some of the latest school-related evidence on pastoral care, disadvantage, disaffection, discipline and disruptive conduct. It is, however, one thing to describe these findings, quite another to suggest ways of combating or overcoming pupils' alienation from schools. We will now endeavour to move the debate forward by making some positive suggestions for improving the practice of pastoral care while, at the same time, preventing disaffected conduct from escalating.

The need for attitudinal change

The daily routine of life inside a lot of comprehensive schools means that far too many pupils do not identify or associate with their institutions and teachers or with the educational philosophy or objectives of present-day schooling. Hence, the prime requisite for combating pupils' alienation is the need to make every pupil feel that he or she matters, that the quality of their work is important, as is their behaviour, attendance and attitude. It is when pupils feel unwanted, rejected, uncared for or disillusioned that they start manifesting their disaffection by staying away, disrupting lessons or underachieving.

In this area, secondary schools could learn a great deal from some of their primary counterparts. In most primary schools, pupils feel a part of the school, as if they were a member of a family. They identify proudly with their peers and teachers. By contrast, in many secondary schools some pupils soon feel 'lost'. They stop identifying with their teachers and they begin to feel that schools are not run for them but for the benefit of the staff. Although it is natural for adolescents to assert their own personas as they mature, they also like to feel cared for and wanted. Too many schools fail to understand the implications of these sentiments as their pastoral provision is situation-specific rather than pupil-centred.

Teachers show pupils that they care for their educational progress and social welfare through the quality of their teaching and in the way they handle their personal relationships, both inside and outside the class-room. They also manifest their concern through the standards they set, by arriving at lessons on time, by thorough lesson preparation, by regular and detailed correction of set assignments, by participating in extra curricular activities, by taking a personal interest in individual pupils, and much more besides. It is regrettable that even such obvious measures are probably not adhered to by all teachers. This is one of the major reasons why the seeds of pupil alienation and disaffection are not being tackled properly. It is especially worrying that some sections of the media are portraying the 1980s as the era of disaffection. Thus, the correlation between disaffection and bad schooling should never be treated lightly as the long-term consequences in society could be devastating (Reid, 1987).

Teachers need to understand this message clearly. Unless substantial changes take place within schools and society, the prognosis for pupils who manifest disaffection will continue to be bleak. In a truly educated and caring society, disaffection needs both understanding and tolerance. But above everything else, it needs to be eradicated if the best use is to be made of our most natural resource – people. The alternative is to allow the inequalities within society to continue and increase as employment opportunities for unskilled labour diminish in a rapidly expanding technological age. If educationalists are unable to solve their problems of ill-discipline, alienation, disaffection and disadvantage, then society is increasingly likely to feel the backlash from an ever-larger pool of dissatisfied adults. Over a period of time, this disenchantment may lead to much more serious consequences than merely expanding the pool of unskilled, unemployed labour and those reliant on social security. It could contribute to a more violent society, something for which our children will never forgive us (Reid, 1984d).

The time is fast approaching when individual teachers, as well as the teaching profession, will have to take a much more objective and closer look at themselves. Such introspection will undoubtedly be to the advantage of disaffected youngsters because the professional problems of teaching are inextricably linked to pupil alienation. Despite the fraught nature of issues like teacher effectiveness, self-evaluation and school accountability, the profession has reached the stage where it is no longer satisfactory to accept unprofessional attitudes and sub-standard teaching.

For their part, employers will have to adapt too. They will have to take cognisance of the present-day and future needs of teachers and pupils alike. Teachers will have to be educated to the point where they understand the objectives of schooling and school management as well as specialised aspects of education. This will mean a rigorous examination of initial and in-service training courses. It will also mean a rapid improvement in the quality and quantity of in-service provision. In particular, if teachers are to tackle their school's problems realistically, they will need more and better courses on such issues as pastoral care; effective classroom and school management; coping with and overcoming disaffected and disruptive pupils through appropriate teaching and curriculum strategies; as well as finding ways of undertaking constructive school and self-evaluation programmes. Suitable initial and in-service courses should enable teachers to learn to detect the kind of potential or actual problems which affect secondary-aged pupils. They should also assist them to implement suitable remedial programmes for disadvantaged and difficult pupils within schools. Only then will many teachers be in a position to show that their schools are well managed, their teaching effective, their curriculum appropriate, and their educational outcomes suitable, satisfactory and meaningful. Only then will teachers *know* they are doing their very best for all their pupils, not just some of them (Reid, 1985).

This is not mere pie in the sky. Schools are first and foremost places where human beings interact. Of course, teachers and pupils vary greatly in the gifts they bring to teaching and learning. Some teachers will inevitably be more effective than others. Nevertheless, schools can do much, through encouragement, co-operative planning and the evaluation of their provision, to ensure that the contribution of every member of staff is as meaningful and effective as possible. An effective school is the sum of *all* its parts.

Similarly, a pupil has to be respected for the progress he or she is making in relation to his or her talents and capabilities. Pupils need to feel a sense of well-being, dignity and purpose. They need to feel they are making progress, not simply standing still or retarding. They need to feel a sense of personal worth and dignity arising from their dealings with *their* school. For pupils of modest academic ability and uncertain motivation, these considerations are critical and pervade most aspects of teaching and learning (Welsh Office, 1984). Within our schools, far too many teachers continue to apply double standards towards pupils; one set of criteria for able, high-fliers, another for less able pupils or for those of moderate ability (Hargreaves, 1967; 1982).

At least educationalists now appreciate more than they once did, thanks to the efforts of the school differences group (Reynolds, 1985). Their research has shown that pupils' experiences in schools present considerable contrasts in context, purpose, teaching styles and quality of provision from which a few generalisations are possible. There is no longer any doubt about the variety of experiences pupils receive as they move from class to class. This is not only true within individual schools but between schools (Rutter *et al*, 1979).

Some of these variations owe much to the quality and interest of different staff. But they also owe a lot to different standards set by staff. It is in the latter regard that schools could do more. For example, staff could agree upon unified policies for combating absenteeism and disruption (Reid 1985; 1986).

Equally, it is clear that local education authorities and schools follow a variety of diverse policies for identifying and dealing with disaffected and underachieving pupils (Bridghouse, 1981). One recurring problem is that schools repeatedly fail to see the precipitating factors which first cause non-attendance or disruptive conduct to occur or underachievement to develop. If this behaviour is not overcome at source it is likely to get much worse as pupils grow in confidence.

Unfortunately, and being realistic, schools often do not have the time or the resources they need to combat some of their problems effectively. Consequently, many pastoral care teams become institution-orientated, fostering disciplinary and administrative codes rather than pupil-orientated policies. Existing evidence suggests that large numbers of disaffected pupils receive very little sympathetic or effective remedial treatment in school. Owing to time and resource constraints, as well as unfavourable teachers' attitudes and training inadequacies, far too many schools are forced to rely solely on punitive measures as their only weapon against disaffected behaviour, supported by whatever help is available from external welfare agencies.

Schools pay a heavy price for these policies. As much so-called pastoral support is ill-conceived and punishment-orientated, middle managers often exacerbate rather than ease tension in particular situations. Therefore, far more imagination is needed by both school personnel and professionals employed in external welfare agencies if disaffected and disruptive behaviour is to be significantly checked or overcome.

Since the early 1970s a number of promising inter-disciplinary initiatives have taken place which appear to be gaining in momentum. Regrettably, however, too many of these initiatives have been hampered by human weaknesses such as territorial imperatives, ignorance and confidentiality. There is little doubt that more thought needs to be given to establishing meaningful and workable links between professionals in different organisations, especially teachers and social workers. Equally, there can be little doubt that implementing effective multidisciplinary approaches is one way of resolving conflict and overcoming problems created and caused by disadvantaged, disruptive and disaffected pupils. There is not, however, a universal panacea; a variety of approaches are needed – in school, between schools and agencies, and between parents and teachers (Reid, 1986).

Despite the dearth of research into this extremely sensitive issue, it is abundantly clear that the quality of staff in schools is a crucial part of the equation. This is particularly true of teachers' attitudes towards pupils, teachers' teaching styles and classroom competence, the school ethos and aspects relating to the curriculum. For example, one eventual measure of the success of the post-Warnock 1980 Education Act will be the extent to which schools are able to combat their non-attendance, disruptive, disaffected and disadvantaged pupil problems through their special needs programmes.

Finally, looming large above everything else stands one clear, succinct message from research into school differences and effectiveness. Schools have it within their own means to determine the strategies and changes they need to make in order to improve the educational experiences of all their pupils. These measures range from the minor to the major. Explicitly, writers are in accord that the free, systematic use of praise is one of the most effective ways of preventing undesirable behaviour from taking place, so is taking an interest in every pupil as a person. Another strategy is the radical restructuring of the secondary school curriculum to improve both its structure and content. Schools can go a long way towards putting their own house in order. Without national leads however, disadvantage and disaffection will never be totally overcome.

Improving pastoral care

Pastoral care systems can be defined as the functions of guidance, support, discipline and administration that schools perform in relation to pupils (Skinner *et al*, 1983). Schools are in a *in loco parentis* capacity when pupils attend them; this means acting in the same manner as *careful* parents.

Schools differ considerably in the way in which they organise their pastoral care systems, depending upon such factors as size, need, the wishes of the local education authority, the attitude and capabilities of staff and the preference of the headteacher, governors and parents. Consequently, the range of staff involved in pastoral care teams includes form and subject teachers, specialist pastoral care staff (deputy head – pastoral and/or girls' welfare; heads of year, house or year sub-groups) and, in some schools, trained counsellors.

The philosophy and emphasis of the pastoral care team in a school are very dependent on the interests and calibre of the staff concerned, particularly key personnel such as deputies, heads of year, counsellors and, of course, the headteacher. It is probably fair to say that only a minority of pastoral staff are trained for their work, although some attend short in-service courses or cover the subject in postgraduate courses for higher degrees and diplomas. Likewise, the quality of postholders is probably equally variable.

Theoretically, pastoral care teams provide a coherent framework within schools to support all pupils. Inevitably, the nature of their work brings certain pupils to their attention more than others. These include pupils with major behavioural problems, or with learning difficulties and those who manifest disaffected tendencies through their non-attendance, lack of effort in class and poor peer group relationships (Bird *et al*, 1980; Johnson *et al*, 1980).

Pastoral care teams also exist to support form tutors and subject teachers in their work by advising them of difficulties being experienced by pupils in their charge and helping them to overcome administrative, behavioural and learning problems. Inevitably, some teachers liaise better with colleagues than others and in large schools communication and co-ordination can pose difficulties. Moreover, some teachers prefer academic rather than pastoral duties and resent the amount of paper work which good pastoral care often engenders (Lewis and Murgatroyd, 1976).

Finally, staff in middle management posts frequently act as the link between parents and schools, not only by organising parents' evenings but also by writing to and seeing parents in times of need on such matters as pupils' non-attendance or minor behavioural problems. More serious behavioural offences or problems of a personal nature are usually dealt with by headteachers, deputies or qualified school counsellors.

The literature is full of case studies which cite good practice in primary and secondary schools (Murgatroyd, 1980b; Galloway, 1981; Jones, 1982). These usually illustrate important themes in pastoral care including: the school's disciplinary policy; liaison with and support for teachers, parents and outside agencies; handling disruptive behaviour within classrooms and schools; providing apposite remedial education; as well as giving descriptions of favourable outcomes with extreme cases (Covill *et al*, 1984).

Form tutors

Effective pastoral care in secondary schools begins with the vitally important work of the form tutor (Button, 1981; 1982). In primary schools, it is the classroom teacher who is the vital cog in the wheel. Without a great deal of dedicated and empathetic endeavour from form tutors and classroom teachers, pastoral care in schools will never be effective. In far too many schools, insufficient notice is taken of this fact. Too often, responsibility is removed from form tutors to middle managers at too early a stage, frequently with negative consequences for pupils' care (Galloway *et al*, 1982).

Form tutors have more opportunities than most teachers to get to know their pupils well. Ideally, good form tutors endeavour to know something about their pupils' home backgrounds, personal interests, strengths and weaknesses, intellectual resources, attitudes and socialization skills. Frequently, this information is vital in preventative work. It can also be invaluable when dealing with instances of underachievement, disruption, non-attendance or general alienation.

Allowing sufficient time for form tutors to get to know their pupils well is a helpful measure in this process. So is following a meaningful pastoral curriculum (Baldwin and Wells, 1979; 1980; 1981; Hamblin, 1986b).

Reid (1986) takes the view that form tutors should rotate with their classes in secondary schools for reasons of consistency and effectiveness. Not everyone shares this opinion, partly because pupils with poor form tutors can suffer considerably. Nonetheless, the advantages accruing from the continuity of a form tutor moving up the age-range from first to fifth year with his or her class, often outweigh any disadvantages. In this structure form tutors learn much more about the temperament, personality, academic ability, behaviour and home backgrounds of their pupils. They also gain crucial insights into their motivation and maturational stages. Furthermore, the continuity achieved by good long-term pupil-tutor relationships can engender confidence in parents, pupils and year tutors alike and lead to greater consistency in approach over a number of years. Successful form tutor-pupil rotation schemes enable staff to be in a better position to advise pupils and parents alike on a range of matters, including subject options and careers, at critical stages in pupils' schooling.

When form tutor-pupil relationships break down, the consequences can be devastating. Pupils, for instance, can feel there is no one to whom they can turn in times of trouble (Reid, 1983c). Problems which teachers should know something about lie undetected. Form tutors have to strive hard to get to know their disaffected pupils very well and treat them equally. This is especially true of disruptive pupils and truants. At the present time, too little is known about how or why some form tutors are more effective than others, especially with disadvantaged or less able groups.

Form tutors need to start from the basis that the quality of their relationship with their pupils is all-important. Nothing should be allowed to endanger this trust. Certainly not bad practice. For instance, once a form tutor is perceived by a class as a mere extension of authority, or as someone who is incapable of retaining confidences, his or her capacity for effective pastoral work is much reduced. This is one of the reasons why the extent to which form tutors and heads of year liaise about pupils' problems and difficulties is always a matter of judgement and style. Certainly, such liaison needs to be handled delicately. Great care should be taken not to break pupils' confidences in case work. Similarly, as a general rule, middle managers should be more prepared to leave routine casework to form tutors rather than interceding unnecessarily. Such intervention often exacerbates rather than reduces tension. It also destroys effective form tutoring. After all, pupils have their own feelings and sense of pride.

Classroom management

Recent research and reviews of research (Docking, 1980; Tattum, 1982; Mortimore *et al*, 1983) tend to suggest that pupils give two main reasons for disrupting classes. As previously mentioned, pupils lay the blame on either situations created by poor teaching strategies ('not being treated with respect,' 'inconsistency of rule application' and 'poor or non-teaching') or aspects related to the structure and organisation of schools ('running down the corridor', 'not wearing school uniform', or 'talking in assembly'). Teachers' expectations of pupils' academic levels can also influence pupil performance adversely or favourably. For instance, a teacher who enthuses about maths and causes the pupils to enjoy the lessons is likely to achieve better performance and conduct in the subject than another who bores the class to tears or is unable to maintain order. This is another reason why changing subject or form teachers often has much greater consequences upon individual pupil and class behaviour than many educationalists seem to realise. Viewed negatively, teachers who expect pupils to display troublesome behaviour probably influence such outcomes; if only unwittingly. Teachers who expect less of pupils get less. Teachers who cannot control classes find they have to combat more misbehaviour than others.

Research suggests that good teachers need to understand some of the lessons from studies into classroom interaction if they are to teach successfully. These show that teaching is far more than standing up in front of a class relating fact to pupils. Teaching is also about understanding individuals and groups of pupils. To achieve this objective, teachers need to spend time finding out what makes their pupils tick. Such time is well spent and will repay them fully. Failure to take an interest in pupils makes them feel that their teachers do not care. Understanding is likely to lead to empathy and, in turn, this will lead to better pupil-teacher relationships, better lessons and less need for overt control. All this makes possible a reduction in the number of opportunities for disruptive conduct to occur.

Research also shows that pupils dislike four particular traits in teachers or 'types' of teacher:
1 Teachers who are 'inhuman' and interpret their role too literally. Such staff are perceived by pupils as being 'a load of rubbish', 'robots', 'faceless . . .' and 'time servers' (Woods, 1984). Therefore, stand-offish approaches are unlikely to work with pupils.
2 Teachers who treat pupils as anonymous (Rosser and Harré, 1976). Despite current teacher-pupil ratios, it is vital that pupils are treated as individuals (Lortie, 1975).
3 Teachers who are soft and/or inconsistent (Marsh *et al*, 1978).
4 Teachers who are 'unfair' and make unreasonable demands on pupils (Rosser and Harré, 1976).

When pupils feel that many of their school's staff fall into one or more of these categories, it is likely that they will manifest their displeasure by rebelling. Research into pupils' perceptions suggests that when children misbehave under such circumstances, there is a rational basis for such conduct. Schools with higher than average numbers of disaffected pupils (with all this implies in terms of violence, vandalism, confrontation and large doses of teacher stress) might well be advised to examine their own professional laurels as well as other factors.

Conversely, research suggests that successful schools are characterised by having a majority of their staff in the following categories:
1 Teachers who are able to keep control at all times (*most* important).
2 Teachers who are able to 'have a laugh' with pupils.
3 Teachers who foster warm, empathetic relationships with pupils.
4 Teachers who like and understand children.
5 Teachers who teach their subjects well, with enthusiasm and in interesting ways.
6 Teachers who teach all the time rather than indulging in aimless activities.
7 Teachers who are consistent and fair.
8 Teachers who treat children with respect and as equals.
9 Teachers who allow pupils a sense of freedom in class.

Managing disruptive pupils in classrooms

Pik (1981) found four distinct phases in incidents of disruptive behaviour in classrooms – the 'build-up', the 'trigger event', the 'escalation' and the 'finale'. He suggests that the first two of these are *promoted* by either the pupil or the teacher or both. However, the escalation and finale always involve both parties. Likewise, Marsh *et al* (1978) describe the sequence in disruptive incidents as generally consisting of an offence by the teacher in the eyes of pupils followed by the pupils' consequent retribution.

Examining differences in teachers' abilities to control pupils, Kounin *et al* (1966) found that too much activity-change, overloading pupils with instructions, and interrupting ongoing activities, all helped to create opportunities for disruptive behaviour. The micro-analysis of normal lessons by Hargreaves *et al* (1975) distinguished between the five phases of 'entry', 'settling down', 'lesson proper', 'clearing up' and 'exit'. The findings suggest that disruption is more likely during some phases than others. Periods of transition from one phase to the next are likely triggers for disruptive behaviour to take place.

The management of control in the classroom has formed part of a number of significant projects including the *Teacher Education Project* at Nottingham (Wragg and Kerry, 1979; Wragg, 1984), Davie's (1980) special course at Cardiff (Philipps *et al*, 1985) and Lawrence's (1980) attempts to work with teachers in schools on various strategies likely to reduce disruption. In addition, a number of anecdotal first-hand accounts of teachers successfully controlling potentially disruptive classes have been published (Francis, 1975; Haigh, 1979; Saunders, 1979).

Lawrence (1980) has suggested three ways of training teachers to develop their skills in order to examine and cope with disruptive behaviour. These include the systematic listing by teachers of all the techniques they use for dealing with difficult children. This sensitises them to the wide range of possible remedial measures which are available in particular situations and helps them to critically analyse their own performance. Lawrence also advises teachers to learn to use and apply Kelly's (1953) repertory grid technique to measure the difficulty of managing classes in schools. The results obtained for these grids can provide invaluable information for headteachers on how to deploy staff effectively, as well as providing an interesting 'picture' of the school. Finally, Lawrence draws attention to a wide range of behaviour modification techniques which are available. These generally utilise positive reinforcement measures for use by staff with difficult pupils (see also Harrop, 1984; Yule *et al*, 1984).

Clarke *et al* (1981) have also reported that teachers can be trained to spot potentially damaging situations in lessons. Their sequence analysis approach shows that critical-choice points can be identified and turned to advantage, thereby reducing the risk of conflict.

By and large, however, much more research is needed into the aetiology and control of disruptive behaviour in classrooms and schools before teachers will be scientifically and intuitively trained to overcome potential and actual misbehaviour. Disruption in the classroom is, and will remain, a major problem for many years ahead. Its causation is both complex and multi-factorial. In the absence of ideal approaches, researchers and teachers alike will have to employ a variety of perspectives and techniques to examine and combat disruptive conduct in schools. In any event, understanding the aetiology of disruption is no guarantee that teachers will be able to control classes or:

1 Monitor the progress of all groups of pupils so that differences in achievement can be identified early, and appropriate remedial action be taken.

2 Consciously strive to raise teachers' expectations of the achievement of pupils from working-class homes, of girls, in some subjects, and of ethnic minorities, in order to reduce the influence of negative stereotyping.

3 Select books and learning materials which are suitable for *all* pupils.

4 Critically evaluate classroom practices so that any unintended biases can be eliminated.

5 Achieve close co-operation between specialist and remedial teachers so that joint approaches to learning problems can be developed.

6 Draw on the new technology to provide individual learning programmes where these seem appropriate.

7 Capitalise on parental influence by showing how pupils can be helped at home.

8 Provide extra learning opportunities such as homework clubs and revision courses to help pupils who have poor facilities for study at home.

9 With regard to sex differences:
a implement a school policy on equal opportunities;
b include at least one physical science in the compulsory core of fourth-
and fifth-year work;
c hold special parents' evenings prior to option choices, in order to focus
on the importance of maths, science and technology for girls.
10 With regard to ethnic groups:
a have a language policy that caters for individual needs and takes
account of the literary heritage of other cultures;
b accept and build upon the diversity of cultures in the school;
c have an agreed school policy on racism. Provide a forum for discussion
of this difficult subject for older pupils within the security of the school.

Mortimore *et al* (1983) consider that these changes will not eliminate
underachievement. They will, however, make school life more profitable
and acceptable for many pupils and, indirectly, make life more
worthwhile for many teachers. Like Hargreaves (1984), Mortimore
believes that the real educational answer to underachievement lies in
reform of the curriculum, the examination system and the internal
organisation of secondary schools. The latter aspect is often forgotten. As
mentioned earlier, few secondary schools, for example, provide pupils
with an opportunity to 'catch up' if they fall behind with their class work
through illness, personal difficulties or for any number of other reasons.
Quite often, once a pupil begins to lose ground, he or she tends to fall
further and further behind his or her peers and may give up altogether.

The Hargreaves report

One of the most influential reports on school improvement in Britain has
been produced by the Inner London Education Authority (Hargreaves,
1984). The Committee's terms of reference were to consider the
curriculum and organisation of secondary schools in Inner London as
they affected pupils mainly in the 11–16 age range. The Committee gave
special attention to pupils who were underachieving, including those
taking few or no public examinations, and those who showed dissatisfac-
tion with school by absenting themselves or through their unco-operative
behaviour.

The Report suggests that substantial changes in the organisation and
structure of schools by local education authorities, headteachers,
teachers and other educational personnel will be necessary if underachievement and disaffection are to be combated successfully. In order to
improve schools, the Committee feels that specific changes and innovations must be introduced in: the teacher/parent partnership; school
attendance; the transition from primary to secondary school; the whole
curriculum; pupil grouping; pupils with particular needs and aptitudes;
pupils for whom English is a second language (ESL) and bilingual (or

multilingual) pupils; skills for independent learning; activities within the fourth and fifth years related to core and option subjects, active learning roles and curriculum organisation and assessment; pupil involvement and participation; learning out of school; links between the schools and community and between schools, industry and the trades unions; and improved alternative provision for disruptive pupils.

For example, the Report suggests that governors and secondary headteachers should ensure that each school has an effective attendance policy. On this matter the Committee believes good practice is associated with:

1 a senior teacher being charged with specific responsibility for pupil attendance;

2 a list of absentees being produced quickly, ideally by morning break, for use by appropriate teaching and office staff;

3 the school devising a sensitive scheme for the immediate follow-up of absentees, for example, by telephoning home or by sending out letters to parents/guardians;

4 form tutors ensuring that records of attendance are as accurate as possible and explanations for absence are produced when pupils return to school;

5 heads of year/house monitoring the work of form tutors;

6 heads of year/house and teachers with responsibility for pupil attendance having regular meetings with education welfare officers, perhaps once a month;

7 regular 'spot checks' for specific lesson truancy and for pupils leaving school before the end of the school day;

8 rewards introduced for individual pupils or classes with an excellent attendance record in the form of praise or prizes;

9 penalties being introduced for pupils who are persistently late;

10 absentees and truants being quietly welcomed back to school upon their return and efforts made to reintegrate them socially and academically (see also Reid, 1982e; 1985).

The Report urges advisers/inspectors to encourage schools with good records of attendance to report their practices to an innovation exchange within the authority. Meanwhile, local education authorities should phase in schemes to attach education welfare officers to every school throughout the secondary sector and devise suitable career and promotion structures for EWOs in the field.

For disruptive pupils, the Committee propose substantial and significant changes in the provision of alternative education and pastoral care. They recommend the creation of a school inspector for pastoral care who, among other things, should be given responsibility for the dissemination of good practice in relation to suspension. In addition, headteachers should ensure that all newly appointed pastoral staff make personal visits to local off-site support units, and should include a visit to an off-site support unit in their induction programmes for probationary teachers. The staff of off-site support units should be invited to make contributions to courses on classroom management for use by teachers in ordinary schools. Finally, governors and other members of appointment committees should regard experience of work in a support unit as advantageous to a teacher seeking promotion.

For underachieving and disaffected pupils, the Hargreaves Committee wish to see a radical change in the secondary curriculum by providing pupils with a distinctive vocational education. On school industry links and work experience programmes, the Report recommends that head-teachers establish their own liaison committees comprised of teachers in charge of personal and social education. The School committees set up to review and co-ordinate school policy on this matter should include teachers of science; craft, design and technology (CDT); careers; geography; history; and the social sciences. Furthermore, the Inspecto-rate should establish a committee of the ten divisional industry/school co-ordinators in the Authority (Inner London) and the staff inspectors for careers, science, CDT, careers, geography, history and social sciences to review present practice and to disseminate good practice.

Like previous reports and research studies (Bullock, 1975; HMI, 1977b; 1979; 1980; 1981; DES, 1981; ILEA, 1981; 1983; Schools Council, 1981; Cockroft, 1982; Galton and Willcocks, 1983; Schools Council for Wales, 1983; Reid, 1985), the Hargreaves Report is right to acknowledge the unsatisfactory nature of much of the secondary school curriculum and its potential and/or actual effects upon pupil learning and behaviour in schools. At present, far too many pupils in our secondary schools are bored and confused by aspects of their curriculum; a situation which urgently needs rectifying. The central importance of the curriculum in combating and reducing absenteeism, disaffection and disruption in secondary schools is well-documented but too little is known about how this can be achieved. The Hargreaves Committee is one of the first which attempts to redress this balance. In its Report, the Committee stresses the need for choice, coherence, breadth, balance and structure throughout the whole secondary curriculum. It also reinforces the important parts played by pupil grouping, teaching styles, the requirements of pupils with particular needs and aptitudes as well as the necessity for pupils to acquire appropriate study skills.

Perhaps, however, the most interesting idea to emerge from the Hargreaves Report is the need to change the curriculum for fourth and fifth year pupils, especially for the betterment of underachievers. The Committee considers that there should be a compulsory curriculum for all fourth and fifth year pupils which should comprise 62.5% of total teaching time. The curriculum would contain six elements: English language and literature (12.5% of teaching time); mathematics (12.5%); science (10%); personal, social and religious education (7.5%); at least one 'aesthetic' subject (art, music etc) (10%); and at least one 'technical' subject (craft, design, technology (CDT) or computer studies) (10%). The remaining 37.5% of school time should be devoted to *either* additional periods in compulsory subjects *or* the free options *or* some of each. Pupils would therefore be able to select from among classical and modern languages, history, geography, economics, commercial and business studies, physical education, additional science subjects, additional 'aesthetic' subjects, additional 'technical' subjects and additional English and mathematics.

As so many fourth and fifth year pupils are disappointed with their secondary school experience and feel that the curriculum-as-it-is-taught is inappropriate to their abilities, interests and aptitudes, the Report suggests and/or recommends that heads of department of all curriculum subjects should ensure that:

a pupils exercise all communication skills − talking, listening, reading and writing − in equal amounts, with the same value ascribed to each;

b topics and relevant issues are raised in classes which stimulate pupils to express opinions, argue, explain and negotiate for a consensus;

c the assessment of oral skills is seen as equally important with the assessment of other skills;

d teachers ensure there is an oral component in any assessment procedure they devise, and pressure external examination bodies to do the same.

To achieve this, Hargreaves suggests making radical changes in the organisation, assessment and teaching of the fourth and fifth year. These may be achieved by implementing formal reviews of schools' existing curriculum programmes; encouraging the development of systems of units and unit credits, leaving certificate and pupil profile schemes; promoting opportunities for creative timetabling; and reducing the pressure on pupils caused by external examinations and existing and outmoded assessment procedures. Moreover, headteachers should ensure that structures exist to provide pupils with experience of taking responsibility and participating in decision-making at various levels (individual, class, year, whole school) and of different kinds in the life of the school. Heads should also make provision for all pupils to have planned out-of-school (off-site) learning experiences throughout the school year, as part of a planned school policy. This could be achieved by the establishment of Urban (and Rural) Studies Centres, Easter and Whitsun revision centres.

The acquisition of good study skills is central to the Report's plans to tackle underachievement. In this respect the Committee recommend that:

a Headteachers, in consultation with the whole teaching staff, instigate a clear homework policy and introduce measures by which its implementation is regularly monitored.

b District inspectors/advisers provide headteachers with support and advice on the matter of homework policy and practice.

c Headteachers ensure that the school fully informs parents about the homework policy and takes measures to enlist their support.

d Headteachers seek to provide opportunities for pupils to complete their homework on the school premises.

e The Authority, in the longer term, investigates the extent to which additional resources are needed for supervised 'extended study' by pupils, and take steps to meet these vital needs.

f Headteachers and teachers ensure the school has a study skills policy and helps pupils both to acquire independent learning skills and to pass examinations. In the latter context, schools and districts within local authorities can play a major contribution by:

  i devising INSET programmes with the aim of creating a body of expertise within each subject area;
 ii preparing study skills booklets for pupils;
iii introducing a teachers' guide which provides ideas and examples of good practice within schools;
 iv devising a booklet for teachers containing supplementary papers on specific topics such as the ILEA (1983) package on *Effective Learning Skills*.

Finally, Hargreaves and his team recognise the key roles played by teachers and adequate resource levels throughout the educational process. Consequently, some of the recommendations made by the Committee include:

1 The Authority advising governors to take account of appropriate experience when considering staff for promotion.

2 The improvement of induction and probationary year schemes.

3 Headteachers ensuring that all heads of department have clear job specifications.

4 Inspectors, when their help is sought by headteachers, giving high priority to improving the effectiveness of heads of department.

5 The Authority providing courses on basic classroom management and on dealing with disruptive pupils especially for teachers in professional difficulties.

6 Heads of department ensuring that members of their subject teams participate in meaningful self-evaluation exercises.

7 Heads of department adopting policies of using classroom observation and co-teaching methods to ensure and/or raise the quality of teaching, as appropriate.

8 Schools pioneering self-evaluation, quinquennial reviews, staff appraisal schemes and course monitoring schemes (see ILEA 1977; 1982).

9 Headteachers designating a deputy as staff tutor with overall responsibility for staff development within the school.

10 Headteachers establishing a representative staff development committee to advise them and the staff tutor on the school's INSET programme.

11 The Inspectorate including a component on staff development and INSET in all management courses for headteachers and senior staff.
12 The Authority giving greater priority to school-focused INSET to meet increasing demand.
13 The Authority giving higher priority and better financial allocation to the in-service education of teachers (INSET) which extends opportunities for teachers to observe and learn from the work of colleagues in other schools.
14 The Authority making financial provision to enable teachers to visit schools outside the ILEA.
15 The Inspector for pastoral care work co-ordinating with a committee the promotion and development of the pastoral curriculum through INSET.
16 The Authority making provision for more local and central courses on the pastoral curriculum and personal and social education a high INSET priority.
17 Headteachers ensuring that all information about the school's INSET programme is on the innovation exchange information sheets.
18 Divisional educational officers enabling schools to satisfactorily replace teachers away on INSET courses.
19 The Authority providing schools with substantially increased administrative assistance.
20 The Authority granting headteachers a half-term sabbatical leave every five years.

Through all these means, and others, Hargreaves seeks to improve the management and organisation of schools, making them more meaningful to a wider range of pupils within them. The Committee emphasises the need for curriculum change, appropriate and better staff development and in-service schemes, and for involving pupils in decision-making, as well as the vital role of community and parental liaison.

The Report is not only innovative, but worthy of discussion by every secondary school and local education authority in Britain. It provides a clear lead for others to follow. The pity of this far-sighted and clear-thinking document is that it was produced in an era of economic restraint in education, cut-backs, falling rolls and low staff morale. It will be a great tragedy for pupils and teachers alike if its lessons go unheeded and the experiments remain untried. As with the case of falling rolls, a great opportunity to innovate will have been missed.

To summarise, there is clearly a great deal teachers, schools, local education authorities and national policy makers can do both to improve pastoral care and to combat disadvantage, disaffection and disruptive conduct. Such changes will take time. They will not be easy. But where there is a will, there is way. Promoting school improvement is one of the greatest and most rewarding exercises currently facing educationalists.

Chapter 8

Teacher research and school self-evaluation

One of the dominant features of the effective school is that it possesses a culture that values reflection. Not the staring out of the window type of reflection, but reflection with a purpose. That is, a commitment to review and seriously consider what one is doing, for the purpose of improving practice. Within a school this activity can be seen at two levels. The first level is that of the teacher; the image one thinks of here is Eric Hoyle's (1972) 'extended professional', Donald Schon's (1983) 'reflective practitioner' or Lawrence Stenhouse's (1975) 'teacher as researcher' who is 'autonomous in professional judgement'. The second level is that of the school itself. Appellations like the 'relatively autonomous school' 'the thinking school' or the 'problem solving school' are descriptive of what is meant here.

Teacher research and school self-evaluation can both be regarded as means for achieving a degree of autonomy for teachers and schools within the educational system. Teacher research emancipates teachers from authoritative forms of knowledge, theory and policy. Similarly, school self-evaluation enables a school to take more control of its curriculum and organisation, and plan its future more effectively and independently. Despite ten years experience of teacher research and school evaluation in the UK, there have been few attempts to link the two approaches into a whole school policy. In this chapter we suggest some ways of doing that.

Our concept of teacher research is well captured by Stenhouse:

... the outstanding characteristics of the extended professional (teacher) is a capacity for autonomous professional self development through systematic self study through the study of the work of other teachers and through the testing of ideas by classroom research procedures.

In the sense that we are referring to it here, teacher research is an act undertaken by teachers either to improve their own or a colleague's teaching or to test the assumptions of educational theory in practice. Classroom research generates hypotheses about teaching from the experience of teaching and encourages teachers to use this research to make their teaching more competent. So when we refer to the teacher researcher, we are not envisioning scores of teachers assuming a research role and carrying out research projects to the exclusion of their teaching. Our vision is of teachers who have extended their role to include critical reflection upon their craft with the aim of improving it.

Teachers are too often the servants of heads, advisers, researchers, text books, curriculum developers, examination boards, or the DES – among others – all of whom influence and constrain a teacher's action. By adopting a critical approach to curriculum and teaching, by taking a research stance, the teacher is not only engaged in a meaningful professional development activity but also in a process of refining and becoming more autonomous in professional judgement. The 'teacher researcher' movement is a prime example of a realistic attempt to achieve this. With its roots in the *Humanities Curriculum Project*, nurtured by the *Ford Teaching Project*, disseminated through the *Classroom Action Research Network* (CARN) and popularised in the work of Elliott and Adelman (1976), Kemmis (Kemmis and McTaggart, 1981, Carr and Kemmis 1983), Nixon (1981) and Hopkins (1985a), the teacher researcher movement has achieved mature status as a recognised research form (*vide* Lawton, 1980). The continuing success of CARN (Holly & Whitehead, 1986) is further testimony to its impact on the educational system generally.

The other level at which emancipation can operate is that of the school. Here it is a question of the school liberating itself from a bureaucratic and control-oriented educational system. The 'ideal' type of emancipated school is that represented by the 'thinking, 'the relatively autonomous', 'creative', or 'problem-solving' school which is also the goal of most school improvement efforts (Hopkins and Wideen, 1984). These 'ideal types' of school organisation were advocated by the OECD (Nisbet, 1973, van Velzen *et al*, 1985) and researchers at the University of Oregon (Runkel *et al*, 1979), amongst others. Bolam outlines the image of the emancipated schools as follows:

Underlying . . . is a theory of educational change which regards teachers within their schools as the most effective vehicle and focus for improving the educational process. In a recent review of educational thinking and practice in OECD member countries I concluded that 'Whatever their traditional approach to innovation, a number of member countries are beginning to recognise weaknesses in the centre-periphery or top-down models', and that they 'are becoming increasingly concerned with the problems of the users (*ie* teachers and schools)'.

Other writers have used different metaphors like 'thinking', 'healthy', 'self-renewing' or 'problem-solving', but the features they are concerned with have a lot in common with the following description which arose from an influential American study (*vide* McLaughlin, 1976) of the change process in education:

The problem-solving that characterizes the initiation of change for the ideal adaptive school system has three main elements:

a The response to external pressures for change is proactive in the sense that it typically anticipates external demands and prepares a local solution before 'exogenous shocks' become local crises.

b Internal demand for change is continually stimulated and considered as legitimate. Needs are assessed and problems are identified on an on-going basis.

c The formulation of proposals in response either to external pressures or indigenous demands and needs consists of a process of mobilizing political as well as organisational resources. The crucial ingredient of this process is that staff of all levels participate in the proposal. By so doing, they can develop a sense of ownership in and commitment to the specific planned changes, and, more importantly in the long run, a sense of trust in the organisation's willingness to change (Bolam 1982: 219).

One way of moving towards this 'ideal type' of school is through School Based Review or School Self-Evaluation (Hopkins, 1985b). A good example of this in the UK is the GRIDS school self evaluation materials (McMahon *et al*, 1984) of which more anon.

There is an obvious link between teacher research and school self-evaluation as both activities share a common set of assumptions and activities. The assumptions are related to individuals and organisations taking more control over their futures. The activities are related to some systematic attempt to review what they (both individuals and organisations) are doing and to proceed to action based on that analysis. Although both activities require similar assumptions and activities, teacher researchers can exist within an alien school environment (albeit with difficulty) whereas a successful attempt at school review for improvement purposes requires a sympathetic school environment. In this sense school evaluation builds on an ethic of teacher research which requires, in most cases, a transformation of the culture of the school (Sarason, 1982). This is difficult to achieve, but it is the implementation of the ideas implicit in this chapter (indeed, in this book) that will bring about changes in the culture of the school. Individual teachers can aspire to the image of autonomy. Schools cannot, unless a significant number of their teachers share that image. But when they do, that school will look very different from those surrounding it.

We hope that this rather grandiose introduction does not appear too theoretical; it is important to draw the connection between teacher research and school self-evaluation because they represent, in our opinion, an extremely important trend – one that has the power to transform our contemporary system of education. In the following two sections we will describe each approach individually but in a similar way. We will first provide a rationale for the activity, then describe some practical approaches and finally give some examples of the idea in action.

Teacher research[1]

The argument that we are using here to support and amplify the teacher researcher concept is that traditional educational research is inadequate to help the classroom teacher improve his or her own practice. There are two aspects to this argument: first, the differing realities perceived by teachers and researchers; second, the limitations of the ubiquitous agricultural botany paradigm for educational research.

One of the most unfortunate aspects of traditional educational research is that it is extremely difficult to apply its findings to classroom practice. The results of research are often either too specific or too general and contain few unequivocal signposts for action. Consequently, teachers often regard educational research as something irrelevant to their lives and see little interaction between the world of the educational researcher and the world of the teacher.

Arthur Bolster (1983) asked the question 'Why has research on teaching had so little influence on practice? His own response is:

The major reason in my opinion is that most such research especially that emanating from our top-ranked schools of education, construes teaching from a theoretical perspective that is incompatible with the perspective teachers must employ in thinking about their work. In other words researchers and school teachers adopt radically different sets of assumptions about how to conceptualize the teaching process. As a result, the conclusions of much formal research on teaching appear irrelevant to classroom teachers – not necessarily wrong, just not very sensible or useful.

Most researchers when they enter classrooms bring with them perspectives derived from academic disciplines. Their view of how knowledge evolves and how it is determined is firmly established by their formal training. The world view that guides researchers' actions is consequently at odds with that of teachers. The teacher derives his or her knowledge of teaching from continual participation in situational decision-making and the classroom culture in which they and their pupils act out their daily lives. So one reason why traditional research is of little use to teachers is because of the differing conceptions of teaching held by teachers and researchers. But there are other problems.

Research in education is usually carried out within the psycho-statistical research paradigm. This approach is based on the agricultural research designs of RA Fisher in the 1930s. It has been increasingly utilised by educational researchers, as can be seen by the myriad of contemporary graduate theses that are conceptualised and executed in this way. The basic idea underlying these designs is that experiments are

1 Based in part on *A Teacher's Guide to Classroom Research* (Hopkins, 1985a) where a fuller discussion of the views can be found.

conducted on samples, usually divided into a control and a experimental group. Then the results are generalised to a target population. The critical point is that samples are randomly drawn and are consequently representative of that target population.

This approach to educational research is problematic, especially if the results are to be applied to classrooms. First, it is extremely difficult to drawn random samples in educational settings. Second, there is a plethora of contextual variables operating on educational settings that are difficult to control. Third, it is difficult to establish criteria for effective classroom or school performance. If this were not enough there are deeper problems that relate to the essence of the teaching/learning process. One is that as teachers we are concerned with the individual progress of pupils, rather than with mean scores from the class or school, yet the agricultural-botany model is premised on measures of gross yield. Stenhouse (quoted in Hopkins, 1985a) puts the paradox like this:

The teacher is like a gardener who treats different plants differently, and not like a large scale farmer who administers standardised treatments to as near as possible standardised plants.

The other deeper problem relates to meaningful action. The teacher-pupil interactions that result in effective learning are not so much the consequence of a standardised teaching approach but the result of teachers and pupils engaging in meaningful action. Meaningful action cannot be standardised by control or sample.

Teacher research is characterised by a set of procedures that involve problem formation, data gathering and data analysis.

Problem formation

This subheading is somewhat misleading. As Kemmis and McTaggart (1981) point out in *The Action Research Planner*:

You do not have to begin with a 'problem'. All you need is a general idea that something might be improved. Your general idea may stem from a promising new idea or the recognition that existing practice falls short of aspiration. In either case you must centre attention on:
    What is happening now?
    In what sense is that problematic?
    What can I do about it?
General starting points will look like –
    I would like to improve the . . .
    Some people are unhappy about . . .
    What can I do to change the situation?
    I am perplexed by . . .
    . . . is a source of irritation. What can I do about it?
    I have an idea I would like to try out in my class.
    How can the experience of . . . be applied to . . .?
    Just what do I do with respect to . . .?

As you read the extract, no doubt certain ideas or topics for classroom research come to mind. It is worth taking a few minutes to jot down these ideas; don't worry about how well they are formed. At this stage it is more important to generate a list of topics from which one can work. Having produced a list, the next step is to evaluate the usefulness, viability and/or importance of the individual topic. There are a number of guidelines that you can use here.

First, do not tackle issues that you cannot do anything about. For example, it may be impossible, in the short or medium-term, to alter the banding or streaming system in your school or to change the textbook that you are using. Because you cannot do anything about it, either avoid the issue or rephrase it in a solvable form. So, although you cannot change the textbook, it may be possible to experiment with different ways the text could be used as evidence in your classes.

Second, only take on small-scale and relatively limited topics, at least initially. There are several reasons for this. It is important to build on success, and a small-scale project satisfactorily completed in a short space of time is reinforcing and encouraging. It is also very easy to underestimate the scale and amount of time a project will take. It is very discouraging to have found after the initial flush of enthusiasm that you have bitten off more than you can chew.

Third, choose a topic that is important to you or to your students, or one that you have to be involved with anyway in the course of your normal schools activities. The topic that you focus on needs to be intrinsically motivating. If not, then again after the initial flush of enthusiasm and when the difficulties begin to build up, you will find that movitation will begin to evaporate.

In summary, when choosing a topic for classroom research make certain, at least initially, that it is viable, discrete and intrinsically interesting.

Implicit in much of what we have written so far is the idea that problems emerge out of a teacher's critical reflection on classroom experience, and are then explored through the use of the classroom research procedures. In other words, both problem formation and problem resolution are grounded in teacher experience.

Problem formation may occur within an open or a closed context. Open problems take as their starting point a teacher's critical reflection on his or her teaching. This reflection culminates in a decision to utilise classroom research techniques to understand more fully and then improve his or her teaching. The open approach is one where the teacher engages in classroom research as a reflective activity and derives from it a hypothesis that can be tested and will provide a basis for action.

The closed approach differs from the open in that many teachers have already indentified a specific problem or hypothesis before engaging in classroom research. In this instance, their classroom research begins with the testing of an hypothesis. So, for example, a teacher having heard about a new teaching method that applied to his/her subject area, would research the effectiveness of the approach in his/her own classroom.

The difference between open and closed contexts reflects the derivation of the problem. In the first instance the hypothesis emerges as a result of critical reflection; in the second it is given – or extant – and the teacher refines it, the proceeds to testing. The important point is that in both instances the research is controlled by the teacher for the purpose of improving practice. The contrast between open and closed problems can be represented in diagrammatic form as in Figure 8.1.

Figure 8.1 Contrast between open and closed problems

Type	Hypothesis
Open	Generating
Closed	Testing

Data gathering

There are a number of criteria to bear in mind when doing teacher research. Two of them are:
- the teacher's primary job is to teach, and any research method should not interfere with or disrupt the teaching commitment;
- the method of data collection must not be too demanding on the teacher's time. As a corollary, the teacher needs to be certain about the data collection technique before using it.

Bearing in mind these criteris, let us outline some ways of collecting information about our own teaching.

Keeping *teacher field notes* is essentially a way of reporting observations and reflecting about classroom events and problems, and the teacher's reaction to them. The notes should be written as soon as possible after the lesson, and can draw on impressionistic jottings made during a lesson. Many teachers we know keep a notebook open on their desk or keep a space in their daybooks for jotting down notes as the lesson and the day progress. Keeping a record in this way is not very time-consuming and provides surprisingly frank information.

Tape recording is excellent for those situations where teachers require a very specific and accurate record of a limited aspect of their teaching, or want a general impression of the flow of a lesson. However, transcribing tapes can be very time-consuming, unless you have secretarial support.

A common practice in some schools is the use of *pupil journals*. Once the pupils have been taken into the teacher's confidence and are aware of the teacher's concern to research his or her teaching, these journals are an excellent way of obtaining honest feedback (particularly when the pupils retain the right to decide whether the teacher has access to the journal). This is also a quick way of obtaining information, as teachers normally peruse pupils' journals as a matter of course.

Information obtained from journals can also act as a starting point for *teacher-pupil discussion*, particularly if a pupil notes any particularly discrepant event or feeling in his or her journal. Because individual discussions are very time consuming it may be more profitable to devote most time to general classroom meetings and only talk individually with pupils (for research purposes) when specific instances warrant it. On the other hand, *pupil-pupil interviews* can form a rich source of data, particularly if the pupil interviewer keeps to an interview schedule prepared by the teacher. It is a good idea to tape-record these individual discussions or interviews for future reference, particularly if the encounters are relatively short.

The *video recorder* is probably the most useful 'wide lens' method that we have available. It allows the teacher to observe many facets of his or her teaching, and provides heuristic and accurate information for diagnosis. Later, the teacher may wish to use a different method to examine specific aspects of his or her teaching that he or she becomes aware of through using the video. Many of the teacher researchers we know use the video on an intermittent but regular basis to enable them to keep in touch with their teaching.

Questionnaires provide a very quick and simple way of obtaining wide-ranging and rich information from pupils. It is important, particularly in the primary grades, to be relatively unsophisticated in the structuring of the questions. We suggest using a Snoopy figure or a happy/sad face for the criteria, keeping the questions simple, and using the 'what did you like best?', 'what did you like least?', 'what would you do differently?' type of open-ended question.

David Hopkins decribes in more detail these and other classroom research techniques in, *A Teacher's Guide to Classroom Research* (1985a). They are basically open-ended methods in so far as they are used most effectively for diagnostic purposes. Although they are described individually it is important to realize that they can be and most often are, used electically and in combination. But each has a specific purpose and is best suited to a particular situation. A taxonomy of the main advantages/disadvantages of each approach is given in Figure 8.2 which summarises ten relatively open-ended methods of gathering data that are generally diagnostic and controlled by the teacher.

Approaches that utilise observation tend to be more structured, require more external help, and are more suited to the testing of hypotheses and

Figure 8.2 Taxonomy of classroom research techniques (based on the work of teachers involved in the Ford Teaching Project)

Technique	Advantage(s)	Disadvantage(s)	Use(s)
Field notes	simple; on-going; personal; aide memoire	subjective; needs practice	• specific issue • case study • general impression
Audio tape recording	versatile; accurate; provides ample data	transcription difficult; time consuming; often inhibiting	• detailed evidence • diagnostic
Pupil diaries	provides pupils perspective	subjective	• diagnostic • triangulation
Interviews and discussions	can be teacher-pupil, observer-pupil pupil-pupil	time consuming	• specific in depth information
Video tape recorder	visual and comprehensive	awkward and expensive; can be distracting	• visual material • diagnostic
Questionnaires	highly specific; easy to administer; comparative	time consuming to analyse; problem of 'right' answers	• specific informa-tion and feedback
Sociometry	easy to administer; provides guide to action	can threaten isolated pupils	• analyses social relationships
Documentary evidence	illuminative	difficult to obtain; time consuming	• provides context and information
Slide/tape photography	illuminative; promotes discussion	difficult to obtain; superficial	• illustrates critical incidents
Case study	accurate; represetative; uses range of techniques	time consuming	• comprehensive overview of an issue • publishable format

to closed types of problems. There are four main approaches to observation: participant observation; clinical supervision; structured observation; and interaction schedules.

A *participant observer* provides the teacher-researcher with the most flexible source of data and also a means of support. We generally try to encourage teachers to engage in classroom research in pairs or small groups for a number of reasons. Perhaps chief among them is the emotional support the teachers gain from each other, particularly as this activity is initially threatening. It is now fairly well established that teachers learn best from other teachers, and take criticism most easily from this source. It is ideal if teachers can act as participant observers for each other, for this mutual exchange of roles quickly breaks down barriers which would be monolithic to outsiders. Participant observers can play any number of differing roles. They can observe a lesson in general, focus on specific aspects, or talk to pupils – all during one observation period.

Clinical supervision is a technique that has enjoyed much popularity in North America, where it was developed as a method of supervising student teachers, but it is also suited for use in classroom research situations. It is a more structured form of peer observation that focuses on a teacher's instructional performance. The process utilises a three phase approach to the observation of teaching events: a planning conference, classroom observation, and feedback conference. The planning conference provides the observer and teacher with an opportunity to reflect on the proposed lesson, and this leads to a mutual decision to collect observational data on an aspect of the teacher's teaching. During the classroom observation phase, the observer observes the teacher teach and collects objective data on the particular aspect of teaching they agreed upon earlier. It is in the feedback conference that the observer and teacher share the information, decide on remedial action (if necessary), and often plan to collect further observational data.

In the previous paragraphs we discussed two approaches to teachers observing each other in action. Sometimes a *structured observation* approach is necessary. Often, all that is required are simple ways of gathering information on basic topics, such as questioning techniques, preferable for teachers to devise their own observation schedules, to 'invent' them for a particular purpose. By doing this, the teacher develops more ownership over the investigation and there is probably a better 'fit' between the object of the observation and the method of gathering data. Before devising the observation checklist, it is useful to ask some organising questions in order to ascertain the purpose of the observation. Examples of such questions might be:

1 What is the purpose of the observation?
2 What teacher behaviours are worth observing?
3 What is focus of the observation?

4 What data gathering methods will best serve the purpose?
5 How will the data be used?

A variety of coding scales can be utilised in specific classroom research situations by teachers. The impetus for coding scales and checklists has come from North America where there is and has been a concern for 'scientific' approaches to teaching. The best known example of coding scales is Flanders' *Interaction Analysis Categories*.

Analysing research data and an example

The methodology for teacher research must be reliable enough to allow teachers confidently to formulate hypotheses and develop strategies applicable to their classroom situations. This is an area where teacher research has not been conspicuously successful. Consequently, it is important to establish a coherent methodology for analysing classroom research data.

The four stages of classroom research are outlined below.
1 *Data Collection* and the generation of hypotheses;
2 *Validation* of hypotheses using the techniques of saturation and triangulation)
3 *Interpretation* by reference to theory, established practice or teacher judgement;
4 *Action* for improvement that is also monitored by classroom research techniques

Jane: an example

As part of the requirements for a course one of the authors taught on the 'Analysis of Teaching', Jane made a videotape of herself experimenting with various models of teaching. In viewing the videotape, Jane made a number of observations. In particular, she felt that she had been rather abrupt in her questioning technique and had given the pupils little time to formulate responses to her questions. It was suggested to Jane that she explore this observation a little further and ascertain whether this was consistent behaviour or an aberration. She did this by taking a further videotape of her teaching, and by asking a colleague to observe her teaching. Jane also developed a short questionnaire on her questioning technique, which she administered to her pupils and subsequently analysed. As a result of this endeavour, Jane realised that she did in fact interject very quickly after asking a question, and quite often answered her own questions.

All well and good, Jane thought, but what does this mean? Thinking that recent research on teaching might help, Jane did some reading and came across an article on think-time. The article reviewed a number of studies on the relationship between amount of time that elapsed after questioning and the quality of pupil response. Jane felt that she was not allowing her pupils enough time to think after she had asked a question, possibly to the detriment of their level of cognitive functioning. So she developed a plan to change and monitor her questioning technique. It took Jane some six months to complete these tasks (teaching is a time-consuming job), but there was no pressure on her to complete the research. In fact, the longer time frame allowed for more valid data, and she was pleased with the results. Not only did she find evidence of higher-level responses from her pupils, but also involving them in the evoluation of her teaching, enhanced the climate of her class through the mutual and overt commitment of both teacher and pupils to the learning process.

As previously mentioned in the classroom research process, the first step is *collecting data*. With the use of, say, a video tape recorder, the teacher gathers information about his or her teaching behaviour. Having collected the data, a sub-stage follows immediately or co-exists with the collection of data – the generation of hypotheses. We are always generating hypotheses to explain classroom events. Even at the earliest stages of research, we are interpreting and explaining to ourselves 'why this is happening' and 'what caused that'. At the end of the data collection stage, not only have we collected our data, but we have also established a number of hypotheses that begin to explain what is happening in the classroom. These hypotheses usually emerge quite naturally from the data gathering process. Jane, in the example, generated a number of ideas about her teaching from viewing the videotape. Among these was an observation that she was too abrupt in her questioning technique and had given her pupils too little time to answer questions. Such hypotheses not only reflect the data but are also an interpretation of it. At this stage, the more hypotheses the better.

The second stage in the process concerns the *validation* of the hypotheses. There are two techniques for establishing the validity of an hypotheses. One is saturation, the other is triangulation. When applied to the classroom research situation, saturation implies that the hypothesis or category generated from observation is tested repeatedly against the data in an attempt to modify or falsify it. Thus, Jane, having decided to explore her questioning technique further, videotaped herself again and found that, in fact, she was quite abrupt in her questioning and interjected far too quickly. In this way, she firmly validated the observation by saturating it.

The other important technique for validation is triangulation. This concept was popularised by John Elliott and Clem Adelman during their work with the *Ford Teaching Project* (Elliot and Adelman, 1976). It involves contrasting the perceptions of one person (eg the teacher) in a specific situation against those of other persons (eg the observer and the pupils) in the same situation. By doing this, an initial subjective observation or perception is fleshed out and given a degree of authenticity.

The third stage in the research process is *interpretation*. T̶
taking a validated hypothesis and fitting it into a frame of re̶
gives it meaning. For the classroom researcher, this mear̶
hypothesis and relating it either to theory, to the norms ̶
practice or to the teacher's own intuition as to what comprises good
teaching. This allows the teacher-researcher to give meaning to a
particular observation or series of observations that can lead profitably
to action. In doing this, the classroom researcher is creating meaning out
of hitherto discrete observations and constructs.

Jane gave meaning to her hypothesis by reading about 'think time'.
That information not only helped her understand the implications of her
behaviour but also suggested a direction for action. Other strategies
might have been to discuss the research with a colleague, visit another
school or attend a course on questioning techniques.

The final step in the process is *action*. Having created meaning out of
the research data, the teacher-researcher is in a position to plan for future
action. Building on the evidence gathered during the research, the teacher
is able to plan realistic strategies which are themselves monitored by
classroom research procedures. Jane did just that. The interpretation
stage gave her information on how to change her questioning technique
which, after some planning, she attempted to monitor and evaluate.

The analysis of data is a very important part of the classroom research
process. It is only at this stage that the teacher can be certain that the
results obtained are valid and reliable. Often teacher-researchers fail to
analyse adequately their data and thus lack a secure platform for action.

School self-evaluation

School self-evaluation has over the past decade become a clearly etched
feature on the educational landscape. The reviews conducted by Elliot
(1980/82) and James (1982) suggest that the appearance, if not the
reality, of school self-evaluation is widely accepted in LEAs and schools
in the United Kingdom. A number of factors may contribute towards an
understanding of school evaluation in Britain. First, there is a tradition of
decentralisation in British schools, which coupled with the emphasis on
school-focused INSET (Bolam *et al*, 1982) makes school-based review
(SBR – a synonym for school self-evaluation) an activity that is logically
and culturally appropriate. Second, because of the decentralised nature
of the British educational system, there have recently been increased
demands for accountability. The recent HMI document *Quality in
Schools* (1985), for example, sees evaluation and appraisal as a means of
maintaining efficiency and quality. Third, a number of LEAs have
initiated schemes for school evaluation: Salford was the first in 1972,
followed by the influential Inner London Education Authority (ILEA)

scheme in 1974, and then by Oxfordshire, Sussex and many others (for a useful critique, see Clift, 1982). Within ten years, school evaluation has become a widespread activity. Fourth, although the original intent of most LEA schemes was accountability, in some cases they were transformed during implementation by influence at the grass roots level, into SBR activities: SBR being the more acceptable face of accountability. Fifth, implementation of self-evaluation schemes reflects regional variations that are a function of the local educational culture.

The purpose of such self-evaluation exercises is often problematic. In his definition of school self-evaluation, Van Velzen (1982) argues for internal development or school improvement as the raison d'être of school self-evaluation. He defines school self-evaluation as:

. . . a systematic inspection (description and analysis) by a school, a sub-system or an individual (teacher, school leader) of the actual functioning of the school . . . frequent diagnosis is a vital and important activity, if for only one reason: it should always be the first step in a systematic school improvement process to gather diagnostic information in order to improve the functioning of the school.

Van Velzen's definition is not universally accepted. In the United Kingdom, for example, many school evaluation schemes have been, and are, characterized by an explicit accountability purpose.

In practice, however, most school self-evaluation projects embody some form of development and accountability function, and can be classified accordingly, as shown in Figure 8.3.

Figure 8.3 Schema for classifying the twin purposes of school self evaluation

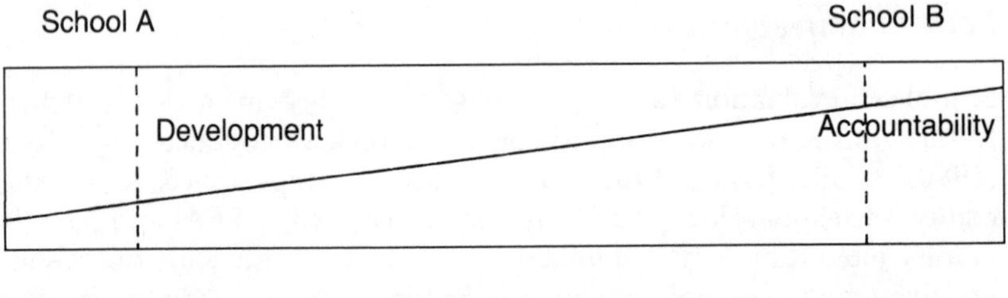

So, for example, School A's evaluation scheme has a major development purpose but it is also minimally accountable to itself and its community. School B's evaluation scheme on the other hand is accountability oriented – the LEA requires a regular and validated evaluation – but as a consequence of doing the evaluation a group of staff worked on improving an aspect of the school's curriculum. Although we are primarily concerned with evaluation schemes that have a development purpose, the message applies equally to those that do not. However, if such schemes adopt practices like those outlined below, then it may be that their purpose will also change.

The outcomes of self-evaluation will obviously vary according to the intent of those initiating the review and the political and cultural context in which the review occurs. But, as part of a school improvement strategy, the goal of SBR is the realisation of the concept of the problem-solving school. This is a contentious statement that has a number of implications, some of which, for the purposes of definition, need to be made explicit.

1 The attainment (or near attainment) of the goal of the problem-solving school implies a radical shift in the concept of schooling. The problem-solving school epitomises values such as democracy, individual automony and co-operation.

2 The concept of the problem-solving school is an ideal goal that schools and school systems can progress towards rather than attain.

3 The focus of school self-evaluation is on process rather than product: a) because the concept of the problem solving school is a process goal; and b) because attempts at improvement through the use of product models of schooling have proven largely unsuccessful.

4 The goal of the problem-solving school cannot be achieved by review alone: review must be linked to a strategy for improvement that involves a signficant proportion of the school staff.

5 Although self-evaluation is an aspect of school improvement the review process itself can be used for different purposes. Consequently, SBR can assume different values in different contexts.

Although it is relatively easy, particularly in retrospect, to be analytically clear about the purpose of a school self-evaluation scheme, there is often vagueness about the procedures involved in actually doing an evaluation: particularly if its prime purpose is to improve the school's organisation. In a recent survey and analysis of the state of the art of school-based review in OECD countries (Hopkins 1985b), little awareness or consensus was found about the organisational issues involved in conducting a school review. Here we will focus on the more complex but less contentious issues of how to enhance a school's effectiveness and problem solving capacity through self-evaluation. In this sense evaluation can be regarded as the link or bridge between the curriculum and the school organisation, as well as a means of improving both.

A matrix for planning school-based review

During our work with the OECD International School Improvement Project (ISIP), we tried to overcome the vagueness sometimes associated with school self-evaluation by developing a matrix that was both descriptive – in so far as it overviewed the whole evaluation process – and prescriptive – because it provided a guide to action (Bollen and Hopkins, 1986). The purpose of the matrix is to identify not only the major roles involved in SBR and the main components of the SBR process, but also to highlight the interaction between them. The matrix arrangement illustrates the roles that various persons play in the SBR process, a consideration that emphasises the different functions assumed by those involved in SBR at various stages in the process. The phases and steps outlined in the matrix provide not only a model for SBR but also a generic school improvement process as shown in the matrix diagram.

In our original design the *horizontal axis* represented the significant persons and groups involved in SBR: pupils, teachers, promoted teachers, internal change agents, school leaders, external support, local education authorities and the environment. Our colleagues suggested that the roles of social workers, parents, governors, and the local community should also be included. When we came to revise the matrix we found that the list of actors had expanded so much that it became unwieldy. A further problem is that various actors can assume different roles in the SBR process at different times (or at the same time) and their perception of their role may also change. So we decided in the revision to focus on role and function rather on than particular actors. We have identified the following roles:

- those who are subject to review;
- those who are doing the review;
- those who are managing the review;
- those who are supporting the review;
- those who are controlling the review;
- those who are influencing the review.

Our original list of actors can be used as a checklist to fit people into various roles and functions, which can be entered into the individual cells of the matrix. Despite this emphasis, the role of the environment in shaping the character of the review must be remembered.

Obviously, within a school self-evaluation project one person or group can fulfil a number of different roles and functions at any one time, so demonstrating different possibilities for various individuals and groups. A teacher could assume the role of 'doing' as well as 'supporting' the review (and all the roles in between). An external support person could equally take a 'doing', 'managing' or 'supporting' role; and an inspector could choose between 'supporting' and 'controlling' the review. This way of identifying role in SBR allows for more opportunity for comparison between cases. Viewed holistically, this arrangement illustrates the interaction of various actors or different phases of the process. For example, in the negotiation stage of the preparation phase, the matrix helps identify who is negotiating with whom about what. It also helps to clarify at any one phase of the process whether action is merely the effort of one or two actors or something based on the common interests of different groups of actors. The matrix arrangement is shown in Figure 8.4.

Figure 8.4 Process and roles in school based review: a matrix

PROCESS	SUBJECT to review	DOING the review	MANAGING the review	SUPPORTING the review	CONTROLLING the review	INFLUENCING the review
Start Condition – Past Experience, History						
Preparation (Readiness) Phase:						
– Initiation						
– Negotiation over –						
• participation						
• control						
• training						
– Decision to proceed						
Review (Initial) Phase:						
– Planning for Review						
– Decision on Instrumentation						
– Data Gathering & Analysis						
– Reporting of Findings						
– Decision to Proceed						
Review (Specific) Phase:						
– Setting Priorities						
– Planning for Review						
– Mobilisation of Resources/Expertise						
– Training for Review						
– Gathering Information						

– Validating Conclusions

– Feedback & Evaluation

– Decision to Proceed

Development Phase:
– Establishing Policy

– Planning for Implementation

– Training (Inset) for Implementation

– Implementation of Policy with particular reference to:–
- school organisation
- materials
- teaching style
- knowledge utilisation
- acceptance of change

– Monitoring and Evaluation

Institutionalisation Phase:
– Monitoring of Action

– Utilisation of SBR Process in other areas of curriculum and school organisation

– Development of problem solving capacity as an organisational norm within the school

The *vertical axis* represents the SBR process and is divided into five major phases: Preparation, Review (initial), Review (specific), Action and Institutionalisation. The *Preparation* phase refers to those activities that precede the review and that ensure readiness for the process. These include the past experiences of review in the school, the initiation or starting conditions of review, the negotiation of participation, control and training, and the eventual decision to proceed (or not) with the review. The *Review (initial)* phase involves the initial review process that gathers general information about the school organisation and curriculum. This results in the decision to proceed to the more specific review phase. The *Review (Specific)* phase involves the setting of priorities for an in-depth review of a particular aspect(s) of the school and results in the feedback of findings amenable to the development of policy should the decision to proceed to action be taken. In the *Action* phase decisions on policy are taken in the light of the findings established during the previous review phase and an implementation plan is put into action. Effective implementation of policy involves change at a number of levels: organisation; materials; teaching style; knowledge utilisation and acceptance. Some of these are, of course, more difficult to achieve than others. Evaluation is an important final step in the action phase. The SBR process can be said to be *institutionalised* within a school's organisational norms when periodic monitoring of previous SBR activity occurs, and when the SBR process is used in other areas of the school's curriculum and organisation. When this is a regular occurrence then the school has developed a capacity for problem solving and improvement.

Obviously the SBR process is not as linear as it is represented in the matrix. But the matrix does provide an indication of the temporal sequence of phases and stages in the process. Similarly, not all the cells of the matrix are represented in any one SBR effort, some cells are 'more equal than others', and some are and remain 'hot' whilst others are predominantly 'cold'. Similarly, the matrix shows us the roles that various actors assume at different phases in the process. Some actors may be involved (in various roles) all the time. At a certain phase all the actors may be involved in some role for a short time. But never will all the actors be involved all the time.

The process of SBR described by the matrix is a generic school improvement strategy. The ultimate goal of the SBR process is the institutionalisation of norms and behaviours consistent with the 'ideal type' of 'problem solving' or 'relatively autonomous' school. It is also important to remember that the whole matrix (process and roles) is embedded in a particular culture and set of values that vary between school districts and national boundaries. These give an individual character to each SBR effort.

Grids

The GRIDS project is a powerful example of a self-evaluation scheme designed specifically to promote internal development in schools rather than to fulfil an accountability function. Its purpose is to place control of the evaluation findings within the school. In 1981, the (then) Schools Council established a joint project with the University of Bristol School of Education which was concerned to develop and pilot materials for assisting whole school staffs to carry out a systematic self-review of policy and practice at their school. The commitment to internal development and school control of the evaluation can be gauged by a list of key principles that characterise the GRIDS approach to school self-evaluation.

1 the aim is to achieve internal school development and not to produce a report for formal accountability purposes;
2 the main purpose is to move beyond the review stage into development for school improvement;
3 the staff of the school should be consulted and involved in the review and development process as much as possible;
4 decisions about what happens to any information or reports produced should rest with the teachers and others concerned;
5 the head and teachers should decide whether and how to involve the other groups in the school, eg pupils, parents, advisers, governors;
6 outsiders (eg external consultants) should be invited to provide help and advice when this seems appropriate;
7 the demands made on key resources like time, money and skilled personnel should be realistic and feasible for schools and LEAs.

The central team outline the GRIDS method in the following quotation from the *GRIDS Handbook* (McMahon *et al* (1984:9).

The central practical recommendation in the GRIDS methods is that the staff should not attempt to make a detailed review of all aspects of the school at once. Instead they should take a broad look at what is happening in the school, on the basis of this identify one or two areas that they consider to be priorities for specific review and development, tackle these first, evaluate what they have achieved and then select another priority. The recommended working procedures may seem unfamiliar at first. The process has been broken down into a series of key steps and tasks which have a logical structure, and a systematic step-by-step approach is recommended throughout. The five stages in this cyclical process are outlined in the GRIDS diagram.

Stage 1 *Getting started*, is where preliminary decisions have to be made about whether or not the GRIDS methods would be appropriate for the school and, if so, how it should be managed. The purpose of Stage 2 the *Initial review*, is to identify the topics that the staff consider to be priorities for specific review and development. Stage 3 is a *Specific review* of the topic(s) that have been identified as priorities; it entails a careful examination of current practice and an assessment of its effectiveness before making recommendations about development. Stage 4 is the *Action* stage when the recommendations are put into practice. Stage 5, *Overview and re-start*, is where evaluation of the development work and of the whole process takes place, and a new cycle of review and development begins.

Figure 8.5[2]   **The five stages of the internal review and development process in planning school-based reviews using the GRIDS approach.**

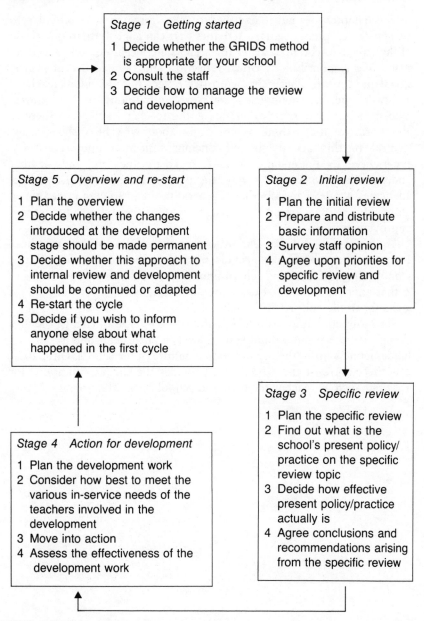

Stage 1   Getting started

1 Decide whether the GRIDS method is appropriate for your school
2 Consult the staff
3 Decide how to manage the review and development

Stage 5   Overview and re-start

1 Plan the overview
2 Decide whether the changes introduced at the development stage should be made permanent
3 Decide whether this approach to internal review and development should be continued or adapted
4 Re-start the cycle
5 Decide if you wish to inform anyone else about what happened in the first cycle

Stage 2   Initial review

1 Plan the initial review
2 Prepare and distribute basic information
3 Survey staff opinion
4 Agree upon priorities for specific review and development

Stage 4   Action for development

1 Plan the development work
2 Consider how best to meet the various in-service needs of the teachers involved in the development
3 Move into action
4 Assess the effectiveness of the development work

Stage 3   Specific review

1 Plan the specific review
2 Find out what is the school's present policy/ practice on the specific review topic
3 Decide how effective present policy/practice actually is
4 Agree conclusions and recommendations arising from the specific review

The diagram mentioned in the quotation is reproduced to give an indication of the problem solving approach adopted by GRIDS (see Figure 8.5). The commitment by GRIDS to inducting a school staff into a problem solving attitude which can be used again in other situations on an ongoing basis is quite apparent.

Commentary

In this chapter we have described teacher research and school self-evaluation as complementary activities that can contribute to our vision of the effective school. Teacher research as a concept embodies features that value responsibility, critical reflection and the exercise of professional judgement. These characteristics reflect the individual teacher's ability to be, in Stenhouse's phrase, 'autonomous in professional judgement'. A major factor in this is the teacher's ability to theorize about practice and to think systematically about what he or she is doing. Central to this activity is self-concious reflection upon classroom experience: to understand it and to create meaning out of that understanding. In a similar way, the process that the GRIDS project advocates is one that embodies a generic problem solving cycle, aimed ultimately at developing a capacity within the school for school improvement.

Arguments like this that lead us to suggest the following propositions:
1 that teacher research can provide important preconditions for effective school self-evaluation and school improvement;
2 that effective school self-evaluation and school improvement requires a change in the culture of the school.

The latter contention is fundamental: effective school change requires change at both personal and system levels and this can only result in a fundamental shift in the organisational culture of the school. Ultimately, it is the culture of the school that provides the shelter conditions for activities such as teacher research and school self-evaluation.

Section E: Creating Effective Schools

Chapters 9 and 10 develop the theme of how to create more effective schools. They examine two important dimensions in this equation. The first is the curriculum. A meaningful, coherent, well-structured and balanced curriculum is essential if any school is to be judged effective. Chapter 9 therefore discusses definitions, perceptions and models, and the stages involved in curriculum development cycles. The second area, elaborated in Chapter 10, is in-service. Few schools are fortunate enough to have totally proficient staff in every respect. Hence, in-service training and staff development programmes are two of the ways in which school managers and individuals can improve themselves and their colleagues, and ensure increased professional competence and effectiveness. This chapter examines ways of putting the partnership model in in-service into practice on behalf of school development, teachers' needs and the professional requirements inherent in effective and efficient teaching. To achieve this, the chapter is sub-divided into three sections: context; countering the cult of the individual; and, some principles which are central to new initiatives. Of necessity – and something for which we do not apoligise, chapter 10 is more theoretical than many of its predecessors. Far too much in-service is atheoretical, leading to few improvements in practice. If schools and teachers are to gain the maximum benefit from in-service work, it needs to be carried out within a proper context so that all engaged in the process can benefit from the acquisition of their new skills and knowledge.

Chapter 9
Beyond the saber tooth curriculum?

One of the most entertaining and perceptive accounts of curriculum development is the parable of *New-Fist-Hammer-Maker*. New Fist, as he is more commonly known, lived in Chellean (early palæolithic) times and, according to Harold Benjamin (1939), was the first great curriculum theorist and practitioner. He is remembered best for the development of the saber tooth curriculum. The saber tooth curriculum had its origins in New Fist's aspirations for a better life for his children and, by the same token, for the tribe as a whole. Motivated by this vision he developed a curriculum that included activities such as saber-tooth-tiger-scaring-with-fire which he taught in a practical way to his children. The benefits of such an induction into these forms of knowledge soon became evident. Despite initial objections by the more conservative and theologically minded members of the tribe (objections that New Fist, being a statesman as well as a curriculum theorist, deftly overcame), tiger-scaring and the other activities soon became accepted as the heart of true education.

All continued well for some generations until the approach of a new ice age drastically changed the environment. The skills acquired through the saber-tooth curriculum were no longer appropriate to the new conditions in the cave realm and the prosperity and equanimity of the tribe suffered. The spirit of New Fist, however, lived on in the new generation, some of whom proposed a new curriculum more suited to the current situation. These radical proposals were ridiculed by the tribal elders as being mere training; and the suggestion that the new activities required as much intelligence and skill as the traditional curriculum was regarded as facetious. Unlike New Fist the tribal elders were neither thinkers nor doers, theorists nor statesmen, as evidenced by statements like:

'We don't teach tiger-scaring to scare tigers; we teach it for the purposes of giving noble courage which carries over into all the affairs of life . . . true education is timelessness. It is something that endures through changing conditions like a solid rock standing squarely and firmly in the middle of a raging torrent. You must know that there are some eternal verities and the saber tooth curriculum is one of them.'

The parable is replete with wisdom. It raises so many issues that we would require another chapter at least to elucidate them. Issues such as education versus training; vocational relevance; transfer of learning; the implementation of innovation; and the calumny of vested interests . . . are all as important now as they were in 1939, let alone Chellean times. Space obviously precludes such discussions but there are three points that we want particularly to highlight. The first is that the term curriculum is an ambiguous one; it is open to many differing interpretations and can be put to many different purposes. The second is that successful teaching is related to thoughtful and systematic curriculum planning. The third is that the responsibility for curriculum development needs to be located close to the classroom. We begin with the saber tooth parable because it is entertaining and illuminating, the lessons one can derive from it provide a context for what follows – the attempt to see how far we have progressed in curriculum development since Chellean times.

In this chapter we will first discuss some of the various definitions, conceptions and models of curriculum that currently abound and see if there is a way through. Second, we will describe in some detail an approach to curriculum development that is sufficiently generic to cover many educational situations. Third, we will discuss some reasons why responsibility for curriculum development should be located close to the classroom door. In our view competence in curriculum development is central to effective teaching and schooling. Unfortunately, teachers often receive no systematic training in curriculum development apart from how to make lesson plans. Tony Flanders, in his report on *The Professional Development of Teachers* (1980), mentions teachers' 'deep sense of bitterness about the lack of support for curriculum development from any quarter'. Similarly, most contemporary approaches to curriculum development underplay the pivotal role of the teacher. In many models of curriculum development the image of the teacher is that of the technician, the 'putter into practice of other people's ideas'; a far cry from our vision of teachers as being confident, flexible, innovative and caring in their professional lives.

Definitions, perceptions and models

Curricula definitions abound. Richmond (1971) sets the scene when he says that:

Curriculum is a slippery word. Broadly defined, it means nothing less than the educative process as a whole. Narrowly defined, as it usually is, the term is regarded as being more or less synonymous with the syllabus, a scheme of work or simply subjects.

This range of interpretation is well illustrated in the following series of quotations. The first three illustrate the broad thesis, the others the narrow.

The curriculum is to be thought of in terms of activity and experience rather than of knowledge to be acquired and facts to be stored. (Hadow Committee, 1931)

... the total effort of the school to bring about desired outcomes in school and out-of-school situations. (Saylor and Alexander, 1954)

Basically the curriculum is what happens to children in school as a result of what teachers do. It includes all of the experiences of children for which the school should accept responsibility. (Kansas, 1958)

The term curriculum would seem, from its derivation, to apply most appropriately to the programme of activities, to the course to be run by pupils in being educated. (Hirst, 1969)

The 'formal' curriculum ... is a programme of worthwhile learning experiences which is planned and implemented within the school. This activity is both conscious and deliberate: it is designed to bring about certain learning outcomes in the child. (Raynor, 1972)

The curriculum of a school is, in the strict sense of the phrase, a statement or programme of its courses of teaching and instruction. (B. of E. – Report on Secondary Education, 1938).

The purpose of presenting these quotations is not so much to argue that one is more correct or appropriate than the others but rather to illustrate the range of opinion that may be encountered. For our part, we tend towards the broad definition and suggest that the word curriculum can apply equally to a unit of lessons produced or adopted by a classroom teacher or to national curriculum projects like SMP or Science 5–13 – including everything in between. For we will argue in the next section that the development process in each of these activities is similar. We find Stenhouse's (1975) definition useful here – 'a curriculum is an attempt to communicate the essential principles and features of an educational proposal in such a form that it is open to critical scrutiny and capable of effective translation into practice'. A curriculum proposal is as much a three-lesson unit on the local environment as it is a major national curriculum innovation such as the *Technical Vocational Education Initiative* (TVEI). The important point is that the principles underlying the curriculum are open to discussion and can be implemented.

Alongside these definitions we must also be aware of the distinction between the 'formal' and the 'hidden' curriculum. The formal curriculum comprises the academic intentions of the course of study; what is supposed to be taught and learned in school. The hidden curriculum, on the other hand, is concerned more with the social side of education; the values and expectations that pupils acquire as a result of going through the schooling process. Although not part of the formal intentions of schooling, the hidden curriculum has the most powerful and lasting impact on most children. It is through the hidden curriculum that we learn about authority and bureaucratic structures, sex-role differentiation, the inequality of the rule of law, and many other positive and negative influences that shape, in a real and enduring way, our futures. One of the most vivid descriptions of the hidden curriculum is given by David Hargreaves:

My argument is that our present secondary school system, largely through the hidden curriculum, exerts on many pupils, particularly but by no means exclusively from the working-class, a destruction of their dignity which is so massive and pervasive that few subsequently recover from it. To have dignity means to have a sense of being worthy, of possessing creative, inventive and critical capacities, of having the power to achieve personal and social change. When dignity is damaged, one's deepest experience is of being inferior, unable, and powerless. My argument is that our secondary schools inflict such damage, in varying degrees, on many of their pupils. (Hargreaves, *The Challenge to the Comprehensive School* 1982)

We are inevitably concerned with the formal rather than the hidden curriculum but this does not reflect their respective importance, either in our eyes or in reality. As Cusick (1973) among others, has argued, high schools tend to spend over 2/3 of their time involved in maintenance (or hidden curriculum) activities rather than instructional (or formal curriculum) activities: and, of course, the two are inevitably connected. The derivation of content for the curriculum – what is taught or not taught (see Eisner's *Null Curriculum*), what subjects are accorded high and low status and who is taught what, are all arguably aspects of the hidden curriculum. So, too, is how we teach the content – because differing teaching styles imply differing classroom climates and levels of pupil participation. The 'nurturant conditions', to use Joyce and Weil's (1980) phrase, are associated with different models of teaching that have a wide and differential impact on pupils – a point that we will touch on again later.

Eisner (1979) argues that these three dimensions of the curriculum – formal, hidden, and null – are the 'curricula that all schools teach'. It is important that we retain this sense of the differential impact of schooling as we read, reflect and teach. Eisner (*vide* 1979) points to five basic orientations to the curriculum that underly the purposes of schooling. Others have described similar influences: Lawton (1983), for example, discusses three or four basic educational ideologies; and Carr and Kemmis (1983) identify eight traditions in the study of education.

The differences between these ideas are less important than the general point. Behind any educational enterprise there is an ideological or philosophical force or forces pushing it forward, which provide a context or set of parameters in which to consider that form of schooling. Schooling and education are always embedded in a set of wider values and although they are often vague, implicit and even contradictory, it is important for us to realise their existence, because to some extent they control and inhibit our freedom of action and inevitably our purpose.

The first of Eisner's orientations is the 'development of cognitive processes'. Here the emphasis is on developing pupils' intellectual capacity and helping them learn how to learn more effectively. The second, 'academic rationalism' refers to the induction of pupils into worthwhile activities and forms of knowledge. The goal is the developing of an educated person, one who is competent in and familiar with the products of humanity's highest achievements. By engaging with these ideas and achievements the individual will inevitably develop rationality and acquire wisdom. The third orientation is 'personal relevance', and its most common expression is the child-centred curriculum. This approach requires that the curriculum and the teacher are aware of each pupil's abilities, experience and predisposition, and that a course of study is developed which builds on those unique qualities. The fourth orientation is 'social adaptation and social reconstruction'. In this approach it is the society's needs that are paramount and the school's purpose is seen explicitly as serving these needs. The billion dollar investment in the USA in science and math curricula in the decade following the Russian success with Sputnik in 1957 is an example of this. So, too, is the recent emphasis on vocational education in the UK and the instrumental nature of many national curricula in the Third World. Finally, Eisner points to the idea of 'curriculum as technology'. Here the emphasis is not so much on the aims or context of curricula but on the means of achieving them. It is an approach that values efficiency, the measurement of observable achievement, and making schools, teachers and curricula accountable. Mastery teaching, standardised tests, systematic instruction and school accountability are all examples of this tendency. The behavioural objectives model for curriculum planning that we will soon be discussing is perhaps the most common example of this orientation.

In this brief description of the five orientations we have tried not to let our personal feelings creep in too much. More importantly, we have not claimed that one orientation is necessarily better than another. Each has been discussed because it enables us more clearly to analyse the purpose of schooling. They provide us with a context within which to consider our own practice and aspirations. Also, it is unlikely that any school or educational system will exhibit characteristics of just one orientation. They are more likely to be found in combination. A useful exercise is to create a matrix using the five orientations and contemporary examples of schooling in England and Wales. Such a matrix would look a little like Figure 9.1.

There are virtually as many models of how to go about developing the curriculum, as there are definitions of the term. Model development is a game that academics play and on the whole it is of little help to teachers, because many models tend to be descriptive rather than prescriptive or

Figure 9.1   The five orientations of schooling

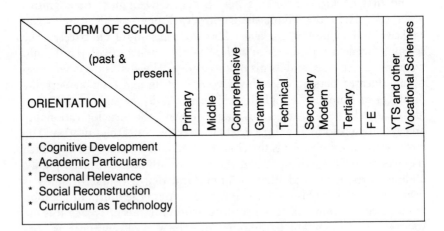

FORM OF SCHOOL (past & present) ORIENTATION	Primary	Middle	Comprehensive	Grammar	Technical	Secondary Modern	Tertiary	F E	YTS and other Vocational Schemes
* Cognitive Development * Academic Particulars * Personal Relevance * Social Reconstruction * Curriculum as Technology									

specific. They describe their originator's somewhat idiosyncratic view of the educational world, which may or may not be very interesting, and give little information to the practitioner on how to proceed. Naturally, there are exceptions, and in the following section we do describe a curriculum model that we believe possesses some practical utility. There are also a number of models that deserve mention on the grounds of tradition, usage or appositeness. To two of these we now briefly turn.

The Tyler model

The best known of the curriculum models is that associated with Ralph Tyler, derived from his seminal book *Basic Principles of Curriculum and Instruction* (1949). So ubiquitous is Tyler's model that many claim that it is the *only* way to develop curricula. Somewhat dismayed by the capricious and whimsical, if not downright sloppy, approach to curriculum development that he witnessed in the US in the 1940s, Tyler proposed as an antidote a systematic and beguilingly simple approach to curriculum planning based around four questions:

1 What educational purposes should the school seek to attain?
2 What educational experiences can be provided that are likely to attain these purposes?
3 How can these educational experiences be effectively organised?
4 How can we determine whether these purposes are being attained?

The so-called 'Tyler rationale' is often expressed in an even more simplified form:

Objectives
↓
Content
↓
Organisation
↓
Evaluation

The Tyler model has been enormously influential, so much so that most curriculum or lesson plans appear to be based on this approach to some extent. Two points should be made about the model at the outset. The first is that by beginning with objectives one begs the question: where do they come from? Some of Tyler's students, who became important curriculum figures in their own right, provided some answers. Benjamin Bloom (1956) and his colleagues produced a taxonomy of educational objectives that provide a ready-made solution for the problem. Hilda Taba (1962) proposed a needs assessment stage that precedes the derivation of objectives. These solutions have served to satisfy most practitioners, but in many ways the problem still remains a real one. The second point relates to the evaluative aspect of the model. The only way to evaluate this type of curriculum scheme is through observing some change in behaviour on the part of the pupil that signifies achievement of the objective. In turn, that objective has to be expressed in behavioural terms so that the achievement can be observed and evaluated. In its pure form the model looks something like the diagram shown in Figure 9.2

Figure 9.2   The flow of the Tyler model

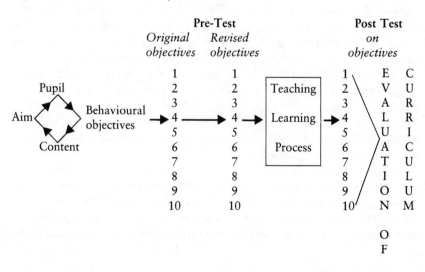

In the diagram, behavioural objectives result from some interaction between the general aim of the curriculum, the content to be taught, and the perceived pupil characteristics. The resulting list of objectives is then tested on the class and as a consequence possibly changed. This provides a base line measure of the pupils' achievement. The teaching/learning process then ensues and the curriculum episode ends with another test that serves to assess the overall pupil achievement on the curriculum. Rarely is the process like this. Testing, particularly the original test, is often omitted. So too is the revision of objectives. Also, the objectives are usually not established with any degree of precision. But the objectives approach is seen in one form or another in most curriculum designs.

Unfortunately, the objectives model is no panacea. Although it is suitable for certain teaching/learning situations its almost universal application is deleterious. There are now a number of well-established critiques of the behavioural objectives model (*eg* Eisner 1979, Stenhouse 1975, Rudduck and Hopkins 1985), but I will briefly rehearse some of the objections here. First, the objectives model trivialises the nature of knowledge. By fitting a subject into an objectives format there is the danger that the essence of, say, history will be reduced to a recitation of the Kings and Queens of England . . . It is very difficult to represent the deep structure of a subject – in this case, the historical method of enquiry, in an objectives format. How does one prepare an objective or series of objectives for appreciating *Hamlet*? So although the objectives approach may be very effective in transmitting information or skills it is unsuited to more complex forms of knowledge. Second, the objectives models tends to make for predictable pupil outcomes. This is to be welcomed when one is concerned with mathematical or scientific formulae, but to be regretted when one is concerned with poetry or art appreciation. Third, the model does not accord with reality. The teaching/learning process in general does not work like that. We teach in a more idiosyncratic and capricious way; often long periods of effort are followed by a sudden burst of understanding. It is only infrequently that we learn in carefully-packaged, uniform and relatively short periods of time. Fourth, the approach, although it often increases the clarity of educational programmes, does little, for reasons already outlined, to increase the quality of educational performance. Finally, the model ignores the ethical, moral and political imperatives surrounding schooling. Questions such as, 'Is this the appropriate content to teach?' are of no importance in this approach.

In discussing the objectives model we have tried to point both to its advantages and its drawbacks. It is the most common form of curriculum design. It has had enormous influence, but is appropriate only in certain, often instrumental, subject areas. Later we will propose a process model as a more appropriate means of dealing with more complex subject areas.

Lawton's Model

The other approach to curriculum design that we will briefly describe, although not as well known or as useful as Tyler's (being descriptive rather than prescriptive), is that associated with Denis Lawton (*vide* Lawton 1973, 1983). His basic idea is of the curriculum as being a selection from the culture and he argues for a cultural analysis approach to curriculum.

A slightly adapted version of his model appears in Figure 9.3.

Figure 9.3 Lawton's Model

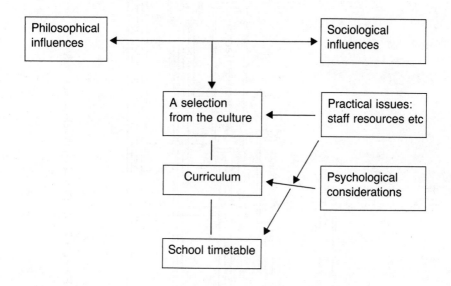

Lawton has an eminently commonsense approach to curriculum in his writing. We find his 'selection from culture' notion very helpful, especially the tension or dialectic that exists between philosophical approaches *eg* Hirst's forms of knowledge, and the sociological or relativist attitude of writers like Young.

Lawton originally envisaged psychology as operating on the selection from the culture, but given current constraints practical issues may be more appropriate. Certainly psychological considerations play (or should play) an important part in shaping the curriculum and in its presentation to pupils. To us Lawton's model has two main virtues: first, its central organising concept of curriculum as a selection from the culture; second, the prominence it gives to philosophical, sociological and psychological

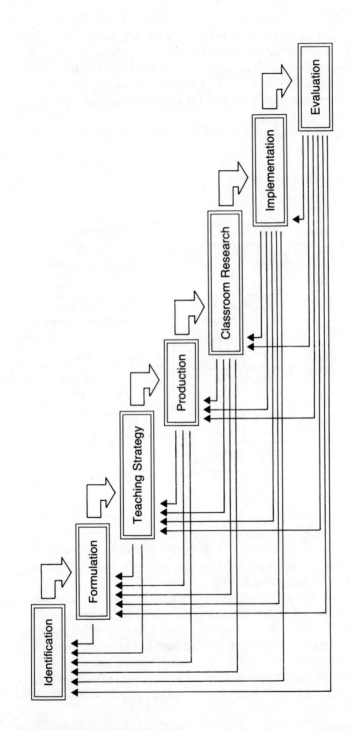

Figure 9.4   A curriculum development cycle

factors in determining the curriculum. But as we said previously, it is a descriptive model and its utility is limited because it gives teachers no indication of how to proceed. It is to a curriculum development model that offers such practical advice that we now turn.

A model for curriculum development

Figure 9.4 represents our model for curriculum development.[1] There are seven major stages in the model; each stage has its own kind of task, its own kind of process and its own product (see Figure 9.5).

Figure 9.5   The seven stages in the curriculum development model

Task	Process	Product
1 *Identify* what job the curriculum has to do	*Analyse* the situation	A clear *purpose* for curriculum development
2 *Formulate* a means of achieving the purpose	*Design* a curriculum concept	A promising *theoretical model* of the curriculum
3 *Select* an appropriate *teaching strategy* for the curriculum	*Establish* principles of procedure for students and teachers when using the curriculum	A specific *teaching/learning* strategy
4 *Produce* the curriculum delivery system	*Develop* the means required to present and maintain the curriculum	An *operational curriculum*
5 *Experiment* with the curriculum on student learning and the school	*Refine* the model through classroom research and regular improvements	A *refined curriculum*
6 *Implement* the curriculum throughout the school in other settings	*Change* general practice to the new curriculum	A *widely used curriculum*
7 *Evaluate* the effects of the curriculum on student learning	*Evaluate* how effective the curriculum is	A *proven* curriculum

At any point in curriculum development, difficulties may emerge which require returning to an earlier cycle and redoing the work. Alternatively,

[1] Based on a 1977 paper by Dr Maurice Gibbons, Professor of Education at Simon Fraser University, British Columbia. Gibbons' work on self-directed learning has had a major impact on education in North America; he is currently committed to developing the Universal curriculum.

an opportunity for a major improvement may emerge which makes reconsideration of the earlier work desirable. When the whole cycle is successfully completed, so much will have been learned in the process that the curriculum developer will be well equipped to begin again.

Although the cycle has seven major stages it is, of course, not necessary to complete each stage in order to produce an effective product. An individual teacher might only engage in the Formulation, Teaching Strategy and Production stages if s/he simply wanted to design a new unit. Another teacher may start with classroom research, then find out that the teaching strategy needs altering and, having done that, go back to classroom research again. Alternatively, a fairly major curriculum innovation would most probably require work in each cycle. In a similar sense, the model is generic in so far as it applies to teachers wanting to develop a unit or a course as well as to curriculum developers on major national projects. The model is prescriptive because, as compared with the descriptive models discussed earlier, it provides a guide to action; it helps teachers and others become more systematic and reflective about the curriculum development task.

The model is also relatively value free, in so far as it represents no overt world view (except one that encourages systematic and self-conscious planning and reflection on the part of teachers). This enables the range of ideological perspectives on the curriculum to be accommodated.

An illustration of this last point is given in Figure 9.6, which summarises a great deal of information about curriculum development. The first column contains the elements of the curriculum development cycle. The second column lists the activities that traditionally occur in each of the seven stages. These are activities that tend to underplay the teacher's role and occur mainly as the result of some external initiative by, for example, the Department of Education. Most teachers will recognise these activities. The third column represents teacher-based activities that can also occur within each of these stages as an alternative to the traditional approach. The table clearly illustrates that teacher- or school-based approaches to curriculum development are both available and viable. The table is not supposed to be taken too literally (or seriously). It certainly does not imply a dichotomy between the two approaches. Its main purpose is to illustrate how a range of experiences, aspirations and activities can be contained within the model. In the following discussion of the stages, however, illustrations of different approaches will be discussed.

Identification
The *identification* stage establishes a clear purpose for the curriculum. It is the rationale; if there is no purpose or rationale then there is no point in proceeding. Curricula are, of course, open to varying purposes, a number of which we have already discussed. A well known polarity

Figure 9.6   Alternative approaches to curriculum development

STAGE	TRADITIONAL	TEACHER-BASED
IDENTIFICATION	Prescribed Curriculum/ Forms of Knowledge	Community based or Pupil Needs
FORMULATION	Behavioural Objectives	Process Model & Principles of Procedure
TEACHING STRATEGY	Teacher centred, didactic	Enquiry/discovery approaches, active learning etc.
PRODUCTION	Centrally produced curricula	Locally developed programs
CLASSROOM RESEARCH	Quantitative analysis	Doing research in your classroom
IMPLEMENTATION	Fidelity	Mutual adaptation
EVALUATION	Quantitive, empirical and objective	Qualitative, illuminative and subjective

within this stage is the distinction between classic and romantic approaches to the curriculum. Lawton's (1973) view of the debate is as follows:

Classical	*Romantic*
Subject-centred	Child-centred
Skills	Creativity
Instruction	Experience
Information	Discovery
Obedience	Awareness
Conformity	Originality
Discipline	Freedom

He continues:

When it comes to questions of knowledge and curriculum the two views might be polarised as follows (but to subdivide in this way may be unfair to the Romantic view as the following list is set out in the Classical framework):

Classical	*Romantic*
Objectives:	*Processes:*
Acquiring knowledge	'Living' attitudes and values
Content:	*Experience:*
Subjects	Real-life topics and projects

Methods:

| Didactic instruction | Involvement |
| Competition | Co-operation |

Evaluation:

| By tests (teacher set) and examinations (public and competitive) | Self-assessment (in terms of self-improvement) |

Inevitably these views are stereotypical but they do give an indication of the types of activities that can flow from such an orientation. The classical view has probably been best stated by Hirst in his concept of 'forms of knowledge.' Hirst (*vide* Hirst and Peters 1970) argues that we can distinguish seven forms of knowledge:

1 Formal logic and mathematics
2 The physical sciences
3 'Our awareness and understanding of our own and other people's minds'
4 Moral judgement and awareness
5 Aesthetic experience
6 Religious
7 Philosophical

Lawton (1973) summarises Hirst's position by saying that he justifies the categorisation of knowledge into these seven forms on the grounds that all concepts belong to distinct categories, which are marked out by 'certain fundamental, ultimate or categorical concepts of a most general kind which other concepts in the category presuppose'. A good example of the influence of this is found in recent DES/HMI publications on the curriculum.

The alternative notion, as represented by the 'romantic' argument, is that the curriculum should be based on the pupils' needs: that we must diagnose them and then build a curriculum around them. The concept of needs can be extended to the community and this provides the rationale for many CSE Mode 3 courses.

From even this brief discussion it can be seen that the identification stage is not only very important but also fraught with opposing views. Two other sources of curriculum purpose, relevant to the contemporary UK scene, need to be discussed. First is the function of curriculum in the eyes of central government. Curriculum innovations like TVEI begin with the government (in this case the MSC) identifying the purpose of the curriculum and then allowing LEAs to complete the curriculum development cycle. The other very powerful source of curriculum initiative is the examination boards. Although times are changing a little, past examination papers still play an important part in the identification stage of curriculum development.

Formulation

The formulation stage involves developing new ideas or improving old ones already developed which promise to fulfil the purpose already identified for the curriculum. In other words it offers strategies for answering the question: what is the best design which can be treated to fulfil the rationale for the curriculum?

As we have discussed already, behavioural objectives are the most commonly used method for formulating the curriculum; but teachers also realise that they are not the only way. Behavioural objectives are an excellent means for teaching skills or evaluating rote learning. However, they can be counter-productive in more complex and sophisticated content areas. For example, it is difficult to formulate behavioural objectives for a lesson on *Hamlet* or poetry appreciation and still remain faithful to the subject matter. The over-use of behavioural objectives has sometimes tended to reduce, say, the study of history to a series of dates or geography to a recitation of capes and bays. Stenhouse (1975) has said that 'Education as induction into knowledge is successful to the extent that it makes the behavioural outcomes of the students unpredictable.' In situations such as these it is better to put pre-specified behavioural objectives aside, and utilise some other organising principle.

The process model is an alternative. This name was coined by Stenhouse to describe his alternative approach to curriculum development as exemplified in the *Humanities Curriculum Project* (*vide* Stenhouse 1975, Rudduck and Hopkins 1985). The process model does not specify the behaviour the student is to acquire after having engaged in a learning activity, rather it describes an educational encounter. It identifies a situation in which children are to work, a problem with which they are to cope, or a task in which they are to engage. By the use of the process model teachers can formulate educational encounters that respect both the child and the integrity of the knowledge with which they interact.

There are three basic approaches to developing a curriculum on a process model. The first is the approach identified with the work of Eisner (*vide* 1979). Like many others Eisner was dissatisfied with the behavioural objectives approach, for reasons similar to the ones previously discussed. He advocated the use of expressive objectives in the areas where behavioural (or in his terms instructional) objectives were inappropriate. The expressive objective defines an educational encounter without specifying what the pupil is to learn from that encounter. Eisner (quoted in Stenhouse, 1975) says that 'an expressive objective provides both the teacher and the student with an invitation to explore, defer, or focus on issues that are of peculiar interest or import to the inquirer. An expressive objective is evocative rather than prescriptive.'
He continues by giving examples:

Statements of expressive objectives might read:
1   To interpret the meaning of *Paradise Lost*.
2   To examine and appraise the significance of *The Old Man and the Sea*.
3   To develop a three-dimensional form through the use of wire and wood.
4   To visit the zoo and discuss what was of interest there.

   What should be noted about such objectives is that they do not specify what the student is to be able to do after he engages in an educational activity; rather they identify the type of encounter he is to have.

While entirely in sympathy with Eisner's argument we find his examples very loose; they provide no structure within which pupils or teachers can effectively explore their new found freedom. The lack of structure, guidance or parameters is a serious drawback and will inevitably lead to aimless teaching and spasmodic learning.

   A more satisfactory avenue for the process model is provided by Jerome Bruner and his concept of structure (Bruner, 1960; 1966). Following the logic of philosophers like Hirst, Bruner argues that each discipline has a structure which determines the way knowledge evolves or is produced within it. In History, for example, knowledge is produced through locating, analysing and making judgements based upon evidence. This historical method determines the way in which historical knowledge is developed. Similarly in science, knowledge advances through controlled experimentation commonly known as the scientific method. Bruner argues that this structure provides an effective model for teaching and learning. Curricula can be formulated by following the method of 'real' historians or scientists; using the historical or scientific method to structure the curriculum. Instead of teaching historical or scientific knowledge we teach how to do history or science and accumulate our knowledge in this way. Bruner would argue that we should introduce pupils to the process of knowledge. In his own words 'Knowledge is a process not a product'. He further argues that 'any body of knowledge can be presented in a form simple enough so that any particular learner can understand it in a recognisable form.' The implication of this is that the historical or scientific approach to learning can and should be introduced in the primary school. These ideas and processes are then refined and become more sophisticated as one goes through the school: hence his notion of the spiral curriculum. Although this approach to curriculum building may appear somewhat novel, many of the Schools Council curriculum projects were built on this model. The *History 13–16*, *Science 5–13* and, of course, Bruner's influential *Man, a Course of Study'* (MACOS) are all examples of these. However, not all curriculum subjects are dignified by the label 'discipline' – so how does one proceed here?

   'Principles of procedure' was the approach that Stenhouse and his colleagues adopted in the *Humanities Curriculum Project*. Faced with producing a curriculum on controversial issues for pupils of school leaving age in a area with no established tradition, they began by specifying the principles upon which the curriculum should be based. The following two extracts illustrate their approach.

The Humanities Curriculum Project, sponsored by the Schools Council and the Nuffield Foundation, was set up in September 1967 to extend the range of choice open to teachers working in the humanities with adolescent pupils.

The work of the Project has been based upon five major premises:
1 that controversial issues should be handled in the classroom with adolescents;
2 that teachers should not use their authority as teachers as a platform for promoting their own views;
3 that the mode of enquiry in controversial areas should have discussion rather than instruction as its core;
4 that the discussion should protect divergence of view among participants;
5 that the teacher as chairperson of the discussion should have responsibility for quality and standards in learning.

If teachers have reserve about any of these premises, the easiest procedure is to adopt them with due scepticism as an exploratory tactic. This will allow them to use the experimental findings of the project for support as they evaluate the likely effects of changing the premises.

The aim of the Project is to develop an understanding of social situations and human acts and of the value issues which they raise. (from Rudduck 1983:8)

In this project, discussion was the main mode of inquiry and the teacher acted as a neutral chairperson. Discussion was informed and disciplined by evidence: that is, items of material from history, journalism, literature, philosophy, art, photography, statistics might be introduced ... Here are summarised the kinds of demand which this curriculum project made on teachers, pupils and schools:

New skills for most teachers
1 Discussion rather than instruction.
2 Teacher as neutral chairperson – that is, not communicating his or her point of view.
3 Teacher talk reduced to about 15%.
4 Teacher handling material from different disciplines.
5 New modes of assessment.

New skills for most pupils
1 Discussion, not argument or debate.
2 Listening to, and talking to, each other, not just to the teacher.
3 Taking initiatives in contributing – not being cued in by teacher.

New content for many classrooms
1 Explorations of controversial social issues, often in the sensitive areas (*eg* race relations, poverty, family, relations between the sexes).
2 Evidence reproduced in an original form – no simplifications of language.

Organisational demands on schools
1 Small discussion groups, each with teacher chairperson.
2 Mixed ability groups found by many schools to be desirable.
3 Non-row formation of chairs – circle or rectangle appearing to be desirable.
(Rudduck 1984:57–58)

From these considerations a set of highly specific principles were developed that provided a structure for both pupils and teachers despite the open-ended nature of the curriculum and the radical teaching/learning process it adopted.

In contrasting the behavioural objectives and process models we are not arguing that one is necessarily better than the other. They are complementary approaches; each has the potential of working well but in different areas.

Teaching strategy

Implicit in the formulation stage is a teaching strategy that transmits the content of the curriculum. In our view the teaching strategy is equally as important as the content that the curriculum delivers. There was a time when many teachers felt that there was only one way to teach . . . the didactic or 'mug and jug' approach . . . but fortunately times change. We are becoming increasingly aware that pupils learn in different ways and all are not amenable to a uniform approach. The Schools Council in their advocacy of enquiry/discovery learning, and the more recent curriculum innovations like TVEI that promote 'active learning', are all moves away from the traditional approach.

It is also important to consider at this stage of curriculum development the various assessment procedures associated with the curriculum. The adoption of profiling, for example, has a powerful impact upon teaching style.

Recently Bruce Joyce (1981) has espoused 'flexibility' as a guiding principle for *professional* development. This represents

'a view of humankind that envisions people-in-teaching and people-in-learning as the creators of themselves through their interaction. Flexibility from that stance, becomes an essential characteristic of the teacher as s/he creates her/himself, offers possibilities to his/her students, and creates the schools of the future.'

A central component of flexibility is the teacher's ability intelligently to use a variety of teaching approaches, to match them to different goals, and adapt them to different student styles and characteristics. To quote Joyce again: 'Competence in teaching stems from the capacity to reach out to differing children and to create a rich and multi-dimensional environment for them.' In their *Models of Teaching* (1980), Joyce and Weil describe four families of teaching approaches; the information-processing; the personal; the social interaction; and the behavioural models. They argue that 'since no single teaching strategy can accomplish every purpose, the wise teacher will master a sufficient repertoire of strategies to deal with the specific kinds of learning problems he or she faces.' They suggest that teachers begin by mastering one model from each family, and then add others as they are found useful to each individual's particular teaching speciality. It is easier to learn models in collaboration with others (*eg* a colleague or student teacher), because the other person can help coach you (and vice-versa) on the finer points of teaching style. We strongly recommend Bruce Joyce and Marsha Weils' *Models of Teaching* as an authoritative and invaluable resource on teaching strategies.

Production

Production is the stage where the ideas and aspirations are operationalised. At the end of this stage the curriculum is ready to go, ready to be used and shared. The scale of production will vary according to the size of the product, whether it be a teacher producing a new unit or a team working on a national curriculum project. Nevertheless, resources have to be collected and organised, staff trained in the new teaching methods and the timetable possibly altered.

The following extract from the original model – although somewhat 'North American' in style – gives a good indication of what is required at this stage (see Figure 9.7).

a production needs
- materials
- methods training
- role changes
- environments
- organisation

b organise for production:
- cover arranged to free teachers regularly for preparation
- time line for completion of materials and arrangements set
- working teams appointed

c produce materials and arrangements:
- planning committee receives materials and monitors arrangements
- critical examination of all materials and other elements of setting: they are revised
- materials pilot – tested and modified from feedback; the gaps are filled and further revisions made

d operational model:
- 'central planning' declares the curriculum operational

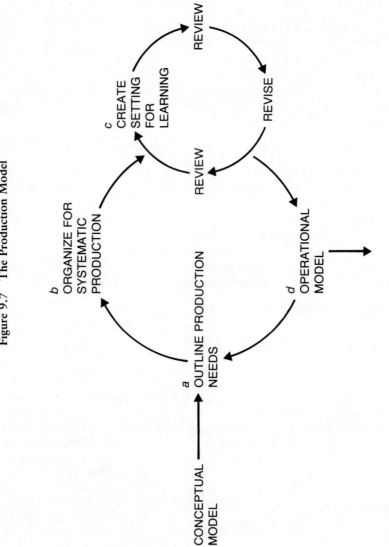

Figure 9.7   The Production Model

Gibbons (1977) describes the strategies required for the production stage like this:

Production: Strategies for making the curriculum operational; producing guides, texts and other materials; creating settings, training personnel, and organising the necessary support systems. Strategies for answering the questions, what must be prepared to make this curriculum design usable? How can this be done efficiently and effectively?

He then gives an example:

The school's curriculum development committee outlined the tasks, divided the work among sub-committees and drew up a production schedule. A new space was found and set up like an editorial room. A teaching handbook of skills and content was written and reproduced. Teaching materials were prepared, reference libraries assembled, and training sessions on the teaching method were provided.

Classroom research

The purpose of this stage is to field-test the curriculum in the classroom, and to refine it through regular improvement. It is important that teachers retain an enquiring and experimental attitude towards a curriculum, irrespective of whether they have produced it themselves or adapted it from elsewhere. A curriculum proposal should never be taken as given but rather regarded as a working hypothetical proposal. Stenhouse (1975) remarks that 'the proposal is not to be regarded as an unqualified recommendation but rather as a provisional specification claiming no more than to be worth putting to the test of practice. Such proposals claim to be intelligent rather than correct.' The ways in which teachers engage in systematic self-study *and* test theory in practice are essentially the same: ie through the use of classroom research methods.

Classroom research is normally associated with outside researchers measuring the effect and outcomes of classroom activity. In a teacher-based context the phrase has a very different meaning. It implies that the teacher is actively engaged in critically reflecting on his/her teaching by utilising classroom based research methods. This is a fundamental role for a teacher who takes professional development seriously, for it is only by understanding our present behaviours, that we can expect to extend or change them. As chapter 8 is concerned mainly with classroom research methods no detail of them is given here.

The purpose of this stage is to revise the curriculum in the light of experience and consequently to produce a better curriculum and so improve the teaching/learning process. This is as far as most teachers need to go. When, however, we are dealing with larger curriculum projects then we need to consider the implementation and evaluation stages. Present trends make this more likely in the future.

Implementation

Implementation is an aspect of curriculum development that has recently
received a great deal of attention. The predominant modality in the
traditional approach is 'fidelity': the expectation that a new curriculum
will be faithfully implemented and exactly reproduced in the receiving
environment. The situation usually occurs when curriculum development
begins centrally and then diffuses outwards. Often this expectation is not
realised because the context of the local environment is not considered.
Under the teacher-based paradigm there is the expectation that the
curriculum will be adapted to the local situation. The norm of mutual
adaptation implies that both the curriculum and the school or classroom
will change as the process of implementation occurs. Thus, the teacher
exercises control over the adoption of curriculum in his/her teaching
situation.

The implementation process is multi-dimensional, involving change at
a number of different levels. Five components of implementation can be
identified. These involve changes in: organisation; materials; role and
behaviour; knowledge; and beliefs.

Changes in organisation (eg restructuring the timetable to
accommodate new options) and materials (eg the introduction of a new
published reading scheme) are achieved relatively easily. Indeed, it is
these two components of implementation that are most often tackled; to
the detriment of the others. Yet it is on the necessary changes in teaching
style, understanding and commitment, that the success or failure of
implementation depends. These are, of course, the most difficult to effect
as they also require heavy involvement in time and inservice provision.
Successful implementation depends on the meanings and attitudes that
teachers give and have towards the curriculum. To recall Stenhouse's
evocative phrase 'there is no curriculum development without teacher
development'.

Evaluation

A distinction is often made between formative and summative
evaluation. The former is concerned with providing ongoing information
to improve the quality of the curriculum. Summative evaluation is
concerned to provide a judgement on the success of the curriculum. The
formative aspects of evaluation occur in our model at the classroom
research stage. This final stage is more concerned with summative
judgement, on how good the curriculum is after it has been implemented
for a period of time. As such, summative evaluation is outside the scope
of our book, but the regular monitoring of curriculum or self-evaluation
is not; this central aspect of the effective school is dealt with in more
detail in chapter 8.

After the conclusion of this cycle, the process of development begins again with the search for new opportunities for growth and new purpose in development.

'No Curriculum Development without Teacher Development'

The hidden curriculum behind the curriculum model is that it is a method that teachers can employ to make their curriculum planning more effective. It is a process not only for curriculum development but also for making teachers more skilful and more effective; of putting them more in control of the curriculum and the teaching/learning process. Only teachers can create good teaching, and thus it is imperative that they occupy a central role in developing curriculum and that *they* develop with the curriculum.

Stenhouse adopted this principle as a central point of his work and it is a theme that will also be developed in chapter 11. But as a conclusion to the discussion of the curriculum model consider this quotation from the work of Lawrence Stenhouse:

'No curriculum development without teacher development', reads one of the poker-work mottoes we hung on our wall during the Humanities Project and haven't taken down. But that does not mean, as it often seems to be interpreted to mean, that we must train teachers in order to produce a world fit for curricula to live in. It means that by virtue of their meangingfulness, curricula are not simply instructional means to improve teaching but are expressions of ideas to improve teachers. Of course, they have a day-to-day instructional utility: cathedrals must keep the rain out. But the students benefit from curricula not so much because they change day-to-day instruction as because they improve teachers.

A curriculum, if it is worthwhile, expresses in the form of teaching materials and criteria for teaching a view of knowledge and a conception of the processes of education. It provides a framework in which the teacher can develop new skills and relate them as he does so to conceptions of knowledge and of learning.

Only in curricular form can ideas be tested by teachers. Curricula are hypothetical procedures testable only in classrooms. All educational ideas must find expression in curricula before we can tell whether they are day-dreams or contributions to practice. Many educational ideas are not found wanting because they cannot be found at all.

We must be dedicated to the improvement of schooling. The improvement of schooling is bound to be experimental: it cannot be dogmatic. The experiment depends on the exercise of the art of teaching and improves that art. The substantive content of the arts of teaching and learning is curriculum. (Rudduck and Hopkins 1985 pp 68–9)

Chapter 10

Moving beyond the cult of the individual

Putting the partnership into in-service collaboration on behalf of school development

"From now on I'm thinking only of me".
Major Danby replied indulgently with a superior smile: "But, Yossarian, suppose everyone felt that way."
"Then," said Yossarian, "I'd be a damned fool to feel any other way, wouldn't I?" (*Catch 22* Joseph Heller 1962)

This chapter is based on four main ideas:
1   School improvement has proved an elusive goal, partly because we have tended to back the wrong horse – the individual teacher.
2   This cult of the individual, as I have chosen to call it, has meant that 'in-service collaboration' has remained an empty vessel.
3   There are growing opportunities, to be explored in this chapter, to focus upon school improvement by moving beyond the cult of the individual and putting the partnership (between teachers, the advisory service, in-service providers, consultants, higher education courses and their tutors, etc) into real collaboration, so that it becomes something more than a notion. The aim is to achieve school improvement through a supportive partnership revolving around school-based research and development.
4   Whereas, traditionally, in-service experience has been gained externally to the school, this chapter rests on the assumption that all kinds of internal involvements fall within the purview of in-service activity. School-based in-service involvement is not considered a 'grey area'; far from it, it is seen as one of *the* central activities leading towards school improvement. In addition, it is considered that higher education, as an in-service provider, will increasingly adopt a crucial supporting role for school-based research and development.

Section One: The Context

This chapter concerns the in-service education and training of teachers (INSET) – a most topical subject. For all those involved in INSET, whether as participants or providers, these are heady days. In an article entitled *Waiting for the Whirlwind* (1986) Wragg claimed that: 'teachers are facing the most radical reshaping of in-service in their professional life-time'.

With the introduction of TRIST (TVEI-related In-Service Training) initiatives during the winter of 1985/86 and the new funding arrangements for INSET to be introduced in March 1987, there is a real chance that, as Wragg points out, Local Education Authorities will eschew a 'short-sighted, instrumental view' and fail to grasp the opportunity of establishing a genuine dialogue between teachers, schools, and in-service providers concerning effective INSET. Effective, that is, in the sense of bringing about genuine teacher and school development. Therein lies one of the questions centrally explored in this chapter – can INSET deliver both?

Sockett (1986), in a recent speech, posed (and answered) the following question:

Who decides what counts as the professional development of the teacher? For most of us here, I guess, we have as individuals decided. We have chosen our career routes which may have involved further study of the Masters kind . . . clearly the balance of concern and resources has to shift to the school as an institution. The University (UEA) has always worked with individuals not institutions: that is its ethos: even projects or INSET programmes which have focused on schools have focused on the enthusiast . . . My belief is that we must continue to support the individual, the enthusiast . . . The danger is that the more locally centralised decision-making becomes in terms of needs and needs assessment, the less the opportunity of individual initiative.

Yet, over the years, INSET has been the haven of individual initiative. INSET, characteristically, has been individualistic, competitive, acquisitive, instrumental, careerist and elitist; sometimes it has been seen as the passport to a 'better life' out of the classroom. In addition, it has seldom led to systematic school improvement. Yet, prior to the recent initiatives, mentioned above, changes in INSET were already afoot; they did not come out of the blue. Such changes were emanating from two sources:

1   A general agreement on the part of many in-service providers and commentators that there should be a shift of focus (on the part of INSET) to *the school* as the unit of change. This led to the emphasis during the 1970s and early 1980s on school-focused, school-centred and school-based INSET activities. While we will contend later in this chapter that these titles are far from interchangeable (they represent different ideological stances), they all point to the importance of matching INSET provision to the needs of teachers, teacher-teams within schools and schools themselves. It had almost reached the point where no-one expected INSET to be successful at the school level. In fact, it has been claimed that:

There is evidence to suggest that the more in-service training is institutionalised, the remoter it becomes from its addressees – the schools. (Bloch, JA, Bunder, W, Frey, K and Rost, J 1983)

In the UK, the James Report (1972) stimulated debate.

'In-service training . . . should begin in the schools. It is here that learning and teaching take place, curricula and techniques are developed and needs and deficiencies revealed. Every school should regard the continued training of its teachers as an essential part of its task, for which all members of staff share responsibility. (DES *Teacher Education and Training*, 1972).

For the first time it became possible to think of school-oriented INSET and staff development as being synonymous. In 1978, a national conference was organised by a sub-committee of ACSTT (Advisory Committee on the Supply and Training of Teachers), a consequence of which was the publication *Making INSET Work* which heralded that the 'process starts in your school'. This influential pamphlet claimed that:

too often in the past it (INSET) has been thought of only in terms of individual teachers attending courses which are designed and provided by outside agencies . . . (there is now a demand for) teachers and schools to plan their own INSET programmes in the light of needs which they have identified.

Pioneering LEAs took up this message and began working in the style described in the publication. The County of Avon, for example, was so serious about initiating such work that officials from this particular LEA approached the Schools Council's Programme One team and asked them to sponsor an LEA-wide project. The MSSD (*Materials for School-based Staff Development*) Project surveyed a range of activities over a two-year period and all this 'good practice' was collated in handbook form (see Oldroyd, Smith, and Lee, 1984). In a wider context, the OECD/CERI organisation supported a six-year programme (1975–81) of research and development into INSET (see Hopkins, 1986).

2   Those involved in providing INSET within higher education were beginning to make changes in their own (largely course-related) practice. Research-based courses began to appear – especially at centres such as CARE at the University of East Anglia and the Cambridge Institute of Education (see Elliott, 1981; Stenhouse, 1983; Walker, 1985)

A major component of INSET has always been secondment to award-bearing courses. Over the last decade such courses have experienced fundamental and radical changes (see Elliott, 1981; Holly, 1984c; Walker, 1985; Dadds, 1986). Elliott contends that

the traditional approach to the education of teachers is based on an instrumental, positivist assumption about the theory-practice relation . . . It is assumed that good practice is derived from a prior understanding of the theoretical principles discovered by researchers. Teachers go off on to courses to study research and develop their theoretical understanding, as temporary inhabitants of a theoretical culture.

Two points are pertinent concerning this traditional model:

a   It creates, and sustains, two cultures: that of the theory-laden researchers and disseminators and that of the practice-oriented teachers and schools (Rudduck, 1977; Holly and Wideen, 1986). When the in-serviced teacher attempts to return to his/her school to apply the principles gained on the course, he/she experiences an 'encounter of cultures'; the re-entry problem in this context constitutes the problem of applying the theory acquired on the course to everyday practice. But does the theory have any meaning for the practice?

b   How committed are the teacher course members to the theory which they have acquired – without active engagement – as passive recipients? Does this traditional model enable the learning teacher to 'own' the material? No wonder then that the teacher is engulfed by the school culture and the theory – his/her temporary garb – can be discarded with impunity. According to Turner (1986):

> For those lucky enough to have used their newly-acquired qualification to secure promotion it is relatively easy to get on with the new task and put off until tomorrow the implementation of all those secondment good intentions . . . For all re-entrants, though, whether promoted or not, the prospects for actually bringing about the kinds of change which secondment has suggested are daunting . . .

In this same article, Turner talks of the 'other staff waiting for the returnee to have 'settled down' and get 'those theories out of her system''. She concludes that to see secondment, as presently constituted, as a vehicle for effecting long-term changes in school practice, is a chimera. Holly and Wideen (1986) contend that the returning teacher can be seen as an 'innovation' (tainted by an alien culture) and Turner points out that 'innovation cannot be achieved unless the environment (the school in the context of the LEA) is receptive to change'. In similar vein, Ron Arnold HMI (as quoted by Elliott, 1981) maintains that:

> Experience has shown that the stimulating effect of an in-service course on one or two individuals has been neutralised on their return by the inability of the school to respond to it and to take advantage of what they have learned . . . it is only when a school has come to a decision as to which direction it should develop in, and analysed its training needs, that it can absorb and act upon the effects of that training.

We find that a reasonable statement. Elliott, however, argues that not only does it rest on the assumption that the theory-practice relation is an instrumental one and that the solution to the re-entry problem is the responsibility of the schools, but also that:

> . . . the contribution of long courses to the improvement of schooling depends on the prior readiness of the receiving institution to utilise the knowledge gained by the student. The individual teacher is utterly dependent on the institution.

One gets the impression that Elliott himself finds this unacceptable. We would contend that individual teachers, if they are to be successful in their change efforts, need the backing of a supportive institutional culture. It is a question of symbiosis.

In fact, in a series of stimulating articles, Elliott (1977, 1981 and 1983) has promoted the importance of the professional development of individual teachers. In so doing he has invited them to pit their course-gained insights against their schools as institutions, which, according to the Elliott line, inevitably promote bureaucratic, instrumental rationality within the line management, managerialist paradigm. What he fails to countenance is that schools and individuals can develop in harmony; change, in his view, occurs solely according to a dialectical, conflict model in which individuals are encouraged to investigate (and then act against) the institutional constraints within which they are labouring (see Holly, 1984a). Elliott's 'blind-spot' will be further explored later in this chapter.

Elliott's solution was to encourage (and equip) teachers as researchers within the framework of award-bearing courses. He aimed to engender self-awareness on the part of the participating teachers whose insights of their particular, concrete situations and their roles within them would lead to committed, counter-cultural action. A further aim was to ground the theoretical inputs of the course in the participants' particular situations, thus encouraging interactive dialogue between what Elliott refers to as naturalistic enquiry, and theoretical and practical concerns. To facilitate this process, research-based courses were introduced on a part-time basis. While, as Elliott admits, this move might prevent 'deep immersion' in the course, it relates theory to practice in a more urgent (that is, weekly) sense. The alternative, of course, to deep immersion in the culture of the course is deep immersion in the culture of the school (Elliott refers to the latter as being 'imprisoned'). But, again, the point rests on the assumption that the culture of the school is alien to the notion of research-based development. Elliott's stance is best described in his own words:

Now, of course, institutional constraints in course members' own schools may prevent them from acting on the insights generated by naturalistic research. But they cannot simply cast them to one side. Individual insight establishes a tension within the practical culture between the goals of the individual teacher and those embedded in the institutional structures he confronts. The individual may have to live with varying degrees of ambiguity but will be motivated to discover ways in which he can share his insights with other colleagues. He will form alliances at various levels of the system and in time the common understandings generated will provide the platform for institutional change. Individuals are not entirely powerless members of the institutions in which they operate.

This view of individually-generated change in schools, referred to elsewhere as a 'gigantic act of faith' (Holly, 1984), permeates the work of

Elliott. This chapter aims to explore an alternative model of research-based development in schools. Elliott himself suggests four directions worthy of exploration. First, while individuals are encouraged to become catalysts for change, they are also exhorted to enter into 'collaboration with key participants' (assuming, of course, that those key participants are still willing to collaborate – see Holly, 1986a). Elliott surmises that the 'more hierarchical control there is in the school over the actions of teachers the more difficult it is for super-ordinates to collaborate in research with sub-ordinates' – and vice-versa?

Second, much 'depends on the institution's capacity to support reflection and discussion among its members'. Again, Elliott hypothesises that the 'staff will only collaborate in naturalistic research when the institution respects the individual as a dynamic force.' It is, therefore, a question of changing the school's culture; the norms, values and expectations which regulate its daily life – this is Elliott's third point. Teacher expectations (and past experience) can militate against collaboration. Teachers have been weaned on the recitation model and the passivity of positivism. As Elliott observes:

In many schools both research and in-service education are perceived as having personal rather than institutional value. They are not part of the practical culture of the schools. Teachers do not expect research conducted by a colleague on an in-service course to make too many demands on their time in school.

Rudduck (1977) maintains that during the process of dissemination of an innovation or of research there are interactive encounters between three cultures – those of the innovation, the disseminator group and the school – and that the 'professional culture of the recipient group . . . is rooted in institutions and in the values represented in the traditional curriculum.' Institutional inertia is a deep-seated, structural and cultural phenomenon which is impervious to individual 'irrationality'. As Rudduck observes:

The question is whether the culture of the workshop (or course) is strong enough to carry the lone individual through when he returns to his home ground, perhaps with the responsibility for introducing innovation into his school.

Miles (1964) sums up this debate when he argues that;

. . . there is a failure of linkage between systems; the detachment and euphoria which make time-limited systems so fascinating and productive, help to blind the participants to what they will be up against when they return to 'ordinary life' . . . the decisions reached on the cultural island may be unworkable, inappropriate or very difficult to communicate to those on the mainland.

Rudduck (1977) reaches the conclusion that disseminators should 'find ways of helping the recipient groups to develop both an understanding of the innovation itself and a capacity to make adaptations that are based on this understanding and on a realistic analysis of the circumstances and pressures of their schools and classrooms.'

Finally, Elliott outlines one solution to the problem of the isolation of the teacher-researcher ('given the constraints outlined the teacher-researcher can feel very isolated amongst his or her colleagues, and unsupported by them'); that of group registration. This entails a small team of staff members joining a research-based course with a negotiated research and development brief. Dadds (1986), Holly (1984c) and Walker (1985) as tutors leading similar research-based, award-bearing INSET courses, have attempted to follow up Elliott's pioneering work – and, in the process, to wrestle with some of the ambiguities of his stance. All three observers have sought ways of helping the individual course-based teacher-researcher cope with the culture clash identified by Elliott and Rudduck. Dadds has identified four approaches to course-based teacher research:

1   *idiosyncratic research*, which is based in the personal interests of the individual teacher. While this approach may 'score' heavily in terms of personal ownership of the research task and motivation – crucial components in any enterprise – it can be seen as an extension of the 'cult of the individual' with the individual teachers 'cocooned in the bubble of their own enthusiasms' (Dadds, 1986).

2   *altruistic research*, which is an extension of the first approach, but which involves the individual teacher researching an area likely to be of interest to his/her colleagues.

3   *negotiated research*, which centres on common ownership of the investigation. Staff involvement in the research project, according to Dadds, can combine both excitement and practical considerations and has a 'huge potential pay off'.

4   *commissioned research*, which is normally undertaken by means of LEA sponsorship.

In the experience of the authors, the last-mentioned approach certainly constitutes a growing trend (boosted by Wilcox, 1985). But as both Wragg (1986) and Dadds (1986) point out, commissioned research could become instrumental and hierarchical and not the manifestation of an organic local partnership (see Goddard, 1985). Negotiated research is the approach which Dadds sees as having the most potential in terms of school-wide 'take-up' of the research findings, as long as personal investment is not jettisoned along the way. It is a question of balance.

Our perspective in this chapter is largely determined by our role (and experience) as course tutors pondering the plight of school improvement while teaching on research-based courses at the Cambridge and West Glamorgan Institutes of Education. Two of us are involved with three such courses: a full-time advanced diploma course, which entails the seconded teachers undertaking a piece of school-based research, normally in a school other than their own; and two part-time courses – an advanced diploma and the MA in applied educational research – which both involve enquiry in the participating teacher's own school. In line with Elliott's earlier assertion, recent experience has taught us that the part-time arrangement, with the teacher having a continuing stake in his/her school is more natural, and more potentially productive, despite certain fairly predictable pitfalls largely arising from the teacher being a 'researcher' among his/her teaching colleagues and having to research within a non-researching, indeed anti-researching school culture.

Two of our recent full-time students arrived on the course without a research brief (from their respective schools). Both wanted to research 'the early months of headship'. One teacher undertook a lengthy search for a school willing to be researched (to earn herself an advanced diploma). She contacted at least six schools without success; yet she had read Schatzman and Strauss (1973) and kept smiling. Another teacher felt that the research 'wan't getting what was there', but got enough to stir up sufficient bad feeling to earn a 'closed release' category for her long study. We can only conclude – who has gained? Who needs it? When asked to speak to a recent conference on the theme of 'enquiry-based courses – implications for the schools', Holly was forced to argue that the title for the speech should read 'Schools (and their improvement) – implications for enquiry-based courses'. 'Unless we tackle the latter, enquiry or research-based courses will be in danger of becoming the latest academic con-trick. Who is fooling who? Who is colluding with the lack of improvement in schools?' (Holly, 1984c).

We mentioned earlier the pitfalls facing part-time students. They often complain that a course timetable does not coincide with the 'heartbeat of school life'; that, despite the rhetoric, course construction is neither negotiated nor conducted in the interests of school development. Moreover, part-timers face what has been called the 'weekly re-entry problem', a schizophrenic attempt to deny (while trying to further) one's research role and to continually combat the pressures towards marginalisation (of the research). There is a pressure to maintain both academic and school credibility – a pressure which is heightened by the school-based nature of the research. This same pressure can force teachers to do covert research and make it look overt; to wave the assignment through the staff room door and later announce its clearance. These teachers have to live with and within the institutional micro-politics; they have to wrestle with the problem of having to produce 'thick descriptions' of the underlying institutional values and assumptions. In doing so they are protected by a negotiated code of ethics; but who is actually protected by such agreements is another matter. Some schools, particularly small primaries, experience research fatigue arising from the headlong rush for personal self-advancement on the part of the researching member of staff. While courses may change, philosophically, their members may be working within a more traditional attitudinal framework.

In bringing schools, teachers and research-based courses into a more meaningful relationship, the general problems are four-fold. First, there is the tension between the right to privacy and the right to know (see Pring's article in Adelman, 1984). Who owns the data? Should confidentiality be respected? What happens to any 'guilty knowledge'? Second, who are the clients for the research? The researched? The head? The whole staff? What is the price of the 'democracy of discomfiture' (see Holly, 1984c)? On whose side is the researcher? Simons (1981) and MacDonald (1981) have both made interesting observations here. Who constitutes the sponsors and who the audience? Third, will the research/enquiry – as a *process* with *products* – have any lasting effects on the school being researched? Will the research be institutionalised (see Holly, 1984b)? Does the research and its findings have a lasting impact on the school – if that, of course, is the object? What is the *extent* of such an *impact over time*? Fourth, what is the nature of the enquiry? What is the relationship between the much-used (often interchangeably) concepts of enquiry, review, research and, indeed, evaluation (see Stenhouse's article in Adelman, 1984). Is there an ideology of enquiry? Does it not only signify a view of teaching and learning, but also an open-ended, autonomous (even emancipatory) explorative research stance? Does it entail *collaboration*? We tend to teach 'enquiry-based courses' collaboratively (the course members cross-reference with each other's research, support each other, etc.), but expect individual research to be conducted in the schools. Is there an illogicality here?

More specifically we would query two phrases often used to describe this kind of research. The first is the term *applied research*. Nowadays, it is not respectable to do un-applied research; even so, however, we would suggest that there are various interpretations of the term 'applied'. Does the phrase entail the application of someone's theory to someone else's practice? This would certainly be the case in what Stenhouse (1982) calls the agricultural-botanical paradigm of research (likewise Elliott's positivism). Is there implied here a division of theory and practice? Jennifer Nias coined the expression, 'action-research is applied research but applied research is not always action-research'. If action-research falls within a certain paradigm, presumably applied research crosses paradigms. Is applied research the modern, respectable and acceptable face of an increasingly unacceptable research paradigm? Perhaps the important question to ask is – in whose interests is the research taking place? Is it conducted in the interests of interest groups? (see Elliott, 1981b) Is it for the head and the senior management team? Or for the *collective* that is the school staff?

Applied research is the central theme explored by Walker (1985) who compares traditional research with the newly-emerging, course-stimulated '*school research*'. What does it look like?, he asks. In answering this question, he makes several pertinent points concerning school research:

- it is applied research in that it is *for* the school and is directly applicable (it is not research *on* schools);
- it aims to relate to an immediate issue in one's institution;
- it is not 'purified' but 'natural' and 'messy';
- it involves data collection, identification of issues and problems (which may not obviously present themselves – they have to be worked on, reformulated and worried over *during* the research), assessment of information sources, design of further enquiries, interpretation, and the *communication* of the improved understanding;
- it is akin to evaluation – of practice, performance and policy – both in teaching and in administration. Walker makes the point that school research is a consequence of, and feeds into, both the increasing professionalisation of teachers and the need for more systematic management of educational organisations.

Walker maintains that school research contains a central paradox – it attempts to combine the 'academic' taste for risk-taking and creativity with the 'applied' school mentality of playing it safe. In line with our own experience, Walker asserts that school research 'can be uncomfortable for the students' (ie the course-based teacher-researchers) and 'embarrassing for institutions' (see Holly, 1986a).

To put it bluntly, he says, no one gets an A for a routine piece of work. As a result some people get caught in a knot in which avoiding trouble is considered a necessity while taking risks is highly regarded.

Walker, in conclusion, argues that school research has five essential differences (as compared with other modes of research).

1 School research has less latitude, less independence; it occurs 'up close' to the train of events, which could be seen as an advantage (excellent access) and a disadvantage (it is trapped within the micro-politics/culture of the school). The teacher-researcher is forced to work within the school reality, within what is possible in the circumstances. Practicability, feasibility, utility and lack of manoeuvrability are important concepts in school research. Because they are immersed in the process they seek to research, it is impossible to approach the research either naively or with objectivity – if that is important. The teacher-researcher will share common understandings (the medium of communication) with the other participants, but must beware what Walker refers to as 'collusive distortion'.

2 School research, as Dadds has maintained, is a different kind of research because it is both negotiated and commissioned. This gives the teacher-researcher a real sense of role conflict; as colleague and researcher, he/she will inevitably have to offer a critique of his/her own culture. One's loyalty is, therefore, in doubt. The question also arises – who to negotiate with? Who constitutes the school? Dadds and Walker

both advocate that the staff should be drawn into taking some responsibility for negotiating the purpose and content of the research – thus becoming the 'contracted' audience.

3   Research, according to Walker, is essentially de-stabilising, there is 'potential to disturbing the existing 'patterns of relationship' and/or balance of power'. This fact renders the teacher-researcher vulnerable, according to Walker (see also Holly, 1984c), who maintains that:

> The researcher learns most, changes most, has most commitment to the project and most at stake if it fails . . . It is the researcher who is isolated and obsessive, working in places where in one sense he or she has little right to be, and so is constantly pitched into precarious and thinly held relations with others.

4   By taking up the researcher role, the teacher can lose the 'cover' of the school's culture (see Holly, 1986a). The research process is 'essentially disruptive of the status quo' because it challenges the 'taken-for-granted understandings' of the school's culture.

5   School-research takes reporting (its findings) seriously. The aim, hopefully, is for the research to have an impact – for it to have practical outcomes – and Walker contends that novel forms of communicating the research are in urgent need of investigation. The fruits of the research must be communicable.

Overall, however, Walker maintains that school research typifies the characteristics of applied research. It could be argued, to extend Walker's viewpoint, that school research is 'real' research in that it is attempting to address real-life, school-level issues. Alternatively, it could be argued that traditional (theoretical) research represents a massive retreat from the rigours of being relevant and meaningful to change and development from *within* the culture of the school, and having to wrestle with all the concomitant problems that such an approach entails.

The second phrase used to describe the approach is *teacher-based research*. It is our contention in this chapter that, within this fairly neutral, innocent-sounding phrase, are bound up conflicting tensions which are dogging the path of genuine school improvement. When we have asked, 'What is teacher-based research?', one answer we have received is that it means nothing more than teachers doing research; that it is school-based means surely that it happens in schools. To us that is a far cry from Stenhouse's vision of the teacher-as-researcher movement. Yet it does allow our students to believe (while researching in other people's schools, problems they have identified) that they are teachers doing research; therefore, it is teacher-based research. This we would call the soft definition of the term. After all, 'teacher-based' might just mean that teachers provide the data – that it is some kind of field research among those anthropological phenomena known as teachers. A harder definition might involve the empowerment (and not the disenfranchisement) of teachers in the research process. In the tradition of action-research, teachers might be encouraged to identify their own problem issues and then take ownership, with appropriate support, of the research into action process. There are, of course, crucial paradigm issues involved in these alternative definitions.

In addition, we would want to argue that the concept of teacher-based research, in the context of school-wide improvement, is an inadequate one. We base our case on three main reasons:

1 The question of which research paradigm is being promoted within teacher-based research. Holly has written a paper on action-research entitled 'Third party, fire and theft' – the third party is the researcher, who, under cover of 'action-research' obtains his/her data (the theft?) while the conflict engendered by the research sets the school alight. Is this teacher-based research?.

2 Returning to our original point, teacher-based research (even action-research itself) involves the perpetuation, philosophically, of the cult of the individual. It is rampant in theories of professional development where the individual teacher dominates the centre of the stage; it is prevalent in higher education where individual teachers compete for careerist (seconded) placements on courses. At the end of their courses these individuals return to their schools and are probably ignored. Yet they will have received 'something mystical arising from our courses' – professional development. In fact, they might well be seen as educational lepers, institutional outcasts, subversives, hot properties. It is worth recording that when Father Neil O'Brien returned to Ireland following his imprisonment in the Philippines, one fellow priest was heard to comment – what happens when Father O'Brien encounters poverty, deprivation and political intrigue in his homeland; will he be able to remain silent? Indeed it is argued (Holly, 1984a) that educational action-researchers are facing similar problems within their working (institutional) lives. Holly, (1984b) also questions whether this individual enlightenment leads to change in schools. He called this the 'act of faith, part one'. Interestingly, Hargreaves (1983) when asking how schools can be made more effective and how improvement can be achieved in practice, poses a similar question:

As it is, we all are in principle committed to school improvement and an astonishing amount of time, energy and personnel are devoted to this goal . . . Inevitably much of this commitment rests on an *act of faith*, and one with which elected members, on the advice of officers and advisers, are fortunately prepared to go along. It is on this act of faith that we obtain funds for advisers and local inspectors, teachers' centres, support teams, advisory teachers and the vast range of INSET courses which vary from a half-day to a full year's secondment. Is our faith justified?

He continues by asserting that a 'harsh critic might say two things . . . that our strategies for school improvement are very heavily *individualised*' (and) 'that our attempts at school improvement are highly *fragmented*' (our italics). He develops both themes:

Much of our effort is directed to individual teachers: we send individuals on courses; we aim to improve the teaching of individual subjects or to solve highly specific problems. We know perfectly well that these efforts bear fruit. Individual teachers can gain much from courses; the teaching of a subject in a school can be improved; a problem can, with help, begin to be solved. Yet we also know that such individual transformations often have a curious evanescent quality. Newly energised teachers lose their enthusiasm more quickly than they should after returning from a course or a secondment. Innovations wither and die with a surprising speed. Many schools have a remarkable, and somewhat mysterious, power to resist the influence of our attempts to improve them through these individualised strategies for change.

Hargreaves points out that 'schools produce deadly antibodies that reject our attempts to graft on the new tissues of improvement'; we do not have an 'educational immunology . . . to forestall this tissue rejection'. On the question of fragmentation he argues that:

There are so many matters requiring attention, so many problems to be solved, so many priorities to be met, that we are forced in practice to try to make improvements on a whole range of fronts at the same time. This means that our resources are inevitably spread rather thinly among the various issues demanding attention, and also that the matters being attended to at any one point do not add up to a coherent pattern of school improvement.

Hargreaves concludes that 'because our approach to school improvement is usually so individualised and fragmented . . . improvements are relatively partial and short-lived.'

This is a central point. The cult of the individual is a deep-seated structural phenomenon which militates against social change. Accordingly, the Schmucks (1974) claim that schools are 'mirror images of the culture in which they operate'; they reflect the norms and values of entrepreneurialism which have permeated society in North America (and the UK?). This philosophy, according to the authors, advocates that strong individuals should be left to their own devices and that, through free enterprise, good will inevitably prevail. Equally, the virtues of independence, self-control and hard work are to be cherished and reflected through life in schools. Competitiveness is the key. According to the Schmucks, the major consequence is 'I-It' relationships, in Martin Buber's terms, ie individual isolation. The irony is that isolated individuals are well fitted to fill the slots in bureaucratic, role-culture organisations.

It is also interesting to note that such diverse authorities as Peters (1966), Lichtheim (1970) and House (1980) all point to the dominance of 'individualism' as the corner-stone of (political) philosophy dating from the enlightenment of the eighteenth century to the present day.

House (1980) argues that all current models of evaluation 'derive from the philosophy of liberalism'. He points out that liberalism itself grew out of the attempt to rationalise and justify freedom of choice, competition and the market society. A 'key idea of liberalism' according to House:

is that of an individualised psychology. Each individual mind is presumed to exist prior to society. The individual is not conceived initially as part of a greater collectivity, although he may submit to one later as in a social contract situation . . . Liberalism is profoundly methodologically individualist in its intellectual constructions.

House supports this statement by quoting from Barry (1973):

The essence of liberalism . . . is the vision of society as made up of independent, autonomous units who co-operate only when the terms of co-operation are such as to make it further the ends of the parties. Market relations are the paradigm of such co-operation . . .

House traces the growth of this philosophy through nineteenth century utilitarianism (an 'extreme methodological individualism ran deep in Mill's philosophy', says House) to the liberal democracy of the twentieth century. But House sees two distinct approaches to the related concept of political pluralism. First, there is the classical tradition in which society is seen as an association of self-determining individuals who co-operate with others for self-interested ends. 'This version of pluralism' says House, 'accepts individual idiosyncracies and interpersonal conflicts as inevitable'. Then there is what he calls the 'US version', 'based on the idea that every person achieves his identity from primary groups; it does not see man as a totally detached individual as does classic liberalism.' Accordingly 'pluralism is based on group rather than individual diversity' and the individual must work through his/her groups; 'immediacy, effectiveness, involvement and participation' are therefore all-important factors, as is the recognition that 'problems are best solved directly by local people close at hand.'

Peters (1966) reviews the importance of both the individual and *fraternity* from his stance within the classic liberal tradition. He accepts the notion that one can only achieve person-hood through being an individual and accepting individual responsibilities, for example respecting other persons. Fraternity gets short shrift; it is seen as a vestige of Marxist excess. Peters, however, does admit that:

It has been assumed to date that rational discussion must take place on the assumption that individuals are concerned about what is to be done in so far as it affects either themselves or other individuals. It is possible, however, *to conceive of a group of beings discussing what ought to be done by the group as a whole, without any concern for the stake of any individual in the future.* They would not, it might be argued, enter such a discussion as individuals with claims and interests to be considered; only as *members of a collective* concerned about the destiny of such a collective. They could be knit together by a feeling of *fraternity* derivative from their common concern as seekers after what was desirable for the collective with no concern for the agonies, relations, or difficulties of any individuals.

But, he continues:

... what would be lacking amongst such a group of rational beings would be any general notion of the importance of individual consciousness or the role of the individual in determining his own destiny ...

... The question, however, is whether a being who deliberates with others about the 'good' of the collective to which he belongs, is guilty ultimately of some kind of incoherence or wooliness of thought if he thinks that there can be any such 'good' which is not that of the individuals who compose it.

In discussing the fraternity of the family, he agrees that:

the common fact of kinship generates a powerful feeling of oneness and belonging which transcends purely personal attractions and animosities ... *It would be strange for a larger association of men to imagine that they were literally kin.*

No wonder that Peters is able to call fraternity 'the much neglected ideal of the French Revolution'. Yet, on the other hand, he is not the champion of unbridled individualism. He argues that 'the concept of being a person ... is derivative from the valuation placed in a society upon the determining role of individual points of view.' Consequently:

In our society being a person matters very much. Individuals are encouraged to judge and choose things 'for themselves'; they are held responsible for the consequences of their actions as individuals and are praised and blamed accordingly; they feel pride for things well done and guilt and remorse for things badly done. They are encouraged to be the determiners of their own destiny and, to a certain extent, they are so because our society encourages this form of individual assertion. This consciousness of being an individual person rather than just a member of a group is therefore both exhilarating and sobering. The sense of mastery and making an impact on the shape of things is mingled with apprehension for the consequences of failure.

Yet, as Peters asserts, people do not stand alone;

This consciousness of being a person reaches its zenith, perhaps, in the experience of entering into and sustaining a personal relationship, which is based on reciprocal agreement, where the bonds that bind people together derive from their own appraisals and choice, not from any statute or institutional position. They create their own world by voluntarily sharing together and mingling their own individual perspectives ...

Peters concludes:

'Respect for persons' is therefore a principle which we must adopt towards others with whom *we are prepared seriously to discuss what ought to be done.* ...

Lichtheim (1970) is a writer whose 'intellectual constructions' belong to the European tradition of 'socialist collectivism' as opposed to what he calls 'liberal individualism' . . .

men have always lived in communities and experienced the need to co-operate. Individualism is a comparatively recent faith, an outgrowth of a particular type of social organisation.

Like House, Lichtheim surveys the development of this bourgeois ideology and its view of 'human nature' through the writings of Hobbes, Locke, Hume and Bentham, culminating in the nineteenth century 'orgy of individualism'. Yet he is also able to describe a different tradition – a conflicting and incompatible vision of man's role in the world – through the writings of Rousseau, Hegel, Owen, and, of course, Marx. Hegel, for instance, partly inspired by Rousseau's view of culture as in some sense contrary to nature, started out:

by asking why European culture was inferior to the classical 'polis' of Greek antiquity, and the reply he gave was that modern society had been fragmented into selfish individuals who cared for nothing but their own interest.

But, according to Lichtheim, it was Rousseau who laid the foundations of the reaction against individualism, who launched the critique of liberalism by developing 'a theory of democracy which was not liberal and individualist in the Lockean sense.' Interestingly, Lichtheim also traces the journey (within left-wing circles) away from liberalism through democracy towards *mutualism* (Proudhon's ideal of a co-operative association of individual artisans) and *collectivism* (Bakunin's vision of collectivity within the commune). For his part, Proudhon 'never renounced the vision of a society in which the producers would own their tools, individually rather than collectively', and clung to his 'worship of *independent craftsmen*', while stressing the importance of 'federation' between workshops of artisans working in mutual co-operation.

We have indulged in this somewhat lengthy philosophical digression for two reasons. First, to stress the centrality within the hegemony of ideas of the cult of individualism; and, second, to make the point that there is in our culture an alternative tradition – virtually unexplored. Teachers are seen first and foremost as crafts people (see Stenhouse, 1973); their autonomy is seen as sacrosanct; their regulation is self-imposed; they are expected, as self-determining individuals, to compete for in-service credentials. As private educational entrepreneurs, their self-interest is seen as the best guarantee of the general welfare of the pupils, the school, and so on. If left alone to compete, at least some of these cannot fail to better themselves and in the long run, or so the theory goes, everyone will benefit. This utilitarian view of teacher development still holds sway according to what House calls the 'instrumental view' of relationships. Each individual views others as instruments in pursuit of his/her private ends. In the meantime, schools stagnate.

3   All this leads to the third shortcoming we would identify in the notion of teacher-based research. It encapsulates an inadequate theory of change. As Holly has argued elsewhere (1984b), enlightened individual teachers (or even small groups of teachers) do not seem to have much success in terms of initiating school-wide improvement. The history of educational innovation is littered with disappointed, disillusioned and embittered would-be educational 'hero innovators'. Perhaps to expect more of individuals is to expect the impossible. Yet the paradox is that real innovation (improvements in teaching and learning) can only occur at individual classroom level. As Fullan (1982) maintains, 'Significant educational change consists of changes in belief, teaching-style and materials which can only come about through a process of personal development in a context of socialisation.'

Stenhouse (1975) recommended that teachers should possess a 'capacity for autonomous self-development through systematic self-study, through the study of the work of other teachers and through the testing of ideas by classroom research procedures'. It could be argued that the teacher-as-researcher movement has spawned many thinking and more effective teachers, but not many thinking schools. Yet Stenhouse was very aware of this problem. Like Rudduck, by adopting a cultural perspective to change in schools ('culture . . . is on the one hand the product of, on the other hand a *determinant* of, systems of social interaction'), he was able to realise that:

the power of the individual teacher is limited. Without his strengths the betterment of schools can never be achieved; but the strengths of individuals are not effective unless they are co-ordinated and supported. The primary unit of co-ordination and support is the school. . . . It is at school level that the problems and potentialities of curriculum innovation have to be negotiated. (Stenhouse, 1975)

This awareness of the problem on Stenhouse's part, however, did not lead to an offer of any real solutions. Even Stenhouse seemed trapped within his own (individualistic) culture. Like Elliott, he saw only one alternative – the managerialism of bureaucratic control, which, given the opportunity, would squeeze the juice out of the artistry of teaching.

The second section of this chapter sets out to trace those developments which have attempted to solve the riddle of how to integrate change in persons and institutions. How to achieve what Fullan calls the 'context of socialisation' for individual endeavour is the central focus.

Section Two: Countering the Cult of the Individual

The first section of this chapter has outlined the 'problem'; the second section attempts to survey the various moves that have been advocated and/or implemented to create this institutional context for the improvement of schooling, central to which is the improvement of teaching and learning in classrooms across the school. As the Schmucks (1974) point out:

Strategies of the future, above all, should be based on collective professional development within the school rather than on individualistic professional autonomy or its opposite, excessive dependence, which have characterised school norms and practices of the past.

We see this 'collective professional development' as *the* avenue to be explored, yet it has been left unexplored by many commentators.

Elliott's work in educational action-research has echoed Stenhouse's emphasis on individual professional development. His description (1980) bears out this fact:

Basically classroom action-reseach relates to any teacher who is concerned with his own teaching: the teacher who is prepared to question his own approaches in order to improve its quality.

But Elliott increasingly became aware of the problems of *institutionalisation* – in terms of the acceptance of individual innovation across the school (see Holly 1984b). He began to see action-research not simply as private reflection; he developed a concept of action research which demands a *community of enquirers* with a general focus in common. All deliberation (building on Schwab, Reid, Holt and the so-called neo-Aristotelians) within this community should be shared for the purposes of discussion and critique, thus creating an intellectually demanding mode of enquiry. This was the aim in the Schools Council Project, *Teacher-Pupil Interaction and the Quality of Learning* (see Elliott, 1981 and 1984). It is interesting that, within recent action-research endeavours, the tendency has been for the research to be collaborative and the action to be personal and individualistic, as opposed to institutional (ie embedded across the institution). Collaboration, in Elliott's sense, is a small group phenomenon. His stance (as described in his papers of 1977, 1981b and 1983) tends to be anti-institutional. School focused INSET, which involves the identification of both individual and school needs, is, in his view, essentially managerial and bureaucratic. According to Elliott (1983), its aim is to produce certain desired changes in teachers' beliefs and behaviour patterns – it is something which is *done* to teachers to rectify deficiencies in their thought and practice, as opposed to a more professional model which would aim to enable and foster the growth and professional development of teachers. Referring to the work of the OECD/CERI INSET project (see Hopkins, 1986) and the DES publication *Making INSET Work*, Elliott (1983) maintains that 'the school is construed as an impersonal functioning system, abstracted from the individuals who live and move and have their being within it.' Elliott assumes that the 'structural functionalist' perspective provides the philosophical underpinnings and organisational theory for school-focused INSET. Thus he concludes that:

INSET focused on the school as a system becomes a matter of rectifying such 'deficiencies' by identifying the malfunctioning parts and allocating the resources necessary to make them fully functional . . . It is therefore hardly surprising that it (the systems perspective) is so embedded in the policy-orientated literature of school-focused INSET. And again one should not be surprised to discover that the discussion of INSET strategies in that literature tends to lean heavily on organisational (sic) development research based on a systems perspective.

Elliott's distaste for Organisation Development (OD) – so great that he mis-names it? – is unfortunate. It is his blind spot referred to earlier in this chapter. While Organisation Development has its weaknesses (see Fullan, 1976) it also has undoubted strengths (ignored by Elliott). One of these strengths is that it goes some way to opening up the possibilities of collegial (staff) development – the alternative channel to be explored in this chapter; alternative, that is, to Elliott's polar approaches of professionalism and managerialism. OD in schools can open up the possibility of harnessing the power of the *collective*.

An introduction to Organisation Development in schools was provided by the Schmucks (1974) in their review of humanistic schooling. Their contention, reflecting a major theme of this chapter, is as follows:

Planting a few humanistically oriented teachers in a closed staff can be disastrous, especially for the humanistic teachers, who must undergo confrontation with strong custodial norms and at the same time face a staff culture that discourages talking out professional differences . . . too many public schools have failed to make proposed changes because they have over-relied on individuals and ignored the power of the organisational structure and strengths of its traditions . . . Thus, we would expect teachers to make some impact on their classrooms, but probably not on the culture of the entire school. Unless a specially trained teacher has support from colleagues, he will either leave the school or revert to the school's prevailing norms.

Given this stance, which is very similar to our own, the Schmucks conclude that successful school development is dependent on mechanisms for change being operated at a number of levels:
- individual
- small-team
- school; whole staff
- institutional; the domain of the school's culture as reflected in the school's organisation.

Accordingly, say the Schmucks;

Humanised learning groups must operate within a larger school culture that encourages and sustains a milieu that is in itself person-oriented . . . (few approaches have) dealt with the systemic and cultural features of the school as a whole in a planned and deliberate way.

An important facet of the Schmucks' work has been their practical emphasis; their 'practical guide to the development of a learning group'; their promotion of team-building and the establishment of shared influence and collaborative decision-making.

Obviously, there is an ideological component in Organisation Development; it attempts to replace individualisation with a common purpose and it embodies the concepts of power-sharing, the democratisation of management, participative/collaborative decision-making, and self-determination/self-renewal. It is serious about achieving school-wide improvement – according to a clear set of values. As Crockett has observed:

The unfinished revolution that we have to face (as OD proponents) is to help the people in our institutions see the importance in the long run of bringing their norms of institutional behaviour, institutional values, and institutional management more closely to the democratic norms . . .

Observers have mentioned the similarities between Organisation Development in schools and the school self-evaluation movement in the UK.

Along with the classroom self-evaluation movement there has been the development of a related phenomenon – School Self-Evaluation, the institutional model resting on a whole school approach. Initiatives in this area have come from over 40 LEAs and the Schools Council (the GRIDS Project). Hargreaves (1983) sees self-evaluation and school-focused INSET as the major recent attempts to avoid the dangers of individualised and fragmented strategies of school improvement. Both recognise, he argues, that 'the school, rather than the individual teacher, should be the target and base for improvement.' They also have the advantage of being much more systematic, but do they really go far enough? he asks. He is not convinced that the dangers of individualisation and fragmentation are avoided 'although in my experience most teachers who have been involved in a school self-evaluation . . . find the self-analysis bracing, few of them report back that as a consequence of the exercise the school is obviously set on a path of fundamental school improvement.'

The next step, Hargreaves argues, is *to help* schools to be able to select from the large list of issues (as identified in a school self-evaluation exercise) a much smaller yet coherent set of issues, which will be given immediate priority. School self-evaluation has tended to be hide-bound by accountability pressures; consequently, the evaluation tends to be descriptive rather than analytical: 'And without such analysis, the prioritisation of issues, and the setting out of carefully designed plans to cope with them, invariably become the badly under-developed section at the end of the final report.'

Hargreaves emphasises that schools need support of two kinds: they need 'a trusting audience who will treat the self-exposure with understanding, confidentiality and a willingness to help' and resource-backing from LEAs. 'Concentration of resources in relation to carefully planned priorities should greatly increase the chances that improvements will be made, and will be seen by all to have been made.'

Alongside the school self-evaluation movement has developed *school-based review* in its many facets – school-based curriculum review, school-based staff development, etc (see Hopkins, 1985). This has great potential; occasionally, however, as with some attempts at school self-evaluation, it may degenerate into some form of top-down managerialism. Whole school curriculum planning and development has also appeared; associated with this development is the trend in schools in some LEAs (eg Oxfordshire) towards the identification of school priorities for development with the LEA's backing (in terms of LEA advisers, consultants and tutors in higher education establishments, heads and teachers are entering into a coherent pattern of collaboration for the benefit of school improvement.) Typically, a school identifies a priority area for development and the LEA, with its in-service apparatus, supports the school in its endeavours eg by seconding teachers with a brief to research the problem area prior to development. The aim is to create an enabling framework for school improvement. Perhaps collaboration at the local level is at last being seen as a manifestation of fraternity rather than fraternisation. Influence is seen as a two-way process; all members in the partnership are prepared to influence and be influenced.

In *Teacher Education for Co-operative Curriculum Review* (1983). Ashton advocates such a movement. She points out that 'School-based work in which classroom practice is both process and product' figures increasingly prominently in initial training courses and INSET provision.

She describes the framework for this activity as 'school-based consultancy type INSET' which is 'school-focused, taking pressing daily concerns identified by teachers as its subject matter.' The aim of the IT-INSET programme is to enhance *cooperation* between college tutors, teachers and students on initial training; the implicit understanding is that:

The quality of a child's educational progress through a school cannot be improved without *all of the teachers* working with each successive age-range (in primary schools) or within each subject (in secondary schools) looking co-operatively at the sum total of their efforts. If students are to acquire the skills for co-operative curriculum review then there would be nowhere better than alongside teachers engaged in the same quest.

Everyone gains. According to Ashton '. . . the tutor can add his area of expertise and experience and, in addition, can revitalise his college based teaching with current involvement in the work of children.' Interestingly, the Open University (where the IT-INSET project has been based) is now contemplating the possibility of validating such school-based work (as indeed is the Cambridge Institute of Education). The term 'school-based' would then have some real meaning; work undertaken in the school, for the school and by the school (with appropriate support) would receive validation.

Significantly, however, while Ashton is able to say that the purpose of bringing together *teams* of teachers, students and tutors was for each member to learn with and from the others, thus giving them experience of 'professional co-operation', she is forced to conclude that this is one area of endeavour which 'remains almost virgin territory':

This is the one of *involving other teachers* in the school. IT-INSET is intended to provide teachers with experience of co-operative curriculum review and also to generate that process in their schools. This did not happen in almost two thirds of cases . . . the major expenditure of time and effort in *individual* classroom IT-INSET programmes is failing to reach its INSET potential while colleagues remain relatively unaffected.

As argued elsewhere (Holly, 1984b), there is a paradox here; by aiming for individual development at classroom level it often proves virtually impossible to make changes in practice across the institution; yet to pitch the effort at the institutional, whole school level often means that the immediacy and the vitality of innovation is lost as the ideas percolate down through the social system. Until this central dilemma is resolved, school development will not be able to move beyond the cult of the individual.

The work of Rudduck (1982), under the auspices of the Schools Council's Programme Two was described in the publication entitled *Teachers in Partnership: Four Studies of In-Service Collaboration*. This project involved school-based study groups, teachers visiting other schools, and teacher-outsider and teacher-teacher partnerships in the observation of classrooms. According to Rudduck (1982):

A particular strength of the four approaches is the centrality of professional discussion: again and again, teachers have stressed the satisfaction of working in a structure that guarantees focused discussion that is more than simply the exchange of opinion. Teachers have also acknowledged the comfort of working in a structure that allows them to examine problems openly. These things are important at a time of low job mobility and low investment in the kind of in-service course that takes teachers away from their own classrooms and staffroom. New sources of professional stimulation have to be found – we think that the approaches we tried out with teachers have such a potential.

Most of the teachers involved had previously participated in classroom research – either in a project or through undertaking appropriate higher degree work. Study groups were established in several schools. One of the significant findings was, perhaps predictably, that:

Public support for the research task is more likely to be found in a school where there is a cohesive and relatively small staff with a habit of professional discussion and an interest in institutional self-scrutiny. In such a school, the staff might invite volunteers to form a working group and commission them to undertake a particular research study. The group would be acting for the school. Support would be guaranteed. The boundary between members and non-members of the working group could readily be crossed, so communicating the progress of the research would be relatively easy. The group would know from the outset that the audience for its research findings would be the whole staff and that the likely occasion of the presentation of these findings would be a staff meeting.

Rudduck, however, mirroring our own experience, admits that the situation was very different in the larger schools. Here institutionalisation often entails gaining a foothold for the research process within the institutional micro-politics (see Holly, 1984b).

In a challenging article, Dow (1984), offering an historical overview of teacher education and development in Australia, contrasts the 'sponsored mobility' view with that of 'contest mobility' (see Turner, 1961). She calls the former the 'aristocratic embrace' and the latter the 'rat race'. She is able, however, to cite new developments in Victoria, Australia, where, in the early 1970s, a combination of teacher unions, the Curriculum Advisory Board and the State Department prompted radical reforms and school-based curriculum innovation (plus banishing inspectors from the schools). At that point 'Schools organised in areas to discuss curriculum revision; areas were then grouped into regions for the same purpose; and finally at a state conference teachers themselves worked out a set of principles for revising secondary school practices and policies.' Following these developments, federal funding was made available to give a 'shot in the arm to local endeavour'; this support, according to Dow, aided and reinforced the development of school-based decision-making. While the Curriculum Advisory Board suggested its own broad guidelines to help schools in their planning – indeed two pilot schools were used which, it was hoped, would have a 'lighthouse effect' – responsibility for curriculum reform was placed directly in the schools. Dow maintains that this policy of school-based autonomy led to many pilot schemes including the establishment of small free (or community) schools within the State system and the division of large schools into mini-schools, with the central purpose of enabling teachers to establish a more supportive school structure. This often entailed the elimination of the practice of 'extreme specialisation'; and when teachers lose their isolation, they are no longer able to hide themselves. It is the de-mystification of teaching; when they are thus exposed and vulnerable, Dow believes that teachers become more self-critical and willing to learn from each other.

Dow also quotes the Swedish experience, where sweeping school reforms were, in her estimation, politically radical, but educationally cautious. High-powered committees of experts revised the curriculum for all schools, leaving the teachers with 'professional constipation'. Dow comments:

The mass of teachers came up the hard way, usually undereducated, underpaid and grossly overworked. In a system that was publicly accountable for what the nation's children were subjected to in its schools, it was considered risky to the point of extreme irresponsibility to let teachers loose in matters educational. Hence they had to remain educational robots. Catch 22 indeed.

If teachers are to control the curriculum, they have to be equipped for the task. If school-based research and development is to be the way ahead, the implications for the support agencies (including higher education) are clear enough. They must offer an enabling framework to facilitate the in-school dialogue. The paradigm is the dialogue; not, we would suggest, between the investigator and the investigated, but between process partners – partners in praxis. The process is one of reflection into action through a collaborative critique. We are all learners; we can all share responsibility for the chosen line of action. Above all, it is this deliberative process that creates control for the participants; control over *their* curriculum and over themselves. We see two developments as of crucial importance here.

First, there is the work of those involved in action-research at Deakin University. Kemmis, in collaboration with Carr (1983), has described the process of *Becoming Critical: Knowing Through Action Research*, which is based on the premise that by using the concepts of critical theory the *consciousness of the school* can be raised – the school can become a critical community by means of action-research placed on an institutional footing. The view is that individual growth and empowerment can occur through research and action *within* staff group collaboration. Henry (1984) has explored this same territory by attempting to move towards an 'understanding of collaborative research in education'. His vision is that of the teacher who:

Undertakes research into practice-based issues of interest through one's own practice, and the rigour associated with one's inquiring and theorising is implied through the collaborative or corporate nature of the research process. Collaboration . . . describes a particular form of participatory involvement in research projects and learning programmes. In collaborative work there is a clear goal of participants working together on shared professional issues. The form of interaction is intended to be associated with non-hierarchical relationships between participants . . . In fact, only by being a researcher can one truly be considered a member of the collaborative enterprise

Crucially, as Henry points out, participants in this kind of collaborative research are 'co-authors of liberating action' (Freire, 1972). Collaboration becomes the social milieu for individual endeavour; it can only occur between people, says Henry:

... after trust, respect, openness and equality of ownership in the research task have been established. These conditions for collaboration are obtained through communication, through dialogue in which all participants are both learners and teachers, and through which critical analysis of practice is developed.

The important issue at stake here is the crucial difference posited by Carr (1984) – largely based on the writings of Habermas, 1972 and 1974 – between 'practical interest' and 'critical' or 'emancipatory' interest. The former view (of the relationship between theory and practice) rests on accounts of what a person is up to in terms of what he (or she) thinks he (or she) is up to. *Thus* this *verstehen* method is based on the understandings and perspectives of practitioners who are assisted, by means of interpretive accounts of their educational situations, to reflect on their practice with the intention of making action decisions about this practice. Practitioners are helped, according to Carr, 'to make morally defensible decisions by developing the art of practical deliberation'. This perspective sees educational practice as a moral activity which requires both a 'disposition to act wisely and prudently in educational situations' and a recognition that moral commitments are realised in and through practice. This view of teaching as a 'moral science' (see Reid, 1981, and Elliott, 1983b) is, in our view, compatible with the stance taken up by Peters – and referred to earlier in this chapter. Each individual, as a constituent facet of his/her personhood, should demonstrate respect for other persons by consistently taking into account their feelings and opinions. Seen from this point of view the willingness to deliberate with others signifies what is essentially an individual morality.

On the other hand, the critical view rests on 'depth hermeneutics' and depends on interpretations that actively criticise and transcend people's own understanding of themselves, challenging their assumptions and offering release from their self-imposed, restricted autonomy. Carr (1984) maintains that this view recognises how a practitioner's own understanding of his/her educational values may be destroyed by various non-educational forces and pressures and how the practical realisation of those values may be impeded by institutional structures and apolitical constraints. The major tasks are to 'expose those false beliefs which sustain practitioners' misunderstandings of their practice' and to 'identify those organisational arrangements which frustrate the pursuit of genuine educational aims and purposes'. The ultimate aim of this *critique* is to convert the accumulating knowledge and understanding into discourse (see Habermas, 1974).

The problem, as Ingleby (1971) has pointed out, is to reconstruct the meaning which has become unintelligible to the author himself. As Freud and Marx both held, it is possible to pay altogether too much regard to people's self-understanding – what if they are mistaken or deluded? Hence the emphasis in Marxism and psychoanalysis on what Habermas calls 'depth hermeneutics' and Marcuse's reference to the 'myth of autonomous man'. The contention is that it is the 'politics of subjectivity' within the 'inner sphere' by means of which individuals are repressed. Both Lacan and Habermas aim to unearth what Ingleby calls the 'social institutions of the mind'. Lacan, (1979) influenced by French structuralist anthropology, sees the structures of the mind, the unconscious, as the 'vehicle of ideology'. But it is the members of the Frankfurt School who have brought into the foreground the question of how and where social conditions are deposited within the individual.

The assertion is that not only do people fail to recognise their own exploitation, they also, through the process of 'internalisation', literally become addicted to it. This is akin to Freud's conception of man as fragmented, self-contradictory and alienated from his own experience. This fragmented individualism is embedded during the process of child-rearing – which, presumably, includes schooling. Teachers, therefore, trapped within a certain kind of personality structure, are seen as creating their pupils in their own image. Habermas attempts to find a way out of this particular spiral. He seeks to create a framework of discussion free from domination, a dialogue between men about the ends of life. 'Hence', says Connerton (1976), 'the paradigm is no longer the observation but the dialogue'; a participative, interactive dialogue between investigator and investigated. As it is, social institutions tend to act in the interests of some, rather than according to any notion of the rights common to all. This stratification is both a conscious and an unconscious phenomenon; the conception of dialogue posited by Habermas, therefore, threatens at both levels.

Thus personal 'responsible autonomy' (as Henry, 1984, calls it) can be enhanced, through a collaborative critical dialogue within an educational community; the promise of emancipation from the non-critical assumption of traditional values can be realised. Action research at this level is more than developing individual competence or taking strategic action within the existing framework (being politically subversive); it is about a different form of group-based, socio-political framework called collaboration.

Because educational action is social action, however, the participatory element of action-research extends beyond individual participation in the process to involvement. The kind of involvement required is collaborative involvement. (Carr and Kemmis, 1983)

The nature of this involvement, we would contend, rests on an alternative conception of personhood and of personal growth through and within collaborative dialogue.

The second point worth noting within the context of this deliberative and collaborative dialogue, is the growing need for urgent research on the workings of groups and review teams – how people behave in such settings (see Handy, 1976) and how they should behave – Habermas on 'symmetrical communication' is relevant here. But it is more than a question of linking Handy with Habermas. There is, for instance, the pioneering work of such initiatives as *Cambridge Group Work* building on the work of the Group-Analytic Society. Teachers need knowledge and experience of the *process* of working together in groups; they need to experience the process of deliberation in order to refine it and gain confidence within it. Reid argues that:

... a moral process of curriculum design needs to be based upon collective deliberation of a very searching kind. That is, our greatest concern in curriculum planning should be about process – about how we get people together to work on problems of what to teach.

Yet, as Hargreaves (1982) points out:

Most secondary school teachers lack the skills needed to work together. . . . They have a defective sense of classroom co-operation. They can co-ordinate with one another, certainly, but in matters of collaboration, the strong form of co-operation, they must be judged remedial.

It is Hargreaves' contention that schools suffer from what he calls the 'culture of individualism', which not only determines attitudes to the pupils but also 'permeates the social relations between teachers'. So much so, in fact, that the teachers cling to their 'addiction to autonomy', which isolates them from their colleagues and insulates them against potential criticism. Hargreaves argues that teaching relationships (and relationships between teachers) are a moral education in themselves. According to his thesis:

Durkheim did not fully resolve the tensions between the two kinds of individualism, between the individual and the group, between independence and obligation, between basic rights and superficial interests. But he did understand that true dignity and morality have a social and corporate aspect. Genuine individuality must be rooted in group life . . . Moral education . . . thus becomes one of the central objectives of schooling. But it cannot be achieved by conventional, direct teaching. It must come through the direct experience of group life. And group life was not merely a means giving people the social skills of co-operation and empathy, but of generating solidarity.

We are well aware, however, that this concluding section looks at the rhetoric, as opposed to the reality, of possible developments. Hopefully, we will be able to explore real ways of realising the rhetoric in terms of an understanding of the kinds of collaborative support necessary for genuine school-based research and development.

Then along came TRIST. A centralist, managerial response maybe, but what is happening 'on the ground'? The rhetoric is certainly in accord with school-determined internal development through the identification of INSET needs, but what is the reality? Imagine this early morning scene in a comprehensive school in the Home Counties.

Time – 9 a.m.   *Location* – head's office.

Those present: LEA TRIST co-ordinator; headteacher; both deputies; four heads of department; and the external (evaluation) consultant, a representative from higher education. The teachers present are the members of the school's TRIST steering committee; one of the deputies, who is acting as the in-school TRIST co-ordinator, has recently attended the induction conference (two and a half days residential) and a one-day workshop.

The head opens the meeting by explaining some background details:
1 they have tried to apply the process guidelines (see Holly, 1986) and have completed their prioritisation of 'key areas of focus'. The curriculum in years 1–3 is their source of major concern, but they can already see that they might have to subdivide this major focus area to look at:
- content issues; its suitability and relevance; any unintentional overlap? any scope to think in terms of inter-disciplinary enquiry or integration of content?
- method issues; teaching and learning styles across the school;
- grouping issues; will the banding policy need to be amended?
- the first term in the first year; should it be so dramatic a departure from the pupil's past experience?

Who identified this priority area? The head's reply was 'intuition . . . grass-roots feeling for some time ... talking to heads of department . . . sounding the water in the staffroom . . . the issues aren't in question.'
2 The history of the school is important; it is often seen as a 'crypto-grammar school' – an image of the school which has proved popular with many parents. In fact, as the head admits, there is some complacency regarding change and development because the school appears to be popular with the customers. It is the only oversubscribed school in the area; it delivers the goods (in terms of excellent examination results); and it is good at doing certain things. But the head talks of the school being in a rut and questions both the quality of experience that the pupils are receiving and the opportunities that exist in the school for lower attaining pupils.
3 Organisationally, the head refers to the school having the 'pavilion model' in which each department works well but in isolation – in its own grand pavilion. He contends that there is an urgent need to encourage departmental colleagues to climb out of their boxes to give a view of the whole curriculum.
4 The TRIST steering committee (those present) had been formed by invitation – the members representing the major curriculum areas. Despite the teacher action, two-thirds of the staff have attended a meeting in which the TRIST scheme was launched, but this was largely informational.

Is there general staff commitment to the scheme? Are they involved? Is it broadly-based? The deputy head (female), who has been nominated the in-school TRIST co-ordinator, assures me that, while the teacher action has made it very difficult to involve all the staff (in a sense the start was inopportune), as the scheme progresses all the staff will become involved. 'Staff have had some bad INSET experiences . . . yes, there's complacency and the pavilion complex . . . they (the staff) feel threatened by observation . . . but they must feel it's coming from them.'

The LEA TRIST Co-ordinator then sketches the background of the scheme for those present. He mentions the emphasis within this particular LEA initiative on school-based INSET and curriculum development (the 'crux of the scheme . . . the core activity'); the new specific grant – to appear in March 1987; the schools' 'ownership of INSET'; and the fact that it is 'such a golden opportunity for schools – can't afford not to do it'.

The in-school co-ordinator then explains the implementation plan.

Phase 1

Step One will involve small groups of staff being 'inducted' into a profile of the whole school; they will be shown the 'tools of management' (the curriculum return sheet), the mechanics of policy decisions, LEA circulars, constraints on policy-making etc.

Step Two will consist of small cross-departmental groups going out for half a day – either across their own school or into other schools – to explore the nature (and variety) of current practice. Observation and pupil shadow studies will be emphasised at this stage. On their return the group members will be encouraged to pool their experience. The idea is to obtain both feedback from these observational visits (including visits to local junior schools) and data concerning their own lower school curriculum.

Step Three will involve the evaluation of this accumulating data. What to measure it against? Staff will be encouraged to find the criteria (with which to judge their own practice) from their visits, from DES reports, etc. Evaluation can then be a matching process – matching the 'practice' as observed, against the best of intentions.

Steps One to Three (Phase One) are scheduled for the summer term 1986. Half their allocation of teacher 'supply days' will be used up during this first phase.

Phase 2

Phase Two will take place during the October of the autumn term, 1986, and will consist of the staff deciding their INSET needs (based on the evaluation of their review of their practice) and then the launch of the crucial stage – the provision of INSET to meet those needs.

Three questions arise from those present (for the LEA) at this point:

• Has money been set aside to resource the changes?

- Have supply teachers (of some calibre) been made available?
- Can we have an 'evaluation skills' workshop to help us evaluate the data during step three?

The meeting closes after both the LEA co-ordinator and the external consultant react to the plans, make some observations and give some suggestions. The evaluation workshop is put in the TRIST diary.

This meeting is probably being repeated (under the auspices of TRIST initiatives) in countless secondary schools up and down the country. Three general points emerge from this particular example:

1 The role of self-evaluation within the developments. This theme will be explored in chapter 11.

2 The fact that the *process* of staff involvement and 'doing TRIST' in this fashion is a 'loosening-up process' (the deputy's words) in itself. The aim is to convince staff that they need to 'open their eyes' and 'climb out of their pavilions' (again, the deputy's words). The irony is that this process of 'awareness-raising' (see Joyce and Showers, 1980) has to be stage-managed by the senior staff. But we were convinced, after talking to this particular management team, that this is not a case of 'managerialism' re-asserting itself. One of the effects of the sustained teacher action has been that heads have been forced to go it alone in terms of 'managing' schools. Staff participation and collaborative decision-making were casualties of the dispute. This particular school, however, has 'staff ownership' of the initiative very high on its agenda.

3 This staff have already made one crucial discovery, that they will need release-time (and supply cover) in order to systematically arrive at a point where they will have identified their INSET needs; they will then have to provide for those needs which will require more release-time and supply cover. Real development is not a headlong rush.

This staff is saying – give us the *time* (and cover) and we'll do a good job. As Wragg (1986) remarked;

Teachers have been asked to underwrite too many novelties, like new examinations, school reorganisation, mainstreaming of handicapped children, mixed ability or mixed age grouping, with no time to reflect, prepare, or visit other schools

The real impact of TRIST will be explored in chapter 11. Suffice to say at this point that TRIST could well be the shape of things to come.

Section Three: Some Reflections

Based on the above discussion, we would identify three central themes which are beginning to emerge from recent initiatives:

1 The external collaborative partnership needed to support the internal collaborative partnership.

2 Internal collaboration itself; the potentialities of collegiality.
3 The importance of school-based development (as opposed to innovation).

The external collaborative partnership

Concerted school development relies on the support of the external collaborative partnership between, for instance, LEA advisers, tutors in higher education and teachers' centre wardens. In the main this kind of support partnership is still in its infancy – although there are certain notable exceptions. 'What is too often missing' says Turner (1986), 'is negotiation between teacher, head and LEA adviser.' She continues, 'It is ironic that schools are encouraged to attempt strategic planning through their own staff development programmes while most LEAs are not attempting the same approach on an Authority-wide scale.'

Bradley (1985), having identified the interrelated activities of change in schools, the professional development of individuals and INSET, stated his belief that 'the task for those involved in INSET – the teachers themselves, teacher educators and educational administrators – is to seek to understand the mechanisms which maximise the positive effects of these relationships and to use them effectively.'

In East Anglia both Bradley and Sockett (see 1986) have endeavoured to establish their respective higher education establishments as co-ordinating sites for the external support partnership mentioned above. According to Sockett, a partnership demands trust, confidence, openness and a shared commitment to the task of school improvement. Such a partnership should hinge on a planning relationship which is organic as opposed to mechanistic (see Figure 10.1).

Figure 10.1   Partnership in school improvement

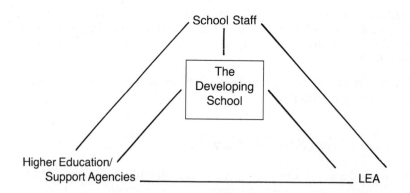

Goddard (1985), in his review of the recommendations for INSET made in 1984 by the Advisory Committee for the Supply and Education of

Teachers (ACSET), explores the interrelated concepts of *brokerage* and *partnership*. Brokerage involves the matching of needs (as identified by the teachers and schools). Goddard maintains that development of partnership is an essential condition for school development. He concludes:

> Much of what currently exists is often divided. Education has the features of a 'top down' system, either from or to local authorities and from schools and institutions to individual teachers. This particular structure does not operate in a way which is going to effect successful development. The findings of the RAND Study (McLaughlin, 1976) indicate that either a 'top-town' or a 'bottom-up' approach on its own, is unlikely to be effective and that collaboration and co-operation and the 'building of teams' (his words) is, in fact, a cornerstone of the successful climate for building a partnership and effective development.

Co-development is the theme here. As Goddard maintains 'partnership is also a development in itself'. In Goddard's own authority, the London Borough of Enfield, heads of schools are being encouraged to become involved in the SID (Supporting Institutional Development) initiative – see Figure 10.2. The SID project is part of a more general Partnership Scheme in which

- LEA officials and school representatives are reviewing their management structures on a supportive, reciprocal basis;
- an LEA-wide climate for co-development is being established, in which all partners within the scheme are beginning to explore the potentialities for change.

Two crucial points arise here:

a Goddard and his colleagues in Enfield are exploring alternative managment styles to the dominant 'line management' model which they see as redundant and a barrier to creative development. Bureaucratic control, as argued earlier in this chapter, preys on individualism. As Goddard asserts:

> The traditions of teaching are that teachers operate individually within their own classrooms. The traditions of the delivery of the curriculum, mean that schools operate individually and separately from the local authority. The tradition has been for local authorities to operate separately and this is certainly true for many of the supporting agencies and higher education.

Consequently, higher education, according to Goddard, needs to switch to a consultancy-based approach to development which is 'directed at teams of teachers and institutions' and targeted on the needs identified by them.

b The general aim is for the LEA, supported by higher education, to establish a climate for development within which the schools feel able to follow suit.

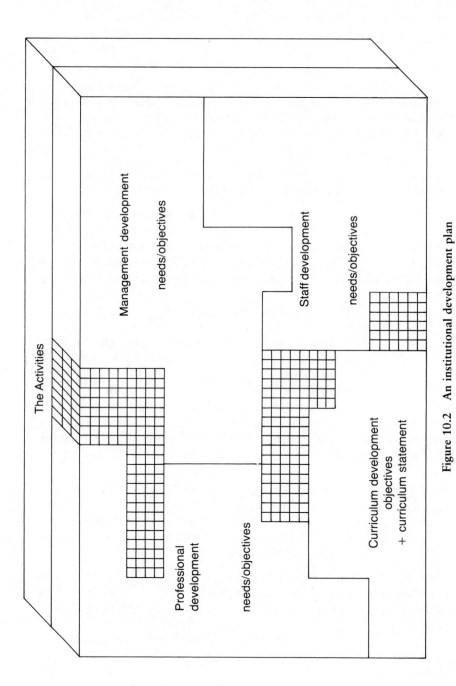

Figure 10.2 An institutional development plan

The internal collaborative partnership

Southworth (1984) has identified four models of staff development:
1 the systems or line management approach — (Elliott's 'positivism') — which is a deficit model in that it aims to rectify perceived deficiencies in individuals' role performances;
2 the laissez-faire approach — the 'purely individualised model' according to Southworth;
3 the pragmatic-expediency approach resting on career promotion and advancement;
4 the organic approach of the 'learning collective'.

The concept of an in-school collaborative partnership demands an exploration of this fourth approach. Cuban (1984), in drawing our attention to the work of Little (1981), maintains that breaking down teacher isolation and cultivating the norm of collegiality can lead to the improvement of classroom practice. He argues that 'New work norms of teachers observing one another, talking frequently about pedagogy, and engaging in joint planning stimulate the sharing of values that nourish school improvement.'

Holly and Southworth (1986) have identified three versions of collegiality in practice:
a *normative collegiality* exists when the staff as a whole collaborate in the formulation of the goals of the school — the 'what' of school development
b *Strategic or procedural collegiality* involves the joint planning of implementation strategies — the 'how'
c *democratic collegiality* in which both the 'what' and the 'how' are agreed by collaborative, participative decision-making.

But, as Southworth (1986) has recently pointed out, collegiality involves a major change in schools — as with 'partnership', it is a radical development in itself. Its importance, however, cannot be underestimated, as Cuban asserts. It can provide the intense interaction, communication and in-school dialogue concerning, say, teaching and learning styles, which is the key to major change. Team-work is crucial. School staffs have the potential to build on the strength of creative synergy leading to combined action. Mutualism — the theme of this chapter — is central; in other words the reciprocity of symbiotic relationships. Yet, as Southworth (1986) illustrates, 'good' relationships need not be cosy and collusive. Disagreement (without personal rancour) could well induce creative dynamism. Team-building needs to countenance this fact.

School-based INSET for school development

Earlier in this chapter we questioned whether the terms school-based INSET, school-focused INSET and school-centred in-service education are actually interchangeable. Our contention is that it is school-based INSET which should be the legitimate title for the kind of activity envisaged — and indeed advocated — in this section.

The school-centred approach as promoted by Bridges and Eynon (1983), which claims, characteristically, to be teacher-initiated, school-located, focused on teachers' practical problems and self-evaluatory of classroom practice seems so much like educational action-research (see Holly and Whitehead 1984 and 1986) as to be virtually indistinguishable from it. Some claim, however, that:

> Taken together these characteristics added up to considerably more than is usually implied by either the term 'school-based' or 'school-focused' . . . What it amounted to was a form of in-service provision which fell virtually exclusively within the professional control of teachers and implied an advanced level of professional responsibility and self-consciousness. (Bridges and Eynon, 1983)

While not wanting to diminish the importance of this approach, which falls fairly and squarely at the professional (ie individual teacher) development end of the INSET spectrum, we would argue that it adds up to considerably less than is implied by the term 'school-based' in this section. The school-centred approach does recognise some central issues, eg teacher responsibility for their own in-service education and the key linkage (explored in this chapter) between self-development, school-oriented in-service education and teacher research.

The school-focused INSET 'movement' which gathered momentum in the 1970s (and which is epitomised in the messages of the DES pamphlet *Making INSET Work*, 1978) has been defined by Perry (quoted in Bolam, 1982) as all the strategies employed by trainers and teachers in partnership to direct training programmes in such a way as to meet the identified needs of the school, and to raise the standards of teaching and learning in the classroom.

As mentioned earlier in this chapter, Elliott (1983) sees the school-focused approach as redolent of 'managerialism' and systems management, a construct from 'organisational theory'. By this sleight of hand (ie identifying all school-focused work with one particular theory of organisations — structural functionalism) Elliott is able to claim that 'INSET focused on the school as a system becomes a matter of rectifying such deficiencies by identifying the malfunctioning parts and allocating the resources necessary to make them fully functional.' According to this approach, claims Elliott, the identification of INSET needs is conducted by the head and the members of the senior management team — they regulate and control the 'system'.

Elsewhere, one of us has outlined five dimensions of the other concept, 'school-based' (Holly, 1985). It means:

a   *school-located* in terms of where the action takes place. Many commentators consider this to be the sole definition of the term. Consider these quotations from *Making INSET Work* (1978):

... a university award-bearing course for a group of staff from the same school includes a substantial school-based component.
Two LEA advisers offer a school-based course of eight weekly sessions on primary maths.
... a teachers' centre warden (was asked) to co-ordinate a term-long school-based course involving outside speakers.

This is what we call the 'weak' interpretation of the term; a stronger definition emerges in this quotation from the same publication:

... some activities, particularly those that are school-based, can be planned and implemented internally.

Two further extracts are pertinent here:

The case has been cogently made that to ensure true implementation of change ... we must work with teachers in the place and in the situation where change is to take place. The case is made with equal cogency that the school-building is the context in which all needs at all levels of the system ultimately come together. (Perry, 1977 — quoted in Hopkins, 1986)

How is technical assistance delivered? Researchers agree that the one-shot workshop in the district office, with no follow-up, is at best symbolic, and at worst trivial. Numerous studies of in-service training state that encouraging teachers and principals at each school site to leave their fingerprints on the training format and content – even to the point of reinventing the obvious — is linked to improved staff performance. While partisans of OD note such findings, others have observed that local site staff training permits teachers to adapt new knowledge and skills to their unique circumstances. Continuous sessions with simple and direct follow-up activities are commonly recommended in these studies. (Cuban, 1984)

A stronger definition of the term 'school-located', then, would have to include different kinds of 'action': planning, implementation, collaboration, involvement in designing courses, etc which are all activities to be carried out in the school.
b *school-centred* meaning in the interests of those who constitute the school — the 'self'. Central to this, of course, will be the teachers — the staff — whose interests are being served. Effective INSET, however, should lead to improved teaching and learning across the school; thus the pupils will also be beneficiaries.
c *school-focused* in the sense that, while the staff will set the agenda, initiate and take responsibility for the INSET activities, they will receive the full support of the other members of the external collaborative partnership mentioned earlier in this section.
d *school-wide* in terms of the scale of staff involvement. Figure 10.3 sets out the pattern, or cycle, of school based improvement through

Figure 10.3   The cycle of school-based improvement through self-evaluation

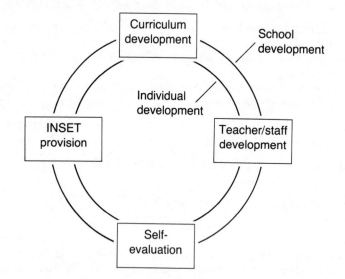

self-evaluation and INSET provision. What is recognised here is that there are different lines (probably more than two) of investment and development. We would make three points; that:

- each line of development is important in its own right;
- there must be a dynamic equilibrium between the lines of development;
- it is essential for the lines of development to be *in dialogue*.

In practical terms this means that the teacher as a 'reflective practitioner' (see Schon, 1983) investigates his/her own classroom performance in terms of, say, the quality of interaction. Teacher teams can also address similar issues and, ultimately, a staff-wide debate can be initiated to investigate teaching and learning styles across the whole school.

e   *school-based* meaning grounded in everyday practice across the school. Mainstreaming could be the term to apply to this positive aspect of the process of institutionalisation. Unlike Elliott, who contends that educational change occurs through the persistence of counter-cultural groups, we would contend that change in schools can occur through organic, collaborative development *within* the culture — *acculturation* as opposed to *proculturation* (see Holly and Wideen, 1986). This approach, however, entails an exploration of the school's present culture and its capacity to tolerate change and development. Innovativeness is the important concept here. As is argued elsewhere (Holly, 1986) there are other important cultural variables such as openness, trust, supportiveness, mutual respect, the acceptance of criticism, etc. Returning to Walker's concept of 'school research', it need not be destabilising of the culture of the school (or at variance with the pace of school development), as long as this same school culture is prepared to countenance the importance of systematic research and evaluation. Self-confrontation could be creatively discomforting, (see the Schmucks, 1974), but this approach needs to spring from the central value system of the school — not in opposition to it.

Three points are relevant here:

1 If this approach becomes organic to the school culture, then, somewhat ironically, effective INSET might become indecipherable as INSET. It becomes one of the 'building-blocks' for school development — a theme taken up in Chapter 8. It could be argued that effective schools need effective INSET (ie school-based in all the dimensions outlined above) to help them to develop effectively.

2 As one of the building-blocks for school development, staff (and professional) development is inextricably linked with curriculum development. To explain these links, Goddard (1985) has used the diagram shown in Figure 10.4.

Figure 10.4 Goddard's Building Blocks

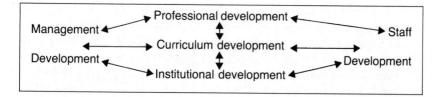

3 Holt (1979) has argued that:

When the focus moves to the school, it moves away from the teacher to the curriculum; a wider concept of professionalism is implied . . . (and) given this wider definition of teacher professionalism, there need be no conflict between personal development and school development.

Both Holt and Reid (1981) have advocated staff-wide deliberation as a means of whole curriculum planning. Their concept of deliberation is very similar to those of collaboration and democratic collegiality posited earlier in this section. In an attempt to emphasise the importance of this 'third force' for school development (which seeks the common ground between Elliott's bipolar view of teacher professionalism versus managerialism), we have constructed the diagram shown in Figure 10.5.

A *Instrumental collaboration* represents what many teachers have come to distrust – sham consultation by means of which the management team aspires to create an impression of 'inclusion' while retaining the reins of power.

Figure 10.5   Staff-wide deliberation

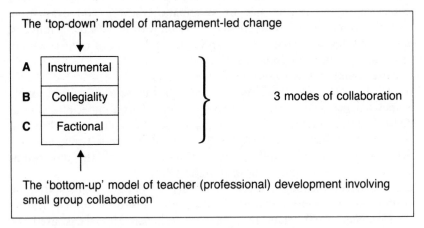

B   *Collegiality* (or democratic collegiality as previously defined) represents the organic approach to school development in which *ownership* is invested in the staff group. Such a staff, working in concert, aims to deliberate, evaluate, investigate – and then take considered action. This organic approach involves systematic development grounded in research. Effective schools, therefore, need to adopt such a school-based approach to research and development – and will need continuing support during these vital processes.

C   *Factional collaboration* represents the micro-political turmoil of small group rivalry. While the individual members are prepared to collaborate within these alliances, the competition between the veto groups prevents school-wide development. In this scenario, 'school research' can often be used to support the claims of one faction or interest group against those of the other groups.

The School Improvement Project

The OECD/CERI's International School Improvement Project (ISIP) – (Van Velzen *et al*, 1985) has concentrated on six thematic areas, the first of which is School-Based Review (SBR) (see Hopkins, 1985). In April 1986, a conference was held at Nene College, Northampton, to disseminate the outcomes of the project. Bollen (1986) and Clift (1986) described the aspects of SBR from the international and UK perspectives respectively. Clift concentrated mainly on LEA schemes for school self-evaluation such as those in use in Oxfordshire, Solihull and Brent. Mention was also made of the GRIDS initiative. Several points arose from their papers relevant to the themes of this chapter.

1   The development of professional organisations (see Handy, 1982 and 1984) will be reliant on the development of an extended professionalism

or 'professionality' (see Hoyle, 1972) which encompasses collaboration as a 'work-norm'. What is required is a highly professionalised teaching force, trained in the skills (in terms both of techniques for evaluation and of inter-personal, collaborative relationships) of institutional review, and acting within a fraternity of professionalism.

2 There is a crucial role for support agencies/higher education (as charted in this chapter) in the provision of those basic skills mentioned above. Research and evaluation skills – those of problem diagnosis, data-collection and data-analysis – will be required for school development through evaluation (including the monitoring of improvement). But the skills to be provided for, and applied by, individuals are for the fraternity that is the school. Ensuring the successful application of research skills for school development should receive the highest priority. What needs to be avoided, however, is mismatch between school needs and support capabilities – sometimes referred to as the 'delivery gap'.

3 SBR can be considered as *the* central process within school improvement; according to both Clift and Bollen, SBR needs to be both systematic and integrated within the management processes of the school. It should be built-in – not a 'bolt-on', fringe activity – and have a profound impact on the school as a social system. SBR has the additional strength of being realistic and 'context-bound' (Bollen, 1986) in the sense that it builds from where the school is now.

4 Politically, SBR is consonant with the concept of the 'relatively autonomous school'. It represents a grass-roots movement, potentially incorporating democratic leadership (see Clift 1986); 'collegiality, fraternity, open communication and co-operation'; a measure of egalitarianism; a tradition for constructive self-criticism; and an open, problem-solving approach. At the same conference, Crandall (1986) drew attention to the power of capacity-building:

The purpose of some external support system activity is to help local schools and school people to develop the ability to identify and solve their own problems, and to plan for and implement their own improvements. Thus, the focus is not on implementing a specific improvement, but on developing the skills and knowledge necessary to be self-directed in improvement-related activities. In some cases, this is done through organisation development activities which may include training in problem diagnosis, problem solving, decision making, goal setting, conflict resolution, and action planning.

SBR is symbolic of both the devolution of responsibility (the decentralised, counter-thrust to centrifugal initiatives) and the mobilisation of the creative power of 'local' human resources. Southworth (1986) concludes:

If this model is to have a reasonable chance of being put into operation on the scale that its promoters imply then teachers will need INSET provision in the area of group and inter-personal skills and understandings. They will also need adequate support at school level. Maybe there is a measure of self-help about this model which is appealing: the staff group could become a network of support within the school for the individual . . . But schools will need help, advice and training to arrive at this.

These are familiar themes in this chapter. Above all, however, as Lavelle and Keith (1985) point out, the top-down paradigm (of centralised decision-making) is being replaced by the 'emergent' paradigm of shared, participative decision-making. According to the authors, the assumption behind this latter model is that the headteacher needs the 'combined resources and understandings of the whole staff team in order that the most effective decisions might be made.' Pro-active development and self-management (aspects of this new mode of decision-making) are elements of both SBR and Organisation Development (OD). Both Lavelle and Keith are members of the OD Unit, attached to the Sheffield Education Department, and are available to:

schools, agencies and departments within the Education Service, helping managers and staff teams identify and address both problems and developmental issues within the organisational and social life of their units, while respecting the autonomy of those concerned. Operating as a neutral third party, it offers insights, drawn from careful diagnosis and consultation, into the relationship between the organisational, cultural and personal aspects of a unit's life and work in a particular setting. These insights then provide the data by which problems may be resolved and developments implemented. (Lavelle and Keith, 1985)

Lavelle (1984) has examined the participative, problem-solving model (or paradigm) which 'places the individual school at the centre of the development process' and which emphasises the internal administration and control of the same process. Implementation, says Lavelle, is in the hands of the teachers; it entails the 'operationalising of new curriculum proposals and the development of strategies to handle the problems created by this process.' Lavelle also charts the repercussions of the tradition of individual classroom/professional autonomy (the cult of the individual); eg the low level of staff interaction and the resulting 'low interdependence' of a school's parts. Stenhouse (1975) makes three points of relevance here:

- teachers need the support of a social climate in order to be prepared to 'face the threat (of honestly examining one's professional performance)';
- the 'highly individualistic conception of teacher autonomy' is increasingly difficult to maintain amid the 'gross disfunctions of practice in a single school';
- the school, therefore, needs to be viewed as a professional community;

creative teachers and head-teachers have been very important to the development of educational innovation in Britain . . . (but) if in the ordinary run of educational life it is the quality of the school as an institution which is the important factor since perhaps the majority of innovations involve groups of teachers, if not entire schools . . . (for) a rich and complex cultural tradition of co-operation through research and development can only thrive in a group which functions as a fully interacting community.

The important concept here is that of institutionalisation (see Holly, 1984b).

In attempting a definition of institutionalisation it is useful to return to Stenhouse (1967 and 1975). Recalling his 'thesis' that creativity can only occur within a cultural framework, it becomes clear that Stenhouse sees institutionalisation as the act of creativity being produced and then adopted by the 'parent' culture through a dialectical process of interaction. Basing his ideas on those of GH Mead (1934), who said 'we can reform the order of things; we can insist on making the community standards better standards', Stenhouse describes this process of trying to induce others to accept our own creative ideas:

We may try to persuade them to adopt our personal innovation as part of the culture . . . A personal innovation attains the status of culture when it is successfully communicated and adopted. Thus, if I develop an innovation in my attitude towards teaching and successfully communicate it to my colleagues so that *we all accept the innovation as a norm for ourselves as a staff*, my innovation becomes cultural rather than personal. (Stenhouse, 1967)

Thus, to Stenhouse, the institutionalisation of innovations occurs when 'they have become norms for the staff, and part of the culture of the establishment.' Stenhouse maintains not only that 'it is by communicating their innovations to a public that individuals contribute to the development of culture', but also, and more generally:

Such a standard, accepted in a single school, is only marginally cultural, however. On the cultural continuum, it is close to the idiosyncratic. Our innovation attains full cultural significance only if it is accepted by a wider group and supported by sanctions deployed by the members of that group.

It would appear that, to Stenhouse, the institution, despite its marginality, is the first point of reference in cultural development. The school witnesses 'the drama of culture set upon a small stage.'

Looking again at his seminal work (1975), we contend that not only is there consistency of message but also that those observers who took the 'teacher as researcher' slogan to be the crux of what Stenhouse had to say, missed a vital half of the message. His initial interest would seem to be in the development of the individual, creatively and critically, but it is his recognition that both these capacities 'grow from the culture and that between the two there is a continuous dialectic' – the process of institutionalisation – that is a central concern. Stenhouse's vision is undoubtedly one of the individual teacher as the school-based curriculum developer and researcher. It is a vision of autonomy and decentralisation, but, we would argue, it is an institutional, not individual, autonomy (see Lavelle, 1984). The object of curriculum development, he argues, is 'the betterment of *schools* through the improvement of teaching and learning . . . the professional development of the individual and the improvement of the creativity of the school proceed simultaneously'. He talks of a school's 'capacity for *action towards change*' and the removal of institutional barriers and constraints; consequently, he argues that it is not only the teacher's professional self-image but also the institutional conditions of work that will have to change. Stenhouse concludes (1975):

I see a move from the idea of a curriculum reform movement to that of institutionalised curriculum research and development . . . The power of the individual teacher is limited. Without his strength the betterment of schools can never be achieved; but the strengths of individuals are not effective unless they are co-ordinated and supported. The primary unit of co-ordination and support is the school . . . (and) it is at school level that the problems and possibilities of curricular innovation have to be negotiated.

We see this process of negotiation (the negotiation of what Stenhouse calls the 'right to experiment') as pivotal in the process of institutionalisation. But this negotiation can have far-reaching effects; for instance, the management of change can lead to a change in management. Is this necessarily a subversive intent? Stenhouse has this to say:

The tendency is to seek a change of organisation which institutionalises innovation in the school and opens the way to a continuous programme of betterment rather than the attempt to leap at a sudden and radical solution of problems.

Above all, Stenhouse attempts to warn against the dangers of his own rhetoric. Reform (he calls it 'gradual adaptation') not revolution is required. While networks of communication offer the fluid, evolving flexibility of a movement – the tactics of dissemination – Stenhouse warns that 'communication is less effective than community in the utilisation of knowledge'. We get the distinct impression that Stenhouse sees networks as the means of spreading the gospel; but that, in his view, it is in schools as educational institutions that real change occurs. He calls teachers educational scientists working in laboratories (their classrooms); the school is their research centre, the unit of the research community. By collaborating within their institution (and institutionalising their research) teachers can achieve what Stenhouse calls the key quality of 'reflexiveness', thus creating a school's 'capacity to review critically and reflectively its own processes and practices' within a systematic review structure.

Autonomy, then, rests with the school rather than with the individual;

it is a case of 'responsible autonomy' (Henry, 1984) with one of the central responsibilities being the obligation to collaborate on a collegial basis (Coulson, 1980). But this collaborative professional partnership envisaged by Stenhouse affects the 'deep structures' of the school (see Hoyle, 1975). The consequent danger is that tissue rejection will occur:

when there is a discrepancy between innovation and the 'pedagogical code' of the school. Many current innovations are underpinned by a 'code' which is quite radically new as far as the adopting school is concerned. This 'code' may perhaps place an emphasis on openness and flexibility in matters of curriculum, methods and the organisation of learning. There are problems of institutionalisation at two levels. At the more superficial level there is the problem of institutionalising not only the medium but also the 'message' which it carries which is derived from the new pedagogical code. The media can be readily adopted by one part of the school; the 'message' requires a switch in code on the part of the school as a whole. (Hoyle, 1975)

SBR, of course, constitutes an innovation which produces other innovations; it is a process with products. Using the terms adopted above, it is both medium and message. SBR, then, impinges on the deep structural and cultural values of the school. It is central to the Developing School – the concept explored in chapter 11.

Section F: Facing the future

Chapters 11 and 12 bring the book to its conclusion. They look towards the future, towards improving practice in schools, to the time when schools become more effective, when teachers are able to make rational decisions based on sound principles and a coherent understanding of theory and practice.

Chapter 11 is necessarily long. It continues the theme begun in the previous section: how to improve and develop schools in order to make them more effective and managerially sound. The first part of the chapter analyses some of the theoretical considerations behind school improvement. The second part focuses on practical guidance in developing effective schools.

Chapter 12 concludes the book by raising some dilemmas which require answers. Both chapters 11 and 12 stress the importance of competent management and leadership to school effectiveness. Thus, the text will have turned full cycle; from the results of ineffective schooling towards effective schools – the theme of this book.

Chapter 11

The Developing School

The individual who fails to learn from experience is forever lost in a chaotic world. He repeats his errors. Worse still, he has no way of navigating among the rocks and shoals of life. One direction is as good or as bad as another. He can make no sense out of his world because he is unable to use his past experience to do better in the future. . . . Organisations, which deal with the collective efforts of men, are devoted to the processing of information and the generation of knowledge. Their ability to test the environment so as to correct error and reinforce truth makes them effective. Inability to learn is fatal yet learning is most difficult because so many men must do it together. (Pressman, JL and Wildavsky, A, 1979)

Some theoretical considerations

This chapter explores, first theoretically and then in more practical terms, the concept of the Developing School. This notion builds on others. Links will be drawn between:
- the Creative School;
- the Thinking School;
- the Learning School;
- the Evaluative School;
- the Problem-Solving School;
- the Relatively Autonomous School;

It will be argued that the Developing School is all these things and more. It consists of six interlocking, yet pivotal elements (Holly, 1985a):
1 An emphasis on the improvement of the process of schooling. The emphasis is on 'schooling' – it is a 'broad-front' approach; nevertheless it should be stressed that curriculum development (the improvement of teaching and learning in classrooms across the school) is the central activity. It is recognised, however, that there are other lines of development which are both supportive of and contributory to curriculum development. Some examples might be:
- the management and organisation of the curriculum. Indeed, it will be argued in this chapter that there is a style of management which is more conducive (than other styles) to the establishment of the Developing School.
- team building; the forging of staff relationships. Southworth (1986)

has pointed out that 'good relationships' might not mean harmonious relationships. It might well be more important to jettison collusive cosiness and 'value difference passivity' (see Holly and Wideen, 1986) in favour of a searching exploration of vital difference. Good relationships could entail challenging relationships.

• the learning of counselling skills to support the pastoral curriculum. Humanised schooling (see the Schmucks, 1974) aims to put warmth and emotion into relationships.

• the provision of awareness-raising experiences, as a first step in the implementation of anti-sexist and anti-racist school-wide policies.
2 The teaching staff are provided with the necessary skills and expertise to play the central roles as researchers, developers and (self-) evaluators. The staff are *the* resource within the Developing School. The art is to unlock their collective experience and capabilities. All the work involved – the research, the development and the evaluation – is undertaken *by* them *for* their school. Consider this quotation:

.. There is plenty of social machinery to check up on a course after it is once launched. The principal of a school, the district superintendent, the college inspector, or the examining board, are all at hand to decide whether the class is doing well in the course. Suppose, however, that by some exercise of wisdom we had reached the conclusion that the subject ought to be thoroughly overhauled. Whom would we expect to do the overhauling? Would the principal regard it as his task? Or the superintendent, or the inspector?

The question arises: Can a substitute for initiative be found in some kind of systematic procedure that will bring to the door of the school new ideas as fast as these ideas are produced? Can we find some way, other than the brilliant inspiration of the reformer, to break into the complaisant routine of the schools. In answer to such questions one can project a plan of organised revision which shall lead to an annual overhauling of the curriculum . . . the re-making of the curriculum with its manifold problems and possibilities seems to offer unbounded and inviting opportunities for the exercise of all the genius that educational workers can contribute. (Judd, CH).

This quotation dates, perhaps surprisingly, from 1922. What Stenhouse, in particular, has led us to realise is that these key 'educational workers' are the teachers themselves. They have the wherewithal to develop their schools, but not, perhaps, up till now, 'power of attorney' in such matters.
3 As we mentioned in Chapter 10, the focus for all this activity needs to be school-based; it is a question of commitment and ownership. The approach required is an organic one. The Developing School rests on the principles of self-determination (within a contextual awareness of what might be termed 'environmental pressures') and systematic development – in the sense that the changes which are considered both desirable and deserving of high priority are grounded in the life of the school, ie institutionalised (see Holly, 1984b, and Holly and Wideen, 1986). While

the emphasis is on innovations being carefully introduced, innovation (in the teacher's everyday conception of the term) is not the order of the day; development is. Innovation, on the one hand, is defined in the dictionary as the introduction of a novelty, a revolution, an alteration, a departure from (or break with) the past; development, on the other hand, consists of the gradual unfolding of growth, evolution, a bringing out of potential, an exploitation of natural resources, a bringing to a more advanced, highly organised state, and an advance through successive stages – a cycle, a spiral. The latter definition underpins the conception of the Developing School. This cyclical orientation to change and development, as embodied in the GRIDS approach (see chapters 9 and 10) is further explored in this chapter.

4 Schools need to be enabled to develop themselves – by both internal (management level) and external support. The latter is increasingly taking the form of the collaborative support partnership as promoted by Bradley (1985) and examined in chapter 10. The role of (external) critical friend or process consultant is crucial within, for example, a formative evaluatory approach. Critical helpfulness (see Drummond, 1986) is the essential ingredient. This role has been explored by the Schmucks (1974), Holly (1984), and both Holly and Hopkins in a new collection of papers (Holly (ed.) 1986). It is a matter of supporting development, within a trusting relationship, by asking the awkward, challenging questions – to break the incestuous circle of introspection and 'navel-gazing'. Major questions arise here, however, concerning the status of what the 'critical friend' has to say. What is its 'authority'? How is it validated? Should the critical friend attempt to 'interpret the situation in terms consonant with those of the actors' (see Terhart, 1982) and thus be subjected to 'communicative validation' (does his/her interpretation ring true in the light of the interpreted person's own experience and judgement of the situation)?. Or should he/she provide a measure of 'argumentative validation' by appealing to the more 'objective' 'unconscious', 'forgotten' or 'routinised elements and conditions' (Terhart, 1982), which are so often neglected because they are so embedded?

5 This collaborative support nexus should involve the presentation of relevant INSET provision (workshops, courses, seminars, conferences, etc) both school-based and centre-based in character. The nature (and quality) of this INSET experience is also crucial; the introduction of more experiential (teacher) learning situations is already receiving close attention, particularly within teachers' centres and other support agencies which are close 'to the ground', and in a position to 'make a difference' by joining in the action on a reciprocal, collaborative basis – the central theme of chapter 10.

6 Self-evaluation is essential in the Developing School for the following reasons:

- it is the basis of what constitutes a systematic research-based development programme, as demanded in chapter 10. It allows for 'front-end' or situational analysis (see Skilbeck, 1975).

- it provides for the maintenance of a data-base concerning current practice; this enables a continuing and coherent re-focusing of tasks to occur.
- it encourages the unlocking and systematic analysis of teacher intuition and 'educated judgement'.
- it provides regular, formative feedback for (curriculum) developers; it offers both evaluation for implementation and the validation of educational improvement. It promotes growth and informed development.
- it creates a platform for critical dialogue concerning classroom practice and the quality of teaching and learning.
- it provides an opportunity for staff involvement in the development process and thus creates the 'occasion' for teamwork, staff inclusion and ownership.
- it can operate on a number of levels, for example

a teacher-based and team-based departmental self-evaluation/classroom action-research leading to teacher professional (and curriculum) development in such all-important areas as: changing teaching and learning styles; new modes of assessment; developing the appropriate skills of guidance, counselling, negotiation (of learning), etc.

b school self-evaluation building on level (a) but also encompassing the evaluation of the whole school performance, as encouraged within the GRIDS approach

c institutional self-evaluation (see below)

The Evaluative School (see Simons, 1980) has self-evaluation built into its sinews. It should be pointed out, however, that the three components of *school*, *self*, and *evaluation* can all be defined in various ways. There is, therefore, a problem of the permutation of meanings. Within the context of the Developing School, the staff (working on the three levels above) constitute the *self*; they focus on certain aspects of the *school* and approach the task with a seriousness of intent (within what we have called '*the democracy of discomfiture*') which makes it a genuine evaluation. We have also argued previously that there are five stages within an in-school evaluation, as illustrated in Figure 11.1 (see Holly, 1984)

A number of points are of relevance here:

a As part of an in-school evaluation, the staff members are responsible for all five stages. In the late 1970s, the hey-day of the 'LEA checklist' approach, the emphasis tended to be on review at the cost of taking any action based on that review. The GRIDS Project aimed to include the action stages as an integral part of the exercise – evaluation for (curriculum) development and improvement.

Figure 11.1   School-based evaluation; a structured approach

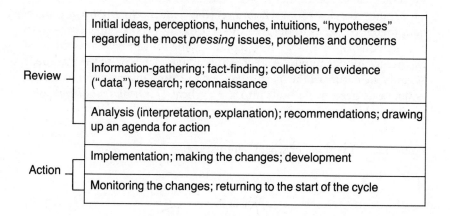

b It should also be acknowledged that evaluation can occur within such a cyclical approach in different forms and at different times as shown in Figure 11.2

Figure 11.2   The holistic approach to evaluation

Curriculum \ Scale of involvement	Individual	Whole school
Intended	1	2
Received	3	4

This two-dimensional model illustrates four kinds of 'curriculum', which require two kinds of evaluation:
- the intended, individual (classroom) curriculum (1)
- the intended whole (school) curriculum (2)
- the actual, received individual (classroom) curriculum (3)
- the actual, received whole (school) curriculum (4)

Two further points are relevant here. First, the intended curriculum (both on the part of an individual and the whole school) consists of what Parlett and Hamilton (1977) refer to as the formal *instructional system*: the elaboration of aims and objectives, the syllabus or scheme of work, curriculum guidelines, lesson notes and plans, a packaged innovation – the domain of the *intentional*. An *intrinsic evaluation* asks such questions as – are these intensions intrinsically worthwhile? Are they realistic? Are our goals misconceived? Are they appropriate – philosophically and psychologically? Second, the received curriculum is what is actually happening, the classroom/school everyday reality. An *empirical evaluation*, therefore, needs to observe and record this process 'up close' and to ask such questions as – what is actually going on here? What is the lived experience for our pupils? And does this actual match up to the intended? What is the nature of the 'performance gap'? Both intrinsic and empirical evaluations need to be built into the cyclical *Spiral of school improvement* (see Figure 11.3).

Figure 11.3   The spiral of school improvement

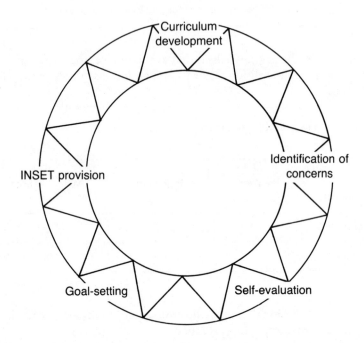

The Developing School is dependent on interlocking lines of development:
- individual (professional) development – the inner line;
- school development – the outer line.

Holly's work for the SIDE (School-based INSET for Development through Evaluation) Project of Cambridgeshire LEA, and for the various TRIST initiatives has convinced us that these lines of development are both crucial: individual and school-wide development both need to be present and *in balance* – the one must not be allowed to take precedence over the other. For far too long (as argued in chapter 10) we have had one without the other – a case of over-developed individuals in under-developed schools? The reverse is now in danger of happening in some schools. What is required is an equilibrium of investment. But this equilibrium does not occur by chance. It has to be striven for. It has to be structured and organised. This is where the synthesising factor – the middle, connecting line – comes into its own. This integrating line comprises *institutional development*, a consequence of the examination and overhauling of the values, norms, expectations, and attitudes which constitute the school's culture, the deep structure of the schooling process which underpins classroom practice and the mode of interaction. We would contend that without (self-) evaluation and development of this deep, structural level, real school development remains out of bounds.

School development depends on cultural development and vice versa. Holly and Wideen (1986) have identified three dimensions concerning cultural change in schools: *proculturation* – the desire to impose a fixed (cultural) agenda on others; *enculturation* – the felt need to resist proculturation and innovation, or the desire to remain unscathed by change and to weed out (or filter) its radical connotations; and *acculturation* – the merging of agendas through (mutual) adaptation and accommodation. Gadamer (1975) has described the latter as the learning process – the engagement of 'the new' with (the application of) one's 'fore-conceptions' in a spirit of openness and interest in adding new knowledge, understandings, skills, etc to one's repertoire. Acculturation is the modus vivendi of the Developing School. It involves the central concept – that of the Learning School.

In the Learning School, learning is not only *the* focus, it is an interactive social, intra-and inter-group activity. Teacher learning about learning can be achieved through action-research and many action-researchers pay homage to the work of Kurt Lewin. His basic planning cycle or spiral has become embedded within many an action-research project. But what about his other messages? Curiously, perhaps interestingly, many of these have been ignored. In his seminal paper published in 1946 ('Action Research and Minority Problems') he talked about the problems of transforming 'serious goodwill' into 'organised efficient action'. Action-research, he argues, leads to social action and, in so doing, deals with problems of 'attitude and stereotypes in regard to other groups and to one's own group'. He continues:

recent research findings have indicated that the ideologies and stereotypes which govern intergroup relations should not be viewed as individual character traits but that they are anchored in cultural standards, that their stability and their change depend largely on happenings in groups as groups.

He also calls the 'workshop setting . . . the most powerful tool' in breaking down these cultural barriers, while recognising that, outside the workshop, each individual group member will be on his/her own. 'Obviously', he states:

... the chances are high that his success will not be up to his new level of aspiration and that soon disappointments will set him back again. We are facing here a question which is of genuine importance for any social change, namely the problem of its permanence.

But what if the culture of the staff group is transformed into a permanent, supportive, workshop setting – the continuous staff conference as Richardson (1973) once called it. Action-research training Lewin concludes is a 'triangle that should be kept together for the sake of any of its corners.' As Piaget (1971) said about pupil learning, so teachers, with suitable help, would be *'free to work with one another'*.

At this point, we would like to describe the activities of one school where the staff appear to be heading in the direction outlined above. It is a high school catering for students in the 13 to 18 age range. As a staff, the teachers decided to explore the concept of autonomous learning in the six curriculum areas within which the staff are all clustered. This exploration began in September 1984. In November, during a residential weekend conference/workshop, over two-thirds of the staff met together to compare notes concerning their exploration thus far. They did this by staging a series of curriculum experiences; each group of staff representing a particular curriculum area attempted to involve the other teachers (as if they were a class) in an experimental lesson – experimental in the sense that it aimed to represent their exploration of the concept of autonomous learning. Teachers became the learners; they experienced the learning process in however many forms of autonomous learning the curriculum teams came up with. The focus was very much on interactive learning with emphasis being placed (at different times) on *independent* learning, *activity* learning, and the *personal and social* aspects of learning (see Figure 11.4). As the observer (and participant in the lessons) Peter Holly felt that he was witnessing and experiencing the personal and social development of teachers; teachers becoming autonomous learners by discussing and enacting the process of autonomous learning. His role during the weekend was not only to observe but also to report back to the staff towards the end of the weekend, in terms of his perspective on their deliberation.

In attempting to hold up a mirror to the staff and their progress. Holly pinpointed five questions:

1 Should a style of learning be matched to a style of teaching? What would 'autonomous teaching' look like?

2 In asking for help in the furtherance of 'autonomous learning', where is the dividing line between organisational support and institutional constraint? In this context he argued that the staff should look to the teachers of personal and social education and drama in particular during the exploration of activity-based, group-based learning.

3 Is there a dichotomy between the declared aims of enhancing the skills of 'communication' (taken to mean induction into the language and

Figure 11.4 The process of autonomous learning

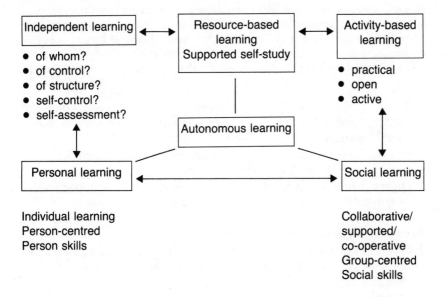

culture, ie socialisation) and 'critique' (the invitation to use those skills to launch a critique of one's culture)? Stenhouse (1967) charts this central dilemma of schooling.

4 Is a 'moral education' involving 'autonomous learning' enhanced by the climate of the school? The 'morally educative school' and the 'just community' (see Power and Reimer, 1981) could provide the framework for 'moral judgement and action'.

5 Is there a mismatch between the rhetoric of progress thus far, as evidenced at the workshop, and the reality – the everyday actuality of the classroom? This question led him to describe the possible potential of the model mentioned earlier in this book – collaborative action-research across the institution; classroom/teacher-based and school-based enquiry.

Following the weekend workshop, the deputy head co-ordinating the development work (interestingly, he had been appointed partly because of a previous involvement in both action-research and collaborative investigations into the process of classroom learning), issued a report to all the staff. This document is a 'record of some of the things that the staff did to develop their own classroom practice in 1984/5' (Pinner, 1985). His introduction contains these comments:

I say some of of the things because every time two teachers meet at the classroom door between lessons to chat about what they've taught, a form of in-service training takes place. The development of classroom practice isn't about the imposition of styles or methods; it's about co-ordinating what is happening already, bringing people together and facilitating their own learning by learning from each other about how best to ply our trade in the interests of young people . . . within the school, we've been involved in the joint enterprise of setting up a new curriculum and many of us have been eager to see that this goes well beyond becoming a 'paper exercise' and that theory is coupled with classroom practice. At the same time, the LEA's own curriculum developments have followed similar lines in that pupil learning rather than teaching has been seen as central.

Included in the report is a description of the 'weekend voluntary conference' and some 'practical steps towards fostering autonomous learning' (as suggested by the Thomsons, 1984).

Practical steps towards fostering autonomous learning include:

a Start from what the pupils know already.

b Engage them actively in what is being offered and allow opportunities for pupils to contribute from their knowledge and experience.

c Question the relevance of what you are offering to pupils. Share with them your reasons for setting a particular task.

d Create opportunities for pupils to develop the following attitudes and values which will enable them to become autonomous learners:

- co-operation
- perseverance
- initiative
- independence
- tolerance
- sensitivity
- judgement
- imagination

e Allow pupils the opportunity to take on more responsibility for their own learning. Help them to find out for themselves instead of telling and showing them what to do.

f Encourage pupils to formulate questions related to what they are learning. The ability to predict, anticipate, hypothesize and speculate all play an important part in learning how to learn in all subjects; whether we are applying those particular qualities to written text, or towards more practically based learning in Science, Craft and Design Technology, or Home Economics.

Also contained in the report is a description of the various experiential learning presentations included during the weekend and news of more recent developments involving 'pupil days' during which members of staff follow pupils 'through a complete working day . . . experiencing something of the total educational context . . .' The idea was that the staff who were doing the following should attempt to enter classrooms as learners and to engage in the act of learning alongside pupils. 'In effect, we moved away from the idea of studying the pupil and used the invitation to visit lessons as a means to experience much of what we had all forgotten – the feeling of being a pupil.' One visiting member of staff is reported as concluding that 'in terms of my own learning I honestly found this one day more useful than any course . . .' (quoted in Pinner, 1985).

Holly's remarks as consultant/evaluator during the workshop (listed above) are also included in the report. This residential weekend was a real learning experience. So much so, in fact, that we have tried to pass on the insights gained to teachers in other schools interested in becoming involved in similar developments. The particular school mentioned above was developing its work on autonomous learning relatively autonomously, ie under its own auspices – within the pre-TRIST situation. More recently, of course, schools have been encouraged to chart similar territory (teaching and learning styles) within the rhetoric of a plethora of national initiatives. CPVE, GCSE, LAPP, RPA, TVEI, and finally, TRIST, have all provided opportunities for advancing the processes of classroom learning. In connection with the introduction of CPVE, a colleague recently observed that:

In a curious way, one hears echoes of the professional debates in the late '60s concerning Plowden philosophy in the primary schools. There is an uncanny resemblance between the spirit of child-centred primary education . . . and the student-centred philosophy that seems to underpin so much of pre-vocational thinking at the present time. The development of skills, learning through experience, group activity with its opportunities for discussion, the importance of good record-keeping as a corollary – it is all there. (Brennan, 1985)

Having taken these comments seriously, Holly was able to organise a DES/Regional couse entitled *Teaching Styles and Approaches to Learning* under the aegis of the Cambridge Institute of Education. With a colleague at CIE, Mary Jane Drummond, tutor for early years education, we were able to discuss with secondary school teachers the relevance of learning in the primary school. It is likely that this dialogue across the 'great divide' (see Derricott, 1984) will become increasingly pressing.

This DES/Regional course was organised in three phases:

- Phase one – March 1986 – Residential Weekend Conference/ Workshop
- Phase two – Summer Term 1986 – Initiation of In-School Development Work
- Phase three – Late June 1986 – A second residential experience designed to meet the needs of the in-school development work.

The initial weekend aimed to achieve 'awareness raising' in terms of the central issues pertinent to changing teaching and learning styles. In a background thoughts paper Holly (1986) was able to identify the following themes:

1 Traditionally, the focus has been on teaching; there is now a new focus on the nature of the process of learning – in all its complexity. Key linkages were identified by means of the schema shown in Figure 11.5.

Figure 11.5   Key linkages in learning

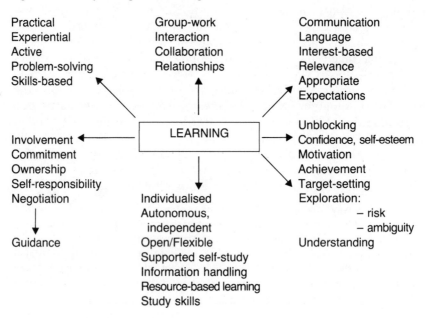

Arising from this schema are some central dilemmas concerning the learning process:

a What happens to learning when it is institutionalised? How can school-based learning be freed from the institutional constraints of location, time and space (see Holly, 1985a)? Very recently the publication of *Sarah's Letters: A case of shyness* (1986) has confirmed the impression that 'one pupil's education is another's incarceration' (Murphy, 1984).

b What is the teacher's role in student-centred learning? How profound are the changes in teaching style necessary for the enabling of learning? How does the teacher remain *in* control without *taking* control?

c What is the purpose of the 'new learning': social understanding as opposed to social control?

Sullivan (1985) has queried whether schools 'really want to produce children who don't accept that teacher knows best'. He points out that –

confident pupils would naturally be displaying their confidence through their behaviour. They would not be overawed by authority, but would challenge assumptions, make independent judgements, work with competence and not seek constant reassurance . . . Most of us actually involved in teaching in classrooms would, I'm sure, feel pretty uncomfortable with children who didn't actually accept that teacher knew best.

Yet Sullivan concludes that 'confident people are more challenging than predictable, passive dull-eyed conformists'. It should be stressed that Brennan (1985), having recorded his observations concerning the student-centred approach, is forced to conclude:

And indeed there are discernible the same constraints which, from society's viewpoint, may well in the final analysis prove necessary ... it is inconceivable that 'the student-centred' model of learning can ever be pursued 'à outrance'. Indeed, given the main function of pre-vocational training, it could be naive to think that this could ever be so.

So what happens to the educational rhetoric amid the political realities? As Elliott (1978) concluded, what happens in classrooms has clear political messages. Is independent learning, therefore, politically subversive or is it a case of being 'independent' to be able to accept a particular (political) agenda? What is certain is that the classroom act is not innocent.

d Does 'negotiated learning' (and the 'negotiated curriculum') result in massive (individualised) differentiation of experience? Are such moves incompatible with the drive towards the common curriculum? Who determines the agenda within the negotiating process? (see Holly, 1986b)
e Is it examination skills versus life skills? Is it a case of one or the other?
f Which is more important, individualised or group learning? Is the latter being neglected at the expense of the former?
g Is the search for relevance and interest-based learning being promoted to the detriment of higher level learning (see Doyle, 1979)? Are success and security being promoted above what Doyle argues are the ingredients of genuine understanding – risk and ambiguity? Taking account of his typologies (see below) are we merely moving from model one to model two? And should learning be easy? Should it be cosy? What is the place, for example, of 'cognitive dissonance' (Festinger, 1962)?
h If motivation is central (see Hargreaves, 1983), is it to be engendered intrinsically or extrinsically? Even Maslow (1981), the arch-priest of self-actualisation and intrinsically inspired learning, was forced to admit that extrinsic motivation has a role to play. Maslow came to realise that students arrive in schools to learn in different states of 'psychopathology' (their previous experience has determined their personality types) and, given this background and biographical detail, some will be resistant to 'new' modes of learning. They expect to receive the same diet as before. The teacher has to struggle with such expectations (see Hull, 1985). Moreover, argues Maslow, in so doing, the teacher will need both to apply the 'discipline' of extrinsic learning (which will be teacher-controlled, in line with the teacher's values and consist of content/skill

education) and to attempt to 'humanise content education so that its relevance is felt'. The teacher must also prevent extrinsic learning from dominating intrinsic learning (gained from profound personal experience). According to Maslow,

relevance is to be attained not by coating substantive ideas with sugar, not by transforming the classroom into an entertainment centre, not by thoughtless worship of spontaneity, but by searching – long and hard – for the natural seductiveness of the subject matter itself.

i How should we assess the 'new learning'? Is profiling the answer? (see Burgess, 1985)

j How should we assess achievement? Is criterion referenced assessment *that* different from norm-referencing? Is the ipsative approach superior to them both?

Figure 11.6   Typology of academic task structures defined by the interation of ambiguity and risk (contained in Doyle, 1979)

Risk

	High	Low
High Ambiguity	Understanding	No task
Low	Memory II	Memory I

2 The efficiency of teacher learning by looking at learning. The experience of classroom action-researchers is invaluable in this context. Rowland (1983) sums up the thinking behind his classroom research into pupil learning as follows:

The most frustrating thing about running a classroom is the lack of time you have to think about what you are doing. We are expected to be accountable for what learning takes place under our supervision, but have little opportunity to reflect upon it as it takes place . . . Children learn while we teach, no doubt. But our understanding of the relationship between teaching and learning seems to be governed more by tradition or fashion than by a close examination of children while they are learning in the classroom.

Following his own investigations, Rowland reaches the following conclusions:

i A necessary condition for successful learning is that the learner is able to exert a degree of control over the purpose, structure and content of his activity.

ii The principles which govern the child's learning are the same as those which govern the adult's learning.

iii The process of analysing children's learning has a direct and positive influence on one's competence as a teacher.

Similar experience has led Holly to conclude that teachers learn by looking at learning. Thus, in the DES/Regional Course described earlier, the participating teachers were encouraged to think seriously about their own classrooms, their teaching and their students' learning experiences.

3 The nature (and characteristics) of the Learning School.
Several threads can be identified. The staff in the Learning School will be encouraged to:
a discuss and explore the dilemmas of learning outlined above.
b take seriously the experience gained in the US by Kohlberg and his colleagues concerning the 'morally educative school' (see below). What are the cultural values and principles of procedure necessary to create a *learning climate*? If the medium really is the message, what is the learning 'medium'? (Power and Reimer, 1980)
These authors chart the generation of 'collective normative values' in a school which ultimately results in a developed 'sense of community'; their quest is to operationalise the linkage between moral judgement and *action*.
c investigate the organisational 'theory' suitable for a more open-ended exploration of learning. How can extended student learning be supported organisationally? The same, of course, goes for teacher/staff (collaborative) learning.
d create a dialogue (concerning teaching and learning styles – in terms of variation and effectiveness) across the school – particularly inter-departmentally.
e explore the possibilities of introducing more humanised schooling (see the Schmucks, 1974) and more open relationships generally.
f introduce control 'after the event' (see Handy, 1984). Handy's 'essay' on schools as organisations is most relevant here. Building on Peters and Waterman (1982), he encourages schools to become proficient at

- problem-finding (as well as problem-solving);
- having an organisational 'fleetness of foot' (which he refers to as a 'bias for action').
- being 'close to the customer'. He contends that 'in excellent schools ... *the children, and their learning,* (our underlining) are what matter'. Handy recommends that schools should 'identify your customers, talk to them; listen to them and find out what they need

and want, lean over backwards to deliver it and monitor the results continually'.

- encouraging 'autonomy and entrepreneurship' throughout the organisation. Schools, says Handy (reminding us of Stenhouse, 1975), should become 'loose networks of laboratories'; ideas (and their communication) should be encouraged.
- offering positive reinforcement (see Rutter *et al* 1979), and should heed the messages of 'expectations theory'.
- establishing an atmosphere that is 'hands on, value driven' in which managers practise what they preach by rolling up their sleeves and working in the classroom with both teachers and pupils.
- 'sticking to the knitting', ie doing what they are best at doing – the organisation of teaching and learning; schools should concentrate on these central core tasks.

Above all, Holly emphasised at the workshop that this particular school seemed to be displaying the necesary 'criteria for take-off' as a learning institution. The following points arose:

1 the symbolic nature of the weekend workshop; the team spirit; openness; communication and pooling of experience.

2 the growing trust and support; the growth of group-based deliberation and the prominence of women teachers. (Is this the 'matrism' explored later in this chapter?)

3 the involvement and engagement with the learning process.

4 the developing space (and autonomy) to explore autonomy.

5 the recognition of the usefulness of the 'external perspective'.

6 the recognition of the importance of evaluation, concerning the quality of the students' learning experiences.

One school staff, therefore, is engaged in the attempt to improve their school through general participation in collaborative action-research.

The Learning School with its central emphasis on the learning process, elevates the importance of the concept of teachers as learners (see Thomson, 1983, and Rowland, 1983 and 1984). The latter is one of the 'building-blocks' which, when assembled in a structured and coherent fashion, constitutes the framework for the Developing School. But 'development' has to be managed . Management Development (see Goddard, 1985) is another of the foundational 'building-blocks'.

It is argued (Holly 1986) that for the successful internal development of a school, there are three crucial issues to take into account:

- is the approach to management in the school and the espoused style of leadership conducive to this kind of work?
- are the members of the senior management team aware that they have certain (supporting) tasks to fulfil?
- are the role(s) of in-school co-ordination being taken seriously?

These three key questions demand some elaboration.

The style of management

For whole school development, the appropriate style of management is one which encourages and enables:

a consultation with, and participation of, the 'body' of the staff, thus invoking their commitment to the enterprise and their involvement in, *and ownership* of, the change process

b supportiveness, collaboration and a willingness on the part of the staff generally to operate as a team (or at least, in teams).

c the realisation that each member of staff is a resource – to be utilised to enhance the development process. Within such an approach the strengths of staff members need to be identified and this expertise orchestrated.

d a critical dialogue to occur between members of staff, but one which is both constructive and positive.

Handy (1977, 1982 and 1984) has explored 'effective management' within the context of effective organisational development. His preferred stance is that of 'management by consent'. Handy maintains that this approach is based on an 'implicit contract' consisting of five principles:

1 the members of staff, according to Handy (1977), are a 'resource which the organisation ought to cherish'.

2 consequently, these same members of staff should be viewed as individuals with personalities and individual rights to be regarded.

3 'deep beliefs' concerning the ways in which people should relate to each other; equality of status and parity of esteem are promoted at the expense of hierarchicalism

4 'authority' is granted by those below not above. It is Locke's social contract before Hobbes' power-coercive, top-down regimentation (what Fullam, 1985, refers to as 'brute sanity'). Those 'in authority' are given the power to make decisions on behalf of others – according to the continuing ratification of this arrangement by those same 'others' (as long as those in authority manage in the interests of those others, remain faithful to the contract, consult with them and honour the agreement to expose themselves to dissent, argument and conflicting opinions). There are two views of the world, two views of human nature, based on Locke's optimism and Hobbes' pessimism. Management by consent rests on the former. Handy (1977) contends that:

It is when a management, un-understanding, infringes the psychological contract by assuming unratified authority that morale is lowered, secrecy and subversion mounts, energy and commitment reduce. Lonely and anxious, management then too often responds with more controls and checks, more assumed rights. Self-fulfilling, the organisation begins to respond only to whips and spurs and everyone wonders what went wrong.

So it is partly a question of resolve ... and the ability to resist the temptation to dive for the controls the first time that a colleague is 'untrustworthy'. It is considered that these two 'world views' demand two kinds of evaluations (Holly (ed), 1986):

The technical-rational approach, according to Cuban (1984) rests on a key assumption – that a body of knowledge and expertise can be applied to increase (teacher) productivity. Cuban writes 'Tighter coupling between the central office and individual schools along particular lines – such as goal-setting, monitoring, evaluating, and specifying outcomes – often gets translated into the familiar pattern of top-down implementation'. According to this view, says Cuban, the teachers are the 'problem, the solution, the scapegoat' . . . but 'few scapegoats have been noted for volunteering'. The other approach aims to 'release local capacities' by harnessing teacher commitment, interest, participation and ownership of the developmental process. Cuban believes that in a climate of an enhanced team-spirit, mutual trust, openness, collaboration and collegiality, 'new work norms of teachers observing one another, talking frequently about pedagogy, and engaging in joint planning, stimulate the sharing of values that nourish school improvement!'

'It is my contention', he concluded, 'that evaluations can be enabling or disabling'. I now want to make the same point concerning styles of – and approaches to – management.

Handy, however, maintains that management by consent does not imply a 'consensus organisation'. Managers, according to his view, are hired to take decisions, although the 'important decisison, the right to institute procedures, must be exposed to possible dissent before implementation'. His model involves consultation, not participative management, through committees which 'are not decision-making forums; rather testing-grounds of decisions . . . platforms for dissenters.' Quite rightly, in our view, Handy's approach aims to avoid the stultifying effects of veto groups, incessant talk (with little action resulting) and the consequent organisational inertia. We would query, however, Handy's rather querulous attitude to staff participation; the latter need not result in non-action. As with all processes, staff participation (and involvement in decision-making) demands structuring – see below.

In 1977 Handy observed two pertinent trends (both contributing to the drive for management by consent): the emergence of managers as semi-professionals and the spread of values more germane to 'matrism' than 'patrism'. His view of managers as semi-professionals is close to the concept of 'entrepreneurialism' much vaunted recently by Peters and Waterman (1982) and Drucker (1985). Handy declares that the semi-professional will endeavour to develop his/her management skills; 'his commitment will be to himself first, his profession next, his organisation third'; and that his/her work will be a 'major source of identity'. Furthermore, these new managers will be both mobile and concerned with self-development. He argues that 'since their career will not necessarily be with the same organisation they cannot expect the organisation to invest too much in their long-term development. They must take responsibility for their own development'.

According to Handy (1977), organisations will tend to be partnerships of mobile professionals who will be managed by consent. He has developed this theme in his essay on schools as organisations (1984). This 'professional culture' seems rather too reminiscent of the cult of individualism – pinpointed in chapter 10. Since 1977, of course, professional mobility in education has slowed down considerably and teachers, whether managers or not, have learnt to stress the development of their organisational – as opposed to their professional – selves. Ironically, therefore, the contracting labour market has contributed to school development.

In identifying a second trend, Handy quotes G R Taylor's 'Rethink' in which the author identified two sets of competing values which he labels 'patrism' and 'matrism'. The former entails the traditional and 'tough' values of order and discipline, respect for authority, self-control and rational behaviour; distinctions between male and female roles; and age and experience elevated above insight and youth. The latter, which is 'radical and tender', belongs to the optimistic school and is concerned with openness, emotional involvement; much less role distinction between the sexes, discussion and dialogue; and a reliance on expertise, youth and imagination. This counter-cultural set of values (that is matrism) has an essential part to play within the Developing School. As Handy asserts,

Management style is neither ultimately right or ultimately wrong, it is only culturally appropriate. The hierarchical style of management may well have been appropriate to a Britain reared by Victorians and Georgians. For the new Elizabethans it seems very probable that the culturally appropriate style is going to be management by consent.

Handy (1977) also poses the question – how does one manage by consent? He gives six answers:
1 recognising the right to disagree
2 controlling by planning not by checking. As mentioned above, this is the evaluative stance utilised within the context of the Developing School. It is evaluation for development, not control (see Holly in Holly (ed.) 1986). Moreover, the GRIDS scheme always aimed to service planning for internal development as opposed to monitoring for external accountability purposes (see Holly 1984). In organisations managed by consent, says Handy (1977),

it is legitimate to plan and to replan or change plans. It is not legitimate to check what others are doing unless their specific agreement has been obtained. Information for planning is willingly vouchsafed, information for monitoring less willingly. The Manager, therefore, has to work with a variety of planning cycles and be clearly seen to use past information as a base for future planning.

3 managing by reciprocal trust (instead of control). As Handy maintains, if you trust someone, there is no need to monitor his/her actions.
4 managing by platoons. Handy argues that individuals find it easier to identify with (and feel that they have greater influence within) small 'primary groups'. Trust, he says, is easier to create in smaller groups, so he utilises Anthony Jay's concept of the platoon and insists that, while 'individuals may be individuals . . . they need a group to identify with . . . Everyone should therefore be a member of at least one platoon.' In the primary school the whole staff can form the ten-member platoon; in the secondary school, with a staff of 65 plus, the problem becomes one of how to establish the platoons. Handy (1984) has since offered mini-schools as one solution; his 'task culture' (problem-solving groups) is another. We hesitate to suggest departmental teams (the 'pavilions' of chapter 10) as they might actually impede school development. Holly once observed that 'whereas a departmental structure was a strength, perhaps in the developing school it is now a weakness' and would prefer to see the platoons formed by interdepartmental groupings. (Holly, 1982b)
5 being yourself. Woods (1979) identified the teacher's person and (school) persona; Nias (1983) has talked in terms of 'situational' and 'substantial' selves. Handy's exhortation is for organisations of consent to be

personal rather than impersonal. You cannot trust a facade. Openness and frankness and sincerity are valued. To act a role is to disappear as a person; whatever your idiosyncracies or habits or values, let them be visible.

6 husbanding your energy. According to Handy (1977), management by consent is exhausting:

to treat individuals as individuals, to welcome disagreement, to tolerate dissent, to listen more than talk, to be true to oneself as well as others – all these . . . require a deal of energy. When energy fails we fall back on routines and general principles, listen less, dictate more.

Handy in fact, while listing the credits ('organisations built on consent sound exciting, sound democratic and in tune with modern ideals'), also admits to some implications on the debit side; managerial burn-out, professional obsolescence (concerning those without the necessary resources of energy), and the temptation to opt out and become 'modular man' – who gets only part of his identity from his work. It is our contention that structured participation on the part of the whole staff could well militate against these repercussions of management by consent. As Nias (1980) has maintained, 'leadership' can be galvanised throughout an organisation.

Moreover, Handy's idea of management by consent is rather dated. It clings to the last vestiges of hierarchicalism and individualism. It also smacks of the instrumental version of collaboration identified in chapter 10. The over-instrumentalism of 'sham consultation' (so distrusted by teachers – see Nias, 1980) has a reactive, other side – factionalism (as Handy himself admits). The more organic, democratic aspects of collegiality can only be achieved through participative decision-making by the staff. But here one has to find categories of this new kind of involvement. Holly and Southworth (1986) have identified three such dimensions:

a normative collegiality, where the value *agenda* (the 'what') is to be discussed and established collaboratively.

b procedural collegiality, where the 'how' is agreed in concert.

c democratic collegiality which involves collaborative planning and decision-making concerning the 'what' and the 'how'. Members of staff know when they are experiencing the reality of democratic collegiality, as opposed to, say, sham consultation. They can smell out instrumentality. Wragg (1982) for instance, has caricatured 'management by all'. He writes about 'Donald', the one member of staff who is not included in the enlarged senior management team comprising the other 39 members of staff, who complains about his predicament to the head of the school. The latter justifies the situation as follows:

You see, as I explained at the staff meeting, we've been through all that dreary stuff about management by objectives, management by consent, we even tried management by embarrassment at one point, but I am sure that my new concept of 'management by all' is most definitely going to set a national trend . . . With a much more mature teaching force we must evolve a style of management that is in accord with the times. That is why I have created the largest senior management team in the country, 39 people, a formidable fighting outfit totally dedicated to the successful running of this school . . . Look Donald I can understand your bitterness at being the only person not in the senior management team, but don't you see that you have been hand-picked for a very special role next year? . . . For management by all to be effective there has to be someone who is actually managed. I've been grooming you for this, Donald. You are the key person in my new plan. You are what I call the 'managee'.

But, asks Southworth (1985), are not the claims made for the collaborative model rather unrealistic in the present circumstances:

A collaborative, collegial staff requires certain pre-conditions (trust, acceptance of each other, stability) and will demand of all staff greater skills in handling group and interpersonal dynamics. To expect teachers to adopt this is, in many cases, far too optimistic.

Perhaps Southworth lacks the courage of his convictions; he seems to believe in the collaborative model but feels bound to retreat into describing 'what is' rather than 'what could be'. He is right to point out the strength of one major constraint: the attitudes of some teachers (who expect not to have to collaborate in the affairs of 'others', ie the management of their schools). This separatist stance, of course, also allows some teachers the luxury of criticising every move made by the members of the senior management team. Hierarchicalism is embedded in some teachers' thinking; they love to hate it.

Southworth (1985) questions whether any individual course-goer has a positive influence on the staff group. Holly's contention is that if the head is the individual course-goer, then the hierarchical 'divide' is in danger of being widened. He would agree with Southworth when he coments: '. . . maybe we should think of all the staff going on a course; or that the staff become the course'.

This attitudinal divide between managers and managed is worsened, according to Southworth (1985), by the current fashion of extracting headteachers from their schools to specifically experience one-term courses of management training. 'What sense of collaboration is this?', he asks, 'when collaboration may well involve schools having lots of leaders – not just the head as leader'?

Southworth (1985) also makes the point that, since the HMI Primary School Survey (DES, 1978), there has been an explosion of interest in the use of scale post-holders as curriculum co-ordinators in primary schools. These 'curriculum consultants' act both as promoters of curriculum review and development in their areas of responsibility and as resources for the rest of the staff group. 'This has coincided,' argues Southworth, 'with increased staff participation in curricular decision-making and evaluation. Quite a lot of this has been promoted to break down some of the inconsistencies caused through teachers working autonomously in 'their' classroom'. But these curriculum co-ordinators will need their own (management) training along with the rest of the staff. He concludes, therefore, that

it is rather paradoxical to focus all the management training on just one leader, the head. There is also the issue that all of those who work collaboratively will be engaged in judgement and decisions more akin to diplomacy and politics than to economics and bulk-buying: yet the industrial model of management is still being offered as a model to emulate.

Handy (1982) has made the same point. Just at a time when schools are aiming to adopt one particular, industrial model of management, industry itself is fast jettisoning this model. 'Perhaps', says Handy, 'in a funny way businesses are going to be more like schools'. Using Handy's categories (1984), they may well trade in their 'role culture' for the 'professional culture' of 'professional organisations' (like educational establishments). These organisations, according to Handy, are/will be staffed full of thrusting, entrepreneurial, risk-taking professional individuals (the cult dies hard!):

they are individuals and they regard themselves in a way as craftsmen and that's what they're about . . . Progress for a professional means doing the same thing but better.

These individuals will be employed on contract work, as 'networkers', and, according to Handy (1983), could well be based in their own homes behind their separate but interlinked (ie networked) computers. The 'organisation' will be purely notional. The atomistic 'society' will have arrived. The pyramid bureaucracy will have given way to the nuclear explosion. Handy (1982) points out that with these professional pathfinders 'doing their own thing', it will be 'difficult for some managers because they like everything to be nice and tidy and well defined'. 'Organisations' will be untidily diffuse. But will the out-workers wear it? Will they countenance the isolation and possible alienation? Will they hanker after the alternative delights of co-operation and collaboration? According to Southworth (1985), sharing ideas and developing plans corporately are the 'building-blocks of healthy communication and commitment . . . as a model it is very appealing because it offers a participative form of management.' But this should not be viewed as being synonymous with consensus decision-making. As Southworth argues there is not a logical connection; creative conflict could well replace cosy consensus. Particularly if the communication is intense (see Cuban, 1984) and the dialogue profound, differences will be identified which may well be disruptive and 'dislocating in terms of changes and improvements'.

Walker (1985) made the same point concerning the impact of 'school research'. It should be remembered, however, that the creative harnessing of value difference is only disruptive to agendas established prior to the collaboration taking place. Collaborative, participative decision-making (like school research) demands suspension of judgement. Agenda-building should arise out of collaboration not preclude it – thus the merging of normative and procedural collegiality in chapter 10, to produce the democratic version. Decisions reached in this manner could be described as 'systematic', 'measured' (over time) and suitably 'considered'. But this model may well rest on the exploration of value difference and the resulting 'conflict' could well be seen as just as untidy and unpredictable from the management perspective as the nuclear diffusion model sketched above. 'Managers' would presumably not opt for either model, but would prefer the cosiness of divided but highly controlled organisations where value difference passivity is highly-prized, ie secondary schools as they are now, which in Handy's terms are a synthesis/permutation of the four work/organisational cultures – the club, role, task and person cultures. Handy, then, sees schools as embodying a 'cultural mix' but with all the attributes of professional organisations. This tendency has five implications:

1 Management by consent is increasingly seen as the norm. The consultative model aims to 'clear' matters prior to implementation; gaining advice, of course, does not necessitate acting upon it. Management by consent, therefore, even when conducted with an earnestness of

intent, could be perceived as instrumental collaboration (as defined in chapter 10).

2 According to Handy, professional organisations sensibly differentiate between administration and leadership. The former, which, he says is 'done for you, not to you', can be dealt with by non-professionals. Handy cites the case of the chief clerk in a firm of solicitors; to combine the two roles in one person, he contends 'is an invitation to stress'. In his extended essay (1984), Handy makes five points, all of which are relevant here. He argues that

a in education there has long been the attitude that there is no time for management; he talks of educational managers running highly complex organisations in their spare time;

b managers are snowed under;

c managers, he adds, are hardly ever un-interrupted, but their inter-personal contacts are fleeting ones (see Stewart, 1982, and Mintzberg, 1973). Indeed, Mintzberg argues that there are ten roles for any senior manager: figurehead, liaison, leader (the inter-personal roles); monitor, disseminator and spokesperson (information roles); entrepreneur, disturbance handler, resource allocator and negotiator (decision-making roles); managing, therefore, tends to be 'superficial', 'quick-fire', 'fragmented' and 'staccato';

d consequently managers have to be 'pragmatic beings', and their working lives consist of 'workable compromises'. According to Hopkins (1986), much of their time is spent 'fire-fighting' and this leads, we would argue, to pragmatism becoming a way of life, even a 'philosophy'. Managing is coping – surviving the vicissitudes of daily organisational life; it is crisis management. An appropriate metaphor is that of the pin ball machine – with the manager projected/bouncing from one crisis to another.

e amidst this frenetic activity, the danger is that the cracks are being (temporarily) filled with Polyfilla, but no-one has the breathing-space to question why the cracks are appearing in the first place. No-one is questioning (or prompting the questioning of) the architectural design. Handy (1984) concludes, therefore, that schools need leaders who are freed from administration. Instructional leadership is, of course, one of the pivotal concepts used in the 'effective schools' literature emanating from the United States.

3 Handy (1984) maintains that this leadership component should be provided by the key professionals. He quotes MacGregor Burns (1978) who maintained that there are two aspects to leadership – transactional and transforming. The former involves 'fixing' and 'dealing' (a necessary part of administration, says Handy); the latter necessitates the 'lifting or transforming of energies with a *common institutional purpose*' (my italics). It includes the 'raising of motivation and morality'. According to Burns, leadership means 'elevating, mobilising, inspiring, exalting,

uplifting, exhorting, evangelising . . . transforming leadership ultimately becomes moral in that it raises the level of human conduct and ethical aspiration.' Thus, transforming leadership can engender organisational 'cohesion through a shared commitment to a cause'. 'Loose coupling' is a characteristic of professional organisations, consequently, the generation of value consensus (the school's culture) could provide a measure of organisational cohesion.

4 Several authors besides Handy have followed this line of reasoning. Gehlen (in Berger and Kellner, 1965); Deal and Kennedy (1982 and 1983) and Deal (1985) have all looked to the positive, unifying effects of a school's or organisation's culture, which is constituted by the sharing of norms, values and expectations (see Holly and Wideen, 1986). More recently, Cox (1986) has explored the importance of 'culture' amid the chaos and uncertainty of value pluralism in schools. From the perspective of these writers, culture becomes a positive (even positivist) force which can be used to combat the unpredictability and untidiness of value pluralism. Cox begins his article by asking whether state education depends 'on some basic consensus about values and can it survive in our divided, pluralistic society?' 'In recent years,' he adds, 'our sense of a cohesive national culture and identity has broken down'. Given the pluralism of values in society (and in families representing that society), what kind of school should the head of any local comprehensive school try to create? Can there ever be agreement, Cox asks, between parents about the schooling they want for their children? He continues:

The battle for the curriculum is not understood by many parents. It's not just a question of whether to introduce topics such as world studies. It affects the way we teach all subjects, the total cultural life of the schools'.

'Cultural', in his usage also means 'political'. The reference to world studies concerns the stance taken by Scruton (1986) against education as indoctrination in favour of a 'good education' which 'depends on arduous study and analysis, on keeping the mind open to conflicting arguments in order to assess facts objectively'. Cox admits, however, that the 'new Left' would argue that objectivity is a subjective construct (see Holly, 1985) and that 'individual freedom to choose between competing ideologies is a bourgeois illusion, a product of the decadent ethos of liberal humanism. . . . The middle classes exert not only political and economic control but also project a particular world view which is accepted as 'common sense', the natural order, by those who are in fact subordinate to it.' Cox is here paraphrasing the work of critical theorists (members of the Frankfurt School – see Lukes, 1976) and structuralists (see Foucault, 1970) all of whom, according to the 'new Right', have higher education in their grip. Cox, in explaining the position of the new Left, asserts that there has always been indoctrination in schools (through 'cultural' activities like history) and that examinations, form positions, team games, prizes, selection, hierarchy etc, amounted to the hidden curiculum which 'encouraged competition and individualism, essential to the working of capitalism'. 'By such means,' he continues, 'some of them trivial, most of us learned to accept unreflectingly a value system'. One gets the impression at this point that Cox, while disliking the content of the value agenda imposed on himself, is impressed by the effectiveness of its imposition. Perhaps, indeed, the content isn't so bad either:

The new Left advocates radical changes to destroy such traditions, to replace competition by compulsory co-operation, and this is why mixed ability teaching is so important to their aims . . . If state education is to commend support, it must retain traditional values, combining study of the disciplines of history, literature, language, mathematics and science, with a concern for individual creativity . . . I join the editors of the 'PN Review' in believing that these attacks on high culture and individual freedom are dangerous. The new ideology devalues the fostering of individual excellence which, after all, benefits the collectivity – and on which the survival of our society depends. (Cox, 1986)

Four points are worth noting here:

- Cox's last sentence is a superb example of the 'liberal' ideology discussed in chapter 10. Adam Smith could not have put it more succinctly.
- By a sleight of hand, Cox has moved from a statement of the aims of the new Left (exposure of the 'structures of the mind' which enthral a person and constrain/or distort his/her individual consciousness) to seeing these same 'critics' as the arch-enemy – the usurpers of this individual freedom.
- Nevertheless, Cox does retain a measure of 'objectivity' when he admits that there are 'no easy solutions . . . the new theories established that most courses in history, literature and the arts involve ideological commitments, and this knowledge cannot be set aside.'.
- Cox also touches on the subtle linkage between 'culture' in the sense of 'high culture' (ie coverage of the tradition of great writers, etc) and the 'culture' of a school – those norms and values which are embedded in the curriculum and which determine the mode of relationships, etc.

5 Referring to the concept of leadership, introduced by Handy as being of central importance, we would contend that professional organisations – like other organisations – have a problem in this area. Is it almost a case of not wanting leaders, but needing them? We would ask three other questions at this point:

a Who are these leaders? Using Handy's categories, are they the charismatic personalities who are the spiders at the centre of his club culture webs? Or the top bureaucrats in the 'role culture'? Or orchestrators (or even commanders) of the task groups? Or key professionals (eg heads of faculty) in the person culture?

b Is 'leadership' a male problem? Do we expect macho leaders? Are we looking for 'Action Man', the messianic executive who will make everything better – the John Wayne of management? On the basis of two pieces of research conducted recently, staffs claim that they hope their new heads will be like 'Moses' (Weindling and Earley, 1985) and lead them out of the wilderness (the list of personal and professional qualities demanded of new heads, according to the researchers, is awe-inspiring), while another report (Lyons, Stenning and McQueeney, 1985) concluded not only that 'heads are still far too autocratic', but also that

There appears to be widespread recognition that a new professional consensus must be forged between headteachers and staff. However, our study suggests that only a small minority of headteachers are initiating debates within their schools aimed at developing mutual understanding and fostering a sense of common purpose among the adult community of the school.

c What of the latter collaborative model? Is it 'leadership' to enable this to happen? Is this the emasculation of leadership? Handy (1984) poses the central question here: whether in professional organisations 'the junior professionals need to go along with the philosophy of the senior professionals or whether they are entitled to hold and practise their own views. Does a head have the right to impose his or her own philosophy?'

Handy (1984) appears to rest on the horns of the leadership dilemma. At times he sways in the direction of leadership both as the facilitation of collaboration and an attribute/quality to be displayed by members of staff generally (democratic leadership, if you like). He recommends a 'bias for action' which means 'discerning the key opportunities for the advancement of the organisations . . . Finding the right problems and doing something about them characterises the lively school'. Drawing on his experience of the GRIDS approach, he concludes that 'some recent experiments in self-evaluation in schools have really been organised approaches to problem finding'. In addition, he underlines the importance of the trust involved in 'control after the event', of 'autonomy and entrepreneurship' (according to which leaders and innovators are encouraged throughout the organisation and the school becomes a 'loose network of laboratories'); of 'productivity through people' (thus forfeiting some control, he argues); and of the approach known as 'hands on, value driven' in which the leaders are seen to practise what they preach. Yet he is also able to talk of the benefits of 'clear lines of command' and of 'tight coupling'. Professional organisations, he says, are composed of autonomous groups 'bonded together for mutual help'. While the energy is within the autonomous groups, he argues, the 'centre' should have the bonding role. Those at the centre should establish normative control – the standards within which the members of staff have freedom to operate. He appears not to countenance the possibility (or even the desirability) of the normative component being collectively deliberated on and established. Leadership, according to Handy, includes 'direction' of the institution; the provision of 'vision' and the initiation of a normative structure which incorporates the establishment of goals and priorities. The dichotomy exists to the last; Handy quotes Peters and Waterman (1982) who extol the virtues of institutions in which 'people can blossom, develop self-esteem, and otherwise be excited participants in the organisation' and then concludes:

Nor is leadership confined to the head . . . Schools close up their policy structure at their peril. Opening up a policy structure does not mean that all staff have to take part in all decisions.

Particular tasks of management

a   To lead by example; to experience the tensions and stresses of being involved in personal change. Holly has already referred to this phenomenon as the 'democracy of discomfiture'. If change is good enough for some, it is good enough for all. In addition, Hoyle's (1972) quotation remains most appropriate: 'Curriculum innovation requires change in the internal organisation of the school. Change in the internal organisation of the school is a major innovation.'

It is a question not only of individual members of the senior management team becoming involved in personal change, but also of these same individuals changing their domain – the school's organisation and management – to keep pace with, and to underpin, curriculum change.

b To attend to the establishment of *pre-conditions* for a school development programme; to set the climate for change and to foster the school's readiness for development. An example of this crucial activity is the instigation of an inter-departmental dialogue concerning teaching and learning styles.

c To promote the ethos of the *Learning School* in which not only is *learning* (and its improvement) seen as the central focus but also, among the staff, *teacher learning* is enhanced by encouraging them to study the *learning process* in their classrooms. In the United States, the phrase 'morally educative school' (see above) is used to describe the moral climate which is capable of communicating messages to all participants. The Learning School aims to have the same impact. Two points are relevant here:

i Fullan (1985) sees 'learning' as the metaphor for the implementation of change. The teachers, committed to the change process, are engaged in institutional learning and problem-solving.

ii Stenhouse (1975) refers to 'principles of procedure' when outlining his process model of curriculum planning and development. Within school-wide curriculum development these 'principles of procedure' include openness, trust, respect, supportiveness, etc. Such principles affect the qualitative dimension as shown in Figure 11.7.

Figure 11.7 Principles of procedure

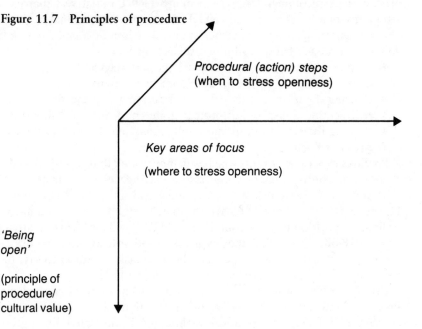

Procedural (action) steps
(when to stress openness)

Key areas of focus

(where to stress openness)

'Being
open'

(principle of
procedure/
cultural value)

Senior members of staff can espouse these 'cultural values' in their everyday actions and relationships – the medium is the message!

d To work at a continuing fusion of individual classroom and whole school, personal and institutional, initiatives. The Developing School will need someone to orchestrate this fusion process.

e To provide support (the demand for which may change over time) during the various stages of the change and development process.

f To encourage staff to go beyond the usual collusive cosiness of 'value difference passivity' and to investigate these value differences as part of the change process. It is important to challenge embedded ideas without invoking unbridled conflict.

g To maintain the framework for development. To set deadlines and encourage colleagues to keep them, to support the cyclical, systematic and structured approach of The Developing School (as embodied in these process guidelines); to promote development before innovation.

h To establish internal co-ordination for the development work.

The role(s) of internal school co-ordination

It is probably inadvisable to create a 'deputy-head in charge of the management of change'. One person cannot change for you; the same person cannot manipulate/pressure you to change – on a lasting basis. But there is a real need for one person, or a small team of colleagues, to co-ordinate, 'manage', support, and encourage the in-school change process. It is recommended, within many TRIST initiatives, that each school appoint a school-based INSET/development co-ordinator, probably of deputy-head/senior teacher status. This senior member of staff will have a range of responsibilities, including:

- liaising with the LEA and external support agencies;
- co-ordinating the in-school developmental activity;
- chairing the in-school INSET team/steering group meetings;
- representing the school at project conferences and workshops;
- training the staff in evaluation and resourcing the staff in the Key Areas of Focus.

Previous experience of this role has demonstrated that this team leader becomes not only an enabler, but also a gate-keeper (the barometer of staff stresses and strains), a fixer, a nurse and an internal consultant. He/she will soon learn the 'art of plate-spinning' (the normal co-ordination position is a horizontal one!). He/she will also learn to attend to what Holly has called the 'expressive and instrumental modes' – soothing staff wounds while keeping them on task. Needless to say, the role is a demanding but crucial one. (See Holly, 1982a)

Co-ordination, however, is not always seen in a positive light. Pressman and Wildavsky (1979) point out that, when implementing changes and facing the political realities of institutional life ('given obstruction, delay, red tape, overlapping, duplication, vacillation, hesitation'), there are two temptations: going outside the bureaucracy, and co-ordination. But, say the authors,

we will show that attempts to circumvent the bureaucracy often create more problems than they solve. And as far as co-ordination, on closer examination we will see that it is a term not for solving problems but for renaming them so they emerge at the end the same as they were at the beginning . . . their quick espousal tends to block deeper consideraton of the nature of organisational difficulties, thus imparing the learning process.

As a reaction to bureaucratisation, or enculturation, as the same phenomenon has been referred to in this chapter, the first temptation is to establish a new organisation within the 'old' one (akin to what Miles, 1964, referred to as a 'temporary system') ie a subculture within the mainstream culture. 'The cost of independence from ordinary bureaucratic constraints', argue Pressman and Wildavsky, 'turns out to be loss of contact with the very political forces necessary to preserve the thrust of the organisation.'

Those involved in moves towards 'debureaucratisation' are condemning themselves to (self-) marginalisation and peripheralisation; they are, culturally speaking, 'out of kilter'. Their work tends to have a 'short-run orientation . . . (and is not) designed to make a permanent and significant difference'. Such personnel, according to Pressman and Wildavsky, have the 'in and out perspective of the anti-bureaucratic stance (but are) unlikely to stick around long enough to shepherd the implementation of their programme after it started'. It was this aspect, of course, that caused us some misgivings concerning Handy's mobile semi-professionals. Changing the culture of schooling demands rather more commitment – and engagement within that same culture. In asserting that cultural embeddedness is an historical phenomenon, Pressman and Wildavsky declare that:

Racial discrimination has existed in America for over three hundred years, and the consequences of racism have left their indelible mark on the differing life chances of black and white in this country. Whatever their proximate causes, the race revolts that began with Watts are *rooted in history* (our italics). All this suggests that it will take a lot of concentrated effort and a long time to eradicate poverty and racism . . . Turning around any American city is something that cannot be accomplished overnight, no matter how dramatic the program. Imagination is needed, but so is perseverance.

Pressman and Wildavsky then turn to their other 'false Messiah', co-ordination. They look to its positive side first – its facilitation of policies which are mutually supportive, its prevention of people working at cross-purposes and its encouragement of a common purpose. What happens, they ask, if there is normative disagreement? Is co-ordination a means of coercion, a form of power? Is it the case that 'everyone wants co-ordination on his own terms'? Their objection to what they call 'bureaucratic co-ordination' (in which clearance is gained from the 'other participants who have a stake in the matter and their consent gained') is similar to our stance towards instrumental collaboration – it is a less than honest attempt to 'sell' one agenda only. It involves the imposition of one definition of the situation; the 'creation of unity where there is disunity', and an attempt to 'expedite what you haven't got – compliance'. Above all, maintain Pressman and Wildavsky, co-ordination might be a means of avoiding the real problem. History will not be changed by denying its existence. The task, therefore, is threefold.

1 to locate the development work – and its implementation – within the mainstream culture and political structure of the school;
2 to build within the bureaucratic set-up by working within it in order to confront the major flow of bureaucratisation
3 to attempt to explore and not to deny the existence of value differences and potential for conflict by constructive management strategies.

As we have already argued in this chapter, the Developing School needs to countenance the exploration of difference.

Section Two: *The Developing School; a practical guide*

Holly has recently prepared a teachers' guide: *Guidelines for Undertaking Internal Development Through Evaluation.* These process guidelines are intended to help secondary schools grasp the TRIST opportunity (Holly, 1986). In the introduction he emphasises that, as with the GRIDS method,

> the central practical recommendation . . . is that the staff should not attempt to make a detailed review of all aspects of the school at once. Instead they should take a broad look at what is happening in the school, on the basis of this identify one or two areas that they consider to be priorities for specific review and development, tackle these first, evaluate what they have achieved and then select another priority . . . a systematic step-by-step approach is recommended throughout. (McMahon, A. Bolam, R., Abbott, R and Holly, P.J. 1984)

In the first section of this chapter we have attempted to provide the theoretical underpinning for this Teachers' Guide. We would now like to provide some flavour of its practical intent by outlining how it can be put into operation, looking first at the structure of the GUIDE:

These process guidelines can be represented in the form of a two-dimensional model (see Figure 11.8)

Figure 11.8   Structure of the GUIDE

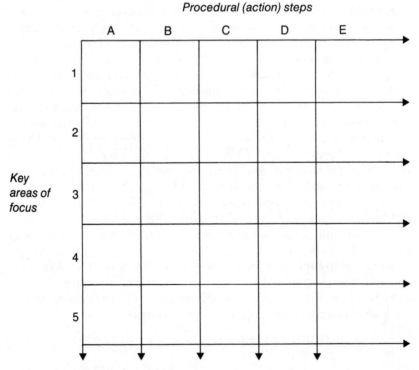

The vertical axis concerns the *Key areas of focus* – which can, for example, be identified within the following schema (see Figure 11.9)

Figure 11.9   Key areas of focus

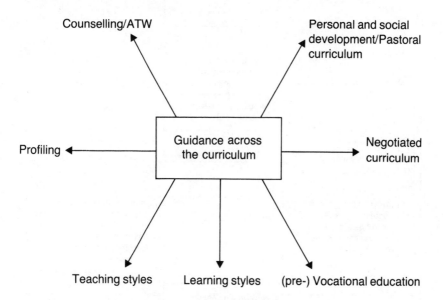

The horizontal axis consists of the *Procedural (action) steps*, the first of which, **A**, entails the establishment of a school-wide forum during which members of staff are able to deliberate and *prioritise*, thus deciding which aspects of the Key Areas of Focus are in most pressing need of review and development. This first step constitutes an attempt to answer the question, *what do we need to look at?* The remaining Procedural (Action) Steps are indended to answer these questions (see Figure 11.10):

- *Where are we now?* An examination of current practice across the school in the key area(s) of focus, using classroom research methods.
- *Where do we want to be?* An investigation of the practice of other schools; a survey of relevant 'theory' (including the messages of DES reports, etc.); the ensuing definition of goals; and the judging of present practice in the light of these goals. An 'agenda for action' should begin to emerge at this stage in the form of an *action* plan.
- *How do we get there?* What are the constraints holding back the development work? The identification of INSET needs is crucial at this stage, in order that they can be provided for *before* moving into action and implementation.
- *How are we doing?* During the implementation stage, the staff should be prepared to mount a continuing programme to monitor the effectiveness and impact of the changes.

Figure 11.10 **The research-based development process**

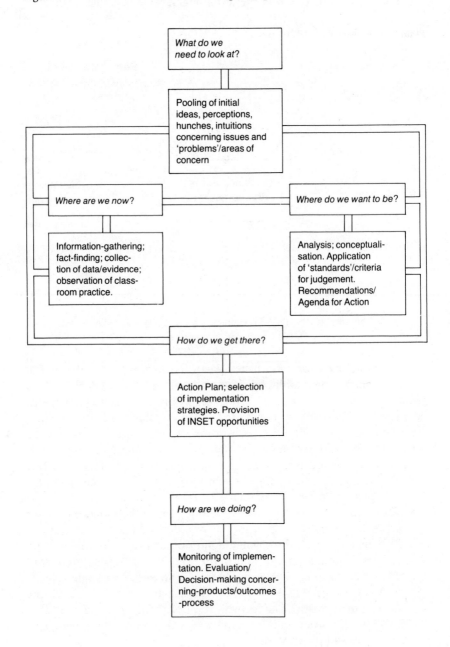

This cyclical approach is, of course, very close to that originally posited by Kurt Lewin in the 1940s (Figure 11.11).

Figure 11.11   Kurt Lewin's action-research process

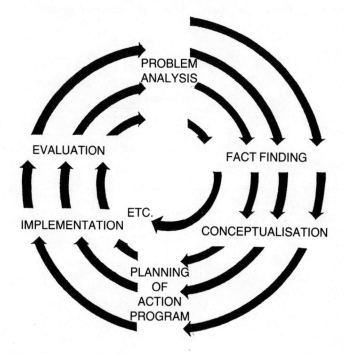

Procedural (Action) Step One

Central question: *What do we need to look at?*

This corresponds to the 'initial review' stage in the GRIDS scheme; its purpose is to survey the work of the school within the Key Areas of Focus and on the strength of this review identify the topics that are considered to be of high priority for review and development.

Conducting the initial review; surveying staff opinion

There would seem to be two methods of eliciting staff opinions:
a circulating a survey sheet (the GRIDS methods);
b conducting a *structured* staff discussion.
Schools may, of course, choose to combine both these approaches.

Using a Survey Sheet

Canvassing staff opinion – using a survey sheet Figure 11.12 is an example of the survey sheet amended to suit the purposes of TRIST/ SIDE. It is divided into two sections: in the first section individual

Figure 11.12   Survey of staff opinion: secondary schools

Section 1. Please indicate (by ticking in the appropriate column):
(i)   the extent to which you feel the following aspects of the school would benefit from specific review and development;
(ii) whether you think each aspect is an area of strength or weakness or is satisfactory.

	(i)			(ii)		
	would benefit from specific review			Strength	Satis-factory	Weak-ness
	YES	NO	DON'T KNOW			
KEY AREAS OF FOCUS						
GUIDANCE						
Counselling; Active Tutorial Work (ATW)						
Personal and Social Development						
Pastoral Curriculum						
Careers Guidance						
Negotiated Curriculum						
ASSESSMENT						
Graded Tests						
Profiling; Records of Achievement						
Continuous Assessment						
TEACHING/LEARNING STYLES						
Autonomous Learning						
Active Learning; problem-solving, etc.						
Resource-based Learning; Supported Self-Study						
Information Technology						
Continuity of Learning						
THE CURRICULUM						
14–16 Curriculum						
16–18 Curriculum						
CPVE: Pre-Vocational Education						
Special Needs/Lower Attainers						

	(i)			(ii)		
	would benefit from specific review			Strength	Satis-fac-tory	Weak-ness
	YES	NO	DON'T KNOW			
Multi-cultural Education	....	....	....	....	....	....
Equal Opportunities	....	....	....	....	....	....
Modular Curriculum						
Work Experience	....	....	....	....	....	....
Residential Experience	....	....	....	....	....	....
Please add any important topics not included above:						
....						
....						
....						
....						

Section 2. Bearing in mind that it may be as valuable to build strengths as to develop areas of weakness, please select up to three aspects of school life from those listed above, including any added by you, and:

in column (i)   write them below in order of priority for specific review and development within available resources *over the next twelve months*:

(ii)   explain what you mean by the topic and what the review should focus upon.

Order of priority	(i) Aspect of school life	(ii) Explanation
1.		
2.		
3.		

members of staff are asked to consider whether different aspects of the school are in need of specific investigation and development; in the second section they are asked to list in order of priority three topics which they think should be selected for review and development over the next 12 months and to explain their choice.

Advice from the GRIDS booklet is as follows:

Past experience indicates that it can take about an hour to complete the survey sheet and that teachers prefer to take it home. The key point to stress is that the teachers should make an individual response and not discuss their views with colleagues beforehand. Individuals are not required to put their names on the survey sheets; they can return them anonymously either in an envelope or by placing them in a box in the staff room. If individuals tick their names on a list when they have done this the co-ordinator can easily check that they have been returned . . . 'The initial review's main strength lies in the opportunity for each contributor to register an opinion' (Primary co-ordinator). Once the survey sheets have been returned, one person, probably the co-ordinator, can tally the results.

Structured staff discussion
There are various models from which to choose; for instance:

1 *Nominal Group Technique (NGT)*
This is a fairly lengthy process (1½ hours) and needs careful chairing. The various steps to take and the time sequences are as follows:
a clarification of task (10 minutes) – by the chairperson, who would need to list the areas of concern from which to select
b silent listing by individuals of the areas giving each one of them most concern (10 minutes)
c 'round robin' during which the chairperson asks each individual in turn for his/her most pressing concern and the items are listed on a flip-chart. The aim would be to go round the staff group more than once (20 minutes)
d item clarification during which any individual can ask another for clarification concerning the point raised (10 minutes)
e selection of issues against the criterion – 'which is the problem you feel most urgently needs investigation?' Silent ranking (5 minutes)
f ranking/tallying (15 minutes)
g discussion of outcomes (20 minutes)

2 *The Diamond* (see Figure 11.13).
This technique is best used to conclude discussion and to determine the concern which takes priority over all others. This is basically a method of organising small group deliberation. The technique is as follows:
a Nine cards (numbered 1–9) are handed to each small group and nine issues/concerns are identified. Each issue is given a number (and a card). Each group is asked to rank the cards/concerns and place them in a diamond shape with the most pressing concern at the top of the diamond and the least pressing concern at the bottom.

Once the survey data has been analysed, the next step is to select the areas for specific review and development in the year ahead. It is possible but rather unlikely that everyone will have identified the same topic as first priority. Where several areas have been highlighted the GRIDS materials recommend that there should be a full discussion to decide between them. The simplest way of doing this is probably to arrange a staff meeting.

Figure 11.13   The Diamond

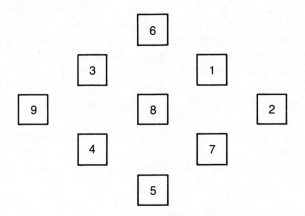

It should be pointed out, however, that the techniques mentioned above can often be incorporated successfully when used in combination, e.g. the diamond being used to follow up a survey sheet. The advice of the GRIDS handbook at this stage is as follows:

> The co-ordinator and team should spend some time beforehand thinking how they are going to organise this meeting. Ideally the staff (and any others involved) should be given a written report of the results a few days earlier so that they have an opportunity to think about the findings. At the staff meeting the co-ordinator can:
> a show how the scores were added up and explain/describe the findings
> b advise the staff about how many specific reviews they can probably realistically tackle given other constraints.
> Schools must be careful not to attempt too much. Two specific reviews are probably the maximum number that a school can handle at any one time.

The process of prioritisation provides an ordered list of (identified) schools needs, thus forming what could be called a *general developmental plan* to be implemented over a period of time. What has not been decided upon at this stage, however, is an *action plan* – how to go about the development programme in a manner that can be strategically implemented (according to the 'art of the possible').

Significant issues
This first procedural (action) step (which embodies the central question – *What do we need to look at?*) rests on four key principles.
1 *Prioritisation* The ability to prioritise makes the review and development programme much more appealing at two levels:
   • it enables the participants to feel that the enterprise is feasible, manageable and practicable.
   • it creates a (correct) impression that there is a seriousness of intent to launch into an in-depth, profound investigation as opposed to a superficial, cosmetic exercise.

2 *Ownership* The emphasis on full-scale staff involvement has a key purpose – that of 'inclusion' – the engendering of participation, engagement and, therefore, a sense of commitment and responsibility.

3 *Segmentalism/Incrementalism* The structure is a cyclical one, in that the list of priorities which emerges from the staff deliberation can be viewed as a development plan – to be tackled systematically and cyclically over a three or four-year period.

4 *Experiential Learning* Having identified the key area of focus, it is acknowledged that, when the staff launch into their review and development programme, they will probably discover that they will need to journey into related areas (within the original schema) during their investigation. This journey of awareness-raising is seen as important in itself.

Procedural (Action) Step Two
Central question: *Where are we now?*

The purpose of this stage (known within the GRIDS scheme as the 'specific review') is to survey work in classrooms across the school pertaining to the key area of focus. What is required, therefore, is a detailed investigation of current practice within the topic area selected as a priority. Three principles are central to such activity;

1 that the investigation is undertaken by a specific review *team* which is representative of the whole staff, ie its membership is interdisciplinary. The aim is to establish an inter-departmental dialogue concerning teaching and learning styles across the school.

2 that their inquiry should take the form of classroom observation by adopting suitable research techniques. The aim of this activity is to complete an *empirical evaluation* by observing 'up close' the classroom reality, the curriculum-as-received by the students.

3 that their research should be 'filed' and a summary document circulated to all members of staff.

It is important to utilise the services of a broad-based team of staff members; not only does this mean that the workload is shared but also that it can be a useful staff development activity for the particular individuals selected. In seeking volunteers, individuals with experience of either action-research, classroom self-evaluation or research techniques should be encouraged to contribute their expertise. Once selected, the team members should meet to decide:

a which aspects of the topic they should focus upon;

b which research techniques would be appropriate.

The team should also draw up a timetable for the review.

It is worth noting the advice contained within the GRIDS handbook:

This is an unpopular task that teachers are inclined to skip but it is one that can be very valuable. When a topic is identified as a priority for development, especially if it is considered a weakness, the inclination is to rush into action. The rationalisation for this is that, since it was identified as a priority, everyone must be dissatisfied and energy and time should be devoted not to examining practice, but to deciding what to do next. However, when the review team do make a detailed examination of present practice this can prove to be one of the most valuable aspects of the whole process as it produces a very solid basis of information on which to proceed.

Within an evaluation it is important to establish the nature/extent of present practice in order to be able to judge the character and impact of the ensuing changes.

The research process

It is crucial at this stage to gather evidence concerning individual practice *across* the school, thus aiming to achieve a full picture in terms of both the *personal* and the *institutional* faces of teaching and learning styles. Questions then arise such as:

- Is there a match or mismatch, between the personal and institutional aspects?
- Is there a variety of practice within departments and across the school?
- Is there a uniformity of practice?
- Is the rhetoric matched by the reality?

There are several different ways of collecting information about present practice. One starting-point is a *documentary search* – an examination of any existing documents and policy statements to clarify what the school or each department says it does about the particular topic in question. Useful sources for such information will be:

- the staff handbook;
- departmental documentation: schemes of work, syllabuses, etc;
- policy circulars from the head and senior staff and curriculum guidelines.

The next step is to collect information from a cross-section of the staff about what they *actually* do in the classroom. There are various ways of doing this. The review team could devise a simple questionnaire for this purpose or ask colleagues to write a brief report. In this context, the advice from the GRIDS handbook is pertinent:

The review team need to think carefully about the advantages and disadvantages of the various methods of collecting information. If they decide to use a questionnaire each question must be thought through carefully – what exactly is the purpose of the question? Will the teachers understand it? How will the data be analysed afterwards? Open-ended questions (eg what are you aiming to achieve in this subject?) can provide fascinating information but they are difficult to analyse. Questions that only require a tick are easier to complete and tally . . .

The review team will almost certainly want to go beyond asking colleagues about their classrooms to observation of their practice. It is crucial to establish a conducive climate for this sensitive work, and to emphasise:

- peer observation; mutual exchanges of information between colleagues; teacher collaboration in this exercise;
- the utilisation of techniques developed by teachers involved in classroom self-evaluation;
- negotiation with colleagues concerning the 'clearance' of the observational data arising from such joint activities. The aim, at this stage, is illumination (of complexity) and understanding (of characteristics), as opposed to appraisal; awareness-raising before judgement.

In the next step, that of collecting data concerning the everyday reality of classroom practice, three approaches may prove useful:

a What is often called the *'quantitative' approach* which entails the use of observation schedules, such as the Flanders Interaction Analysis Categories (FIAC) and that used by the ORACLE Project. These schedules enable the users to identify percentages of classroom-time spent on various kinds of task. Intensive *shadow studies* of pupils (throughout their curriculum) can be conducted using this technique.

b The *'checklist' approach* can be useful to sensitise teachers to the issues that are important (important, that is, according to the compilers of the checklist!) An example is shown in Figure 11.14

Three questions arise concerning this approach:

- Is the list of checklist items a comprehensive, exhaustive one?
- What lies behind each question? For instance, to avoid a one-dimensional (yes/no) response to the question concerning 'display' other questions need to be triggered – by whom? all the pupils? Is it quality work? How long has it been up on the walls? What is its relevance to the present topic/class-work etc?
- Is it important to discuss the implicit contradictions between the items (eg creativity versus control)?

c The so-called *'qualitative' approach* which includes the use of observation notes, diary-keeping, interviewing, video recording and playback, audiotaping, etc. Ebbut (1983) has usefully differentiated between those techniques which need specific apparatus/equipment and those which do not. His paper is available as a ready guide for teachers working within this field. Again, the GRIDS advice is useful in this context:

An interview needs to be planned as carefully as a questionnaire. Consider whether you want to conduct a fairly tightly structured series of interviews (eg draw up a list of questions beforehand and then ask everyone the same questions) or one that has a much looser focus (eg what provision should we make for gifted children?) A major task is to decide how the answers will be recorded. Taking detailed notes may limit your time for asking questions. If you tape the interview, consider what you will do with the tape afterwards, bearing in mind that it can take several hours to transcribe a thirty-minute interview.

d No matter how the data has been collected and what range of

Figure 11.14 One approach to a "checklist"

KEY ASPECTS	OBSERVATION NOTES
LEARNING	
UNDERSTANDING	
ENJOYMENT	
INTEREST	
CONTROL	
CHALLENGE	
PRODUCTIVITY	
CREATIVITY	
FLEXIBILITY	
INVOLVEMENT	
ORGANISATION	
RELATIONSHIPS	
PRESENTATION	
ATTITUDES	
EFFICIENCY	
DISPLAY	
etc.	

key questions to ask:

(i) are these aspects the worthwhile ones to be looking for?

(ii) what is the available evidence?

(iii) what is the quality/effectiveness of what is being evidenced?

data-collecting techniques has been utilised (an ecletic approach is always advisable), the specific review team have the onerous responsibility of analysing the data (at this stage this amounts to collating, categorising and distilling). They must also make it available, in an accessible, public form, to their colleagues. The format of such a document/discussion paper may well prove crucial.

Furthermore, if these same colleagues have been involved in the classroom research process, an important 'spin-off' at this point might well be personal engagement in the professional development of individual classroom performance, alongside the more concerted, holistic institutional approach embodied in these guidelines. In other words, individual investment in the improvement of both teaching and learning within the teacher's classroom could well arise from this more institutional focus on the 'instructional system' (see Holly, 1984).

Many teachers, when investigating their own classrooms, have found the Open University/Schools Council pack *Curriculum in Action* very useful. The materials cluster around six basic questions:

1 What did the pupils *actually* do?
2 What were they learning?
3 How worthwhile was it?
4 What did I (the teacher) do?
5 What did I learn?
6 What should I do now?

It should be pointed out that, while some of the questions are highly relevant to this particualar stage of the review and development process, others (eg How worthwhile was it?) concern stage three, which focuses on the evaluation process.

Procedural (Action) Step Three
Central question: *Where do we want to be?*

Procedural (Action) Steps Two and Three do not have to be arranged sequentially. Two working parties could meet simultaneously, one filing evidence of present practice and the other preparing the criteria with which to judge this same practice.

1 It is important to co-opt other members of staff to join the deliberative team. The aim of this group-work is to 'brainstorm', in a structured fashion, an *intrinsic evaluation*. This term was used by Scriven (1967) to denote a set of judgements concerning the structure of an educational programme, its design and assumptions. According to a more recent study, that of McCormick and James (1983), within an intrinsic evaluation:

the focus is on what ought to be taught, the intended curriculum . . . the principal concern must be for the worth and value of the planning activities . . . This type of evaluation can be contrasted with empirical evaluations . . which require a consideration of the curriculum as experienced by the pupils.

According to the same authors, intrinsic evaluation 'requires the skills of the philosopher.' It undoubtedly embodies a philosophical intent; it is the realm of 'vision', ideals, aspirations, and aims and objectives; of goal-setting. It encapsulates values and the generation of criteria for judgement concerning the worth-whileness, quality and effectiveness of educational provision.

2 As part of the GRIDS initiative in Haringey LEA, a structured series of sessions was instituted to complete an intrinsic evaluation:

- Step one: team meets to brainstorm the insider view of good practice in the topic area;
- Step two: team organises various kinds of input representing the external view of good practice, eg a literature search, a guest speaker, description of relevant past experience, etc;
- Step three: team meets to merge the internal/external perspectives to its own satisfaction
- Step four: team identifies a set of 'bench marks' concerning worthwhile or effective provision, with which to judge the present practice as surveyed and filed within the previous stage of the development programme. (The new 'vision' can also be used to judge the quality of the present school policy in this area. It is a question of scrutinising and evaluating intentions).

3 When the school's present practice is judged in the light of the internally-conceived measures of quality control, it is possible not only to identify a 'performance gap' (between these reformulated intentions and the realities of classroom life), but also to begin to prepare an agenda for action in terms of recommendations. At this stage what began as a general plan is being modified into an action plan.

4 If the deliberation has been confined to the membership of the working groups, it now becomes vital to negotiate these recommendations with staff colleagues. What is sought is their commitment to the suggested changes.

The organisation of this 'dissemination' can be the special responsibility of the school-based INSET co-ordinator.

Procedural (Action) Step Four
Central question: *How do we get there?*

At this stage the recommendations arising from the specific review are to be put into practice. Within the GRIDS scheme, this stage is significantly titled, *Action for Development* – the action that is needed to prepare for, and provide support during, the envisaged changes.

The question *How do we get there?* concerns the strategic planning that goes into preparing the ground for implementation; it is the formulation of these implementation strategies which constitutes an action plan. These strategies can be of two kinds:

- the removal of constraints;

- the promotion of positive supports (eg INSET provision to help the staff cope with the new demands on them).

To our mind these two aspects are interrelated. For instance, Menlo (1985) has argued that teachers have a more positive attitude to change than is generally recognised. Their negative feelings arise from what he refers to as the sense of loss (eg being de-skilled) that change brings with it. His contention is that if developers help teachers cope with such fears, the positive feelings will be allowed to dominate. One coping strategy is to make available appropriate INSET experience *prior to* the implementation of the changes.

What is crucial is that this INSET experience is provided before, and not after, the changes are implemented (as was often the case in the 1960s – the hey-day of innovation – See Figure 11.15)

Figure 11.15   Inset changes over time

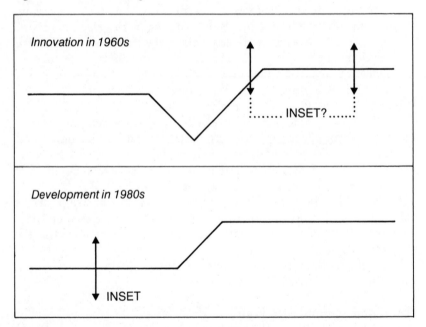

While each school will have particular INSET needs according to its own focus for development, it could well be the case that more than one school in the same location will have identified similar needs. It would be sensible and cost-effective to provide the necessary INSET support at the local teachers' centre – to be attended by the appropriate members of staff from both schools. DES/Regional courses can also be utilised to provide the necessary 'input' for school-based development.

It will be important, of course, to evaluate this INSET experience in terms not only of its intrinsic worthwhileness but also its effectiveness in meeting the needs of its individual members of staff and the school's development programme, 'Quality' INSET experience is as important as the question of timing.

Procedural (Action) Step Five
Central question: *How are we doing?*
This is very much the stage for 'taking stock' and asking such questions as:

- How are we doing?
- What should we do next?

According to the GRIDS advice:

the three main purposes at this stage are: first, to complete one cycle of the review and development process; second, to start a further cycle of review and development using the GRIDS method, if desired; and, finally, to consider whether any additional people should be informed about what happened during the first cycle. The head and school co-ordinator must be centrally involved at this stage in the process.

This 'stock taking' consists of 2 levels of evaluation:

a *Monitoring* – the maintenance of a continuing, cumulative data base concerning the ups and downs of implementation. This formative screening or profiling of daily performance (in the sense of monitoring as 'checking on transmission': is the message getting across?) enables the staff to move to the second level by obtaining sufficient data to be able to validate/evaluate the nature of the improvements.

b *Evaluation* – the digestion and analysis of this data in order to make judgements concerning the impact, extent, quality, effectiveness and 'success' of the developments over time. The important point at this stage is to heed the advice of Sarason (1971) and to avoid being blinded (by enthusiasm) to the faults of the innovation and, in the terms used by Doyle and Fonder (1977/78), to remain a pragmatic sceptic. That is, to remain somewhat distanced from the change in question and to be open to the possibility that, within the ethos of development, the aim is to synthesise the best of the 'old' with the best of the 'new'.

It is also important to investigate the effectiveness of both the process (the mode of development) and the products (the outcomes of the development work). Both aspects will need to be *institutionalised*. Crucial questions must be asked at this stage concerning the re-start of the cyclical development programme:

- when?
- how?
- who to be involved?

The decision to give an account (or not) of the development work is an important one. What is crucial is to steer clear of the climate (and constraining effects) of accountability. As the GRIDS handbook maintains, it is probably unwise to attempt to achieve internal development at the same time as responding to accountability pressures. The latter could well defeat the former. The concept of the Developing School is now central within the *practice* of TRIST arrangements. Over twenty comprehensive schools in Hertfordshire LEA are, at present, using the Teachers' Guide (summarised above) in their efforts to initiate curriculum change and school development under the auspices of this particular TRIST scheme. The guidelines were offered to the schools following the induction conference for school co-ordinators (and their colleagues) in January 1986. One school co-ordinator introduced the scheme in her school by circulating the following report-cum-discussion paper:

To all members of staff

TRIST – INTRODUCTORY MEETING

Background
In-Service Training
The present system of authorities planning their INSET in an ad-hoc way seems set to end in April 1987. From then on, the DES will be asking for each authority to plan a year long programme of INSET and to submit the plan. If it is deemed acceptable, an award will be made by the DES to cover the programme.

TRIST (TVEI – related INSET) can be seen as a precursor to this. For use until April 1987, some money has been channelled through TVEI/MSC to enable certain LEAs to plan programmes of INSET which will suit their needs. However the use of TVEI is just a device to get the money to the authorities – the INSET has no other links with TVEI.

In this LEA, two districts have been chosen to use the money, and programmes were submitted last summer.

The complete programme includes INSET on:

Information Technology
Business Education
Physical Science and Technology
Cross-curricular implications of Mathematics
and Curriculum change, Guidance and Monitoring

The details of all the schemes are set out in the Introductory TRIST booklet. The meeting attended by the Head and Deputy Head on Friday, related to the INSET on Curriculum Change, Guidance and Monitoring, which is seen as the work which will set all the other courses in context.

The Authority's View
The Chief Adviser said that the LEA viewed the INSET being organised by TRIST as very important. It will enable co-ordinated developments; will give schools the chance to give a lead in curriculum change; will help provide staff with skills and understandings they need for future developments, and will give a valuable introduction to the Authority's INSET, starting in 1987.

How is the 'Curriculum Change, Guidance and Monitoring' going to be introduced?

Each school will be given the opportunity to identify areas that they wish to work on. Examples of areas are teaching styles, learning styles, special needs, profiling, guidance and equal opportunities. Guidance of pupils, in the widest sense, is seen as a key element.

They will then, it is hoped, work through a number of stages leading on from this to bring about developments, and evaluate them.

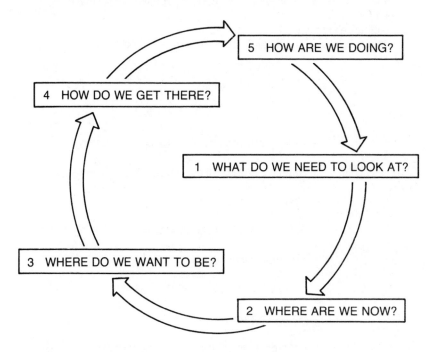

Throughout all these stages, there will be back-up from TRIST in the form of residential and day conferences, organised to fit the demands of schools, plus the opportunity to fund school-based INSET. A school co-ordinator will act as a liaison with the TRIST staff.

The Induction Conference

This is being held on January 20th–22nd and three members of staff will be attending. This opening conference is designed to set in motion the programme as outlined above.

(Young, 1986)

. . . .

(More recently, the same school has produced a 'statement of intent' concerning its promised development plans)

Initial Statement of Intent for TRIST

Identified areas of concern

Staff have identified the following areas of interest and concern – both very wide but at this stage it seems wise to leave all options open.

They are:
1   An overview of pastoral care.
2   An examination of teaching styles and their relationship to pupils' motivation.
Sub-headings as identified by staff are:–
1   *Pastoral Care* – Tutorial and House System – vertical etc.

Monitoring of pupils

Discipline

Role of the form teacher/form periods/training

Personal and social education

Behavioural problems

Individual social responsibilities

Personal relationships

Co-ordination between staff involved

Review of present practice

Co-ordination of guidance/caring/discipline /counselling

Awareness of outside agencies/resources

2   *Teaching styles* and their relationship to pupils' motivation –

Problem solving

Critical appraisal of active learning approaches

Feasibility studies

Individual learning

Active learning

Relationship to new exam methods

Methods of learning

Discussion techniques

Team teaching

Underachievement

Study skills

Relevance

Breaking through 'boredom' thresholds

Reluctant learners

Long term perspective of education

Short-term goals

Other areas of concern

The next area prioritised by staff was Special Needs. We feel that the two areas already identified may well cover some ground associated with Special Needs, though it may be necessary at a future stage to consider this as a separate entity.

In addition the 'structure of the school day' was seen as an important area of concern. We would be interested in this if any INSET was planned, but would probably consider an internal review as well.

The plans of other schools involved can be summarised as shown in Figure 11.16. TRIST, and its successors, can provide for, and realise, the Developing School in action.

Figure 11.16   The clusters of priority areas as identified within one TRIST initiative

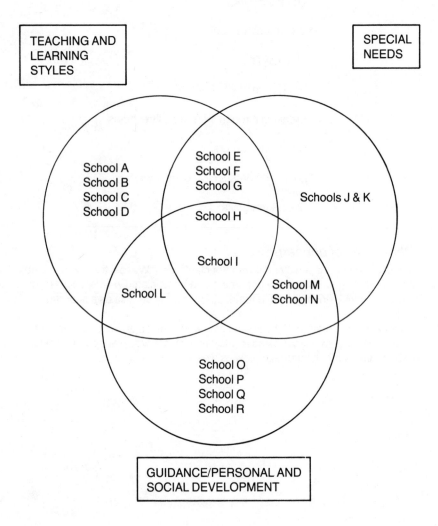

Chapter 12

Effective Schools: some dilemmas

The inclusion of the word 'towards' in the title of this book was intended to signify a measure of both uncertainty and provisionality in our understanding of what constitutes an effective school. There is much more certainty to be found in the American educational literature. Some American observers, however, are embarrassed by this lack of scepticism (see Cuban, 1984). Like the Berlaks (1982), these commentators prefer to identify the dilemmas that still remain. The 'dilemmas' approach, according to the Berlaks, is intended to capture the 'dynamic of everyday school life, the lived contradictions of schooling and curricular practices'; it enables us to analyse the 'personal, social and cultural' tensions within schooling. Elsewhere Holly (1986a) has adopted this approach and identified the dilemmas arising from the 'effective schools' literature. Here we will concentrate on just three central dilemmas:

- the efficacy of which leadership style?
- school culture; maker or breaker of innovation?

Leadership

As Manasse (1985) notes the last few years have seen a resurgence of attention given to the importance of leadership in shaping effective schools. Whether any individual – including the head or principal – can be so effective as to make the school effective is a moot point; nonetheless, as former Secretary of State for Education, Sir Keith Joseph recently argued, a good head teacher is the 'closest thing to a 'magic wand' for a primary school' (quoted in the *Times Educational Supplement*, 11/4/86).

But how to judge head-teacher effectiveness remains a central question. Would it be valid, asks Manasse, to use such indicators as student achievement scores, community satisfaction, staff satisfaction (as evidenced by attendance and turnover) and a common sense of purpose? Manasse (1985), like Hopkins (1986), queries whether heads are controlled by the pace of events. Is it an indication of strong 'leadership', he asks, when they manage to rise above the hurly burly of daily life? Manasse then summarises the dimensions of 'principal effectiveness' arising from research in the US. He lists the following:

Basic competencies	'Optimal' competencies
Commitment to 'mission' (purpose and direction)	Monitoring
	Ability to recognise patterns
Concern for image	Perceptual objectivity
Participatory management style	Analytical ability
Tactical adaptability (involving consensus management)	———
Coaching skills	Sense of control
Firmness in enforcing quality standards	Persuasiveness
	Commitment to quality
	Focused involvemement in change

Above all, says Manasse, heads/principals should have both a strong sense of themselves as leaders and the vision, initiative and resourcefulness to go with it. Herein lies the central dilemma. Manasse maintains that the principals should not only have an 'underlying picture of their schools as they want them to be', but also a vision based on clearly articulated, personal values ('in their image'). Heads establish the goal agenda (the 'set priorities') and the 'strategies designed to achieve that picture'. But the central task then becomes one of generating the commitment of others to the same agenda; thus, the importance of incentives and 'symbolic leadership' involving high energy, strong communication, human relations skills and high tolerance for stress. 'Purposing' means that the head/principal has to galvanise both consensus and commitment. 'We must allow principals', argues Manasse, a 'fair measure of building level autonomy' in order that they can 'set appropriate agendas for their particular circumstances.'

It should be remembered, of course, that strong principalship is an innovation in the United States; it could even be argued that, fueled by research findings, American principals are being exhorted to strive for the kind of managerial leadership position that heads in the UK are being invited to relinquish. It is significant, for instance, that leadership and principalship are synonymous terms in the US; not so, we would argue, in the UK context. It is also interesting to note that Manasse, in quoting the work of Little (1981), defines her favoured approach – collegiality – as the 'notion that the work of teachers is shared'; continuous staff interaction leading to continuous teacher involvement in the improvement of instructional practice. But this interpretation of 'collegiality' entails staff involvement in the 'means' but not the 'ends'; it constitutes 'instrumental collaboration' – the staff dancing to the head's tune. Manasse claims that different leadership styles (directive or facilitative, authoritarian or democratic) can be equally effective (although, he says, 'laissez-faire principals give teachers too much power'). We would then ask – but what are the socio-political messages emanating from the continuing practice of a particular leadership style?

The Berlaks (1982) contend:

In contrast to the evolving common wisdom that the school principal must take charge in order to maintain standards, we argue that 'effective' schools in a democracy require collaborative, non-hierarchical relationships between building–administrators, teachers, educational professionals and parents.

Authoritarian leadership breeds authority dependency; heteronomy within (head-teacher) autonomy. And, as Handy (1984) points out, 'old habits, particularly of dependence, die hard.' In turn, as Southworth (1986) asserts, collaboration 'cuts across autocracy and deference to the head'. Hierarchicalism, it can be argued, rests on two dimensions:

1 The active assertion of 'authority' by those 'in authority'; and the concomitant, passive affirmation by those 'under' authority.

2 The maintenance of the pathological divide between managers and managed. But both 'sides' need the will to break down this divide for collaboration to become a reality.

According to Nias (1980), teachers become alienated by dictatorial leadership. Her research, building on that of Yuki (1975), indicated that teachers welcome 'positive-type' leadership which is a combination of the following:

Initiating structure: the head sets high professional standards and has a high level of personal involvement in the school;

Consideration: the head is readily available, especially for discussion, and is interested in the development of the teaching staff.

Decision-generalisation: the head gives a lead in establishing the aims for the school, but encourages participation in both goal-setting and decision-making – normative collegiality.

As usual, Wragg (1981) finds the words to describe this situation:

My favourite leadership style seems to be on the increase in all those schools where many of our most capable men and women heads, deputies and several other key people in the school, have managed to secure a degree of commitment, professionalism and enjoyment that should be the envy of other professions. It is like the traditional way Viennese conductors have of standing before their orchestra, violin in hand, joining in the playing, and occasionally waving their bow in time to the music. I suppose if a tuba player ever became leader it might be called the double hernia style. . .

Stuff Musgrove's aloof, withdrawn, study bound prisoner sending down memos that look as if they have been written by a silicon chip. I'm right behind the tuba-playing, participant merrymakers. Let's have some joy in the world. Remember, however, to indent for a free National Health Service truss in next year's estimates.

The school culture

Philosophically, Arnold Gehlen (see Berger and Kellner, 1965) provided the rationale for institution-building through the medium of 'culture'. His basic argument is that 'man' is biologically unstable; stability is achieved by sociological means through interaction with the environment 'through structures produced by himself.' Therefore, 'he must construct his own world. This world, which is culture, must aim at the firm structures which are lacking biologically'.

According to Berger and Kellner, Gehlen saw these man-made structures as being continuously produced and reproduced in human activity. Given the inherent (biological) instability, however, these structures (ie 'culture') are 'precarious and predestined to change'.

As mentioned earlier in the book, Gehlen's views have been recently resuscitated by commentators like Deal and Kennedy (1982 and 1983). Deal (1985) has argued that

Effective schools are those that over time have built a system of belief, supported by cultural forms that give meaning to the process of education. Just as with businesses these schools will display shared values and beliefs, well-known and widely celebrated heroes and heroines, well-attended and memorable rituals and ceremonies, positive stories, and a dedicated informal group whose members work diligently to maintain and strengthen the culture.

Manasse (1985) points out that a principal's task is to balance organisational stability and change initiatives (which are, potentially, destabilising). But, paradoxically, the strength of the organisation's culture (the shared norms, values and beliefs) might be too strong for any innovative efforts to cope with. As Deal himself asserts:

. . . norms – or informal rules – of autonomy and equality dictate how teachers relate to one another and undermine efforts to introduce innovations such as open space architecture and team-teaching . . .

This raises the question of the quality of a school's culture and its value (in)compatibility with the values embedded within various innovations. While Deal and Kennedy (1983) can argue that 'strong schools have strong cultures' ('the importance of culture is an old-fashioned idea that great business leaders have known for years . . . Many school principals also spend considerable time building cohesive school cultures'), they are able to cite the power of school culture, as demonstrated by Sarason (1971), to undermine innovation, which experiences 'cultural domestication' (see Holly, 1984b). Deal and Kennedy (1983) conclude, therefore, that 'when the culture works against you, it's nearly impossible to get anything done.' But having made this observation, the authors leap to the conclusion that, if a negative culture acts to veto innovation, a positive one will enhance it. They declare that the problem is to make something powerful and ill-defined work for us and to show that building strong school cultures is intimately tied to improving educational performance.

Within this particular act of faith, they ignore two possibilities:
a that the particular characteristics (within time and place) of a school's culture might operate for some innovations and against others – but not on behalf of innovation generally; there has to be a cultural match within what amounts to a filtering process (see Holly and Wideen, 1986).
b that there is someting about the process of institution-building through the agency of a school's culture which will always operate in the interests of stability, predictability and control. Change bears the promise of instability and a 'sense of loss'. (Menlo, 1985).

In addition, as Holly and Wideen (1986) acknowledge, innovations are representative of sub-cultures, interest groups and pluralist values, which "pull the school in several directions". Innovations which embody sub-cultural values, therefore, endanger the cohesiveness of the overall culture. Can the latter ever totally erase this unpredictability and untidiness? Indeed, is the power and cohesiveness of a school's culture something of an illusion? Deal and Kennedy (1983) maintain that the 'internal squabbling' and 'mixed signals' emanating from a school serve both to lower its reputation and lose parental support. A school, then, cannot afford to display the social reality that is value pluralism (Hutchinson, 1986); it is forced to create the myth of value cohesion (see Tangerud, 1986).

Indeed, Tangerud has questioned the efficacy of the harmony, consensus model which tends to pervade school improvement research and practices. He is sceptical for example, of the 'McKinsey 7–S Framework for Organisational Diagnosis' (see Figure 12.1) (as promoted by Henley, 1986) which is based on the centrality of strong, shared values. Given his conflict perspective, Tangerud (1986) maintains that this (mythical) concept is not representative of the reality of competing interests, antagonism and dis-harmony. If a shared value is a myth, of course, a myth could be a shared value. If colleagues are encouraged to behave cohesively, then they may come to believe in this cohesiveness. A myth, like culture, might serve to support the social fabric. One senses, however, that Tangerud believes that this myth-making can expect what amounts to only temporary, impermanent success. The reality of dissension will re-assert itself. Entrepreneurs (ie those with vested interests), argues Drucker (1985), will exploit innovations and, thus, defeat the attempts of 'bureaucracy' to deny the perceived anarchic presence of innovation.

Dalin (1973) maintained that

major innovations will always be based on changes in educational, social, political or economic objectives. These changes reflect changes in values and thereby value conflicts in Society.

Figure 12.1   McKinsey 7–S framework for organisational diagnosis

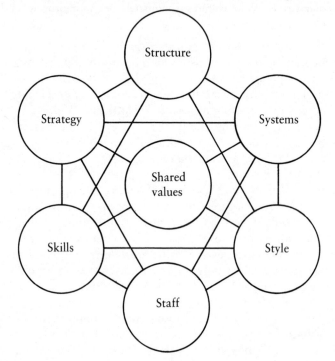

These societal value conflicts are inevitably reflected within the views of the staff at a school. Yet, more often than not, these deep-seated value conflicts are 'put to bed', and allowed to remain dormant. Menlo (1985) refers to 'value difference passivity' which serves to mask the (potential) value divergences regarding fundamental principles. But 'innovation' threatens to invoke this value difference debate. Organisationally and also personally, then, innovation is threatening. Teachers have an intuitive awareness of this fact. There are three possible responses to the predicament:

1 to affect and maintain the *status quo* of comfortable, cosy, even collusive harmony (enculturation).

2 to storm the 'cultures', ride roughshod over the competing agendas and for the head to impose, unilaterally, his/her own value agenda. The message is: forget your differences and agree to this agenda which is being imposed on your for the good of us all (proculturation).

3 to take up the stance of 'accommodation', adopt the 'sluicegate' approach to change and acknowledge the gradualism of this developmental perspective in which no one personal agenda holds sway. Within acculturation people influence and are influenced. This is not a radical approach; it is the developmental, gradualist stance of SBR schemes such as GRIDS.

It could be agreed that SBR, like school improvement strategies generally, belongs to the 'harmony/consensus model'; it involves collaborative planning and decision making and is procedurally *systematic*. It is a good example of collegial displacement; procedural collegiality is given prominence at the expense of normative collegiality. Working together (in partnership) is promoted before the exploration of fundamental value differences. The 'how' is put before the 'what'. The danger, then, is that it becomes too systematic – at the expense of the quality of the debate. Another danger is that its systematic nature will 'bureaucratise' the changes and produce minimalist, domesticated, neutralised innovation – innovation without change at the fundamental level. Even when SBR is seen as the medium for exploring value conflict, precautionary measures are taken and are labelled the 'management of conflict' (a contradiction in terms?). As Stenhouse (1975) contends, there is a need to 'manage conflict within the school, rather than pretend that it does not exist . . . the exercise constitutes a major management task'.

The dialectical nature of change makes management problematical. For instance, within the kind of non-productive culture described by Sarason (1971), change initiatives are forced to go 'underground' – factional collaboration. Such activity, from the management's perspective, could be seen as subversive and the head may attempt to right the balance by encouraging instrumental collaboration (according to his/her agenda). A power struggle (for control of the normative agenda) might ensue. The Developing School, as described both theoretically and practically in chapter 11, faces this major dilemma. It attempts to resolve the dilemma by establishing what could be termed a *development culture* which embodies:

- a gradualist, thorough-going perspective;
- the collaborative spirit of democratic collegiality;
- a willingness to explore value difference.

Culturally speaking, however, as Southworth (1986) has argued, collaboration and collegiality might be 'against the grain'. Those who, like ourselves, have faith in collaboration as 'the way forward' will assume (wrongly) that there will be:

- a uniformity of response and enthusiasm from teacher colleagues.
- a similar level of interest and involvement in INSET activities across the staff. Hall (1978) has exploded this myth with his research into differential 'stages' of teacher investment, involvement and interest in the "concerns-based" approach.
- a continuing presence of 'change supportive norms' (Henley, 1986)
- the existence of ideal conditions, e.g. teacher goodwill, ample time and resources, etc.
- an agreed understanding of collaboration as a proper professional activity.
- an absence of other (competing) innovations. According to Bolam

(1985) there are, especially nowadays, scores of innovations – all being promoted by pressure groups – baying at the doors of schools and demanding entrance (ie adoption) and simultaneous implementation.

an absence of both micro-political intrigue and hostility and the destructive agenda of 'wreckers'. As Tangerud (1986) maintains, the first myth is that of institutional loyalty; the second is an interest (on the part of the staff) in school improvement.

SBR, from the political perspective, tends to mirror the politico-cultural 'norms' of society (see Bollen, 1986). On occasions, however, SBR could well incorporate political norms and values at variance with those of the social environment. Perhaps, therefore, the collaborative, collegial, participative form of SBR is too decentralised, too democratic, and not hierarchical enough for the schools' 'political masters'. The central dilemma (for those at all levels of the educational system) is whether to insist on control through line management or to promote collaborative team-work (or both!). DES officials, Chief Education Officers and headteachers face the same dilemma. Is 'society' ready for democratic schools? Moreover, are the schools ready for democracy and collegiality? asks Southworth (1986). Given the authority-dependence mentioned earlier in this chapter, what are the prospects for the democratisation of schooling? When introducing the GRIDS scheme to a group of heads of secondary schools in shire constituencies in the south of England, Peter Holly was stopped in his tracks by their collective, anguished cries. 'we can't do this', they said, 'We are the 'liberals' in our schools – if we open up the debate we'll be opening the reactionary floodgates – we'll have corporal punishment, uniform, etc. pushed through in no time'.

Democratic procedures, therefore, do not necessarily lead to 'democratic' codes or innovations. Personal and group value agendas might well determine the nature of the changes. Phenomenologists, on the one hand, argue that individuals seek to further their own personal ends within institutional life; these same individuals have not only levels of need (see Maslow, 1954) but also three central desires – for stability and security (Gehlen's point), – for (the excitement of) involvement in change – for personal advancement; self interest (see Figure 12.2).

Individuals also have personal lives (and biographies) outside schools; if their personal lives are in turmoil and full of ambiguity, they will naturally seek security at school and vice versa.

Structuralists, on the other hand, argue that the process of 'structuration' (see Giddens, 1985) occurs within institutions as a continuous dialectical tension between institution-building, institution-maintenance and institution-renewal.

According to this view, individuals combine within institutions and are then structured institutionally over time. They create and are created; they grow attached and become addicted. As Henry (1964) noted:

Figure 12.2 The change process in action

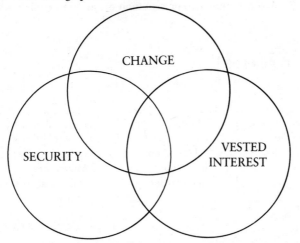

A social organisation really has no 'shape' . . . rather, the image that a culture has of an organisation represents, in part, the way in which people in that culture expect things to get done – that is, a set of values. In our culture, these values include responsibility, authority, command, obedience, dominance and submission.

The challenge, however, is to probe these deep-seated inter-connections between teaching 'codes', the hidden (or para-) curriculum, and the school's culture, climate or ethos. As Reynolds (1985) acknowledges, the concept of a school's culture is allied to the 'hidden, informal world of the school' and is 'that part of the school which is most difficult to look at and most difficult to change'. Apple (1979) concludes:

As investigators of the hidden curriculum and others have noted, the concrete modes by which knowledge is distributed in classrooms and the commonsense practices of teachers and students can illuminate the connections between school life and the structures of ideology, power, and economic resources of which schools are a part . . . the school is a well-established institution, and it may be that neither the teacher nor the children can perceive more than marginal ways to deviate to any significant extent from the commonsense rules and expectations that distinguish schools from other institutions.

Holly and Wideen (1986) are attempting to explore some of these inter-relationships by charting the 'key linkages' within the 'Culture Club' – the process of institutionalisation (see Figure 12.3 which attempts to set out the conceptual framework.) This, and future findings from published studies, will continue to add to our knowledge base. We are on the way, but we have a great deal further to go, before we can be precisely certain of what an effective school is and how we can change ineffective schools into effective ones. We suggest that contributing to this debate is one of the most exciting challenges facing educationalists today.

Figure 12.B   A diagrammatic representation of the 'culture club' phenomenon

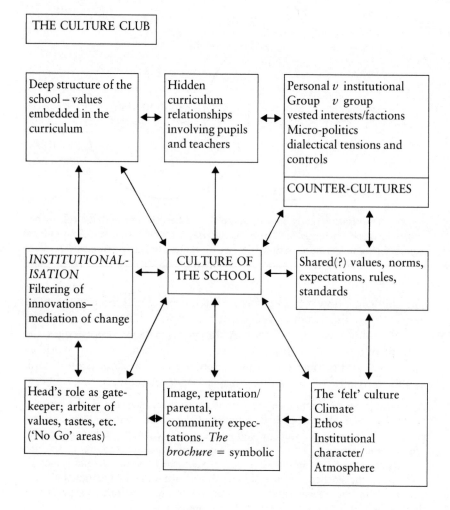

Further Reading

To do justice to the complex theme of school effectiveness, it is probably necessary to read a large proportion of the articles, reports and books referred to throughout this book. However, for those interested in our approach to the topic we recommend the following introductory reading list.

Bolam, R. (ed) (1982) *School Focussed In-Service Teacher Education* Heinemann.

Bollen, R. and Hopkins, D. (1986) *School Based Review: Towards a Praxis* ACCO.

Crandell, D. and Loucks, S. (1983) *A Roadmap for School Improvement* Andover, Mass: The Network Inc.

Elliott, J. and Adelman, C. (1976) *Innovation at the Classroom Level: a Case Study of the Ford Teaching Project* Unit 28 Open University Course E203, Curriculum Design and Development Open University Press.

Fullan, M. (1982) *The Meaning of Educational Change* Toronto: OISE Press.

HMI *Quality in Schools* HMSO.

Holly, P. and Whitehead, D. (eds) *CARN Bulletin* Cambridge Institute of Education.

Hopkins, D. (1985a) *A Teacher's Guide to Classroom Research* Open University Press.

Hopkins, D. (1987) *Improving the Quality of Schooling* Falmer Press.

Hopkins, D. (ed) (1986) *Inservice and Educational Development* Croom Helm.

Hopkins, D. and Wideen, M. (1984) *Alternative Perspectives on School Improvement* Falmer Press.

Hoyle, E. and McMahon, A. (1986) *The Management of Schools* Kogan Page.

Huberman, M. and Miles, M. (1984) *Innovation Up Close* Plenum.

James, M. (1982) *A First Review and Register of School and College Initiated Self Evaluation Activities in the UK* Educational Evaluation and Accountability Research Group Open University.

Kemmis, S. and McTaggart, R. (1981) *The Action Research Planner* Deakin Press.

Lawton, D. (1980) *The Politics of the School Curriculum* RKP.

McCormick, R. (ed) (1982) *Calling Education to Account* Heinemann.

McCormick, R. (1983) *Curriculum Evaluation in Schools* Croom Helm.

McMahon, A. et al (1984) *Guidelines for Review and Internal Development in Schools* Longman.

Nixon, J. (ed) (1981) *A Teacher's Guide to Action Research* Grant and McIntyre.

Nuttall, D. (1981) *School Self Evaluation: Accountability with a Human Face* Longman.

Nuttall, D. (*et al*) (1986) *Cases in School Evaluation* (provisional title) Falmer.

Reid, K. (1985) *Truancy and School Absenteeism* Hodder and Stoughton.

Reid, K. (1986) *Disaffection From School* Methuen.

Reid, K. (ed) (1987) *Combating School Absenteeism* Hodder and Stoughton.

Reynolds, D. (ed) (1985) *Studying School Effectiveness* Falmer Press.

Rudduck, J. and Hopkins, D. (eds) (1985) *Research as a Basis for Teaching* Heinemann.

Runkel, P. et al (1979) *Transforming the Schools Capacity for Problem Solving* C.E.P.M.

Sarason, S. (1982) *The Culture of the School and the Problem of Change* 2nd edn., Allyn and Bacon.

Schmuck, R. and Runkel, P. (1985) *The Handbook of Organisation Development in Schools* (3rd ed) Palo Alton CA: Mayfield.

Schon, D. (1983) *The Reflective Practitioner* Basic Books.

Stenhouse, L. (1975) *An Introduction to Curriculum Research and Development* Heinemann.

Van Velzen, W. (1982) *Conceptual Mapping for School Improvement* OECD.

Van Velzen, W. et al (1985) *Making School Improvement Work* ACCO.

Walker, R. (1985) *Research for Teachers* Macmillan.

Bibliography

APU (1981a) *Language Performance in Schools* London: HMSO.
APU (1981b) *Mathematical Development* London: HMSO.
APU (1981c) *Science in Schools* London: HMSO.
Acton, T. A. (1980) Educational criteria of success *Educational Research* 22 163–9.
Adelman, C. (ed) (1984) *The Politics & Ethics of Evaluation* London: Croom Helm.
Anderson, R. R. (1980) *From List D to Day School* Dundee: Dundee College of Education.
Apple, M. W. (1979) *Ideology & Curriculum* London: Routledge and Kegan Paul.
Armor, D., Conry-Oseguera, P., Cox, M., King, N., McDonnell, L., Pascal, A., Pauly, E. & Zellman, G. (1976) *Analysis of the School Preferred Reading Programme in Selected Los Angeles Minority Schools* Santa Monica, California: Rand.
Ashton, P. (1983) 'Teacher education for co-operative curriculum review' *Forum* Autumn, 26, (1).
Auld, M. (1976) *Report of the Committee of Inquiry into William Tyndale School* London: ILEA.
Austin, G. R. (1978) *Process Evaluation: a Comprehensive Study of Outliers* Baltimore: Maryland State Department of Education.
Austin, G. R. (1979) 'An analysis of outlier exemplary schools & their distinguishing characteristics' Paper presented at the meeting of the American Educational Research Association San Francisco, April 1979.
Austin, G.R. (1981) *Exemplary schools & their identification* (unpublished Manuscript) Centre for Educational Research and Development University of Maryland.
Averch, H. *et al* (1971) *How Effective is Schooling?* New York: Englewood Educational Technology Publications.
Ayllon, T. A. and Roberts, M. D. (1974) Eliminating discipline problems by strengthening academic performance *Journal of Applied Behaviour Analysis*, 7, 71–6.
Baldwin, J. and Wells, H. (1979, 1980, 1981) *Active Tutorial Work – the First – Fifth Year* Oxford: Basil Blackwell.
Banks, O. (1979) *The Sociology of Education* London: Batsford.
Barker, R. and Gump, P. (1964) *Big School, Small School* Stanford: Stanford University Press.
Barnes, D. (1982) *Practical Curriculum Study* London: RKP.

Barnes, J. H. and Lucas, H. (1974) 'Positive discrimination in education'. In Leggatt, T. (ed) *Sociological Theory and Survey Research* London: Sage.

Barr, R. and Dreeben, R. (1981) *School policy, production, and productivity* (unpublished manuscript) Chicago: University of Chicago.

Barrow, R. (1984) *Giving Teaching Back to Teachers* London: Wheatsheaf.

Barry, B. (1973) *The Liberal Theory of Justice* London: Oxford University Press.

Bayh, B. (1977) Challenge for the third century: education in a safe environment *Final Report on the Nature & Prevention of School Violence & Vandalism* Washington DC: US Government Printing Office.

Benjamin, H. (J. A. Peddiwell) (1939) *The Saber Tooth Curriculum* New York: McGraw Hill.

Berger, P. and Kellner, H. (1965) Arnold Gehlen and the theory of institutions *Social Research* 32 Part 1 110–115.

Berlak, A. and H. (1982) 'Toward a non-hierarchical conception of school inquiry and leadership' *Curriculum inquiry*.

Best, R., Jarvis, C. and Ribbins, P. (1980) *Perspectives on Pastoral Care* London: Heinemann Educational books.

Best, R., Jarvis, C. and Ribbins, P. (1983) *Education and Care* London: Heinemann.

Beynon, J. and Delamont, S. (1984) 'The sound and the fury: pupil-perceptions of school violence,' In Frude, N. and Gault, H. (eds) *Disruptive Behaviour in Schools* Chichester: John Wiley.

Bird, C., Chessum, R., Furlong, J. and Johnson, D. (eds) (1980) *Disaffected Pupils* Brunel: Brunel University Educational Studies Unit.

Blackham, H. J. (1978) *Education for Personal Autonomy: an Inquiry into the School's Resources for Furthering the Personal Development of Pupils* London: Bedford Square Press.

Bloch, J. A., Bunder, W., Frey, K., and Rost, J. (1983) 'Institutionalised in-service training for science teachers' *European Journal of Science Education* 5, 2, 157–169.

Bloom, B. *et al* (1956) *The Taxonomy of Educational Objectives 1. Cognitive Domain* London: Longman.

Bolam, R. (ed) (1982) *School-Focussed In-Service Training* London: Heinemann.

Bollen, R. (1986) 'School-based review in the perspective of educational policy' Paper presented at the ISIP, UK Dissemination Conference, April, 1986.

Bollen, R. and Hopkins, D. (1986) *School Based Review: Towards a Praxis* Leuven, Belgium: ACCO.

Bolster, A. (1983) 'Towards a more effective model of research on teaching' *Harvard Educational Review* 3, No 3, 294–308.

Bowles, S. and Levin, H. M. (1968) 'The determinants of scholastic achievement – an appraisal of some recent evidence' *Journal of Human Resources*, 3, 1–24.

Brace, J. (1982) 'The educational state of Wales' *Education for Development* 7, 2, 63–72.

Bradley, H. 'Why must INSET be a Partnership?' Conference paper Klagenfurt University December, 1985.

Brennan, E. J. T. (1985) 'On the eve of CPVE, – some impressions of the changing pre-vocational scene *Cambridge Journal of education*, 15, 1.

Bridges, D. and Eynon, D. (1983) *Issues in School-Centred In-Service Education* Cambridge: Cambridge Institute of Education.

Brighouse, T. (1981) 'An LEA perspective on underachievement' *Secondary Education Journal*, 12, 3, 21–23.

Brimer, A., Madaus, G. F., Chapman, B., Kellaghan, T and Wood, R. (1978) *Sources of Differences in School Achievement* Slough: NFER.

Brookover, W. B., Beady, C., Flood, P., Schweitzer, J. and Wisenbaker, J. (1979) *School Social Systems & Student Achievement: Schools Can Make a Difference* New York: Praeger.

Brookover, W. B. and Schweider, J. M. (1975) 'Academic environments and elementary school achievement' *Journal of Research and Development in Education* 9, 82/91.

Brophy, J. E. and Good, T. L. (1974) *Teacher-Student Relationships: Causes and Consequences* New York: Holt Rinehart and Winston.

Brunel, B. (1960) *The Process of Education* New York: Vintage Books.

Bruner, J. (1966) *Towards a Theory of Instruction* Boston: Harvard University Press.

Bryan, K. and Digsby, A. (1983) 'Pupil performance and school effectiveness' *Westminster Studies in Education* 6, 33–53.

Buist, M. (1980) 'Truants Talking' *Scottish Educational Review* 12, 1, 40–51.

Bullock (1975) *A Language for Life* (The Bullock Report) London: HMSO.

Burgess, T. and Adams, E. (1985) *Records of Achievement at 16* Slough: NFER/Nelson.

Button, L. (1981) *Group Tutoring for the Form Teacher 1* London: Hodder and Stoughton.

Button, L. (1982) *Group Tutoring for the Form Teacher 2* London: Hodder and Stoughton.

California State Dept of Education (1980) *Report on the Special Studies of Selected ECE Schools with Increasing & Decreasing Reading Scores* Sacremento, California: Office of Program Evaluation and Research.

Carroll, H. C. M. (ed) (1977) *Absenteeism in South Wales: Studies of Pupils, their Homes & their Secondary Schools* Swansea: University College of Swansea Faculty of Education.

Carr, W. (1984) 'Theories of theory and practice' Unpublished conference paper London University Institute of Education.

Carr, W. and Kemmis, S. (1983) *Becoming Critical: Knowing Through Action Research* Victoria: Deakin University Press.

Children's Defense Fund (1975) *School Suspensions: Are They Helping Children?* Cambridge MA: Children's Defense Fund.

Clarke, D. D., Parry-Jones, W., Gay, B. M. and Smith, C. M. B. (1981) 'Disruptive incidents in secondary school classrooms: a sequence analysis approach' *Oxford Review of Education* 7, 111/17.

Clarke, D. *et al* (1984) 'Effective schools and school improvement' *Educational Administration Quarterly* 20, 3, Summer, 41–68.

Clegg, A. and Megson, B. (1973) *Children in Distress* London: Penguin Education.

Clift, P. (1982) 'LEA schemes for school self evaluation: a critique' *Educational Research*, 24, 4.

Clift, P. (1986) 'SBR: the UK Scene' Paper presented at the ISIP UK Dissemination Conference April, 1986.

Cockroft (1982) *Mathematics Counts* (The Cockroft Report) London: HMSO.

Cohn, E. (1968) 'Economies of scale' *Journal of Human Resources* 3.

Coleman, J. (1965) 'Methods and results in the ILEA studies of effects of school on learning' *Review of Educational Research* 45, 335–86.

Coleman, J. S., Campbell, E., Hobson, C., McPartland, J., Mood, A., Weinfeld, F. and York, R. (1966) *Equality of Educational Opportunity* Washington DC: US Government Printing Office.

Comber, L. C. and Whitfield, R. C. (1979) *Action on Indiscipline: a Practical Guide for Teachers* NAS/UWT in association with the Department of Educational Enquiry, University of Aston.

Connerton, P. (ed) (1976) *Critical Sociology* Harmondsworth: Penguin.

Corrigan, P. (1979) *Schooling the Smash Street Kids* London: MacMillan.

Coulson, A. A. (1980) 'The Role of the Primary Head' In Bush, T. *et al* (eds) *Approaches to School Management* London: Harper and Row.

Court Committee (1976) *Fit for the Future* London: DHSS.

Covill, N., Martin, F., Taylor, J. and Tyson, M. (1984) 'Implications from extreme histories' In Frude, N. and Gault, H. (eds) *Disruptive Behaviour in Schools* Chichester: John Wiley.

Cox, B. (1986) 'Competing cultures' personal column *TES* 24/1/86.

Crandall, D. P. 'External support for school improvement: constructs of the International School Improvement Project' ISIP Conference Paper Nene college, Northampton, April, 1986.

Cuban, L. (1984) 'Transforming the Frog into a Prince: effective schools research, policy & practice at the district level' *Harvard Educational Review*, 54, 2.

Cusick, P. (1973) *Inside High School* New York: Holt Rinehart and Winston.

Cuttance, P. (1980) 'Do schools consistently influence the performance of their students?' *Educational Review* 32, 267–80.
Cuttance, P. (1985) 'Frameworks for research on the effectiveness of schooling' In Reynolds, D. (ed) *Studying School Effectiveness* Lewes: Falmer Press.
DES (1972) *Teacher-Education and Training* (The James Report) HMSO.
DES (1975) *Survey of Violence, Indiscipline & Vandalism in Schools* London: Department of Education and Science.
DES (1977) *Ten Good Schools: a Secondary School Enquiry* carried out by H.M.I. London Dept. of Education & Science.
DES (1978) *Making INSET Work* London HMSO.
DES (1979) *Aspects of Secondary Education in England: a Survey of HM Inspectors of Schools* London: HMSO.
DES (1981) *The School Curriculum* London: HMSO.
DES (1982) *The New Teacher in School* London: Department of Education and Science.
Dadds, M. (1983) 'Learning the Role of an Action-Research Consultant mimeograph Cambridge Institute of Education.
Dadds, M. (1986) 'The School, the Teacher-Researcher and the In-Service Tutor' In Holly, P. J. and Whitehead, D. (eds) *CARN Bulletin No. 7* Cambridge, CIE.
Dalin, P. (1973) *Case Studies of Educational Innovation IV Strategies for Innovation in Education* Paris OECD/CERI (Centre for Educational Research & Innovation).
David, J. L. (1982) *School Based Strategies: Implications for Government Policy* Bay Area Research Groups Mimeograph.
Davie, R., Butler, N. and Goldstein, H. (1972) *From Birth to Seven* London: Longman in association with the National Children's Bureau.
Davie, R. (1972) Absence from school *Education Guardian* 12 September, 1972.
Davie, R. (1977) 'The interface between education & social services' In Kahan B. (ed) *Working Together for Children and Their Families* Cardiff: DHSS/Welsh Office HMSO.
Davie, R. (1980) 'Promoting school adjustment' In Pringle M. K. (ed) *A Fairer Future for Children* London: MacMillan.
Deal, T. E. (1985) 'The Symbolism of Effective Schools' *The Elementary School Journal* 85, 5 (University of Chicago).
Deal, T. E. and Kennedy, A. (1983) 'Culture & School Performance *Educational Leadership* 40, (5), 14–15.
Deal, T. W. and Kennedy, A. (1982) *Corporate Cultures: The Rites & Rituals of Corporate Life* Reading Mass: Addison-Wesley.
Delamont, S. (1976) *Interaction in the Classroom* London: Methuen.
Delamont, S. (1980) *Sex Roles and the School* London: Methuen.

Derricott, R. (1985) *Curriculum Continuity: Primary to Secondary* Windsor: NFER–Nelson.

Docking, J. W. (1980) *Control & Discipline in Schools: Perspectives and Approaches* London: Harper & Row.

Doss, D. and Holley, F. (1982) *A Cause for National Pause:* Title 1 schoolwide projects (ORE Publication 81:85) Austin, Texas: Office of Research & Evaluation, Austin Independent School District.

Douglas, J. W. B. (1964) *The Home and the School* London: MacGibbon and Kee.

Dow, G. (1984) 'Viewpoint: sponsored and mobility revisited: tensions for teachers' *Sociological Review*, 32, 2.

Doyle, W. (1979) 'The tasks of teaching & learning in classrooms' North Texas State University (Mimeograph)

Doyle, W. and Ponder, G. A. (1977–78) The practicality ethic in teacher decision-making *Interchange* 8, 3.

Drucker, P. F. (1985) *Innovation and Entrepreneurship* London: Heinemann.

Drummond, M.-J. (1986) 'Focus on learning' DES/Regional course teaching styles & modes of learning Unpub. Conference Paper.

Duffy, G. G. (1980) *Teacher Effectiveness Research Implications for the Reading Profession* East Lansing Institute for Research on Teaching, Michigan State University.

Dunham, J. (1977) '*Educational Review* 29, 3, 181–7 (See also article in *Educational Research* 23, 3, 205–13.)

Durkheim, E. (1961) *Moral Education* New York: Free Press.

Ebbutt, D. (1983) 'Specific methods and techniques for collecting and analysing information from the classrooms' Cambridge CIE Mimeograph.

Edmunds, R. R. *et al* (1978a) *Search for Effective Schools* Cambridge Massachusetts: Harvard University Centre for Urban Schools.

Edmonds, R. R. (1978b) 'A Discussion of the Literature & Issues Related to Effective Schooling' *Paper presented at CEMREL'S National Conference on Urban Education* St. Louis, July 1978.

Edmonds, R. R. (1979a) 'Effective Schools for the Urban Poor' *Educational Leadership* 37, 15–27.

Edmonds, R. R. (1979b) 'Some Schools Work and More Can' *Social Policy* 9, 28–32.

Edmonds, R. R. (1981a) 'Making public schools effective' *Social Policy* 12, 56–60.

Edmonds, R.R. (1981b) 'A Report on the research project Search for Effective Schools . . . and certain of the designs for school improvement that are associated with the project' Unpublished Report Prepared for NIE Institute for Research on Teaching, Michigan State University.

Eisner, E. (1979) *The Educational Imagination* New York: MacMillan.

Elliott, G. (1980/82) *Self Evaluation and the Teacher: an Annotated Bibliography & Report on Current Practice* (4 vols) London: Schools Council.
Elliott, J. (1977) 'Evaluating in-service activities: from above or below?' *Insight*, November, 1977.
Elliott, J. (1978) 'The politics of classroom organisation' *Forum* 20, 2.
Elliott, J. (1980) 'Implications of classroom research for professional development' In Hoyle, E. and Megarry, J. (eds) *World Yearbook 1980* London: Kogan Page.
Elliott, J. (1981a) 'The teacher as researcher within award-bearing courses' In Alexander, R. J. and Ellis, J. W. (eds) *Advanced Study for Teachers* Teacher Education Study Group Society for Research into Higher Education, London: Nafferton Books.
Elliott, J. (1981b) 'In search of an alternative power base' *Education and Urban Society* 13, 4 August.
Elliott, J. (1981c) 'Action-research: a framework for self-evaluation in schools' CIE/Schools Council TIQL Project Working Paper.
Elliott, J. (1983) 'School-focused INSET and Research into teacher education' Cambridge Journal of Education 13, 12.
Elliott, J. (1985) 'Educational theory, practical philosophy and case study' CARE. Mimeograph, April.
Elliott, J. and Adelman, C. (1976) '*Innovation at the Classroom Level: A Case Study of the Ford Teaching Project* Unit 28 Open University Course E.203: Curriculum Design and Development, Milton Keynes: Open University Press.
Essex County Teachers' Working Party (1976) article in *Education* 145 350 quoted by Tattum, D. (1982) in *Disruptive Pupils in Schools and Units* Chichester: John Wiley.
Feldhusen, J. F., Thurston, J. R. and Benning, J. T. (1973) 'A longitutinal study of delinquency and other aspects of children's behaviour' *International Journal of Criminology and Penology* 1, 341–51.
Feldhusen, J. F., Roeser, T. D. and Thurston, J. R. (1977) 'Prediction of social adjustment over a period of 6 or 9 years' *Journal of Special Education* 11, 29–36.
Festinger, L. (1962) 'Cognitive Dissonance' *Scientific American* October.
Finlayson, D. S. and Loughran, J. L. (1976) 'Pupils' perceptions in high and low deliquency schools' *Educational Research* 18, 2, 138–45.
Flanders, T. 1980 *The Professional Development of Teachers* A report to the Teacher Federation, Vancouver B.C.
Fogelman, K., Essen, J . and Tibbenham, A. (1978) 'Ability grouping in secondary schools and attainment', *Educational Studies* 4, 3, 201–212. See also *Child* 4, 1, 41–58; *Concern* 29, 19–25; *Educational Research* 20, 2, 143–151; *Educational Studies* 4, 2, 122–130; *British Journal of Educational Studies* 26, 1, 8–23.

Fogelman, K. (1976) *Britain's Sixteen-Year-Olds* London: National Children's Bureau.

Fogelman, K. and Richardson, K. (1974) School 'attendance; some results from the National Child Development Study' In Turner, B. (ed) *Truancy* London: Ward Lock Educational.

Foucault, M. (1979) *The History of Sexuality 1: An Introduction* Harmondsworth: Pelican.

Francis, P. (1975) *Beyond Control? A Study of Discipline in the Comprehensive School* London: Allen and Unwin.

Frazer, B. (1981) 'Learning environment in curriculum evaluation: a review' *Evaluation in Education*, 5, 3–93.

Frazer, B. and Walberg, H. J. (1981) 'Psychological learning environments in science classrooms', *Studies in Science Education* 8, 67–92.

Freire, P. (1972) *Pedagogy of the Oppressed* Harmondsworth: Penguin.

Frude, N. (1984) 'Framework for analysis' In Frude, N. and Gault, H. (eds) *Disruptive Behaviour in Schools* Chichester: John Wiley.

Frude, N. and Gault, H. (eds) (1984) *Disruptive Behaviour in Schools* Chichester: John Wiley.

Fullan, M. (1976) In Morgan, C. with Pritchard, G. *Organisation Development (OD): The Case of Sheldon High School* Open University E321 Unit 6 Management in Education, College Press.

Fullan, M. (1982) *The Meaning of Educational Change* New York: OISE/Teachers' College Press.

Fullan, M. (1985) 'Change Processes and Strategies at the Local Level' *Elementary School Journal* 85, 3, 391–421.

Furlong, J. (1976) 'Interaction sets in the classroom' In Hammersley, M. and Woods, P. (eds) *The Process of Schooling* London: RKP.

Gadamer, H. G. (1975) *Truth and Method* London: Sheed and Ward.

Galloway, D. (1976a) 'Size of school, socio-economic hardship, suspension later and persistent unjustified absence from school' *British Journal of Educational Psychology* 46, 1, 40–7.

Galloway, D. (1976b) 'Persistent unjustified absence from school' *Trends in Education*, 4, 22–7.

Galloway, D. (1981) *Teaching and Counselling: Pastoral Care in Primary and Secondary Schools* London: Longman.

Galloway, D. (1985) 'Pastoral care and school effectiveness' In Reynolds, D. (ed) *Studying School Effectiveness* Lewes: Falmer Press.

Galloway, D., Ball, T., Blomfield, D. and Seyd, R. (1982) *Schools and Disruptive Pupils* London: Longman.

Galloway, D. and Barrett, C. (1983) 'Disruptive pupils: a result of teacher strees as well as a cause?' *New Zealand Post Primary Teachers Association Journal*, Term, 2, 40–4.

Gallup (1977) 'Ninth annual gallup poll of the public attitudes toward the public schools' *Phi Delta Kappa* 59, 1, 33–48.

Galton, M. and Willcocks, J. (1983) *Moving from the Primary Classroom* London: RKP.

Garbarino, J. (1973) 'High School size and adolescent social development' *Human Ecology Forum*, 4, 26–29.

Garbarino, J. (1980) 'Some thoughts on school size and its effects on adolescent development' *Journal of Youth and Adolescence*, 9, 169–182.

Garbarino, J. and Asp, C. E. (1982) *Successful Schools and Competent Students* New York: Lexington Books.

Gath, D., Cooper, B. and Gattoni, F. (1971) 'Child guidance and delinquency in a London borough' *Psychological Medicine* 2, 185–191; See also: Gath, D., Cooper, B., Gattoni, F. and Rockett, D. (1977) *Child Guidance and Delinquency in a London Borough* Oxford: Oxford University Press.

Gawthorne-Hardy, J. (1977) *The Public School Phenomenon* London: Hodder and Stoughton.

Geddes, D. (1982) Series of articles on disruption in schools *The Times*, 2–5 March, 1982.

Gibbons, M. (1974) 'Walkabout: Searching for the right passage from childhood and school' *Phi Delta Kappa*, May 596–602.

Gibbons, M. (1976) *The New Secondary Education*, Bloomington, Indiana: Phi Delta Kappa.

Gibbons, M. (1977) *A Model of Curriculum Development* Simon Fraser University Mimeograph.

Gibbons, M. *et al* (1980) 'Toward a Theory of self-directed learning: a study of experts without formal training' *Journal of Humanistic Psychology* 20, 2, Spring 41–56.

Giddens, A. (1984) *The Constitution of Society: Outline of the Theory of Structuration* Cambridge: Polity Press.

Gillham, B. (1984) 'School organization and the control of disruptive incidents' In Frude, N. and Gault, H. (eds) *Disruptive Behaviour in Schools* Chichester: John Wiley.

Glenn, B. C. (1981) *What Works? An Examination of Effective Schools for Poor Black Children* Cambridge Mass: Centre for Law and Education, Harvard University.

Goddard, D. (1985) 'ACSET: its Implementation in a Wider Context' *School Organisation*, 5, 3.

Goldstein, H. (1980) 'Fifteen thousand hours: a review of the statistical procedures' *Journal of Child Psychology and Psychiatry*, 21, 364–6.

Graham, P. and Rutter, M. (1968) 'The reliability and validity of the psychiatric study of the child: II Interview with the parent' *British Journal of Psychiatry* 114, 581–92. See also *British Medical Journal* 3, 695–700.

Gray, J. (1980) 'Guidance in Scottish secondary schools: a client evaluation' *British Journal of Guidance and Counselling* 8, 2, 129–145.

Gray, J. (1981a) 'School Effectiveness research: key issues' *Educational Research* 24, 1, November.

Gray, J. (1981b) 'Towards effective schools: problems & progress in British research' *British Educational Research Journal* 7, 1, 1981.

Gray, J. *et al* (1983) *Reconstructions of Secondary Education* London: RKP.

Grunsell, R. (1978) *Beyond Control? Schools and Suspension* London: Writers and Readers.

Grunsell, R. (1980) *Absent from School: the Story of a Truancy Centre* London: Writers and Readers.

HMI (1977) *Curriculum 11–16: The Red Book* London Department of Education & Science.

HMI (1979) *Aspects of Secondary Education in England* London: HMSO.

HMI (1980) *A View of the Curriculum* London: Department of Education and Science.

HMI (1981) *Curriculum 11–16: A Review of Progress* London: Department of Education and Science.

HMI (1985) *Quality in Schools* London: HMSO.

HMSO (1981) *'West Indian children in our schools:' Interim Report of the Committee of Inquiry into the Education of Children from Ethnic Minority Groups* London: HMSO.

Habermas, J. (1972) *Knowledge and Human Interests* London: Heinemann.

Habermas, J. (1974) *Theory and Practice* London: Heinemann.

Haertel, G. D. and Walberg, H. L. (1981) 'Socio-psychological environments and learning' *British Educational Research Journal* 7, 27–36.

Haigh, G. (ed) (1979) *On Our Side; Order, Authority and Interaction in School* London: Temple Smith.

Hall, G. E. (1978) 'Concerns-based in-Service teacher training: an overview of the concepts, research and practice' Paper Presented at Conference on School-Focused In-Service Training' March, 1978, Bournemouth.

Hall, G. E. and Loucks, S. F. (1977) 'A developmental model for determining whether the treatment is actually implemented' *American Educational Research Journal* 14, 3, 263–276.

Halpin, A. (1966) *Theory and Research in Administration* New York: MacMillan.

Halsey, A. H. *et al* (1980) *Origins and Destinations* Oxford: Oxford University Press.

Hamblin, D. (1973) 'A model of counselling for the British secondary school' *Further Education Staff College Reports* 5, 19, 17–20.

Hamblin, D. (1974) *The Teacher and Counselling* Oxford: Blackwell.

Hamblin D. (1977) 'Caring and control: the treatment of absenteeism,

In Carroll, H. C. M. (ed) *Absenteeism in South Wales* Swansea University College of Swansea Faculty of Education.

Hamblin, D. (1978) *The Teacher and Pastoral Care* Oxford: Blackwell.

Hamblin, D. (ed) (1981) *Problem and Practice of Pastoral Care* Oxford: Blackwell.

Hamblin, D. (1986a) 'The failure of pastoral care' In special edition of *School Organisation* 6, 1.

Hamblin, D. (1986b) *The Pastoral Curriculum* Oxford: Blackwell.

Handy, C. (1976) *Understanding Organisations* Harmondsworth: Penguin.

Handy, C. (1977) 'The organization of consent' In *The Changing University* Piper D. & Glatter, R. (eds) Windsor: NFER.

Handy, C. (1978) *Gods of Management* London: Pan, Books.

Handy, C. (1982a) 'Contraction in organisation' Schools, Council Programme One Seminar Paper.

Handy, C. (1982b) 'Where management is leading' *Management Today*, December.

Handy, C. (1984a) *Taken for Granted? Understanding Schools as Organisations* York: Longman/Schools Council.

Handy, C. (1984b) *The Future of Work* Oxford: Blackwell.

Hanushek, E. A. (1981) 'Throwing money at schools' *Journal of Policy and Management* 1, 19–41.

Hargreaves, A. (1979) 'Strategies, decisions and control: interaction in a middle school classroom' In Eggleston, J. (ed) *Teacher Decision-Making in the Classroom* London: RKP.

Hargreaves, D. (1967) *Social Relations in a Secondary School* London: RKP.

Hargreaves, D. (1979) 'Durkheim, deviance and education' In Barton, L. and Meighan, R. (eds) *Schools, Pupils and Deviance* Driffield: Nafferton Books.

Hargreaves, D. (1980) 'Classrooms, schools and juvenile delinquency' *Educational Analysis* 2, 2, 75–87.

Hargreaves, D. (1982) *The Challenge for the Comprehensive School* London: Routledge and Kegan Paul.

Hargreaves, D. (1983) 'School self-evaluation' *Inspection and Advice* 19, Autumn.

Hargreaves, D. (1984) *Improving Secondary Schools* Report of the committee on the curriculum & organisation of secondary schools, London: ILEA.

Hargreaves, D., Hester, S. K. and Mellor, F. J. (1975) *Deviance in Classrooms* London: RKP.

Harrison, B. (1986) 'Sarah's letters: A case of shyness' Bedford Way papers, 26, London University Institute of Education.

Harrop, A. (1984) *Behaviour Modification in the Classroom* London: Hodder and Stoughton Unibooks.

Hastings, D. J. (1981) 'One school's experience' In Gillham, B. (ed) *Problem Behaviour in the Secondary School* London: Croom Helm.

Henley, M. (1986) 'The development and implementation of school improvement policies by education authorities' ISIP UK Conference Paper April.

Henry, J. (1954) 'The formal social structure of a psychiatric hospital' *Psychiatry* 17, 139–152.

Henry, J. (1984) 'Towards an understanding of collaborative research in education' Deakin University. Since reprinted in Holly, P. J. and Whitehead, D. (eds) *CARN Bulletin* 7, CIE.

Hersh, R. H., Carnine, D., Gall, M., Stockard, J., Carmack, M. A. and Gannon, P. (1981) *The Management of Education Professionals in instructionally Effective Schools: Toward a Research Agenda* Eugene Centre for Educational Policy and Management, University of Oregon.

Hirst, P. and Peters, R. (1970) *The Logic of Education* London: RKP.

Holden, A. (1969) *Teachers as Counsellors* London: Constable.

Holden, A. (1971) *Counselling in Secondary Schools* London: Constable.

Holly, P. J. (1982a) 'Facilitating action-research in schools' Conference Paper Klagenfurt University, December.

Holly, P. J. (1982b) 'Monitoring the teaching and learning processes in a comprehensive school' Schools Council Programme One Seminar Paper.

Holly, P. J. (1984a) 'Action-research: a cautionary note' reprinted in Holly, P.J. and Whitehead, D. (eds) *CARN Bulletin No. 6. Action-Research in Schools: Getting it into Perspective* Cambridge Institute of Education.

Holly, P. J. (1984b) 'The institutionalisation of action-Research in schools' *Cambridge Journal of Education* 14, 2, Easter term.

Holly, P. J. (1984c) 'Beyond the cult of the individual: putting the partnership into in-service collaboration' Unpub. Conference Paper Downing College, Cambridge.

Holly, P. J. (1984d) 'Clarifying the concepts involved in institutional self-evaluation: an introductory paper' *Conference Paper* CIE, October.

Holly, P. J. (1985a) 'The developing school' *CIE/TRIST Working Paper* Cambridge CIE.

Holly, P. J. (1985b) 'With due regard to objectivity; a subjective view' *CIE Open Lecture/Seminar papers* 7, 10, 85.

Holly, P. J. (1985c) 'Researching the personal within the institutional' *CIE Open Lecture/Seminar Paper* 21/10/85.

Holly, P. J. (1986a) 'Action-research: third party, fire & theft?' In Holly, P.J. and Whitehead, D. (eds) *Collaborative Action-Research* CARN Bulletin No. 7, CIE.

Holly, P. J. (1986b) 'The Teachers' Guide' CIE/TRIST Working Paper Cambridge CIE.

Holly, P. J. (1986c) 'Northamptonshire LEA's interpretation of the DES brief, regarding the Lower Attaining Pupils Programme: A critique' Paper commissioned by the Further Education Unit.

Holly, P. J. (ed) (1986d) 'Developing a "professional evaluation"' In special edition of the *Cambridge Journal of Education*.

Holly, P. J. (in press) 'The central dilemmas of change initiatives in schools' *School Organisation* (forthcoming).

Holly, P. J. with Southworth, G. W. (1986) *Inside Judgements: Self Evaluation in the Primary School* (forthcoming).

Holly, P. J. and Wideen, M. (1986) The Culture Club, chapter in *OECD/CERI ISIP publication* (forthcoming).

Holly, P. (ed) (1986) *CARN Bulletin* Cambridge: CIE.

Holt, M. (1979) 'Reshaping the strategy of in-service training' *Education* 26/10/79.

Holt, M. (1982) 'Whole curriculum planning in schools: some research implications' *Journal of Curriculum Studies* 14, 3, 267–276.

Hooper, R. (1978) 'Pupil perceptions of counselling: a response to Murgatroyd' *British Journal of Guidance and Counselling* 6, 2, 198–203.

Hopkins, D. (1985a) *A Teacher's Guide to Classroom Research* Milton Keynes: Open University Press.

Hopkins, D. (1985b) *School Based Review for School Improvement* Leuven, Belgium: ACCO.

Hopkins, D. (1986a) *Instruments and methods for School Based Review* Leuven: Belgium ACFO (forthcoming).

Hopkins, D. (1986b) 'The change process and leadership in schools' *School Organisation* 6, 1.

Hopkins, D. (ed) (1986d) *In-service Training and Educational Development: an International Survey* London: Croom Helm.

Hopkins, D. (ed) (1987) *Improving the Quality of Schooling* Falmer Press.

Hopkins, D. and Wideen, M. (1984) *Alternative Perspectives on School Improvement* Lewes; Falmer Press.

House, E. R. (1980) *Evaluating with Validity* Beverley Hills; Sage Publications.

Hoyle, E. (1972) 'Educational innovation and the role of the teacher' *Forum* 14, 42–44.

Hoyle, E. (1972) 'Creativity in the school' unpublished paper given at OECD workshop in Portugal.

Hoyle, E. (1975) 'The creativity of the school in Britain' In Harris, A. Lawn, M. and Prescott, W. (eds) *Curriculum Innovation* London: Croom Helm/Open University Press.

Hull, C. (1985) 'Pupils as teacher educators' *Cambridge Journal of Education*, 15, 1.

Hunter, M. G. (1979) *Final Report of the Michigan Cost-Effectiveness Study* East Lansing; Michigan Dept of Education.

Hutchinson, B. (1985) 'The Public Image of HAP' Interim Report 3 Herts. Achievement Project, December.

ILEA (1977) *Keeping the School Under Review* London: ILEA (first version).

ILEA (1981) *Attendance Survey, 1981* Inner London Education Authority Research and Statistics Branch, Document RS 791/81, ILEA.

ILEA (1982) *Keeping the School Under Review* London: ILEA (second version).

ILEA (1983) *Effective Learning Skills* Learning Resources Branch, London: ILEA.

Ingleby, D. (ed) (1981) *Critical Psychiatry* Harmondsworth: Penguin.

Insell, P. and Jacobson, L. (1975) *What Do You Expect?* California: Cummings Publishing Co.

James, M. (1982) *A First Review and Register of School and College Initiated Self Evaluation Activities in the UK* Educational Evaluation and Accountability Research Group, Milton Keynes: Open University.

Jencks, C. *et al* (1972) *Inequality; a Reassessment of the Effect of Family & Schooling in America* New York: Basic Books.

Johnson, D., Ransom, E., Packwood, T., Bowden, K. and Kogan, M. (1980) *Secondary Schools and the Welfare Network* London: Allen and Unwin.

Jones, A. (1980) 'The school's view of persistent non-attendance' In Hersov, L. and Berg, I. (eds) *Out of School* Chichester: John Wiley.

Jones, A. (1984) *Counselling Adolescents: School and After* (2nd edition) London: Kogan Page.

Jones, D. (1976) 'Bunking off' *Teaching London Kids*, 5, 3–8.

Joyce, B. *et al* (1981) *Flexibility in Teaching* London and New York: Longman.

Joyce, B. and Showers, B (1980) 'Improving in-service training: the messages of research' *Educational Leadership*, February.

Joyce, B. & Weil, M. (1980) *Models of Teaching* (2nd ed) New York: Prentice Hall.

Judd, C. H. (1922) 'The scientific technique of curriculum making' *School and Society*, 367.

Kahan, B. (ed) *Working Together for Children and Their Families* Cardiff DHSS/Welsh Office: HMSO.

Kamin, L. J. (1974) *The Science & Politics of IQ* Harmondsworth: Penguin.

Kelly, G. (1955) *The psychology of Personal Constructs* (2 vols), New York: Norton.

Kemmis, S. and McTaggart, R. (1981) *The Action Research Planner* Victoria, Australia: Deakin University Press.

Knutton, S. and Mycroft, A. (1986) 'Stress and the deputy head' *School Organisation*, 6, 1.

Kounin, J. S., Friesen, W. V. and Norton, E. (1966) 'Managing emotionally disturbed children in regular classrooms' *Journal of Educational psychology*, 57, 1–13.

Kyriacou, C. and Sutcliffe, J. (1978) 'Teacher stress; prevalence sources and symptoms' *British Journal of Educational Psychology* 48, 159–67.

Lablow, W. (1975) 'Academic ignorance and black intelligence' In Insell, P. and Jacobson, L. (eds) *What Do You Expect?* California: Cummings Publishing Co.

Lacan, J. (1979) *The Four Fundamental Concepts of Psycho-Analysis* Harmondsworth: Penguin.

Lacey, C. (1970) *Hightown Grammar* Manchester: Manchester University Press.

Lacey, C. (1977) *The Socialization of Teachers* London: Methuen.

Lavelle, M. (1984) 'The role of consultancy in curriculum and organisation development innovation in education' *School Organisation* 4, 2, 161–170.

Lavelle, M. and Keith, D. (1985) 'Planning for headteacher staff development' Introductory paper OD Unit Sheffield Education Department.

Lawrence, J. (1980) *Exploring Techniques for Coping with Disruptive Behaviour in Schools* University of London, Goldsmith's College Educational Studies Monograph.

Lawrence, J. *et al* (1981) *Dialogue on Disruptive Behaviour: a Study of a Secondary School* London: PJP Press.

Lawrence, J., Steed, D. and Young, P. (1984) *Disruptive Children – Disruptive Schools?* London: Croom Helm.

Lawton, D. (1973) *Social Change, Educational Theory and Curriculum Planning* London: Hodder and Stoughton.

Lawton, D. (1975) *Class Culture and the Curriculum* London: RKP.

Lawton, D. (1980) *The Politics of the School Curriculum* London: RKP.

Lawton, D. (1983) *Curriculum Studies and Educational Planning* London: Hodder and Stoughton.

Lawton, D. *et al* (1978) *Theory and Practice of Curriculum Studies* London: RKP.

Lehming, R. And Kane, M. (eds) (1981) *Improving Schools* New York: Sage.

Levine, D.U. & Stark, J. (1981) *Extended Summary and Conclusions: Institutional and Organizational Arrangements and Processes for Improving Academic Achievement at Inner-City Elementary Schools* Kansas City: Centre for the Study of Metropolitan Problems in Education University of Missouri – Kansas City, August 1981.

Lewin, K. (1946) 'Action-research and minority problems' *Journal of Social Issues*, 2, 34–46.

Lewis, D. J. and Murgatroyd, S. J. (1976) 'The professionalisation of counselling in education and its legal implications' *British Journal of Guidance and Counselling* 4, 1, 2–15.

Lewis, I. (1985) 'Teacher action-research and award-bearing courses: a course organiser's view' York: York University School of Education.

Lezottee, L. W., Edmonds, R. and Ratner, G. A. (1974) *A Final Report: Remedy for School Failure to Equitably Deliver Basic School Skills* East Lansing Dept of Urban and Metropolitan Studies, Michigan State University.

Lichtheim, G. (1970) *A Short History of Socialism* London: Weidenfeld and Nicolson.

Little, J. W. (1981) 'School success and staff development: the role of staff development in urban desegrated schools' Final report to National Institute of Education.

Lortie, D. C. (1975) *Schoolteacher: a Sociological Study* Chicago: University of Chicago Press.

Lukes, S. (1976) *Power: A Radical View* London: MacMillan.

Lyons, G., Stenning, R. and McQueeney, J. (1985) *Employment Relations in Maintained Secondary Schools* Bristol: National Development Centre for School Management Training.

Lytton, H. and Craft, M. (1974) *Guidance and Counselling in British Schools* (2nd edn). London: Edward Arnold.

MacDonald, B. (1976) 'Evaluation and the control of education' In Tawney D. (ed) *Curriculum Evaluation Today* Tawney, D. (ed) London: Schools Council/MacMillan.

MacDonald, B. (1981) 'Mandarins and lemons – the executive investment in program evaluation' *AERA symposium paper* April.

MacMillan, D. L. and Morrison, G. M. (1979) 'Education Programming' In Quay, H. C. & Werry, J. C. (eds) *Psychopathological Disorders of Childhood* (2nd edn). New York: Wiley.

Madaus, G. F. (1980) *School Effectiveness* New York: McGraw-Hill.

Madaus, G. F. *et al* (1979) 'The sensitivity of measures of school effectiveness' *Harvard Educational Review* 49, 207–230.

Manasse, A. L. (1985) 'Improving conditions for principal effectiveness: policy implications of research' *The Elementary School Journal* 85, 3.

Majoribanks, K. (1979a) *Families and their Learning Environments* London: RKP.

Majoribanks, K. (1979b) 'Family and school related characteristics of intelligence, personality and school-related affective characteristics' *Genetic Psychology Monographs* 99, 165–183.

Marland, M. (1974) *Pastoral Care* London: Heinemann.

Marsh, P., Rosser, E. and Harre, R, (1978) *The Rules of Disorder* London: RKP.

Maslow, A. (1954) *Motivation and Personality* New York: Harper and Row.

Maslow, A. (1981) 'What is a Taoistic Teacher?' In Rubin, L. J. (ed) *Facts and Feelings in the Classroom*, London; Ward Lock Educational.

Mays, J. D. (ed) (1972) *Juvenile Delinquency, the Family and the Local Group* London: Longman.

McCormick, R. (ed) (1982) *Calling Education to Account* London: Heinemann.

McCormick, R. and James, M. (1983) *Curriculum Evaluation in Schools* London: Croom Helm.

McDill, E. L. (1969) 'Educational climates of high schools' *American Journal of Sociology* 74, 567–86.

McGuiness, J. B. (1982) *Planned Pastoral Care: a Guide for Teachers* New York: McGraw-Hill.

McLoughlin, W. (1983) 'Understanding how schools fail children' *International Review of Education*, XXIX, 59–72.

McMahon, A., Bolam, R., Abbott, R. and Holly, P. (1984) *Guidelines for Review and Internal Development in Schools* Primary and Secondary School Handbooks, York: Longman/Schools Council.

McMahon, A. *et al* (1982) The GRIDS Project *Educational Management and Administration* 10, 217–222.

McNamara, D. (1975) 'Distribution and incidence of problem children in an English county,' quoted in Laslett, R. (1977) 'Disruptive and violent pupils: the facts and the fallacies' *Educational Review* 29, 3, 152/62.

Mead, G. H. (1934) *Mind, Self and Society* Chicago: University of Chicago Press.

Menlo, A. (1985) 'A reconceptualisation of resistance to change and its application to the institutionalisation process' Paper prepared for ISIP seminar, Lucerne, June 1985.

Miles, M. B. (1965) 'Planned Change and Organisational Health: Figure and Ground' In Carlson, R. D. (ed) *Change Processes in the Public School* Eugene: Oregon Centre for the Advanced Study of Education.

Miles, M. B. (ed) (1964) *Innovation in Education* New York: Teachers' College Press: Columbia University.

Miller, W. B. (1958) 'Lower class life as a generating milieu of gang delinquency' *Journal of Social Issues* XIV, 3, 5–19.

Millham, S. *et al* (1982) *Issues of Control in Child Care* London: HMSO.

Mills, W. P. C. (1976) 'The seriously disruptive behaviour of pupils in secondary schools of one local education authority' Unpublished MEd Thesis University of Birmingham.

Mintzberg, H. (1973) *The Nature of Managerial Work* New York: Harper and Row.

Moore, B. M. (1971) *Guidance in Comprehensive Schools: a Survey* Slough: NFER.

Moos, R. H. (1979) *Evaluating Educational Environments* San Francisco: Josey Boss.

Mortimore, P. (1980) 'Misbehaviour in schools' In Upton, G. and Gobell, A. (eds) *Behaviour Problems in the Comprehensive School* Faculty of Education, University College, Cardiff.

Mortimore, P. (1982) 'Underachievement: a framework for debate' *Secondary Education Journal*, 12, 3, 3–6.

Mortimore, J. and Blackstone, T. (1982) *Disadvantage and Education* London: Heinemann Educational.

Mortimore, P. and Mortimore, J. (1981) 'Making the most of the nightschool shift!' *The Guardian* 7 April, 1981.

Mortimore, P., Davies, J., Varlaam, A., West, A., Devine, P. and Mazza, J. (1983) *Behaviour Problems in Schools: an Evaluation of Support Centres* London: Croom Helm.

Mortimore, P. and team (1985) 'The ILEA junior school study: an introduction,' In Reynolds, D. (ed) *Studying School Effectiveness* Lewes: Falmer Press.

Mullin, S. P. and Summers, A. A. (1981) 'Is more better? a review of the effectiveness of spending on compensatory education' Unpublished manuscript, University of Pennsylvania.

Murgatroyd, S. J. (1977) 'Pupil perceptions of counselling: a case study' *British Journal of Guidance and counselling* 5, 1, 73–8.

Murgatroyd, S. J. (1980) Research cited by Reynolds, D., St. Leger, S. and Murgatroyd, S. J. in 'School factors and truancy' Chichester; John Wiley.

Murnane, R. J. (1980) *Interpreting the Evidence on School Effectiveness* Working Paper No. 830 New Haven Connecticut, Institution for Social and Policy Studies, Yale University.

Murphy, J. (1984) 'Giving Ignorance a Bad Name' *TES article* 9, 11, 84.

NEA (1979) Teacher opinion polls 1978–79 *The Weekly Educational Review* 9 August, 1979; National Education Association.

NIE (1978) *Violent Schools – Safe Schools* Washington DC: US Department of Health Education and Welfare.

NUT (1976) *Discipline in Schools* London: National Union of Teachers.

Nash, R. (1976) *Teacher Expectations and Pupil Learning:* London RKP.

Newsom, J. and Newsom, E. (1983) 'Perspectives on children's behaviour at school' In Frude, N. and Gault, H. (eds) *Disruptive Behaviour in Schools* Chichester: John Wiley.

New York State Dept of Education (1974a) *Reading Achievement Related to Educational and Environmental Conditions in 12 New York City Elementary Schools* Albany, NY, Division of Education Evaluation.

New York State Dept of Education (1974b) *School Factors Influencing Reading Achievement: a Case Study of Two Inner City Schools* Albany NY: Office of Education Performance Review, ERIC Document Reproduction Service No ED 089211.

New York State Dept of Education (1976) *Three Strategies for Studying the Effects of School Processes* Albany NY: Bureau of School Programs Evaluation.

Nias, J. (1980) 'Leadership Styles and Job-Satisfaction in Primary Schools' In Bush, T. *et al. Approaches to School Management* London: Harper and Row.

Nias, J. (1983) 'The definition and maintenance of self in primary teaching: values and reference groups' Paper presented at Conference at St Hilda's College, Oxford, on Teachers Lives and Biographies.

Nisbet, J. (ed) (1973) *Creativity of the School* Paris: OECD.

Nixon, J. (ed) (1981) *A Teacher's Guide to Action Research* London: Grant and McIntyre.

Nuttall, D. (1981) *School Self Evaluation: Accountability with a Human Face* York: Longman.

Nuttall, D. *et al* (1987) *Cases in School Evaluation* Lewes: Falmer.

Oldroyd, D., Smith, K., and Lee, J. (1984) *School-Based Staff Development Activities: A Hand Book for Secondary Schools* York: Longman/Schools Council.

Olweus, D. (1978) *Aggression in the Schools: Bullies and Whipping Boys* Washington DC: Hemisphere.

Olweus, D. (1984) 'Aggressors and their victims: bullying at school' In Frude, N. and Gault, H. (eds) *Disruptive Behaviour in Schools* Chichester: John Wiley.

Ouston, J. (1981) 'Differences between schools: the implications for school practice' In Gillham, B. (ed) *Problem Behaviour in the Secondary School* London: Croom Helm.

Pablant, P. & Baxter, J. C. (1975) 'Environmental correlates of school vandalism' *Journal of the American Institute of Planners* 241, 270–279.

Pack (1977) *Truancy and Indiscipline in Schools in Scotland* (The Pack Report) Scottish Education Dept, London: HMSO.

Parry, K. (1976) 'Disruptive children in school: the view of a class teacher and head of house' In Jones-Davies, C. and Cave, R. (eds) *The Disruptive Pupil in the Secondary School* London: Ward Lock Educational.

Patrick, H., Bernbaum, G. and Reid, K. (1982) *The structure and process of initial teacher education within universities in England & Wales* School of Education, University of Leicester.

Perry, P. (1977) quoted in Hopkins, D. (ed) (1986) 'In-service training and educational development: an international survey' London: Croom Helm.

Peters, R. S. (1966) *Ethics & Education* London: George Allen and Unwin.

Peters, T. and Waterman, R. (1982) *In Search of Excellence* Lada: Harper and Row.

Phillips, D. (1978) *The Children We Fail* Available from 260 Wendover, Thurlow Street, London SE17 2UW.

Phillips, D., Davie, R. and Callely, E. (1985) 'Pathways to institutional development in secondary schools' In Reynolds, D. (ed) *Studying School Effectiveness* Lewes: Falmer Press.

Phillips, D. and Callely, E. (1981) 'Pupils views of comprehensive schools or "what do they think of it so far?"' *Links* 7, 1, 32–6.

Phillips, D. and Callely, E. (1982) 'Teacher-Researchers – in search of topics?' *Links* 6, 1, 16–17.

Phi Delta Kappa (1980) 'Why do some urban schools succeed?' Bloomington Ind, *The Journal*.

Piaget, J. (1971) *Science of Education and the Psychology of the Child* London: Longman.

Pik, R. (1981) 'Confrontation situations and teacher-support systems', In Gillham, B. (ed) *Problem Behaviour in the Secondary School* London: Croom Helm.

Pinner, M. (1985) *School Internal Report: Development of Classroom Practice* (1984/5).

Pollard, A. (1980) 'Teacher interests and changing situations of survival threat in primary school classrooms,' In Woods, P. (ed) *Pupil Stategies: Explorations in the Sociology of the School* London: Croom Helm.

Power, M. J. *et al* (1967) 'Delinquent schools' *New Society* 10, 264, 524–3.

Power, M. J., Benn, R. T. and Morris, J. N. (1972) 'Neighbourhood school and juveniles before the courts' *British Journal of Criminology*, 12, 111–32.

Power, C. and Reimer, J. (1981) 'Moral atmosphere: an educational bridge between moral judgement and action' In Damon, W. (ed) *New Directions For Child Development: Moral Development* San Francisco: Josey-Bass.

Pressman, J. L. and Wildavsky, A. (1979) (2nd edn) *Implementation* Berkely: University of California Press.

Purkey, S. and Smith, M. (1983) 'Effective schools: a review' *The Elementary School Journal* 83, 427–452.

Purkey, S. C. and Smith, M. S. (1985) 'School reform: the district policy implications of the effective schools literature' *The Elementary School Journal* University of Chicago, 85, 3.

Rafalides, M. and Hoy, W. K. (1971) 'Student sense of alienation and pupil control orientation of high schools' *The High School Journal* 55, 101–111.

Reid, K. (1981) 'Alienation & Persistent School Absenteeism' *Research in Education* 26, 31–40.

Reid, K. (1982a) 'The self-concept and persistent school absenteeism' *British Journal of Educational Psychology* 52, 2, 179–187.

Reid, K. (1982b) 'Case studies and persistent school absenteeism' *The Counsellor* 3, 5, 25–30.

Reid, K. (1982c) 'Absent, sir' *Social Work Today* 13, 42, 12–13.

Reid, K. (1982d) 'School organisation & persistent school absenteeism: an introduction to a complex problem' *School Organisation* 2, 1, 45–52.

Reid, K. (1982e) 'Persistent school absenteeism' *Westminster Studies in Education*, 5, 27–35.

Reid, K. (1983a) 'Institutional factors and persistent school absenteeism' *Journal of Educational Management & Administration* 11, 17–27.

Reid, K. (1983b) 'Restrospection and persistent school absenteeism' *Educational Research* 25, 2, 110–15.

Reid, K. (1983c) 'Differences between the perception of persistent absentees towards parents and teachers' *Educational Studies* 9, 3, 211–19.

Reid, K. (1983d) 'The management of decline: a discussion paper' *School Organisation* 3, 4, 361–70.

Reid, K. (1984a) 'Some social, psychological and educational aspects related to persistent school absenteeism *Research in Education* 31, 63–82.

Reid, K. (1984b) 'The behaviour of persistent school absentees' *British Journal of Educational psychology* 54, 320–30.

Reid, K. (1984c) 'Disruptive behaviour and persistent school absenteeism' In Frude, N and Gault, H. (eds) *Disruptive Behaviour in Schools* Chichester: John Wiley.

Reid, K. (1984d) 'More than a matter of opinion' *Times Educational Supplement* 5, October 1984, 4.

Reid, K. (1985) *Truancy and School Absenteeism* London: Hodder and Stoughton.

Reid, K. (1986) *Disaffection from School* London: Methuen.

Reid, K. (ed) (1987) *Combating School Absenteeism*, London: Hodder and Stoughton.

Reid, K., Bernbaum, G. and Patrick, H. (1980) 'Future research issues in teacher education' *Educational Review* 33, 2, 143–50 See also: Reid, K. and Patrick, H. (1980) 'The class of 79' *Times Education Supplement* 20 June, 1980.

Reid, K., Bernbaum, G. and Patrick, H. (1981) 'On course: students and the PGCE' Unpublished paper presented at UCET Annual Conference Oxford, November 1981. See also: Patrick, H., Bernbaum, G. and Reid, K. (1981) 'The way we were: the staff of University Departments of Education' *Ibid*.

Reid, K. and Jones, K. (1983) 'Poor relation that's ripe for research' *Times Educational Supplement* 25 March 1983, 4.

Reid, W.A. (1981) 'The whole curriculum: problems and possibilities' *Cambridge CIE conference paper*.

Reynolds, D. (1975) 'When teachers and pupils refuse a truce: the secondary school and the creation of delinquency' In Mungham, G. and Pearson, G. (eds) *Working Class Youth Culture* London: RKP.

Reynolds, D. (1976) 'The delinquent school' In Woods, P. & Hammersley, M. (eds) *The Process of Schooling* London: RKP.

Reynolds, D. (1979) 'Bringing schools back in' In Barton, L. (ed) *Schools, Pupils and Deviance* Driffield: Nafferton Books.

Reynolds, D. (1982a) 'A state of ignorance' *Education for Devleopment* 7, 2, 4–35.

Reynolds, D. (1982b) 'Towards more effective schooling' special issue of *School Organisation* 2, 3.

Reynolds, D. (1982c) 'School effectiveness research: a review of the literature' *School Organisation and Management Abstracts* 1, 1, 5–14.

Reynolds, D. (1984) 'The school for vandals: A sociological portrait of a disaffection – prone school' In Frude, N. and Gault, H. (eds) *Disruptive Behaviour in Schools* Chichester: John Wiley.

Reynolds, D. (ed) (1985a) *Studying School Effectiveness* Lewes: Falmer Press.

Reynolds, D. (1985b) 'The effective school' *Times Educational Supplement* 17 September 1985.

Reynolds, D. (1985c) 'The effective school' TES 20/9/85 announcing *Studying School Effectiveness* London: Falmer Press.

Reynolds, D., Jones, D. and St Leger, S. (1976) 'Schools do make a difference' *New Society* 37, 721, 223–5.

Reynolds, D. and Murgatroyd, S. J. (1977) 'The sociology of schooling and the absent pupil: the school as a factor in the generation of truancy' In Caroll, H. C. M. (ed) *Absenteeism in South Wales* University College of Swansea Faculty of Education.

Reynolds, D., Jones, D., St Leger, S. and Murgatroyd, S. (1980) 'School factors & truancy' In Hersov, L. and Berg, I. (eds) *Out of School* Chichester: John Wiley.

Reynolds, D. & Murgatroyd, S. J. (1981) 'Schooled for Failure' *Times Educational Supplement* 4 December 1981.

Reynolds, D. & Sullivan, M. (1981) 'Bringing schools back in' In Barton, L. A. (ed) *Schools, Pupils and Deviance* London: Nafferton Books

Reynolds, D. and Reid, K. (1985) 'The second stage – towards a reconceptualisation of theory and methodology in school effectiveness studies' In Reynolds, D. (ed) *Studying School Effectiveness* Lewes: Falmer Press.

Richardson, E. (1973) *The Teacher, the School and the Task of Management* London: Heinemann.

Richmond, K. (1971) *The School Curriculum* London: Methuen.

Rist, R. (1970) 'Student social class and teacher expectations – a self fulfilling prophecy in ghetto education' *Harvard Educational Review* 40, 411–451.

Rist, R. (1974) 'Student social class and teacher expectations' In Insell, P. and Jacobson, L. (eds) *What Do You Expect?* California: Cummings Publishing Co.

Robinson, P. (1983) *School Effectiveness: the Primary School Context* 6, 21–32.

Rosenshine, B. (1970) 'Evaluation of instruction' *Review of Educational Research* 40, 279–300.

Rosenshine, B. (1978) *Instructional Principles in Direct Instruction* Illinois: University of Illinois.

Rosenshine, B. and Furst, J. (1971) 'Current and future research in teacher performance and criteria', In Smith, B. W. (ed) *Research on Teacher Education* Englewood Cliffs: Prentice Hall.

Rosenthal, R. (1975) 'Toward to what do you expect?' In Insell, P. and

Jacobson, L. (eds) *What Do You Expect?* California: Cummings Publishing Co.

Rosenthal, R. and Jacobson, L. (1968) *Pygmalion in the Classroom* New York: Holt Rinehart and Winston.

Rosser, E. & Harré, R. (1976) 'The meaning of disorder' In Hammersley, M. and Woods, P. (eds) *The Process of Schooling* London: RKP.

Rowan, B., Bosserts, S. and Dwyer, D. (1983) 'Research on effective schools: cautionary note' *Educational Research* 12, 4, 24–31.

Rowland, S. (1983) 'Educating Ourselves' *Forum* 25, 2, Summer

Rowland, S. (1984) *The Enquiry Classroom: An Introduction to Children's Learning* London: The Falmer Press.

Rubel, R. J. (1977) *The Unruly School* Lexington MA: Lexington.

Rudduck, J. (1977) 'Dissemination as the Encounter of Cultures' *Research Intelligence*, 3, 1.

Rudduck, J. (1983) *The Humanities Curriculum Project: an Introduction* (revised edition) Norwich: UEA/Schools Council.

Rudduck, J. (1984) 'Introducing innovation to pupils' In Hopkins, D. and Wideen, M. (eds) *Alternative Perspectives on School Improvement* Lewes: Falmer.

Rudduck, J. and Hopkins, D. (1985) *Research as a Basis for Teaching* London: Heinemann.

Runkel, P., Schmuck, R., Arends, J. and Francisco, R. (1979) *Transforming the Schools Capacity for Problem Solving* Eugene: Oregon: CEPM.

Rutter, M. (1967) 'A children's behaviour questionnaire for completion by teachers: preliminary findings' *Journal of Child Psychology & Psychiatry* 8, 1–11.

Rutter, M. (1975) *Helping Troubled Children* Harmondsworth: Penguin.

Rutter, M. (1979) *Changing Youth in a Changing Society* London: Nuffield Provincial Hospitals Trust.

Rutter, M., Tizard, J. and Whitmore, K. (eds) (1970) *Education Health and Behaviour* London: Longman.

Rutter, M., Yule, W., Berger, M., Yule, B., Morton, J. and Bagley, C. (1974) 'Children of West Indian Immigrants: I rates of behavioural disturbance and of psychiatric disorder,' *Journal of Child Psychology & Psychiatry* 15, 241–62.

Rutter, M., Cox, A., Tupling, C., Berger, M. and Yule, W. (1975a) 'Attainment and adjustment in two geographical areas: I the prevalence of psychiatric disorders' *British Journal of Psychiatry* 126, 493–509.

Rutter, M., Yule, B., Quinton, D., Rowlands, O., Yule, W. and Berger, M. (1975b) 'Attainment and adjustment in two geographical areas: III some factors accounting for area differences' *British Journal of Psychiatry* 126, 520–33.

Rutter, M., Yule, B., Morton, J. and Bagley, C. (1975c) 'Children of

West Indian Immigrants: III home circumstances and family pattern'
Journal of Child Psychology and Psychiatry 17, 35–36.
Rutter, M. and Madge, N. (1976) *Cycles of Disadvantage* London:
Heinemann.
Rutter, M., Maughan, B., Mortimore, P., Ouston, J. and Smith, A.
(1979) *Fifteen Thousand Hours: Secondary Schools & Their Effects on
Children* Cambridge Mass: Harvard University Press and London: Open
Books.
SED (1977) *Truancy & Indiscipline in Scotland* (The Pack Report)
Edinburgh: Scottish Education Department.
Sarason, S. B. (1971) *The Culture of Schools and the Problem of Change*
Boston: Allyn and Bacon.
Sarason, S. (1982) *The Culture of the School and the Problem of Change*
(2nd edn) New York: Allyn and Bacon.
Saunders, M. (1979) *Class Control and Behaviour Problems*
Maidenhead: McGraw-Hill.
Schatzman, L. and Strauss, A. L. (1973) *Field-Research: Strategies for a
Natural Sociology* Englewood Cliffs: Prentice-Hall.
Schmuck, R. A. and P. A. (1974) *A Humanistic Psychology of Education
Making the School Everybody's House* Mayfield: National Press Books.
Schon, D. (1983) *The Reflective Practitioner* New York: Basic Books.
Schools Council (1973) *Cross'd with adversity: the Education of Socially
Disadvantaged Children in Secondary Schools* London: Evans/Methuen
Educational.
Schools Council (1981) *The Practical Curriculum* London: Schools
Council.
Scriven, M. (1967) The Methodology of Evaluation *AERA Monograph
Series on Curriculum Evaluation. No. 1.* Chicago: Rand McNally
39–89.
Scruton, R. (1985) *Education or Indoctrination?* London: Institute for
European Defence & Strategic Studies
Seabrook, J. (1974) 'Talking to truants' In Turner, B. (ed) *Truancy*
London: Ward lock Educational.
Sharp, A. (1981) 'The significance of classroom dissent' *Scottish
Educational Review* 13, 2, 141–51.
Shepherd, M., Oppenheim, B. and Mitchell, S. (1971) *Childhood
Behaviour and Mental Health* London: University of London Press.
Shostak, J. (1982) 'Black side of school' *Times Educational Supplement*
25 June 1982, 23.
Siann, G., Draper, J. and Cosford, B. (1982) 'Pupils as consumers:
perceptions of guidance & counselling in a Scottish school' *British
Journal of Guidance & Counselling* 10, 1, 51–61.
Sidaway, N. D. (1976) *No Small Change* Carlisle: Cumbria County
Council.

Simons, H. (1980) 'The Evaluative School' *Forum* 22, 2.
Simons, H. (1981) 'Case Studying Superordinates: the Power Politics of Policy Evaluation' AERA symposium paper.
Skilbeck, M. (1975) 'School-based Curriculum Development and Teacher Education' Reprinted in Prescott, W. & Bolan, R. *Supporting Curriculum Development* Milton Keynes: Open University.
Skilbeck, M. (1984) *School Based Curriculum Development* London: Harper and Row.
Skinner, A., Platts, H. and Hill, B. (1983) *Disaffection from School: Issues & Interagency Responses* Leicester: National Youth Bureau.
Smithells, R. (1977) 'Confidentiality' In Kahan, B. (ed) *Working together for Children and their Families* London: DHSS/Welsh Office HMSO.
Smith, I. (1978) 'Guidance and the social order of the school' *Scottish Educational Studies* 10, 1, 34–36.
Sockett, H. (1986) 'The new INSET arrangements' *Conference Paper* Cambridge: UEA.
Southworth, G. W. (1984) 'Development of staff in primary schools' *British Journal of In-Service Education* 10, 3.
Southworth, G. W. (1985) 'Changing management in primary schools' *Education* 22, 11, 85.
Southworth, G. W. (1986a) 'Managerialism revisited' *Education* 14, 3, 86.
Southworth, G. W. (1986b) 'Primary school headship and collegiality' *School Organisation* (in press).
Spartz, J. L., Valdes, A. L., McCormick, W. J., Myers, J. and Geppert, W. J. (1977) *Delaware Educational Accountability System Case Studies: Elementary Schools Grades* 1–4 Dover, Delaware Dept. of Public Instruction.
Spooner, R. (1979) 'Pastoral care and the myth of never ending toil' *Education* 2 march 1979, 251–2.
Stallings, J.A. (1981) 'What research has to say to administrators of secondary schools about effective schools and staff development' Paper presented at the Centre for Educational Policy and Management Conference on Creating the Conditions for effective teaching; Eugene, Oregon.
Stallings, J. A. and Hentzell, S. W. (1978) 'Effective teaching and learning in urban schools' Paper prepared for CEMREL's National Conference on Urban Education St Louis, July 1978.
Stenhouse, L. (1967) 'Culture and Education' London: Heinemann.
Stenhouse, L. (1975) *An Introduction to Curriculum Research and Development* London: Heinemann.
Stenhouse, L. (1978) 'Curriculum Research and the Art of Teaching' UEA/CARE Mimeograph.
Stenhouse, L. (1982) 'The Conduct, Analysis & Reporting of Case Study

in Educational Research & Evaluation' In McCormick, R. (ed) *Calling Education to Account* London: Heinemann.

Stenhouse, L. (1983) *Authority, Education and Emancipation*, London: Heinemann.

Stewart, R. (1982) *Choices for the Manager* New York: McGraw-Hill.

Stott, D. H. (1963) *The Social Adjustment of Children*, London: University Press.

Sullivan, M. (1985) 'Confidence Trick' *TES* article.

Taba, H. (1962) *Curriculum Development: Theory and Practice* Harcourt Brace; Jovanovich.

Tangerud, H. (1986) 'The development and implementation of school improvement policies by education authorities' *Paper Presented to ISIP* UK Dissemination Conference April 1986.

Tattum, D. (1982) *Disruptive Pupils in Schools and Units* Chichester: John Wiley.

Taylor, M. (1981) *Caught Between: a Review of Research into the Education of Pupils of West Indian Origin*, Slough: NFER/Nelson.

Teachers' Action Collective (1976) 'Pastoral care: the system of control' *Teachers' Action* 5, 22–27.

Terhart, E. (1982) 'Interpretative approaches in educational research' *Cambridge Journal of Education* 12, 3.

Thomas, D. (1985) 'Initial training needs of special education teachers' In Hopkins, D. and Reid, K. (eds) *Rethinking Teacher Education* London: Croom Helm.

Thomas, J. A. (1962) 'Efficiency in education: a study of the relationship between selected inputs and mean test scores in a sample of senior high schools' Unpublished PhD dissertation Stanford University School of Education.

Thomson, E. (1983) 'Teachers as learners' *Forum* 25, 3.

Thomson, E. & A. (eds) (1984) *What Learning Looks Like* York: Longman/Schools Council.

Tomlinson, T. M. (1980) 'Student ability, student background and student achievement: another look at life in effective schools' Paper presented at Educational Testing Service Conference on Schools New York, May 27–29 1980.

Topping, K. J. (1978) 'Consumer confusion and professional conflict in educational psychology' *Bulletin of the British Psychological Society* 31, 265–7.

Topping, K. J. (1983) *Educational Systems for Disruptive Adolescents* London: Croom Helm.

Trisman, D. A., Waller, M. I. and Wilder, C. A. (1976) *A Descriptive & Analytic Study of Compensatory Reading Programmes: Final Report* 2, PR, 75–26 Princeton NJ: Educational Testing Service.

Turner, D. (1986) 'Is secondment cost-effective? *Education* 14, 2.

Turner, R. H. (1961) 'Modes of social ascent through education:

Sponsored and contest mobility' In Halsey, A. H., Floud, J. & Anderson, C. (eds) *Education, Economy & Society* New York: Free Press.

Tyerman, M. J. (1968) *Truancy* London: University of London Press.

Tyler, R. (1949) *Basic Principles of Curriculum and Instruction* Chicago University Press.

U.C.C.A. (1982) *Statistical Supplements to the 17th & 18th Reports* London: Universities' Central Council on Admissions.

Varlaam, A. (1974) 'Educational attainment and behaviour at school' *Greater London Intelligence Quarterly* 29, 29–37.

Van Velzen, W. G., Miles, M. B., Ekholm, M., Hameyer, U., Robin, D. (1985) *Making School Improvement Work: A Conceptual Guide to Practice* OECD/ISIP Leuven: ACCO.

Venezky, R. L. and Winfield, L. F. (1979) *Schools That Succeed Beyond Expectations in Reading* Studies on Education Technical Report, No. 1. Newark University of Delaware ERIC Document Reproduction Service ED 177484.

Wadsworth, M. (1979) *The Roots of Delinquency* London: Martin Robertson.

Walberg, H. J. (1969) 'The social environment as a mediator of classroom learning' *Journal of Educational Psychology* 60, 443–448.

Walberg, H. J. and Anderson, G. J. (1972) 'Properties of the achieving urban class' *Journal of Educational Psychology* 63, 381–385.

Walker, R. (1985) *Doing Research. A Handbook for Teachers* London: Methuen.

Walker, R. (1985) *Research for Teachers* London: MacMillan.

Warnock Report (1978) *Special Educational Needs: Report of the Committee of Enquiry into the Education of Handicapped Children and Yound People* Department of Education & Science/Welsh Office/Scottish Office, London: HMSO.

Weber, G. (1971) *Inner-City Children Can Be Taught to Read from Successful Schools* Washington DC Council for Basic Education.

Wedge, P. and Proser, H. (1973) *Born to Fail* London: Arrow, in association with the National Children's Bureau.

Weindling, R. and Earley, P. (1985) Reported in *TES* 6/9/85; NFER/Nelson (forthcoming).

Welsh Office (1984) *Response to Underachievement: a Discussion of Practice in Secondary Schools* Cardiff: Welsh Office HMI Report.

West, D. J. and Farrington, D. P. (1973) *The Delinquent Way of Life* London: Heinemann Educational.

Wicker, A. (1969) 'School size and students' experience in extra curricular activities' *Educational Technology* 9, 44–7.

Wilcox, B. (1985) BERA Conference Address, Sheffield (August).

Williams, T. (1976) 'Teacher prophecies and the inheritance of inequality' *Sociology of Education* 49, 223–235.

Willis, P. E. (1977) *Learning to Labour: How Working Class Kids Get Working Class Jobs* Kent: Saxon House.

Wiseman, S. (1964) *Education and Environment* Manchester: Manchester University Press.

Woods, P. (1979) *The Divided School* London: Routledge and Kegan Paul.

Woods, P. (1984) 'A Sociological Analysis of Disruptive Incidents' In Frude, N. and Gault, H. (eds) *Disruptive Behaviour in Schools* Chichester: John Wiley.

Wragg, E. C. (ed) (1984) *Classroom Teaching Skills* London: Croom Helm.

Wragg, E. C. and Kerry, T. L. (1979) *Classroom Interaction Research* Nottingham: University of Nottingham School of Education.

Wragg, T. (1981) 'Resort of the desperate' *Personal Column* TES 29/5/81.

Wragg, T. (1982) 'Management by all' *Personal Column* TES 23/7/82.

Wragg, T. (1986) 'Waiting for the whirlwind' *TES* 31/1/86.

Wright, D. (1973) 'The punishment of children' In Turner, B. (ed) *Discipline* London: Ward Lock Educational.

Wright, H. J. and Payne, T. A. N. (1979) *An Evaluation of a School Psychological Service: the Portsmouth Pattern* Hampshire: Hampshire Education Dept.

York, R., Heron, J. and Wolff, S. (1972) 'Exclusion from school' *Journal of Child Psychology & Psychiatry* 1, 259–66.

Yuki, G. (1975) 'Toward a behavioural theory of leadership,' In Houghton, V. *et al The Management of Organisations & Individuals* London: Ward Lock Educational.

Yule, W., Berger, M. and Vigley, V. (1984) 'Behaviour modification and classroom management', In Frude, N. & Gault, H. (eds) *Disruptive Behaviour in Schools* Chichester: John Wiley.

Index

Ability grouping 2
absenteeism 36, 37, 42, 43, 48, 53, 57, 70,
    86, 101, 111
absentees 72, 73, 76, 94, 110
abusive behaviour 54
academic achievement 57
academic aims 9
academic attainment 89, 91
academic values 27, 78
accommodation 59, 267
accountability 4, 6, 8, 23, 26, 36, 100, 127,
    128, 134
acculturation 198, 215, 267
achievement 4, 25, 27, 40, 60, 83, 84
action-research 172, 179, 185, 187, 196,
    212, 215, 216, 222
active learning 156
administration 79, 103
advisers 63, 124
'aesthetic' subjects 112
agenda-building 231
aggression 44
aims 25, 38, 72
alienation 45, 63, 70, 73, 81, 89, 99, 100,
    231
anti-school feelings 95
anti-social behaviour 51
apathy 55
applied research 170, 171, 172
appraisal 127
assessment 6, 8, 13, 39, 46, 86, 93, 110,
    112, 155, 156, 171, 212
atmosphere 5, 25, 28, 79
attainment 4, 57, 77, 87
attendance 35, 88, 109
audiotaping 251
authority 93, 94, 105, 142, 225, 227, 264
autonomous learning 216, 217
autonomy 24, 25, 115, 117, 129, 136, 177,
    188, 204, 205, 224, 235, 264
award-bearing courses 166, 168
awareness-raising 219, 249

'Bampton School' 48, 49
behaviour modification 100

behavioural difficulties 86
    objectives 14, 153
    problems 42, 57, 183
bias 100
bilingual pupils 109
black children 85, 86
'blackboard jungle' 54
brainstorming 253
bullying 30, 39, 44, 66, 81, 85, 90, 96
bureaucratisation 238

Capitation 88
career aspirations 84
charisma 61
checklist approach 251
child development 8
child guidance 57
child-centred curriculum 143
classroom observation 113, 124, 249
classroom research 120, 122, 124, 158, 253
climate 3, 4, 18, 20, 25, 29, 79, 84
co-operation 25, 129, 201, 218, 231
co-ordination 104, 237, 239
cohesiveness 26, 78
collaboration 12, 162, 167, 182, 187, 192,
    197, 199, 201, 204, 225, 229, 231,
    264, 268
collaborative partnership 192, 195, 197,
    205, 211
collaborative planning 18, 229, 268
collegiality 12, 100, 201, 229, 264, 268
commitment 19, 210
communication 11, 14, 19, 42, 104, 171,
    195, 201, 204, 216
communication skills 112
competition 96, 234
compulsory core 109
compulsory curriculum 111
conflict 59, 108
confrontation 35, 39, 59, 60, 61, 71, 90, 94,
    95, 107, 199
consultation 226
cost-effectiveness 6
counselling 69, 71, 74, 75, 83, 212
counselling skills 210

counsellors 63, 68, 79, 103
CPVE 219
'creative school' 11, 289
criterion-referencing 13, 22
cult of the individual 162, 173, 174, 183
culture 3, 20, 117, 136, 190, 215, 262, 265, 266
curriculum 2, 6, 18, 24, 27, 30, 39, 55, 58, 63, 66, 78, 81, 101, 109, 138
curriculum development 7, 8, 17, 21, 149, 150, 151, 159, 168, 209, 236
curriculum planning 148, 236
cut-backs 114

Data collection 125, 171, 201
decentralisation 127, 201, 204
decision-making 17, 36, 59, 75, 112, 118, 127, 181, 184, 195, 201, 204, 238, 264, 268
delinquency 35, 37, 45, 57
democratic collegiality 195
Developing School 205, 209, 210, 211, 215, 224, 227, 237, 238, 248, 256, 261, 268
deviance 39, 53, 59, 66, 72, 76, 81, 86, 88, 93, 94, 95
Diamond (the) 244
disadvantage 34, 35, 37, 39, 41, 67, 81, 82, 88, 99, 100, 102, 103
disaffection 34, 35, 36, 37, 39, 42, 43, 45, 47, 63, 78, 79, 81, 86, 88, 91, 96, 98, 99, 100, 103, 111
   disaffected behaviour 74, 82
   disaffected pupils 54, 62, 66, 72, 73, 94, 101, 102, 105, 107, 111
discipline 5, 12, 23, 24, 25, 26, 34, 39, 41, 44, 47, 52, 54, 57, 58, 59, 61, 93, 99, 103
discussion 123, 155
disenchantment 55
displays 7
disruption 34, 36, 37, 43, 47, 51, 54, 55, 58, 84, 86, 88, 91, 94, 96, 101, 108, 111
   disruptive behaviour 43, 52, 78, 87, 89, 99, 104, 107, 108
   disruptive pupils 42, 57, 61, 62, 72, 101, 102, 107, 110, 113
diversity 109
documentary evidence 123
documentary search 250
drama 15

Education Welfare Officer 75, 110
effective school(s) 2, 5, 12, 15, 16, 19, 21, 22, 24, 28, 29, 32, 137, 138, 200, 262

effectiveness 4, 6, 7, 8, 9, 11, 12, 23, 30, 31, 63, 129, 200
empathy 59, 68, 88, 186, 187
employment prospects 45, 55
encouragement 42, 89, 94, 101
enculturation 215, 238
engagement 224, 248
enquiry/discovery learning 156
enthusiasm 106, 107, 120
entrepreneurship 223, 235
equal opportunities 85, 89, 109
ESL 189
ethnic groups 85, 92, 109
ethnic minorities 100
ethos 2, 3, 4, 20, 24, 25, 29, 50, 62, 70, 79, 84
evaluation 6, 13, 15, 17, 28, 32, 58, 100, 101, 127, 134, 159, 168, 171, 199, 201, 210, 213, 224, 238, 249, 256
   evaluation skills 191, 192, 201
Evaluative School 209, 212
examination boards 152
examinations 6, 23, 25, 26, 48, 84, 109, 112, 221, 233
expectations 9, 18, 19, 26, 27, 28, 30, 32, 39, 66, 70, 77, 78, 81, 84, 91, 92, 106, 108, 167, 221
experiential learning 248
'extended professional' 115, 200
extortion 51, 96
extra-curricular activities 7, 63, 100
extroverts 88

Factional collaboration 200
falling rolls 114
family background 32, 84
feedback 27, 30, 84, 122, 124, 212
field notes 121, 123
flexibility 25, 156
form tutors 69, 70, 71, 76, 78, 79, 103, 104, 105, 110
formal curriculum 141
formative evaluation 160
fourth and fifth year 111, 112
fraternity 175, 182, 201
friendship groups 95

Girls 18, 84, 85, 100
goals 9, 10, 11, 18, 19, 264
governors 6, 43, 63, 103, 110, 111, 113, 130, 134
'great divide' 219
GRIDS 13, 117, 134, 135, 136, 181, 200,

211, 212, 227, 235, 240, 243, 249, 250, 251, 254, 255, 267, 268
group dynamics 60
guidance 8, 69, 73, 74, 76, 80, 103, 212
guidelines 6, 25, 57, 89, 250

Handicapped children 56
Hargreaves Report 109–111
hidden curriculum 141, 161, 234
hierarchy 58, 89, 168, 225, 228, 234, 238
high-fliers 6, 62, 101
higher education 83, 84, 164, 185, 192, 193, 201
'Hillbourne Comprehensive' 47, 49, 50
home background 36, 42, 56, 69, 83, 84, 88, 104, 105
home-school links 39, 45, 70
homework 27, 44, 45, 70, 84, 112

Imagination 218
immigrant pupils 48
improvisation 15
incrementalism 248
independent learning 110, 112, 216, 221
indiscipline 51, 53, 54, 55, 57, 58, 63, 91
individualism 228, 234
indoctrination 233
induction 111, 113
innovation 110, 148, 167, 178, 183, 211, 236, 266
INSET 6, 7, 8, 12, 15, 17, 18, 26, 29, 31, 61, 68, 100, 101, 113, 114, 138, 162, 164, 165, 179, 181, 182, 188, 190, 192, 197, 198, 199, 211, 238, 241, 254, 255, 268
institutionalisation 179, 184, 198, 202, 204, 205, 256, 278
intrinsic evaluation 253
interaction 11, 18, 19, 63, 94, 106, 146, 198, 202, 215
interpretation 125, 251
interviews 123, 251
introverts 88
intuition 62
involvement 224, 226
ipsative approach 222

Job satisfaction 25
job specifications 113

Key areas of focus 189, 241, 243, 148

Language policy 109
LEA support 18

leadership 9, 11, 14, 18, 19, 24, 26, 28, 29, 31, 32, 52, 94, 108, 224, 228, 232, 234, 235, 262, 263
learning climate 223
learning difficulties 7, 72, 81, 103
Learning School 209, 215, 223, 224, 236
learning-centred approach 30
less-able pupils 6, 37, 60, 89, 92, 93, 101, 105
liaison 42, 114
life skills 221
line management 193, 195
location 22, 36, 62

Malaise 36, 79
management 2, 6, 8, 23, 24, 25, 26, 34, 58, 59, 63, 70, 72, 84, 100, 105, 124, 200, 209, 224, 225, 226, 230, 232, 235, 236
by consent 228, 231
skills 62
mandation 9, 10, 15
maturation 55
middle management 69, 70, 78, 86, 102, 104, 105
minority groups 38, 85
misbehaviour 100
mixed ability groups 93, 155
monitoring 6, 9, 10, 11, 21, 27, 28, 32, 100, 201, 256
moral education 217
morale 25, 54, 71, 84, 114
motivation 5, 57, 83, 89, 105, 168, 221
multilingual pupils 110

Negative attitudes 45
negative reinforcement 55
negotiation 204, 212, 150
networkers 231
neutral chairperson 155
Newsom 43
norm-referencing 13, 222
normative collegiality 185, 229

Objectives 38
approach 146
observation 122, 125, 127
notes 251
schedules 251
off-site support units 57, 110
one-parent families 39, 83
option choices 109, 110
oral skills 112
order 25, 26, 29, 47, 62, 93, 94

Organisation Development (OD) 17, 100, 181, 197, 202
outcomes 16, 27, 36, 77, 96, 101, 141
ownership 168, 200, 210, 212, 225, 248

Parent-child relationships 41
parent-school relationships 57, 88
parent-teacher contact 24
parental attitudes 42
parental involvement 7, 18, 27, 29, 36, 42, 100
parental perspective 29, 43
parents' evenings 46, 104, 109
participant observation 124
participation 30, 133, 224, 238, 248
partnership 138, 162, 168, 192, 193, 227
pastoral care 7, 39, 47, 61, 66, 67, 68, 69, 70, 71, 72, 73, 74, 77, 79, 89, 99, 100, 103, 110
pastoral curriculum 104, 114, 190
pastoral-academic dichotomy 68
peer group influence 83
peer group relationships 39, 55, 66, 81, 90, 95, 103
peer observation 124, 150
physical assault 51
physical attractiveness 92
physical punishment 29, 77
policy documents 6
positive discrimination 35
positive reinforcement 100, 223
power-sharing 101
praise 26, 36, 40, 42, 89, 94
primary education 30
primary schools 80, 96, 99, 104, 219
prioritisation 248
probationary teachers 111
problem finding 223
   formation 119, 120
   resolution 120
   solving 17, 27, 116, 136, 223
'problem-solving school' 16, 21, 115, 129, 209
procedural (action) steps 241
procedural collegiality 195, 229
process factors 20, 21
   guidelines 248
   model 153, 156
proculturation 198, 215
professional development 156, 166, 173, 192
profiling 156
public examinations 38, 84, 109
punishment 29, 55, 57, 58, 61, 77, 89

pupil care 2, 24, 29
pupil diaries 123
pupil grouping 109, 111
pupil participation 77, 110, 142
pupil profiles 6, 78, 112
pupil-centred provision 99
pupil-power 91
pupil-pupil interviews 122
pupil-teacher ratio 28, 77
pupil-teacher relationships 105, 106
pupils' perceptions 46, 40, 66, 75
   perspectives 78, 79

Qualitative approach 251
quantitative approach 251
questioning 124, 125
questionnaires 122, 123, 250
quinquennial reviews 113

Racism 83, 85, 109
rape 51
reading 2, 14, 24, 27, 28, 30, 32, 41, 83
recognition 89
record-keeping 70
   of achievement 6
'reflective practitioner' 115, 190
review 115, 129, 138
'relatively autonomous school' 116
remedial action 74, 100, 124
   education 59, 72, 93, 104
   measures 100
   programmes 101
resources 5, 6, 16, 20, 22, 26, 31, 36, 60, 78, 84, 85, 86, 88, 112, 117, 158, 202
responsible autonomy 187
retribution 107
rewards 29, 60, 77
robbery 51
role conflict 69, 171
rote learning 153
rules 19, 26, 39, 57, 59, 66, 69, 70, 81, 90

Sabbatical leave 114
saber tooth curriculum 139
salaries 31, 32, 79
sanctions 72
SBR 128, 129, 138, 122, 201, 202, 205, 267, 269
school buildings 2, 29, 32
   climate 77
   counsellors 104
   development 12, 138, 163, 199, 201, 214
   effectiveness 2, 14, 35, 66, 68, 77, 78
   evaluation 5, 128

improvement 17, 19, 21, 97, 114, 129, 136, 162, 173, 201, 268
School Improvement Project 200
leaving age 55, 91
research 170, 171, 172, 198, 200
self-evaluation 98, 115, 117, 127, 136, 101, 102
size 2, 24, 31
school-based research 185, 188
school-centred INSET 196
school-focused INSET 127
school/community links 6
schooling 209, 215
secondment 164, 165
self-actualisation 221
-awareness 166
-concept 59, 81
-control 174, 227
-determination 210
-development 196
-discipline 59
-esteem 81
self-evaluation 5, 17, 100, 101, 113, 128, 129, 130, 134, 181, 191, 192, 196, 198, 211, 212, 215, 135
self-fulfilling prophecies 92, 93
sensitivity 218
sex differences 100, 142
sex stereotyping 92
sexism 83, 84
SIDE 214
sixth-form colleges 91
'slack' 20
social background 84, 91
class 36
disadvantage 83, 84
outcomes 37
workers 40, 41, 128
socially-deprived areas 26
socio-economic background 22, 47, 63
special educational needs 7, 38, 70, 72, 83, 88, 102
special units 86
staff appraisal 113
staff development 8, 18, 20, 21, 25, 27, 31, 61, 113, 114, 138
handbook 250
involvement 14
meetings 72
relationships 209
training 15
turnover 55
strategic collegiality 195

stress 45, 62, 63, 70, 83, 94
strictness 94, 95
structured staff discussion 243
student-centred learning 220, 221
study skills 111, 112
sub-cultures 96
subject choices 83
summative evaluation 168
suspension 57, 72, 75, 110
systematic self-review 134
systems management 195, 196

Tape recording 121, 123
teacher as researcher 115, 203
teacher education 6, 30
teacher research 98, 115, 117, 118, 125, 136, 196
teacher-based research 172, 178
teacher-parent partnership 109
teacher-pupil discussion 122
teacher-pupil interaction 119
teacher-pupil ratio 26, 55, 77, 106
teacher-pupil relationship 29, 39, 48, 55, 63, 66, 78, 80, 81, 90, 92, 93, 94, 95
teaching skills 153
team building 181, 209
teamwork 195, 212
'technical' subjects 112
technology 6, 100, 143
testing 15, 136
'thinking school' 16, 115, 209
top-down model 200
paradigm 202
strategies 8
transfer of learning 148
transition 107, 109
TRIST 163, 188, 189, 190, 191, 192, 214, 219, 238, 148, 156
truancy 36, 37, 52, 53, 75, 84, 105, 110
TVEI 81, 152, 156

Underachievement 36, 37, 39, 66, 70, 81, 82, 83, 85, 86, 109, 111, 112
unemployment 39, 47, 83

Validation 125, 126
vandalism 36, 37, 51, 52, 59, 107
verbal abuse 52
video recorders 122, 123, 125, 126, 251
violence 36, 51, 52, 107
vocational education 111

Warnock Report 102
welfare 12, 27